Peoples of the Earth

Peoples of the Earth

Ethnonationalism, Democracy, and the Indigenous Challenge in "Latin" America

Martin Edwin Andersen

Foreword by
Robert A. Pastor

LEXINGTON BOOKS
A division of
ROWMAN & LITTLEFIELD PUBLISHERS, INC.
Lanham • Boulder • New York • Toronto • Plymouth, UK

Published by Lexington Books
A division of Rowman & Littlefield Publishers, Inc.
A wholly owned subsidiary of The Rowman & Littlefield Publishing Group, Inc.
4501 Forbes Boulevard, Suite 200, Lanham, Maryland 20706
http://www.lexingtonbooks.com

Estover Road, Plymouth PL6 7PY, United Kingdom

British Library Cataloguing in Publication Information Available

Library of Congress Cataloging-in-Publication Data
Andersen, Martin Edwin.
  Peoples of the Earth : ethnonationalism, democracy, and the indigenous challenge in
"Latin" America / Martin Edwin Andersen.
      p. cm.
  Includes bibliographical references and index.
  ISBN 978-0-7391-4391-9 (cloth : alk. paper) — ISBN : 978-0-7391-4391-9
  1. Indigenous peoples—Latin America—Ethnic identity. 2. Indigenous peoples—
Politics and government. 3. Indigenous peoples—Latin America—History. I. Title.
  GN564.L29A53 2010
  980'.00498—dc22   2009048284

⊖™ The paper used in this publication meets the minimum requirements of American
National Standard for Information Sciences—Permanence of Paper for Printed Library
Materials, ANSI/NISO Z39.48-1992.

Printed in the United States of America

Contents

Tables and Figures

To my parents,

Edwin M. and Angelina N. Andersen

Columbus arrived in the New World in 1492, but America has yet to be discovered.
—Jack Weatherford, *Indian Givers; How the Indians of the Americas Transformed the World*

One always loses when, instead of defending something real, it is mythologized because as such it is useful.
—Editorial, *Pukara* (Bolivia), April/May 2009

There is a whole nation that we don't know, that we are not a part of, but which has a claim to this land they still consider valid. What we have here is an indigenous, pre-Colombian movement that rejects not only what is white, but also the mestizo. We are sitting on the top of a volcano and don't even know it.
—Amparo Menéndez Carrión (1981)

The indigenous community is the only social institution that can and will guarantee the rights and access to land and resources of its members. The community itself is the social security system of the rural poor.
—Søren Hvalkof

Building sovereignty means building hope.
—John Merritt, Inuit Tapiriit Kanatami

We have to admit that until now the problem of nationalities has not been resolved by any revolution or counterrevolution, by any reform or counterreform, by any independence or annexation, by a coup or countercoup.
—Demetrio Cojtí Cuxil, Guatemalan Indian nationalist (1991)

In the end we will conserve only what we love.
We love only what we understand.
And we will understand only what we are taught.
—Senegalese saying

Foreword

The Last Frontier of De-Colonization in the Americas: Indigenous Peoples

By Robert A. Pastor

In the mid-1970s, after a long history of dictatorship, and a briefer history of swings between democracy and authoritarianism, Latin America finally began a steady journey to democracy. By 1991, every country in the Americas—with the exception of Cuba—had a democratically elected government, and an OAS General Assembly that summer approved the "Santiago Commitment," a procedure for collectively defending all the democracies. This was a remarkable step around the narrow, restrictive principle of non-intervention. That commitment was strengthened in Lima, Perú, on September 11, 2001, when the OAS governments unanimously signed the Inter-American Democratic Charter.

The Charter was signed on a day that represented another watershed. A few moments before the OAS voted on the charter, the United States was attacked by a small group of Islamist nihilists. The United States turned toward fighting a global "war on terror" and away from the challenge of breathing life into the Inter-American Democratic Charter. Latin America looked in another direction as it began to absorb the full implications of its thirty-year march to democracy.

Two distinct but intersecting trends emerged from this new democratic wave, and both are the subjects of this path-breaking book:

- Native or indigenous groups that had long been exploited, persecuted, or simply marginalized began to organize and find their voices in their countries and the region; and

- New populist leaders, like Hugo Chavez of Venezuela, Evo Morales of Bolivia, and Rafael Correa of Ecuador, emerged from these groups or from other sectors and began to bend the boundaries of democratic institutions for the declared purpose of redistributing wealth and power to the indigenous groups.

Together, these two trends offered the Americas a chance to de-colonize the "First Nations", who had never achieved full liberation since the Europeans arrived five hundred years before. In a thoughtful analysis, Martin Edwin Andersen chronicles both trends in a scholarly manner, but he does not conceal his sympathy for the struggle of the indigenous groups and his uneasiness with the new populist leaders, who seem more determined to dismantle the checks and balances of democratic institutions than wanting to help guarantee a place in the political firmament for indigenous peoples.

Andersen explores how the expansion of the franchise in an age of the Internet has altered the very concept of the state and the meaning of democracy. He is convinced that the only way to ensure that the indigenous groups' rights will be respected is within a democratic framework. If the populists of the left undermine that very framework to help indigenous people, a shift to the right would leave indigenous people without the structures essential for defending those rights. In the end the best way to assure that this last frontier of colonialism is definitely closed, and minority rights are always preserved, is to guarantee democratic institutions.

Re-Emergence of the Natives

At some level of consciousness, most people in the Americas know that the European "discovery" of the new world was not really a discovery. When Christopher Columbus arrived in the Western Hemisphere, he thought he had reached the Indies and therefore called the inhabitants, "Indians." The name stuck even though people soon realized that he had not reached the Indies, and that the people classified under that one term represented literally thousands of groups of people with different languages and cultures and spread over two vast continents.

Among the many peoples were two vast civilizations—the Mayan/Aztec civilization in the Mexican and Central American plateau and the Inca/Aymara/Quechua people in the Andes. Both peoples had developed advanced civilizations with a population that exceeded Spain and much of Europe. However, conquistadors led by Hernan Cortes in Meso-America and Francisco Pizarro in Perú were able to defeat and suppress these civilizations with a combination of boldness, more advanced military technology, and disease. They then imposed a three hundred year imperialistic system that treated most of the native population as virtual slaves. The lives of the natives did not improve after the local Creoles gained their independence from Spain. Although some of the groups rebelled, they could not sustain a war against the Creoles or Europeans. By and large, indigenous peoples suffered quietly.

At the present time, there are about thirty five to forty million native peoples in the Americas, with the largest numbers in Mexico (12 million or 14 percent of the Mexican population), Perú (with 9.3 million and nearly half of the country's population), Bolivia (5.6 million; 81 percent), Guatemala (4.1 million; 66 percent); Ecuador (4.1 million; 43 percent); and Chile (1 million or 10.3 percent). In a total population of about five-hundred million in Latin America, these figures are not large, but in the context of the six countries identified above, indigenous peoples have the power of numbers.

Only when democracy began to take root did non-governmental organizations and indigenous leaders began to collaborate to help natives defend their rights and their land. As these groups organized, new leaders emerged, and a new discourse was articulated to connect the nation's history with the culture of the native peoples. Some people see the indigenous movements motivated by an anti-neo-liberal, anti-globalization, and a neo-Marxist philosophy, but Andersen disputes that. He argues that, at base, the newly politicized native movements are more concerned about defending their culture, language, and rights and that may seem to overlap with leftist philosophies, but there are also examples of these groups utilizing globalization to their interests. But there is no question that the new populist leadership in the Americas—notably Evo Morales of Bolivia, Hugo Chavez of Venezuela, and Rafael Correa of Ecuador, together with less widely-known leaders in Perú and Guatemala—are using the language of anti-Americanism and anti-neo-liberalism to consolidate power and disrupt or dismantle the checks and balances that are at the heart of democracy. Is this good for indigenous peoples?

In some ways, what they are doing is good. When the new Ecuadorian Constitution, approved in a referendum on September 28, 2008, recognizes the state is multicultural, that represents a much-needed step forward. When the new leaders adjust state expenditures to assist the poor rather than protect the rich that is positive. But when the President consolidates power by eliminating the countervailing force of the Congress or the Courts, then that spells danger for minorities, and he fears that may be the direction that some of these populists are heading. Even if the new populists are dedicated to helping the poor and the indigenous leaders, the history of the region suggests that they will not last, and if they have destroyed the very institutions needed to preserve the rights of the minorities, then if their successors want to erase their legacy and re-marginalize the indigenous groups, they will not be constrained.

In the end, Mick Andersen argues for the "pluri-national character of the state and recognition of groups' rights and effective citizenship that allows for self-determination, including common territory, culture and language." But it is by no means clear that this will occur. If the leaders are more interested in past injustices than in future inclusion, and if they try to divide their people, then the result could be "vengeance between races and cultures" and a new authoritarianism. Only within a democratic framework can the rights of the excluded be defended and more effective forms of incorporation can be found. "Such efforts," he concludes, "will help to make democracy real for millions of people still outside the arc of its benefits, address the unfinished business of decolonization in the hemisphere, and offer a broad assurance that the clock will not be turned back on Indian progress." The signal contribution of this book is to help us to understand that the new wave of democracy offers the chance to finally incorporate those who have been left behind, but if that is done poorly, then democracy itself will be placed at risk. This path-breaking volume helps us to see clearly the risk and the opportunity. If this transition to a more complete democracy succeeds, all of the countries of the Americas will be the richer for it.

Robert A. Pastor is Professor of International Relations at American University and is Co-Director of the Centers for Democracy and Election Management and of North American Studies.

Acknowledgments

Seeking to understand the workings of a true democracy, Benjamin Franklin, one of the United States' founding fathers, studied the participationist simplicity of the liberty-loving People of the Long House—also known as the Six Nations, or the Iroquois—whose territory was once roughly the size of the old Roman Empire.[1] Since that time, the example of the nation-state Franklin helped build—the United States of America—has been a beacon to countries around the world, even if the U.S. itself did not always live up to its promise with allies, friends and admirers around the globe, or with large portions of its own people—as happened in the last hundred or so of the three centuries of warfare against Indians that ended at Wounded Knee on December 28, 1890. Thus an important part of the transcendant example, of what former President Jimmy Carter calls the United States' "vast ... moral footprint," that was set down for generations after the events of the 1770s, was given to us by Indian tribes in this country. That gift is a necessary first acknowledgment for any freedom-loving non-Indian seeking to address issues concerning indigenous peoples, democracy, the rule of law and respect for human rights.[1]

The analysis contained in this work was also enriched by the insights and support of a number of friends, colleagues and mentors, all of whom I admire

---

1. More prosaically, but no less importantly or heroically, as George Washington's army camped in desperate wintry circumstances at Valley Forge, it was a group of Oneida Indians who risked their lives to trek hundreds of miles to bring the Revolutionary Army food, including more than 600 bushels of corn. See the Appleton (WI.) *Post-Crescent*, Nov. 16, 1995, p. B-3; "The Oneida Indians of Wisconsin," online at: http://www.jefflindsay.com/Oneida.shtml, and "Oneidas brought corn to Washington's starving troops at Valley Forge," online at: http://www.oneidaindiannation.com/ pressroom/morenews/36439904.html.

and whose time they have spent with me I cherish. I owe a debt of gratitude to my former professor at the University of Wisconsin-Parkside, the noted and quietly charismatic applied cultural anthropologist Dr. Henry F. Dobyns, for ideas and perspectives that more than three decades later I find offer a uncommon bedrock for investigation that is still yielding rich benefits. Similarly, one of Dobyns' colleagues, Dr. Richard Stoffle, another of my professors at UW-Parkside who is now at the University of Arizona, served as a role model on the important contributions that could be made in the pursuit of serious academic study.

My current professors at the Catholic University of America, ethno-nationalism scholar Dr. Jerry Z. Muller and Latin American expert Dr. James D. Riley, the current and former History Department chairs, respectively, were both generous with their time and encouragement of this project, as well as with the insights of years of research and meditation on issues this work seeks to address. It was a class taken with Dr. Muller on nationalism in Europe during the twentieth century that first raised the idea of the universality of ethno-historical analysis and its potential for application to the phenomena of indigenous mobilization in the Western Hemisphere.

Amstrong Wiggins and Leonardo Crippa took time from their important work at the Indian Law Resource Center in Washington, D.C., to give me the benefit of insights without which this book would have been noticeably poorer. Dr. Richard Millett, professor emeritus of history at Southern Illinois University at Edwardsville, has been a friend in the best sense of the word, including the encouragement by example of a creative, inquiring mind and generous soul. The following people offered comments on various drafts of this paper that not only improved what it provides the reader, but likely also spared me from certain embarrassment along the way, and I thank them for their time, interest and friendship: Alan Thomas, my former colleague at the Office of U.S. Senate Majority Whip Alan Cranston, who also cast a discerning eye on my first book, *Dossier Secreto: Argentina's Desaparecidos and the Myth of the "Dirty War"* (Cranston, a wonderful employer and friend, ended his distinguished twenty-four-year in the Senate by making his last legislative achievement the requirement, by law, that the U.S. Department of State include a section on indigenous rights in its annual human rights country reports); Ambassador John Maisto, a distinguished former special assistant to the President and White House senior director for Western Hemisphere Affairs; Steven M. Tullberg, the former Washington office director of the Indian Law Resource Center; Associated Press Latin America Correspondent Nestor Ikeda; Chilean development expert Carolina Koch; Dr. Melina Selverston, founder of the Coalition for Amazonian Peoples and Their Environment; Dr. Jennifer S. Holmes, associate professor of political economy and political science at the University of Texas at Dallas; the Mexican sociologist, Professor Araceli Burguete Cal y Mayor; Peruvian defense expert Luis Giacoma Macchiavello; Frank McGurk, my former supervisor at the

National Defense University and a member of the Mi'kmaq tribe; Dr. Wm. Dean Rudoy, *mensch maggiore* and secretary of the board of the Robert F. Kennedy Center for Justice and Human Rights; Dr. Frederick M. Nunn, dean of academics at the Center for Hemispheric Defense Studies; Robert D. Lamb of the U.S. Office of the Deputy Assistant Secretary of Defense for Policy Planning; Dr. Louis Goodman, dean of the School of International Service at American University; Dr. William Ratliff, a research fellow and curator of the Americas Collection at the Hoover Institution of Stanford University; Dr. Oswaldo Jarrín Roman, a former Ecuadorian defense minister and professor with the Latin American Faculty of Social Sciences (FLACSO), and Dr. Thomas Fingar, the Payne Distinguished Lecturer in the Freeman Spogli Institute for International Studies at Stanford and the former chairman of the National Intelligence Council. The Oxford-educated historian and former colleague, James L. Zackrison deserves a special mention for his patient and always insightful questions and his fine editor's pen. Thanks are in order, too, to his anthropologist father, James W. Zackrison, for his own comments on religious issues and native peoples. Dante Caputo, the former political secretary of the Organization of American States and the head of its Democracy Project, hired me to write the organization's consultant paper on indigenous rights, itself a great honor and a chance to participate in an important hemispheric dialogue, as well an opportunity that allowed me not to have to obsessively focus on the bottom line while I was racing to finish up this book. And, as this book neared completion, a wondrous trek my wife and I were able to take on the Amazon near Manaus was led by our guide Rubens Billy, whose example reaffirmed the vast storehouse of plant and animal knowledge that indigenous peoples possess and are willing to share.

Important encouragement and advice were provided to me as well by Dr. Howard Wiarda of the University of Georgia and Dr. Orlando Pérez of Central Michigan University. Dr. Walker Connor, whose inestimable influence upon the scholarship of nationalism makes it a challenge for any writer to adequately describe in a volume much in less a sentence, read an early chapter that became the foundation for this book and found reason for encouragement, and I am honored that he did so. I further owe an intellectual debt to Barry Scott Zellen of the Center for Contemporary Conflict at the U.S. Naval Postgraduate School. Although it was Steve Tullberg who first suggested to me important answers to indigenous concerns in "Latin" America might be found in the examples of Native peoples living in the Arctic, finding Zellen's important work—*Breaking the Ice: From Land Claims to Tribal Sovereignty in the Arctic* and *On Thin Ice: The Inuit, the State, and the Challenge of Arctic Sovereignty*—while almost at the end of my own research, helped clarify my own thinking about how and why human security, tribal security and national security are conceptions that are inexorably tied together. I would also like to thank José Torres, a librarian at the National Defense University, who has always been a source of encouragement and an indefatigable intellectual resource at one of the best libraries in Washington, D.C. I very much appreciate, too, the generosity of Drs. Cynthia H. Enloe of Clark University and Andrew Canessa of the University of Essex, for sharing with me and the readers of *Peoples of the Earth* the creativity and insight illustrated by their map of a nation-state's ideal ethnic security and graph of contending political and religious appeals in highland Bolivia, respectively.

And, of course, when someone one has admired for such a long time—someone like Dr. Robert Pastor—agrees to sign on with a Foreword to a labor of love, there are few words to express the gratitude and the joy at the company one occasionally keeps. (A few names I have omitted here upon those persons' request; if I have forgotten anyone, my sincere apologies.)

The timely availability of a book depends heavily on the editorial team working to bring it forward. In that regard, I was very fortunate to be able to count on the fast and highly professional team at Lexington Books, led by Acquisitions Editor Joseph C. Parry and ably supported by Assistant Editor Jana Wilson and Editorial Assistants Tawnya Zengierski and Mirna Araklian. I appreciate their support, as well as their accessibility.

My daughters, Carla Thais and Kelly Carina, and my parents, Edwin M. and Angelina N. Andersen (to whom this book is dedicated), have been steadfast in their love and support in what must have appeared a never-ending story that impinged on family time that should be, and is, the best and most precious fortune I have.

Finally, the person to whom I owe special gratitude for both understanding my need to write and for offering a joyous and reflective domestic life that makes me want to do it from home, is my wife, Dr. Barbara (Basia) Borzuchowska Andersen. Basia is my North Star, beckoning me through the good and the less good, inspiring me to do my best to fulfill life's promises along the lines of excellence, like she herself is doing, at work as well as in our home.

Martin Edwin Andersen
Churchton, Maryland

Part I

Chapter One
Introduction

"The past is never dead. It's not even past."
—William Faulkner
Requiem for a Nun

"It is impossible to awaken someone who is pretending to sleep."
—Navajo proverb

In 1992, the five-hundredth anniversary of Christopher Columbus' "discovery" of the Americas was a catalyst for unprecedented indigenous peoples' mobilization throughout the Hemisphere. That year, an important Indian leader from Ecuador visited Washington, D.C., for the first time. At the end of his stay, when the cold winds of late autumn had already forced a small army of homeless people onto subway grates to keep warm, the soft-spoken man was asked how he felt about his visit. "You know, for a city that has so many poor people on the streets, you certainly have a lot of big houses for your cars," he responded, alluding to the many parking garages downtown. His view, so different from that of many visitors to the U.S. capital, reflected the values of the culture in which he was raised.

One hundred and eighty-two years earlier, Shawnee Chief Tecumseh asked William Harrison, governor of the Indiana Territory, a question revealing of the cultural abyss between Native Americans in what was then United States territory and the white settlers who were then moving onto their lands, dispossessing the original inhabitants:

How can we have confidence in the white people? When Jesus Christ came upon the earth, you killed him—the son of your own God—you nailed him up!

You thought he was dead, but you were mistaken. And only after you thought you killed him did you worship him, and start killing those who would not worship him. What kind of a people is this for us to trust?[1]

The two stories are separated by nearly two centuries but are united in their themes of cultural difference, and the frank questioning of the values of a dominant society. They offer a viewpoint from which to understand one of the most vexing challenges of the twenty-first century: What can be done to bring the First Nations of the Americas into new democratic compacts that respect their rights, broadly considered, while retaining the region's relatively harmonious nation-state boundaries (a "Zone of Peace," as some call it). And what can be done to ensure respect for individual liberties, critically important to civilian-led rule of law? This last consideration is itself complicated. Since the time of the Spanish Conquest relations between indigenous peoples and the nation-state has run predominantly along a militarized axis; the armed forces (when not the Catholic Church) have been the primary representatives of the usually physically and culturally remote capital city, those whom Native Americans saw and with whom they interacted. With such a history, the emergence of peoples who share ancestral, cultural, language or religious ties and common identities—some thirty-five to forty million historically disadvantaged Native Americans—as influential political actors in Central and South America and Mexico poses important challenges for policymakers throughout the Hemisphere. The issue of their full and just incorporation as citizens, on their own terms, becomes even more important as demands for Indian self-determination, and the possibilities of ethno-sectarian violence, are cast as a direct threat to the security policies—and thus the sovereignty—of several nation-states of "Latin" America.

As the region prepares to celebrate its bicentennial marking independence from Spanish colonialism even as it engages in an unprecedented hunt for resources, indigenous scholars, activists and others hotly dispute the ownership of the laurels from that historic time, long the known property of those tracing their own descent at least in part to Spain and other countries of Europe. The former say the regional liberation in 1810 from which Native Americans' own forefathers did not tangibly benefit was nonetheless a commonweal for which they can claim, in the name of their forbearers, a large measure of credit. The enduring presence of the past, where the selection of narratives itself involves a competition for public memory, thus becomes a weapon in political and cultural clashes over both the contours of national identity and the direction of state institutions..[2]

Looming in the background and reaching even farther back into history, in several countries of South America, in Nicaragua, and from Guatemala to southwestern United States, are voices raised challenging contemporary political boundaries of nation-states by comparing them, and their utility and their equitability, with those of pre-conquest civilizations. These and other emerging phenomena, some based on readings of history, others ground in the here and now, suggest that the eventual course of challenges to the political legitimacy of ruling elites and the distribution of resources upon which contemporary indigenous mobilization is based remains an open question—witness the bloody clash, a tragedy foretold, in June 2009 in Bagua, Perú. History does not concede optimism: the largely unheralded genocide against Indian peoples in Perú and Guatemala occurred as late as the waning years of the twentieth century, while today indigenous peoples' forbearance across the region is wearing exceedingly thin. Centuries-old grievances, contemporary humiliation, and the continued lack of real political empowerment and effective mechanisms to peacefully address those injustices continue to be played out, precariously, along one of the hemisphere's deepest fault lines. In Bolivia, Perú, Ecuador and other countries (including Chile, a country frequently held up by international critics as a model in other social, political and economic spheres), what has been a pent-up potential for backlash against the established elite is now in the process of boiling over. As the poet Langston Hughes famously wrote, sometimes dreams deferred explode.

Although far greater inclusion and effective democratic institutions are needed, the situation today is unlike that of just two decades ago, when indigenous peoples were irremediably underrepresented in the democratic politics of what is commonly referred to as "Latin" America. Yet, until recently, indigenous movements often appeared to bask in a broad appeal spanning class and ethnicity, pioneering U.S. political scientist Donna Lee Van Cott noted in early 2009. "Today [however] the outlook is more muddled," she wrote shortly before her own tragic death.

> Some indigenous parties have maintained their regional strength and expanded geographically, but others have become fragmented, lost public support, or failed to achieve their potential. A backlash against indigenous movements threatens to overturn historic gains in policies and rights and to sap movement momentum by forcing indigenous parties to adopt a defensive posture. . . . After 20 years, indigenous movements have lost their novelty as fresh political faces with the ability to introduce new ideas to the political agenda.[3]

Indigenous activism is arguably the final frontier—and the unfinished business—of a century-long (or more than two centuries-long, if the U.S. revolution is the starting point), process of global de-colonization. As Indian rights activist Steven M. Tullberg noted, "Like other colonized peoples throughout the ages, indigenous peoples have suffered under the domination of settler populations who denied them self-government, suppressed their cultures, languages, and religions, expropriated their lands and resources, and impoverished them." Even when not overtly victimized, indigenous peoples were still ignored; their voices—offering different ways to view and appreciate the world—went unheard. Using the term "peasant" for peoples whose resurging ethnic identity has meant that it has been increasingly replaced by "indigenous" or "First Nations" since the time he wrote, historian Steve J. Stern found pessimism in the human costs—social, cultural, economic—associated with what dominant societies continue to call "development." Incorporating primarily peasant territories into the modern global capitalist economy, he noted, had at least in the medium term a destructive impact on those peoples' lives.

> Even those who see "modernization" as ultimately beneficial would now be inclined to concede that it first exacts a heavy price. . . . Traditional values and social relations come under assault; local institutions that once provided a measure of economic security and income redistribution become ever more precarious; time-tested political strategies vis-à-vis lords or the state prove increasingly obsolete. The net result breaks down the viability of an earlier way of life, and provokes political unrest and mobilization.[4]

This relentless marginalization is not without its reasons and, ultimately, its potential costs, perhaps even more so today. "In the context of globalization, characterized by an intense circulation and exchange of people, goods and information," wrote Peruvian anthropologist Gisela Cánepa, "the tendency has been to assume that 'difference' precedes the cultural encounter, while on the contrary 'difference' is generated precisely" in their context. "For that reason, cultural difference is not a neutral value, or marginal to politics. Rather it is one central field where hegemony is pursued."[5]

Indigenous peoples' struggles today have implications for political stability, long-term trends in political inclusion, and economic development throughout the region. The legitimacy and urgency of their struggle stem, in part, from the fact that, in the aftermath of the Allied powers' defeat of the Axis in World War II, race-based political hierarchies and the resulting usurpation of rights (and resources) have been challenged and eroded, when not overturned. It is now far less acceptable in the court of world public opinion, and according to international law, to turn back the clock to a time when such primitive ideologies emanating from the global North altered societies' perception of democracy and the rule of law.

Although given up for dead by most of a generation of academics, nationalism at the beginning of the twenty-first century fuels popular aspirations and internecine conflict around the world. (We distinguish here between "civic nationalism," the name often used for a people already in possession of a state or territorial unit of government, and "ethnic nationalism," used to describe those who do not.) "Unlike other isms, nationalism has never produced its own grand thinkers: no Hobbeses, Tocquevilles, Marxes or Webers," Benedict Anderson pointed out in *Imagined Communities Reflections on the Origin and Spread of Nationalism*. As such it is related more to diffuse ideas of kinship and religion. Yet as sociologist Craig Calhoun has noted, it "remains the pre-eminent rhetoric for attempts to demarcate political communities, claim rights of self-determination and legitimate rule by reference to 'the people' of a country. . . . Neither ethnic conflicts, nor the discourse of national identity, nor the practical power of nationalist mobilizations has receded into the premodern past, despite the confidence of many earlier social scientists (an embarrassment especially for Marxists)." In fact, as political scientist Donald L. Horowitz underscored, Marx's idea of class as being both an inherited and determinative membership (that one's class position is his "inherited and inescapable fate") works far better when applied to ethnic groups than to social classes, particularly when predicting which has greater conflict potential.[6]

The challenges posed by native peoples' mobilization in the Americas include but are not limited to a more equitable political inclusion and a fair share of economic development. They also include whether a new consensus can be reached that will help indigenous peoples protect their lands, their access to resources, and to protect their cultural inheritance through an expanded democratic franchise. As the U.S. National Intelligence Council's 2020 Project, "Mapping the Global Future: New Challenges to Governance," notes: "Increasing portions of the population [in Latin America] are identifying themselves as indigenous peoples and will demand not only a voice but, potentially, a new social contract. Many reject globalization as it has played out in the region, viewing it as a homogenizing force that undermines their unique cultures and as a U.S.-imposed, neo-liberal economic model whose inequitably distributed fruits are rooted in the exploitation of labor and the environment."[7]

A global economy that erodes once-inviolate national borders also helps to undermine the solidity of national identity within a nation-state and exacerbates inequalities; this adds to the impetus for Native Americans to seek new cultural references, in some cases those offered by ethno-nationalism. At the same time, it might be argued that indigenous peoples are less in opposition to the amorphous term "globalization" per se, than they are to specific free trade agreements and other nation-state institutional arrangements that challenge their land ownership and other rights and neither offer nor honor protections for Native peoples. The case of Guatemala is instructive, from a Western perspective, of the cross-cutting outlook inherent in the attitudes of many indigenous peoples. "The Mayanist movement is at once predominantly conservative on the cultural plane and predominantly innovative and revolutionary on the political and economic plane," noted indigenous leader Demetrio Cojtí Cuxil. "For that reason, it is said that the Maya movement's path leads not only to Tikal (traditionalism) but also to New York and Tokyo (modernism)."[8]

Compare the examples of some Native peoples such as Ecuador's Otavalo (who have been able to maintain their centuries-old traditions, dating to even before the Inca invasion, as textile makers and business people) and Guatemala's Mayan farmers who produce broccoli for a New Age market, prospering in the globalizing economy,[9] with the early-1990s example of Chiapas, Mexico. An authoritarian Mexican President Carlos Salinas de Gortari, intent on successfully negotiating the North American Free Trade Agreement with the United States, officially ended agrarian reform and "modernized" agriculture by modifying Article 27 of the Mexican Constitution, which provided for the inalienable right of land ownership by Native communities. With this act, and his regime's insistence on promoting the image and concerns of a monolingual, monocultural and monoethnic modern state in a country with large sections of the population who had been marginalized, Salinas succeeded in detonating protests by many of the country's 56 indigenous groups, with the uprising in the state of Chiapas in particular capturing the popular imagination.[10] Similarly the confrontation of Native peoples with Peruvian state security forces in Bagua had a strong component of rejection of a free trade agreement with the United States seen by the indigenous communities as prejudicial, as well against the pretension of a corrupt central government anxious to bypass prior consultation accords with the indigenous communities in favor of multinational corporations. (According to a 2009 report by the international watchdog group Transparency International, fully 70 percent of Peruvians surveyed see government anti-corruption efforts as ineffective, with the judiciary and the political parties leading the list of the institutions viewed as corrupt.)[11]

The examples from Ecuador and Guatemala, compared to those of Mexico and Perú, show that it is a mistake, as historian Marc Becker noted—in an observation not without criticism of the trend he discerns—"to assume that ethnic-based movements are necessarily opposed to the neo-liberal capitalist system. In fact, neoliberalism is highly capable of accepting and integrating ethnic expressions into its agenda." On the other hand, as Danish land reform expert Søren Hvalkof pointed out, "although indigenous communities and their organizations may seem to be in accord with neoliberal arguments regarding the inflated and incompetent bureaucracy and (cost) inefficient state obstructing the development of decentralized competitive markets, they are at the same time fierce defenders of strong State regulations and efficient control institutions safeguarding their rights and equal access to land and financial and productive resources and, as such, absolutely against [deregulating] the State and its instruments." And neoliberal arguments cut across the interests of indigenous communities in other ways as well. As anthropologist Kay Warren has underscored regarding the experience of Guatemala's Mayan peoples, it is also important to note "the contradictory pressures of international funders who in the name of neoliberalism pressure the government to trim bureaucracies and social services and in the name of peace offer very specific kinds of support for the strengthening of civil society and democracy."[12]

Throughout the 1990s and the beginning of the twenty-first century, indigenous peoples have been most successful arguing their case for the right to self-determination and autonomy before international forums. In fact, as political scientist Virginia Q. Tilley has chronicled, a transnational indigenous peoples' movement has emerged, a "global network of native peoples' movements and representatives—and of sympathetic institutions, non-governmental organizations (NGOs) and scholars—which, through decades of international conferences, has formulated certain framing norms for indigenous politics now expressed in several international legal instruments." Over time, this movement has become "an omnipresent influence in indigenous ethnopolitics around the world, partly by generating new transnational resources for indigenous movements, such as legal expertise, political leverage, funds for travel and consultation or communication technology, but more broadly by fostering an international human rights climate that has helped to cultivate political openings, to indigenous demands for group rights, within national areas." However, these new vistas of cooperation have at the same time already fostered overheated alarums by non-Indians invested in the status quo. Writing about the contemporary demands of Argentine and Chilean Mapuche Indians, conservative political analyst Malú Kikuchi darkly warned: "For almost two decades, growing stronger, counting on international support that includes supplying money, media attention and even weapons, Latin American indigenism advances without being met by forces to confront their demands; few of them just and the majority, absurd."[13]

The recent mobilizations of indigenous peoples in Bolivia and Ecuador that resulted in several non-Indian civilian presidents being overthrown arguably presented the specter of "failing states" —weak states in which the central government has little practical control over much of its territory and which thus may, although not always do, serve as breeding grounds for terrorism, ethnosectarian violence, or other globalization-related maladies. "The Failed States Index 2007" published in *Foreign Policy* magazine, places countries such as Mexico, Guatemala, Ecuador, Perú, and Bolivia—all nations where indigenous mobilization is a significant factor in recent past or potential violent internal conflicts—in their "warning" category.[14] And in mid-2009, political scientists Mitchell A. Seligson and John A. Booth, examining a year's worth of regional polling data to see if the situation in Honduras was a system-challenging crisis foretold in the numbers, found that—after the Central American republic and the hemisphere's perennial "sick man," Haiti—the next countries whose democratic political stability was threatened by their citizens' low perceptions of political legitimacy were Guatemala, Perú and Ecuador. They pointed out that each of these countries with large Indian populations were characterized by "low consolidation of democratic norms and high dissatisfaction with government performance and institutions." According to the polling data, each had "larger proportions of antidemocratic, institutionally disloyal, and economic performance-frustrated populations." "Having large populations of disgruntled citizens may encourage elites to risk antidemocratic adventures," they noted, the most common form of challenge to democracies. Only historically coup-prone Bolivia, the country with the largest percentage of indigenous populations in the Americas, appeared to escape such a fate, for reasons that will be explained elsewhere in this work. What is more, the failure to conciliate and remediate real and perceived injustices can have expansive waves extending beyond coup-prone polities. In his own work on Central and Eastern Europe Rogers Brubaker shows how a "triadic nexus" of competing nationalisms repeatedly plunged that region into bloodshed. Under this scenario, "homeland nationalism"—arising when members of a group are politically separated from their ethnic homeland—leaves the dispossed with the choice of assimilation, becoming a national minority demanding collective rights, or irredentism, choices that have had, to varying degrees, echo in several countries in Latin America. And, as economists José G. Montalvo and Marta Reynal-Querol note, "the index of ethnic polarization is a significant explanatory variable for the incidence of civil wars." At minimum, business as usual is not possible in a society with a high level of potential ethnic conflict, since this situation affects all levels of economic activity."[15]

In their book, *Armed Actors: Organized Violence and State Failure in Latin America,* University of Utrecht professors Dirk Kruijt and Kees Kooning, warn that the proliferation of "armed actors" in the region is due in part to ethnic tensions in various countries, particularly in the central Andean region of Ecuador, Perú and Bolivia.[16] At the same time, as political scientists Joshua S. Goldstein and Jon C. Pevehouse point out, when conflicts take on an ethnic cast, they become harder to resolve, "because they are not about 'who gets what' but about 'I don't like you.' . . . Almost all the means of leverage used in such conflicts are negative, and bargains are very hard to reach. So ethnic conflicts tend to drag on without resolution for generations." The conflicts are more intractable because they are based not only on material interests, but also on psychological and emotional factors.[17]

From any map of the territories in the region that are seen as trending toward the status of "ungoverned spaces"—areas in which a state faces significant challenges in establishing control, where drug production and their distribution northward, rest areas for insurgent and terrorist groups, and other illegal or anti-democratic activities flourish (including, in a few instances, curious efforts at proselytizing by violent Islamist groups) —one can see that these geographic neighborhoods mesh largely, albeit imperfectly and not exclusively, with areas where indigenous peoples live, and where they frequently fall victim to these phenomena. "The indigenous inhabit the most remote regions, particularly those along international borders," noted political scientist Van Cott, in a study published in 1997 by the *Air & Space Power Journal.* "Guerrilla groups and drug traffickers inhabit these regions for the same reasons: they are excellent places to evade the state, to launch offensive operations from which they can escape over international borders. As a result, in places where guerrilla movements, drug traffickers and the indigenous share territory, most notably in Colombia, Guatemala and Perú, the Indians must fight to establish a relationship between themselves and the diverse armed groups in the region."[18] Along the Brazil/Colombia border, the Tikuna and other native peoples find themselves victims of drug and alcohol abuse due to their proximity to drug traffickers, who, because the indigenous peoples' superior knowledge of the nearly impenetrable rain forest and river networks, use them as drug mules to transport cocaine to Brazil's booming market. And in large swathes of territory in Guatemala, much of it home to more than two dozen Mayan peoples, Mexican narcotics traffickers are truly kings of the forest, lords who now pay their local "mules" and hit men with cocaine rather than with money, and who are leaving a growing trail of home-grown addicts.[19] In 2007, of the eight cases examined by the RAND Corporation around the world in its study *Ungoverned Territories; Understanding and Reducing Terrorism Risks*, two were in Latin America—the Colombian-Venezuelan border and the Guatemala-Chiapas (Mexico) border. Both areas home to large Indian populations, RAND found the first to be an example of "contested governance," of a region where local forces "actively disputing governmental control, seek to create their own state-like entity, either to realize aspirations of independent self-rule or to profit from illegal activities without the interference of state authorities." In the case of Guatemala, the think tank noted that the government could not maintain "a competent, qualified presence stronger than competing power centers. . . . Local officials, where they exist, are inept or are co-opted by criminal organizations."[20]

Although some governments view the activism of indigenous peoples in those the so-called "ungoverned" areas as real or potential threats to national sovereignty, just as surely those risks are exacerbated by the failure of those same nation-states to consider solutions that allow Native American communities to survive as nations within those nation-states. Proof of the possibility of enhancing national-state sovereignty through recognition of Indian nationality— by means of what historian Shelagh D. Grant has called tribal "'self-government' within a non-ethnic government"—can be found in the writing of Barry Scott Zellen. He noted that one of Canada's "most powerful claims" to that its sovereignty in the frozen north is the "increasingly supportive, collaborative, and interdependent relationship to the Inuit [Eskimo] of the Arctic, their enduring stewardship over the Arctic lands, seas, and wildlife since time immemorial, and the mutual recognition of each other's sovereignty through the resolution brought forth by Native land claims."[21] U.S. military historians, too, offer special insight into the potential fruits of effective sovereignty when they point out that Native Americans in the United States have the highest record of service in the armed forces per capita when compared to other ethnic groups, a subject that we will return to later in this book.

For indigenous peoples, the possession of commonly held ancestral land goes beyond mere economic survival—although it also serves tens of millions for that purpose as well. As is the case with Native Americans in the United States, for the indigenous peoples of Mexico and Central and South America the ability to govern themselves, to establish and maintain group rights and territorial control of lands that form part of their cultural inheritance, to empower themselves through education and to protect their languages and cultures, means that as a people they can also hope to survive in a way that allows them to pass their ethnic identity as well as their traditions to their children. The increased political mobilizations of indigenous peoples in Brazil, Colombia and Mexico in the 1970s can all be traced to increases in outside pressure on native peoples' lands. Since that time, the number of countries facing similar challenges has grown, from Guatemala south, on both sides of the Andes and down the Cordillera to Punta Arenas, Chile, the southernmost city on Earth.

Those concerned about human rights, regional security, and environmental protection can find in the subject of indigenous rights common interests and, potentially, common cause. By juxtaposing a map of where most indigenous peoples live in the Americas, with diagrams of the region's most vulnerable so-called "ungoverned areas" and what is left of the hemisphere's pristine natural inheritance, one is rewarded with a remarkable territorial overlay and new possibilities for collective action. Native peoples' homelands, in many cases the last remote forests, savannas, mountains and wetlands of Latin America, are facing a ruthless onslaught by multinational corporations, lawless cattle ranchers, cash-hungry loggers and landless peasants. In Mexico, an estimated 70 percent of indigenous land is forest; the Sierra Madre Occidental in Chihuahua state is one of the richest biosystems in North America, with a stunning variety of plants and animals. Yet the region's fifty thousand Tarahumara Indians remain at risk, victims of an unholy alliance of large landowners and drug traffickers.[22] During November 2008, the Conferencia de Nacionalidades Indígenas de Ecuador (Confederation of Indigenous Nationalities of Ecuador/*CONAIE)*, a native peoples' organization composed of fourteen different Indian peoples of differing languages and cultures that claims to have some two million members, threatened the government of leftwing populist Rafael Correa with a nationwide uprising against it to protest mining legislation the group said was prejudicial to the environment. Correa's cabinet, CONAIE complained, was carrying out a "genocidal" and "neoliberal extractionist" policy on natural resources. That year the Correa government received plaudits internationally for elevating indigenous rights in its new Constitution by describing the country as "intercultural, plurinational"—a phrase of important significance to Native peoples. Yet the government also protected its own definition of development, and its own money trail, by not including in the new magna carta a clause on "previous informed consent" to govern resource exploitation on Indian lands—something that is a key demand of indigenous groups around the world. Then again, in 2009, the Correa government faced indigenous mobilization over its plans to permit, without their prior consent, extractive mining on Indian lands and the placing of water resources under the control of the government in Quito.[23] (The title of this book, *Peoples of the Earth*, borrows from the Mapuche of Chile and Argentina the English translation of their people's name and their view of their harmony with the environment—how land and life are synonymous—a conception shared to a greater or lesser degree by indigenous peoples throughout the Americas. As *Peoples of the Earth* goes to press, the Mapuche in Chile confront the government in Santiago, occupying ranches and logging compounds in the country's south, torching some, and demanding schools, clinics and a return of their native lands.)

In a region in which the failure to protect property rights is an Achilles' heal for democratic governance and economic growth, experts say that securing legal protection for Indian lands is the greatest challenge faced by native peoples as they seek to preserve their own ways of life, and the ecosystems that sustain them. These protections must be part of a systematic effort to encourage indigenous peoples living in fragile environments to conserve their resources by ensuring their rights and their ability to defend their land and resource base, and to help them meet their needs in a modern world, without losing their time-honored resource management methods suddenly seeming more relevant in a globally warming world.

Framed largely in the words, perspectives and history forged in the global North, concepts such as race and ethnicity, statehood and nationalism, and modernity and civilization rest uneasily and uncertainly on the current debate over indigenous peoples' rights and their places within nation-states. At the same time, the challenge of indigenous peoples' political struggle does include crises of *participation* (where "sizeable segments of the population, heretofore excluded from the system, demand effective participation in the political process"), *legitimacy* (where "sizable portions of the politically relevant population challenge or deny the normative validity of claims to authority made by existing leadership"), and *distribution* (in which "sizable portions of the politically relevant population demand a redistribution of societal rewards and benefits, often economic").[24] As seen in the first decade of the twenty-first century, the unwillingness of society to deal with any one of these crises can precipitate a rolling eruption of the others, in a self-destructing chain of events with an uncertain finale, but one in which the imploding norms and rules of political participation of the status quo will remain neither viable nor attractive. What makes consideration of the issues included in this book all the more imperative is the fact, as noted by historians and social scientists such Jerry Z. Muller, Chaim Kaufmann, and others, that "once ethnic antagonism has crossed a certain threshold of violence, maintaining the rival groups within a single polity becomes far more difficult."[25]

At the time this monograph was begun, 2008, when the independence of Kosovo occupied the front pages of the world's newspapers, a focus on the nationalist experience in other regions began to offer a useful—although certainly not a defining—comparison with the rise of native peoples' nationalism in the Americas. Not all indigenous movements have remained within the parameters of emphasizing their cultural values and their desire for full citizen rights, but all explicitly recognize the differences between Indian and non-Indian traditions, mores and customs. Reflecting chasms of culture and disputed ideas over state and ethnic-group boundaries, as well as conflicts concerning political rights and civil liberties, indigenous demands also bring with them the potential for ethnic conflict of four types categorized by political scientists. The communal conflicts in "Latin" America range—as either potential or real, inchoate or full-blown— from *ethnic violence* (two or more groups involved in aggressive acts against each other) and *rebellion* (where one group revolts against another to wrest control of the political system), to *irredentism* (the effort by an ethnic group to secede from one state to join ethnic group members in another state) and *civil war* (where one group seeks to create new political system based on ethnicity.)[26] The challenge for policymakers in capitals around the region who are interested in increasing both political stability and democratic legitimacy is how to support Indian mobilization in a way that actually strengthens state cohesion. Although few in number, the example of the Inuit of Canada, examined later in this book, is particularly relevant, given its insights into the necessary balancing of rights and obligations as they relate to traditions, but also about the more difficult issues of land ownership, development and environmental stewardship.

The cases of Perú and Bolivia, in particular, have important implications about indigenous peoples' mobilization along broad-based or ethnic, nationalist lines, what role ideology plays in these political and cultural movements, and who can and should be their allies. Their example, together with that of Ecuador, are critical for understanding the ongoing but often overlooked tensions between Marxist and neo-Marxist ideology and questions of race and ethnicity, issues that arguably bear the seeds of potential disunity among Indian peoples themselves. (As we will see later, in Chapter Seven, Indian opponents of President Evo Morales echo this complaint.) Guatemala—together with Perú one of the countries in the region where racism against Indians is most prevalent—also offers an interesting counterpoint to the "popular" jargon of the Left. As Kay Warren has noted, while the Left came to express support for cultural respect and the autonomy of indigenous peoples, that was not enough. "On the whole Mayanists judged the *popular* model as calling for their assimilation into national society . . . *Popular* organizers were seen as externalizing injustice by focusing their critiques on U.S. imperialism and colonialism—and more recently on global 'neoliberalism'—rather than giving high priority to patterns of Guatemalan racism, internal colonialism, and cultural distinctiveness."[27]

Just as important, part of the gathering confrontation in the region has its roots in a history that far pre-dates Cold War loyalties and arguments that persisted after the fall of the Berlin Wall. For example, in April 2009, the Miskito Indian council of elders, angered by unfulfilled promises of autonomy offered by the post-Marxist Sandinista government in Managua, declared that the impoverished and isolated Caribbean coast—more than half of Nicaragua's national territory—had seceded from the Central American country and was now the Independent Nation of Moskitia. In announcing that they were taking control of all local government offices—and that all land titles, concessions and contracts issued by the Nicaraguan government were invalid and would have to be renegotiated—the new authorities said that while they hoped for a peaceful transition to self rule, they were also forming an army to defend their claims. The group pointed to a series of historic treaties from the nineteenth century to support their claim to their own nation on Indian lands. They also appointed a defense minister.[28]

As Indian voters become political forces to be reckoned with, regional left-wing populist leaders—whose social justice banners have been adapted to mirror the cultural concerns of indigenous peoples—have sought to monopolize their activism for their own ends. At mid-year 2009, indigenous activists in Honduras rallied in support of Manuel Zelaya, remembering how the recently deposed president had opened his doors to them. The U.S. newspaper *Indian Country Today* reported that largest indigenous organizations in the Central American republic "assert that the new administration is trying to hide the real reason for the coup, which was that the opposition feared a new constitution that could provide more rights and protections to indigenous and other Hondurans." While a desire to quash Indian interests was unlikely to have been the primary motivating factor for the quasi-coup—other clashes over money, power and international geopolitics were also involved—the claim appeared grounded in an ugly reality. The *de facto* Honduran regime that replaced Zelaya quickly moved to expel the medical staff of the community-run Indigenous Garifuna Community Hospital, forcing them to discontinue their work. The facility had opened in 2007 under an agreement with the Zelaya government in keeping with the International Labor Organization convention that supported locally managed health services for tribal and indigenous peoples. Rotary International had named the hospital director, Dr. Luther Castillo, "Honduran Doctor of the Year" that year.According to Castillo, the hospital's ten Garifuna doctors—all graduates of the Latin American Medical School in Havana—treated over one hundred and seventy five thousand cases since the facility opened its doors.[29]

Unfortunately, when it comes to indigenous issues in the region, a tragic observation about Latin American politics remains particularly apt: While the Latin Left too often falls into the thrall of latter-day populist and violence-prone Jacobins, the underlying orientation of political conservatives and free market mavens is reminiscent of that in colonial white-run Rhodesia.

The scene in Tegucigalpa, however, is not new in Latin America and has encompassed populists of both right and left. As Argentine novelist Ernesto Sábato sensitively wrote from the northern Argentine city of Salta following the overthrow of elected military strongman Juan Perón:

That September night in 1955, while we doctors, farm-owners and writers were noisily rejoicing in the living room over the fall of the tyrant, in a corner of the kitchen I saw how the two Indian women who worked there had their eyes drenched in tears. And although in all those years I had meditated upon the tragic duality that divided the Argentine people, at that moment it appeared to me in its moving form. . . . Many millions of dispossessed people and workers were shedding tears at that instant, for them a hard and sober moment. Those two Indian girls who wept in a kitchen in Salta symbolized great multitudes of their humble compatriots.[30]

Today's leftwing populists, while claiming to deconstruct the checks and balances of democratic institutions in the people's interest, often actually dismantle them to their own benefit—a point made clear in the writings about contemporary Ecuador of leftwing historian Marc Becker. And as we will examine later in this book—as promises remain unfulfilled and disenchantment replaces hope—in the end the self-interested efforts of the leftwing populists and other non-Indian elites may serve only as a portal through which important numbers of Native American groups emerge to make common cause with violent extra-continental extremist groups, including Islamist fundamentalists. Such a phenomenon, posing an uncomfortable question that nonetheless surely needs answers, is already beginning to take place in Mexico and Venezuela.

In some respects the struggle of indigenous peoples might appear revolutionary in Western, or European senses of the word. However, increasingly, in their search to remake the existing social order, their demands and also the pattern of their resistance—their rebellion—are based on what they consider an older, legitimate political order, one of shared identities that include longstanding sets of beliefs and images. In response to centuries of discrimination, some radicalized native peoples are channeling legitimate demands for effective political participation, cultural integrity and access to resources through ethnosectarian appeals to a racially based nationalist counter-reaction, a response that should constitute a dead letter to the democratic community in the Information Age. The threat posed to the rule of law can only get worse if the security challenges implicit in this undercurrent are ignored. "The changing configuration of nation-states provides the building blocks with which diplomats must seek to build peace and security even in the face of transnational forces such as terrorism," warns political scientist Philip G. Roeder. "Nation-state crises have been extraordinarily destabilizing," he adds. "[I]n recent decades projects to create new nation-states have been the single most common agenda of terrorists."[31]

Among the indigenous movements that want more than to simply emphasize their cultural values and the desire for full citizenship rights is an articulation and a frank recognition of the differences between Indian and non-Indian traditions, mores and customs. Today, Native American nationalists seeking meaning in their particular historical epic find in "imagined communities"—a phrase coined by Benedict Anderson that refers to a nation comprised of a community that is socially constructed and ultimately imagined by the people who perceive themselves as part of that group[32]—the means of recovering a collective identity. Identifying each other through symbols of a common heritage and a potentially shared future becomes both a rationale for, and a means of, challenging nation-states that reflect neither their values nor past or current possibilities of constructive participation.

As the twenty-first century progresses, other voices demanding the conservation or the reconstruction of pre-Colombian institutions, practices and borders are being increasingly noted, even when these are only partly documented and understood, and major differences exist in their interpretation, though for all intents and purposes such a history has earlier been described in the North American context as "nonexistent, an unheard wailing."[33] Peruvian and Bolivian Indians dream of uniting the countries of the Andes, from Colombia in the north to Argentina and Chile to the south, in a reprise of *Tawantinsuyu*, the Inca Empire that brought together the Quechua and Aymara peoples living along the spine of the Andes before the Spanish conquest in 1532. Thousands of Indians belonging to what they term the "Guarani nation," have called for the "resurrection" of an Indian homeland for an indigenous community that extends from southern Brazil, through Paraguay, Bolivia and northern Argentina.[34] A new indigenous political party in Chile, Wallmapuwen, whose name means Tierra Mapuche (or in English, Mapuche Land), proposes a new self-governing nation in the *Wallmapu*, the Mapuche Indian territory spanning the Andes that encompasses lands in both Chile and Argentina, including the "restitution" of *Puelmapu*, the easternmost Mapuche territory whose federal capital is Buenos Aires. (In September 2009, Mapuche Indians living in the Argentine province of Neuquen were accused by area cattlemen and large landowners of forming a guerrilla organization supported by members of the Colombian Revolutionary Armed Forces [*Fuerzas Armadas Revolucionarias de Colombia/FARC*] and the Basque Homeland and Freedom [*Euskadi Ta Askatasuna/ETA*] armed nationalist separatist organization. These, they claimed, were already clandestinely working with Mapuche groups in the south of Chile. One prominent businessman, scion of a leading regional political family, charged that the Indians had created "a regime of terror and insecurity" in the province. Mapuche leaders, supported by labor unions and human rights organizations, countered by saying the accusations were an attempt by powerful interests to expropriate their ancestral lands. "We couldn't be supported by violent independence movements like ETA or the FARC because we are only demanding autonomy as a people in the context of the laws of this country," countered Mapuche leader Jorge Nahuel.) The Mapuche case in particular makes it important to remember that, as Goldstein and Pevehouse have pointed out, when ethnic challenges result in wars of secession, conflicts "can be large and deadly, and they can easily spill over international borders or draw in other countries. *This spillover is particularly likely if members of an ethnic or religious group span two sides of a border, constituting the majority group in one state and a majority in a nearby region of another state, but a minority in the other state as a whole."*[35] (Italics added.)

In the northern Amazon region, a row between a group of Indian tribes and rice farming squatters in the Raposa Serra do Sol reservation—where 4.2 million acres are home to 18,000 Indians—turned so violent that in 2008 Brazil's Supreme Court warned that it might escalate into civil war. According to an *Associated Press* report: "Top military generals warn that too much land in Indian hands, especially along Brazil's borders, threatens national security and could lead to tribes unilaterally declaring themselves independent nations." Among the Brazilian armed forces, European examples of ethnonationalism were considered, for instance improbably comparing the situation in the Amazon to Kosovo, which broke away from Serbia in February, 2008. It was only in May of the next year that the Supreme Court ordered the rice farmers to leave the disputed land.[36]

Concerns about the effects of unrest, potential, real, and imagined, is not limited to south of the Rio Grande, either, but are now raised across the Americas. As will be seen later, in southwestern United States, migration from southern Mexico, Guatemala, Belize, El Salvador, western Honduras, the Pacific lowlands of Nicaragua and northwestern Costa Rica—those countries comprising what is known as "Mesoamerica"—has brought in its wake nascent identification with, and proto-activism in favor of, pan-Indian allegiance, a loyalty forged (sometimes with outside encouragement) through a putative common bond with ancient Mayan and Aztec civilizations, even among Central American Indians whose ancestors belonged to rival tribes and peoples. (In El Salvador, tourism interests and non-Indian factors have resulted in the "mayanization" of that country's indigenous peoples even though neither the Nahuat nor the Lenca "are Mayan in any linguistic or pre-Colombian cultural sense.")[37]

Possibly apocalyptic scenarios are not only the elucubrations of Brazilian generals, Argentine landowners, or non-Indian elites in Perú and Bolivia, either. They have also emerged in Canada, a country that—unlike the United States—has largely eschewed "melting pot" nostrums, and in the process has recently done much to empower its indigenous peoples in the frozen north. In late 2009, Douglas L. Bland, Chair of Defence Studies at the School of Policy Studies at Queen's University in Kingston, Canada, sought to rock his country's consciousness with the publication of a novel, *Uprising,* about a future Indian rebellion there. His publishing house promoted the book by claiming it an "urgent" work of a security specialist accustomed to offering advice to Canada's most important political leadership: "Combining wide-ranging experiences, extensive military knowledge, historical research, travels in strife-torn regions of the world, and his long-held interest in the theory and practices of revolutionary warfare, Douglas Bland now masterfully presents in *Uprising* a chilling national narrative about a future aboriginal 'people's war' in Canada." It advertised the work not only as fiction, but also pertaining to the categories of "aboriginal issues," and "USA and Canadian public affairs." In *Uprising,* Bland, echoing a perspective offered by author and indigenous rights theoretician Zellen nearly two decades earlier, warned that:

> A root cause of terrorism in far-away countries, Canadians are told, is poor, desperate young people who turn their frustrations and anger on their 'rich oppressors.' *Uprising* brings this scenario home to Canada. . . . [The Indians] know their minority force cannot take on all Canada. They don't need to. A surprise attack on the nation's most vulnerable assets—its abundant energy resources—sends the Canadian Armed Forces scrambling and politicians reeling. Over a few tension-filled days as the battles rage, the frantic prime minister can only watch as the insurrection paralyzes the country. But when energy-dependent Americans discover the southward flow of Canadian hydroelectricity, oil, and natural gas is halted, they do not remain passive.[38]

In the case of *Peoples of the Earth,* the challenges a growing and in some ways new indigenous activism pose to the concept of the nation-state itself, particularly in the Andean region, are examined and assayed based on available evidence, historical precedent and regional and international trends. It looks at whether such activism can be channeled through multi-cultural, multi-ethnic and pluri-national citizenship, or whether it portends a future of centrifugal forces tearing apart the fragile consensus around democratic governance in nations that mostly were just a generation ago under white or mixed-race authoritarian rule. It probes particularly how new linguistic, religious and other cultural awakenings, and their related definitions of group identity with a nation-state, coincide with existing national boundaries, and whether these can contain them. It defines "political culture" as being, in the words of historian Robert Whitney

> about the ability and *the power* to bestow meanings on things, people, social relations of production, and ideas within specific historical contexts and social struggles. This power to bestow meanings, in turn, is often realized within the context of historically specific collective action and mass mobilization. . . . Political culture refers to the living collective memories, struggles, and values of social groups who create their own identities and political meanings not only to resist dominant political discourses and practices but also to create alternative ways of living.[39]

The study also employs what Stern called multiple time frames of analysis, offering views that extend from the welter of conflicts and divisions found at a certain time among and within contending social classes and ethnicities, to the perspectives offered by a larger sweep of history. These multiple time frames are, Stern notes, both

> relatively short time frames ('conjunctural' and 'episodic') to understand the recent changes that make rebellion or insurrection more likely and possible, and to appreciate dynamic changes that emerge during the course of violent con-

flicts; and longer time frames spanning centuries to understand the historic injustices, memories and strategies that shape the goals, consciousness, and tactics of the rebels.[40]

By way of example, in the case of Bolivia, multiple timeframes help understand
how the historical memory of both the politicized Aymara and their non-Indian
opponents have been linked over two centuries, while an examination limited to
a half-century's events prior to their contemporary rebellion is inadequate to
understand the dynamics of political consciousness on the *altiplano*. "The most
distant and distinct point in relation to the uprising of 1780 is perhaps the agrarian revolution which took place in Bolivia in response to the Agrarian Reform of
1953," wrote Xavier Albó, a Bolivian linguistic anthropologist. Albó traced the
collective memory that linked the rebellion of Aymara Indians by Tupaj Katari
in 1781 in La Paz to the emergence of a powerful peasant movement in the early
1980s. This more contemporary group's most militant members like to call
themselves "kataristas," and their leader came from a community not far from
Katari's birthplace. "But what catches the eye is that after the reform and the
lethargic two decades that followed, the Bolivian peasantry has begun to agitate
once again in a manner reminiscent of that distant Katari of the colonial period,"
Albó noted. "(I)t is evident that the Katari/katarista nexus, spanning across two
hundreds years, has an ideological element: a unifying and mobilizing historical
memory."[41]

    Another example of how the use of multiple timeframes helps to understand
the issue is the largely un-remarked aspects of the political situation in southern
Mexico. According to one respected author, "even now militant organizations
deep in the jungles of the state of Quintana Roo practice ancient rituals and
resist Occidental cultural and political hegemony, including the Gregorian
calendar."[42]

    To understand the insertion of ancient indigenous peoples' practices and be-
liefs into contemporary society requires both original and surer ways to concep-
tualize political, economic and cultural aspects of identity construction—
composed of particular collective memories, values and visions of the world,
always more distant to the outsider because the time, place and circumstance are
not hers. And to do so means understanding how these relate to the political and
institutional contexts in which they now occur. To put their struggle within the
context of the evolving concept of the nation-state offers the chance to view
with greater granularity, in the words of political scientist Joel Migdal, "the
transformation of people as they adopt the symbols of the state and the transformation of the state as it incorporates symbols from society."[43]

    Just three decades ago, many social scientists and others still thought that
Latin American indigenous peoples were immune to the attractions of nationalism, given their culturally neutral ascribed status as "peasants" as well as their
social fragmentation and their being seen as "deprived of the cultural resources

for a collective response to their subordinate status." Until very recently the countries of "Latin" America and the Caribbean have largely been free of explicitly ethnicity-based parties competing against other, more traditional political movements of left, right and center through which nation-state elites have expressed their differences and settled accounts.[44]

By means of surveying contemporary experience in Bolivia, Perú, Ecuador, Guatemala, Chile, and other countries, *Peoples of the Earth* juxtaposes the emergence of the Indians' cultural agenda, including respect for native languages and religion, with the types of ethnic-based populism (characteristic of Bolivia's Indian president Evo Morales[45]) and ethnic nationalism gaining ground in the region. It examines how new and sometimes-contradictory bonds of indigenous solidarity are being projected across national boundaries, and to what extent native peoples' mobilization threatens regional stability. Or how such mobilization creates an opportunity to construct a more lasting democratic consensus (democratizing democracy) rooted in the full citizenship and participation, including in economic development, by all of a nation-state's peoples, perhaps by constructing federal-type devolution of power and income to subnational units.

Although multidisciplinary in scope, *Peoples of the Earth* does, in some ways, eschew generalized behavioral explanations that social scientists tend to offer for past events. It also consciously attempts to balance the contributions of social history to clarity, empathy and understanding, with traditional standards of scholarship, at the same time avoiding what David Hackett Fischer once called "the Fallacy of the Lonely Fact." Emerging ethno-nationalist perspectives used in the debate over the challenges faced and posed by indigenous peoples makes this work necessarily tentative, when not speculative. The unique saga of the native peoples in Mexico and Central and South America requires a broad, eclectic vision, one that hopes to help light the way, to paraphrase the words of novelist Norman Mailer, for nations to discover the deepest colors of their character.[46] As Oxford professor Alan Knight has observed, "the historian is not obliged to subscribe to a general . . . theory. The historian should, of course, frame hypotheses and make them clear. . . . [U]ltimately, it is fruitfulness—the payoff in terms of historical understanding—which counts."[47] The primary aim of this book is, no more and no less, to increase the bounty of our common understanding of a discordant past and a conflictive present, with the purpose of assisting others divine a possibly more hopeful future.

Chapter Two
The "Miner's Canary" of Democracy

"An evident principle runs through all the programs I have outlined. It is the principle of justice to all peoples and nationalities and their right to live on equal terms of liberty and safety with one another, whether they be strong or weak."
—Woodrow Wilson, speaking about his *Fourteen Points* program, January 1918[1]

"Like the miner's canary, the Indian marks the shift from fresh air to poison gas in our political atmosphere, and our treatment of Indians, even more than the treatment of other minorities, reflects the rise and fall of our democratic faith."
—Felix S. Cohen, *The Erosion of Indian Rights 1950-1953*[2]

In 1962, *CBS News* anchor Walter Cronkite presented a program segment, "So That Men are Free," reported by the peripatetic newsman Charles Kuralt. The account, from what Cronkite observed was one of the most remote areas of the world, was from Vicos, a former hacienda two hundred miles north of Lima, two and a quarter miles up to the snow line of the Andes and, as Kuralt noted evenly, "just ten years out of the sixteenth century." There, beginning in 1952, four leading U.S. social scientists—Allan R. Holmberg, Paul L. Doughty, Henry F. Dobyns and Harold Lasswell—and Peruvian counterparts like Cornell University-educated Mario Vázquez would come to work on an experiment at giving Indian peasants at the hacienda increased and unheard-of initiative in making decisions about the thirty-thousand-acre estate. The learned outsiders then attempted to measure the consequences of that process and other experimental inputs associated with modernization and democratization. The Cornell Peru Project ended up becoming, as the university itself later noted, "a paradigm for international development in the third world" in the later half of the 1960s and early 1970s. What they were doing in practice, Dobyns recalled years later, went far beyond dry theorems of academia. The experiment was challenging at a most basic level, he said, the assumption rife among non-Indians in Perú, an inheritance of Spanish colonialism, that Indians could not safely and soberly administer their own lives and fortunes, and under no circumstances could be trusted.[3]

Those working the hacienda, Kuralt reported for *CBS*, were "descendants of the once all-powerful Inca whose forebears created a civilization rivaling that of Ancient Egypt, full of a great art that is cherished in museums throughout the world." Yet just outside Vicos, he noted, were many other haciendas

> where the Indians with the same heritage are serfs willing to bow down their heads in submission to the man who owns or rents them. If they are unwilling to submit they may starve slowly or they may move to Lima and live in slum shacks on the edge of the city and starve slowly there. Here at Vicos, the Indians neither submit, nor leave for Lima, nor starve. They hold their heads high, stay and prosper because they have learned something, something which in ten years has carried them from sixteenth century serfdom to freedom in the twentieth. What they learned is a simple thing, that all sane men are equal, including Indians.[4]

The global struggle for de-colonization over the past century remains perhaps one of the under-heralded odysseys of contemporary time, the period having "restored a large measure of freedom and dignity to one billion colonized people and [therefore] must be ranked as one of the greatest human rights achievements in the twentieth century."[5] That struggle was conducted almost entirely in the homelands of indigenous peoples, a wide array of humankind linked by a common term. As José Martinez Cobo, the special rapporteur of the U.N. Subcommission on the Prevention of Discrimination and Protection of Minorities defined: "Indigenous communities, peoples and nations are those which, having a historical continuity with pre-invasion and pre-colonial societies that developed on their territories, consider themselves distinct from other sectors of the societies now prevailing in those territories, or parts of them. They form at present non-dominant sectors of society and are determined to preserve, develop and transmit to future generations their ancestral territories, and their ethnic identity, as the basis of their continued existence as peoples, in accordance with their own cultural patterns, social institutions and legal systems."[6]

The activism of indigenous peoples—those who inhabited a land prior to it being taken over by colonial societies and who believe themselves to be distinct from most of those who currently govern those territories—can no longer be ignored. Although a much devalued currency in today's political debates, surely the word "genocide" applies to the legacy of colonial and neo-colonial treatment of indigenous peoples throughout the Americas, as measured in the numbers of Indian nations obliterated, cultures destroyed, languages lost, and lands stolen from them.

The legitimacy of the native peoples' struggle stems in part from the fact that since World War II, race-based political hierarchies and the resulting usurpation of rights are no longer viewed as acceptable in the court of world public opinion. It is no accident that one of the champions of the legitimization of native peoples' politics in the Western Hemisphere, the Colombian intellectual Gregorio Hernandez de Alba, grounded his beliefs in his experience in Europe during the late 1930s and early 1940s. These "made him supremely aware of the issues of race and the dangers of discrimination against people for ethnic or religious reasons," and pointed out "the absurdity of a 'civilized' nation seeking to exterminate people for their religion or race."[7]

In the Western Hemisphere, historically marginalized Native Americans share a legacy of centuries of colonization, discrimination, poverty, and loss of control over their lands, traditions and natural resources along with others of the estimated two hundred and fifty million individuals belonging to five thousand distinct indigenous communities in 70 nation-states around the world.[8] As part of a fourth stage of global democratic development—the first three being the struggle against overseas colonialism and national dictatorships, and the consolidation of "Western" democratic institutions and practices—native peoples have emerged as key political actors in several countries in the Americas. They seek to strengthen traditional cultures, languages, governments and economies while ensuring respect for and control of their lands and access to natural resources.

Also known as "indigenous peoples," or members of "First Nations," the estimated forty million of the poorest peoples in Mexico and Central and South America have for more than two decades awakened to the prospect of seeking political power, although not exclusively through the democratic process. At the same time, as the United Nations' Economic Commission for Latin America and the Caribbean (ECLAC) noted, "consciousness is growing that, in order to overcome poverty, states can no longer search for formulas based on traditional strategies, but they ought to reformulate their historic relationship with indigenous peoples."[9] Indigenous peoples' increasingly ambitious demands, Mixtec Indian lawyer Francisco López Bárcenas suggests, "require a profound transformation of national states and institutions that would practically lead us to a re-founding of nation-states in Latin America. . . . Indigenous peoples in Latin America struggle for autonomy because in the twenty-first century, they still are colonies."[10]

Throughout Central and South America and Mexico, native peoples face the continuing effects of class-based and ethnic discrimination and *de facto*, when not *de jure*, domination.[11] With between 5.3 and 12 million Indians each, Mexico, Perú, Guatemala and Bolivia have the largest indigenous communities in "Latin" America. In five countries in the region, including relatively prosperous Chile, Indians account for between six hundred thousand and one million people; in Brazil there are an estimated seven hundred thousand indigenous people, about four hundred thousand who live on reservations. In Nicaragua, El Salvador and six other countries, Native Americans make up less than half a million each. Although most native peoples live on or near their ancestral lands, urban populations have swelled, particularly as conditions in a globalizing economy have made subsistence agriculture unsustainable. While some 671 indigenous peoples are recognized by their ethnic or tribal affiliation by nation-states, a *Socio-Linguistic Atlas of Latin American Indigenous Peoples,* published in November, 2009, by UNICEF showed that more than a fifth of the 420 languages spoken by the region's indigenous peoples are in danger of extinction. More than 100 Indian peoples have already abandoned their original languages and now speak only Spanish or Portuguese.[12]

A 2007 study by the World Bank showed that 80 percent of the indigenous peoples in Latin America live in extreme poverty, and that governments in the region had relatively few social programs specifically designed to meet their needs. In Guatemala, for example, a country that UNICEF ranks as the sixth worst in the world with respect to chronically malnourished children, the national average of half of the young population unremittingly hungry reaches 80 percent in rural areas where the population is overwhelmingly Mayan Indian. In a country UNICEF points out is rich enough to prevent the widespread hunger, some Indian children are so malnourished that, in the words of the *Economist,* "their black hair has turned blond, their faces are chubby from fluid build-up as their organs fail, the veins in their legs become a visible black spider-web and their face muscles are too weak to smile."[13]

Native peoples' demands for greater inclusion and control of their destiny are aided by the "unprecedented recognition"[14] of indigenous status and rights resulting from the networking possibilities opened by the internationalization of non-state forums.[15] At the same time, the easy availability of alternative means of communication, such as the Internet and cellular phones, has meant that indigenous nations, such as Chile's well-organized Mapuche people, have been able to share ideas, programs and strategies across the globe, as well as deepen and expand beyond personal experience and oral traditions the recovery of a historical memory that remains largely outside their countries' formal educational systems.

Yet the emergence of these new voices is not without risks. In May 2008, indigenous advocates called on the United Nations to draft laws that protect native peoples' rights to own media and that provide for the prosecution of those who kill or persecute indigenous journalists. A list of recommendations called "The Right to Communication and Free Expression of Indigenous Peoples," presented at the U.N. proposed models for legislation that drew heavily on Article 16 of the U.N. Declaration on the Rights of Indigenous Peoples, and a new Community Radio Broadcast Law adopted in Uruguay. The demands were made in the wake of the murder of four Indian journalists in Oaxaca, Mexico, the month before.[16]

Indigenous populations, ranked by countries' total numbers of Native Americans in 1990s

Country	Thousands of Indians	% of population
Mexico	12,000	14.1*
Perú	9,300	46.5
Bolivia	5,600	71.2
Guatemala	5,300	66.2
Ecuador	4,100	43.2
Argentina	1,000	3.1*
Chile	998	10.3*
Colombia	44	2.2*

*High regional concentrations of indigenous populations.

Note: Argentina included because of the Mapuche connection; Colombia because of the Andean connection.

Sources: Estimates based, for most countries, on data from the early 1990s used by the Inter-American Development Bank, the Pan-American Health Organization, and the Economic Commission for Latin America and the Caribbean. The percentages of population are based on population at the time the data was compiled.

From: Latin American Newsletters, *Latin American Special Report*, July 2007

Globalization, with its "steady flow of persons, capital, arms, and ideas," is nonetheless bitterly opposed by many indigenous activists and their allies. Ironically, the phenomenon has arguably had the effect of shrinking the role and importance of states at a time of increasing indigenous peoples' demands that they receive the critical services the existing nation-states say they offer to their citizens.[17]

Most native peoples' activism in the Americas has remained peaceful, even in the face of armed repression; Indian violent protests and insurgencies represent mostly a fitful response to crushing economic crises and efforts by national governments to forcibly remove them from ancestral lands and/or renege on agreed-upon legal agreements protecting their communal rights. It remains to be seen, however, if and how the challenges posed by native peoples' mobilization can continue to be peacefully and productively incorporated as part of a more equitable political inclusion and economic development, particularly as indigenous populations have become, like the rest of the region's population, more urbanized. The question of how native peoples become an integral part of a nation's political community while the same time pressing their demands for cultural and political autonomy remains a Gordian knot that, as legal expert Felix

Cohen pointed out in the U.S. context, "reflects the rise and fall of our democratic faith."

It is not at all certain that the once pent-up pressures that now fuel Native American activism can be contained within the boundaries of regional nation-states that were mostly drawn up two centuries ago by exclusionary non-Indian elites. As López Bárcenas noted, suddenly at issue are the very structures of these nation-states and their future institutional viability. And with it, the once ironclad certainty that national borders would remain inviolate and contribute to the stability, if not prosperity in Central and South America and Mexico. "Interstate conflict (conflict between nations) has been relatively limited on the continent," Strategic Forecasting, Inc. (Stratfor), noted in a recent report. Although many South American states have long histories of conflict within its territory, "often between various indigenous groups or between European-blooded elites and rural inhabitants," this fact, together with geographic circumstances, have helped keep the potential for interstate conflict "low."[18]

Yet the geopolitical model that postulates "Latin" America as a "zone of peace" may be, at least in the future, at risk.[19] A January 2008 report by Stratfor took note of the divide between Bolivian President and Aymara Indian Evo Morales and his allies in the poor Native American highlands on one hand, and rebellious, more affluent residents of European ancestry in the country's eastern lowlands on the other. As a result, Strafor warned, "Bolivia's chaos will raise a question that has not been addressed on the continent in a century: Are South America's borders inviolable?"[20] In other words, will nation-states find themselves obligated to redraw their common frontiers in a way that calls into question national identities and regional loyalties? The announcement in April 2009 that Nicaragua's Miskito Indians were seceding from that country, taking with them control of more than half the national territory, suggests that process might already be taking place. Echoes of such challenges are also beginning to be heard elsewhere. As this work was headed to press, a radicalized Chilean Mapuche organization declared "war" on the government in Santiago, renouncing both their Chilean citizenship and any future attempts at dialogue. (At the same time, it should be noted that the secession card can be played as a bargaining chip in the hope of negotiating greater power or spoils; in the United States the Inupiat people recurrently "study" secession, using the prospect of an inquiry to bargain with the State of Alaska.)[21]

For their part, some indigenous activists claim that, "The war on terror is a new source of abuses of human rights; it is threatening to expand to Latin America, targeting indigenous peoples that are demanding autonomy and protesting market policies and neo-liberal globalization." National Autonomous University of Mexico anthropologist Pedro Ciciliano defends, "Indigenous people can be considered a threat, because they are poor and are pressing for their rights, but they don't represent a terrorist threat." Those holding such views point to events in several countries of the region, including Colombia and Chile to back their case, pointing to what they said is nothing less than the "criminalization" of social movements. "We are the victims of this criminalization and persecution . . . for the thousands of instances of human rights violations in our territories we have requested this hearing," Miguel Palacin Quispe, chair of the Andean Coordinating Committee of Indigenous Organizations (CAOI) and president of the National Confederation of Peruvian Communities Affected by Mining, told a March 20, 2009 hearing of the Inter-American Commission on Human Rights (IACHR), a consultative body to the Organization of American States. Palacin Quispe said that Peru's "extractive model" has allowed oil and other large companies to engage in "irrational exploitation," with "enormous damage and pollution" to Indian lands. "These new neighbors, the multinationals, have located their battles in our territories, and they have put us in a position where we have to defend ourselves." In one instance three years earlier, he testified, twenty nine indigenous activists requesting a dialogue with mining company and government representatives who appeared on Indian territory without consultation, were held hostage and then tortured for three days by the Peruvian National Police. "It is now known," Palacin Quispe added, "that eighteen Colombian ethnicities are in danger of extinction and for them we mobilize, for them we protest and there is no mechanism for dealing with this. . . . we have become the objects of assassination, torture and imprisonment. . . . In many areas, they are preventing us from our constitutional right to mobilize and protest; and the strategy of the state is now to change laws . . . so they criminalize dissidence, and in Chile, against the Mapuche, they use the anti-terrorist law. They also seek to privatize public land and along with this they are increasing the military presence in our territories."[22]

Without question, however, neo-Marxist populists, narcotics traffickers and even in two or possibly three, albeit limited, cases, radical Islamists, have appeared to manipulate, or attempt to manipulate, legitimate native peoples' mobilization for their own purposes, even if doing so puts the nascent progress of the indigenous communities, as well as regional democracy, at considerable risk. As we will see later in this text, in some respects these efforts are reminiscent of attempts in the 1920s by the Soviet-run Comintern to promote indigenous nationalism in Central and South America and Mexico. Others remind of the 1930s, when European and American Nazis sought to capitalize on discontent on U.S. Indian reservations in order to create a potential pro-Reich fifth column in North America in the run-up to World War II.

For now, the potential for native peoples' activism to result in hyper instability borne of ethno-sectarian strife is just that—mostly potential. However, other warning signs also exist, such as incipient disaffection of Native Americans from radicalized leftist politics as well as from Christian faiths ranging from traditional Catholicism to the charismatic, the Pentecostal, and the fundamentalist.[23] This suggests the possibility of both political and religious entropy—that is, nature tending from order to disorder—and a portal through which unforeseeable numbers of Native American groups may emerge to make common cause even with violent extremist groups from outside the Americas, such as radicalized Islam. What is potentially just as bad, it must be noted, is the xenophobic reaction of non-Indian elites, who use the contacts between some Indian leaders and peoples to reinforce their own racial and social prejudices. For example, fulminating against "bloodthirsty Indians" in his own country, political commentator José Brechner—a founder of the political party of a former rightwing military dictator, Hugo Banzer Suárez—characterized the alliance of the government of President Evo Morales with the Iranian dictatorship and militant Islam in this way:

> There is fear in Bolivia, and a lot of it, because those who do not know the frantic Indians do not know terror. The closest to the Bolivian altiplano indigenous are the hordes of Muslim fanatics. It is not by chance that the Arabs are strengthening bonds with Morales; they have through the Indians the human material propitious to expand the Jihad. The Muslim savagery fits perfectly with that of the Bolivian altiplano.[24]

The unprecedented political *protagonismo* of native peoples in Central and South America and Mexico has indeed shaken up the status quo in the region. As historian Eric Foner once remarked about black emancipation during the U.S. Civil War, it is a time of "millennial expectation of impending change." Like African Americans at war's end and during Reconstruction, Indians in Latin America find themselves transformed "in ways unmeasurable by statistics and in realms far beyond the reach of the law." The particular moment is due to a number of factors. East-West Cold War divisions around the world, but particularly in the region, have receded, replaced by long suppressed demands for freedom and autonomy of peoples within existing nation-states. The jarring internal and international migrations of rural peoples that social scientists until recently rotely gave the class-based moniker of "peasants" meant that these return to their former homelands more aware of their cultural differences and more willing to make those part of their political agenda. The international community has also become more aware of the plight of indigenous peoples generally and those of the Western Hemisphere in particular, for a variety of reasons. New international agreements on human rights have promoted a substantive discussion about both the individual and the collective rights of tribal and other indigenous peoples. In an Information Age characterized by cheap and ubiquitous communications, non-government organizations and ethnic communities communicate and coordinate responses to challenges to indigenous rights and to new opportunities for collective action. And, given the fundamental questions posed by indigenous mobilization to modern national concepts of "citizenship," native peoples find they share among and between themselves a "surfeit of identity"— ironically in much the same way several small European populations did, which resulted in their establishing their own nation-states as a result. This flood of ethnic consciousness underlies their demands for greater autonomy and, perhaps, independence from existing nation-state models.[25]

It is in this context that the extraordinary vitality of those communities' activism offers a chance for the indigenous agenda to be fitted into the warp and weave of constitutional, rather than ideological, politics. The expansion of the liberal democratic franchise can, when open to creative new ideas, steer clear of the creation of new sets of winners and losers in a zero-sum game that destroys any chance for social peace. Conversely, because the emerging tectonic shifts in regional politics and society—of the type the historian of identity Elie Kedourie presciently warned about in another time and in a different context (the Middle East of the twentieth century)—these could also result in intractable and unremitting ethno-sectarian strife. Among the changes that are already taking place: a revival of historic disputes, the fresh recollection of old humiliations, and disowning stultified exclusionary political and social structures.[26] "What Latin American elites are learning is that poor, 'apathetic and fatalistic' masses are prime targets for charismatic demagogues," Amy Chua wrote in a 2003 work, suggestively titled *World On Fire; How Exporting Free Market Democracy Breeds Ethnic Hatred and Global Instability*. "Increasingly, indigenous leaders . . . are offering the region's demoralized majorities a package that is hard to beat: a natural scapegoat (rich, corrupt 'whites') and a sense of pride, ownership, and identity. Sometimes that identity is 'Aymara'—the Aymara are a fiercely independent people whose ancestors created architectural marvels many centuries before the Incan conquest; other times, it is 'Quechua,' 'Mayan,' 'Inca,' or just 'indio.'"[27]

Some writers view the role of Native American ethnic parties in Latin America as a net gain, deepening what historian Frederick M. Nunn mordantly calls the region's "low-intensity democracies" by increasing their inclusiveness, legitimacy and levels of participation.[28] Those who argue in favor of channeling native peoples' mobilization into an expanded and more humane democratic contract point out that participatory ideology seeks, through the lens of self-determination and cultural autonomy, to increase both access and effective citizenship in a nation-state's political and social life.[29] The Confederation of Indigenous Nationalities of Ecuador, one of the most powerful Indian umbrella organizations south of the Rio Grande, framed the debate thus:

> The plurinational state is the construction of new political structures: administratively decentralized, culturally heterogeneous, and open to the direct and participatory representation of all indigenous nationalities and social sectors, particularly those that have been marginalized and excluded from the state structure and dominant socio-economic development models . . . implying . . . an institutional expansion . . . within a new concept of State, Development and Citizenship.[30]

In part, the native peoples' struggle for recognition and power today has been carried out within the framework of increasing the legitimacy of democratic regimes in the process of consolidation, a time in which also "the attraction of states is obviously waning . . . suffering serious competition from a host of new identity symbols and forms of political and economic association."[31] That the traditional nation-state concept has been particularly susceptible to challenge is due in large measure to the fact that U.S. and European models of nation-states, contrary to the view from the North, have had only partial relevance or applicability for how these functioned in the Global South, with

> political parties and elections providing 'the bare procedural minimum of democracy' in Latin America, without providing effective representation and accountability. In response, social movements have developed alternative visions of democracy and national identity, and have searched for alternative links between society and state based on those visions. . . . Latin American indigenous movements are key players in these processes; their insistence on cultural difference and collective identity challenges nations to redefine belonging, and challenges states to enable active, multicultural citizenship.[32]

This "bare procedural minimum of democracy"—too often a parlor game played by a small, cohesive and entrenched elite alternating with demagogic populists often of the same social extraction—exists in one of the world's most violent regions, one with its most unequal income distribution as well as seething ethnic rivalries. In addition, as this author suggested a decade ago, in 1999, public corruption may have become Latin America's biggest security threat because it robs democratic governments of the legitimacy they need to combat the growing challenges of street crime and transnational crime—through partnerships with civil society.[33]

Nonetheless, elite discourse continues to find refuge in the trappings of political modernity, rather than programmatic and organizational renewal. For more at least two decades traditional non-indigenous "Latin" American political parties have sought the advice, techniques and messages of campaign strategists from the United States. As the *Wall Street Journal* reported in 1999, the already-reduced scope of election debates at the end of the Cold War opened up a market for U.S. consultants offering foreign elections an "American cachet" characterized by "slick TV ads and centrist platforms." Or, as U.S. consultant Sergio Bendixen was quoted as saying, "Politics is being restricted to a very narrow lane. . . . We are experts at making campaigns out of narrow points."[34] Native American demands, urgent and impossible to ignore, reside outside these narrow lanes.

With such trends increasingly dictating the restricted contours of national campaigns, it is no wonder that the lack of a real representative democracy has largely conspired against development of the kind of effective redress dispossessed (not to say "minority") ethnic groups need in order to be able to opt for inter-ethnic cooperation, even while strengthening their nonmaterial values (history, culture, language, traditions and forms of organization) and protecting their lands and access to other resources, rather than exaggerated ethnic nationalism. Emphasis on the latter "is most likely to develop in environments that are devoid of the institutions and practices—for example, enforceable contracts and impartial state institutions—that protect people from being taken advantage of by others."[35] The relative absence of those institutions and practices, then, is precisely related to the "'the bare procedural minimum of democracy' in Latin America," where "effective representation and accountability" are lacking.

In this view, it is the lack of democratic institutions and practices, rather than challenges to them, that pose the greatest threat to stability: "The real destabilizing factor is the narrow-minded attitude of some states, like the Chilean state, which refuse to recognize the country's multi-ethnic nature and to design mechanisms that permit it to be expressed," says Chilean lawyer and Indian rights activist José Aylwin. "A state that recognizes that multi-ethnic nature and establishes political and territorial rights for indigenous people to allow them to develop within their own cultures has much fewer problems in terms of stability than states which deny that reality."[36] In this benign formulation, nationalism might thus be framed as "a broad vision for organizing society, a project for collective identity based on the premise of citizenship—available to all, with individual membership beginning from the assumption of legal equality," the national being emerging from "a series of competing discourses in constant formation and negotiation."[37] In this context, it is unsurprising that indigenous peoples, like other ethnic groups in emerging democracies, would choose to "vote identity," selecting "the party representing the demographic with which they most strongly identify."[38]

Native communities in the region are today embarked on a course that can either strengthen democracy or replace it with nationalist leaders whose platforms could lead to even greater strife, or even civil war, as nation-state boundaries are challenged as part of an illegitimate colonial and neo-colonial inheritance. In societies deeply divided along ethnic lines, establishing or maintaining a fragile or emerging democracy is not a foreordained, or even necessarily likely, outcome. While ethnicity—defined as the use of presumed physical or cultural attributes, such as race, ancestry, language, religion, work habits, clothing, etc.—can inspire loyalty and solidarity, it can also offer grounds for alarm and set the stage for new persecution, albeit of members of different groups or even minority subsets of coalitions attaining power. At least part of what is happening in the Americas at the beginning of the twenty-first century may be an inchoate movement towards irredentist, winner-take-all ethno-nationalism, a powerfully parochial movement of the sort that has wreaked havoc in the Balkans for more than a century.

Taken by themselves, the marquee forays of Native Americans into the political arena paint a different, less pacific and notably less sanguine picture than those highlighted by the proponents of democratic, franchise-expanding, or participationist scenarios. They include the more than fifteen-year-old Zapatista sitz-rebellion in southern Mexico, the "first to make an impact on global audiences . . . [but one that] did not identify as an ethnic-related movement, but as one defending the interests of Maya peasants."[39] They also include decisive participation in civilian-led or civil-military putsches against elected presidents in Ecuador and Bolivia, and the inauguration in 2006 of a neo-Marxist, coca growers union president as head of state in La Paz. Leon Zamosc notes, for example, that although the Ecuadorian indigenous peoples experienced a breakthrough in participation in the country's public life, allowing them to exert influence on government policies and to become a force to be reckoned with in the struggle for power, their participation in a coup attempt meant that their political coming of age showed a lack of an unambiguous commitment to the rules of democracy.[40]

Those indigenous activists and their non-Indian allies who embrace radical populism or Marxist praxis see their "popular" appeal as based on broad support for ideologically specific visions of the future. However, in the words of the Argentine post-Marxist political theorist Ernesto Laclau, mass mobilization often merely "represents the ideological crystallization of resistance to oppression in general,"[41] rather than the unambiguous purchase of a particular dogma. The reason for the desperation accompanying emerging Native American militancy is reflected in the fact that, of the four countries—Bolivia (where native peoples are the poorest people in South America's poorest country), Guatemala, Ecuador and Nicaragua—that arguably come closest to the designation of "failing states," the first three are also those where native peoples form a numerical majority or, grouped together, comprise the largest ethnic bloc.

Some Indian movements and demands have only slender, if any, links to either Marxist or radical populist political thought, though embracing a worldview that emphasizes ethnicity in the context of nationalism. Peruvian and Bolivian Indian nationalists' dream, cited earlier, of uniting the countries of the Andes contains the potential for all four types of communal conflict: ethnic violence, irredentism, rebellion and civil war. Less incendiary are the demands by six Andean indigenous organizations and five others from Argentina, Bolivia, Chile, Ecuador, Colombia and Perú grouped together in an Andean Coordinator of Indigenous Organizations (*Coordinadora Andina de Organizaciones Indígenas*). These insist that their countries be "re-founded as plurinational states" and demand absolute autonomy to native peoples, who are to be ruled by indigenous traditions.[42] Brazilian Indians and those of four other South American countries who claim to belong to what they call the "Guarani nation," an entity that they say needs to be "resurrected" from southern Brazil, through Paraguay, Bolivia and northern Argentina—suggests a similar, if more remote, possibility for communal conflict.[43] A new party led by Chilean Mapuche intellectuals, *Wallmapuwen*, calls for the "restoration" of eastern Mapuche territory across the Andes in Argentina. Such irredentist (where one ethnic group tries to secede from one state to join co-ethnics in another) claims, based on strong ethno-national tension along the two countries' common border, are seen by some as a potential threat to Chile's national sovereignty.[44]

In the southwestern United States, while the mainstream media in the United States focuses on illegal immigration from "Mexicans" and others from Mesoamerica across the southern border, what passes virtually unnoticed is that in states like California, "many of the men and women who immigrate to the United States are not necessarily Latino in the general sense of the word, but are Indian people."[45] Some activists believe that the day laborers looking for work in the American Southwest "are not illegal migrants, but migrants returning to their ancestral homeland," part of the Mexican pre-Colombian civilizations emanating from a place called *Aztlan,* the legendary ancestral home of the *Nahua* people, which includes those territories wrested from Mexico after the Mexican-American War. The workers are the "descendants of the indigenous people who have been migrating across the Americas for millennia, long before Europeans created national borders."[46] The largest growing population in California is that of "new unknown immigrants" from Meso-America, ranging from Mexico through Central America.

> According to the *Frente Indígena Organización Binacional* (FIOB), a California nonprofit for immigrants, the majority of the people who are labeled Mexicans are natives from the Mixtec, Zapotec and Chatino tribes. FIOB estimates that there are 70,000 to 80,000 indigenous workers from Oaxaca throughout California. The Mexican Consulate in San Francisco indicates that there are more than 10,000 Maya Indians from the Yucatan Peninsula of Mexico currently living in Marin County alone and about 18,000 throughout the Bay area. . . . *for most indigenous people, it's safer to be identified as Latino than as Indian.*[47] (Italics added.)

The semi-nomadic ancestors of today's native peoples living along the desert expanses of the U.S.-Mexican border—such as the Tohono O'odham, whose Connecticut-size reservation runs along it for some sixty miles—knew no such boundaries until at least 1854. As late as the 1990s, an estimated one-third of the O'odham reservation families "retain close ties to Mexico . . . keep households in the Mexican villages, shop in Mexican stores, and pray in the Mexican churches. They attend festivals and visit friends."[48] The digging up of graves in Arizona of Tohono O'odham ancestors and the secret alleged removal of their remains while building the U.S.-Mexico border fence has become, at the end of the first decade of the twenty-first century, a rallying cry for groups such as the Indigenous Alliance without Borders, which seeks to maintain traditional ceremonies and mobility in ancestral territories.[49] In February 2009, eight members of the U.S. Congress wrote President Barack Obama to complain about the impact the border fence, pointing out that

There are several tribal nations on the US-Mexico border; during the pushing of
the fence these nations were not consulted and in many instances their sovereignty was undermined. Basic protections and rights under the National Preservation Act and the Native American Graves Protection and Repatriation Act
were violated. One example was the destruction of 69 Tohono O'odham graves
south of Tucson in 2007. [50]

Questions about the legitimacy and reach of borders goes beyond that separating the United States and Mexico and extends to that separating the United
States and Canada. Adam Beach, the Manitoba-born Indian actor, provided an
insight into such thinking.[51] Asked about the irony of a Canadian representing
two iconic World War II U.S. images—those from the battle at Iwo Jima and
that of Native American "code talkers" in the Pacific theater—both of which
represented U.S. Indian patriotism, sacrifice and partnership with the federal
government, Beach replied: "Indians don't really look at our borders; Canadian,
American, we're all peoples that share North America. We see each other as
people sharing this land." [52]

The challenge posed by some Indian activists to the borders' authority and
authenticity is also underlined in the works of Leslie Marmon Silko, a Native
American writer from the Laguna Pueblo tribe and one of the second-generation
leaders of what has been called the "Native American Renaissance." In two essays, "Fences against Freedom: and "The Border Patrol State," published in her
book, *Yellow Women and a Beauty of the Spirit, Essays on Native American Life
Today,* Silko contends that contemporary colonialist attitudes in the United
States, enshrined in the country's laws, treat American Indians as foreigners of
uncertain and potentially criminal allegiances. The differing treatment accorded
to U.S. Indians and Mexican-Americans at and around the southwest border, she
says, is evidence of the fluid nature of the border itself, as, by their actions, U.S.
authorities in effect redraw it with the treatment they mete out to non-whites. In
her novel, *Almanac of the Dead,* Silko uses the Native American tradition of
story telling to challenge (in what *The New York Times* called "a passionate in-
dictment") an Anglo justice system that allowed white settlers to lay claim to
land contained in communal land grants in Arizona and New Mexico protected
by the Treaty of Guadalupe Hidalgo. In *Almanac,* she tells of English-speaking
elected officials and legal officers who replaced those Spanish-speakers who had
come before, certifying white claims on prime land and water resources, quietly,
without fanfare and without the residents from time immemorial knowing what
was being done to their precious inheritance. The latter hung onto the belief that
the Treaty of Guadalupe Hidalgo protected the land grants and titles the King of
Spain had recognized as theirs.[53]

Silko's novel rarified the Indian claims, but was true to them. A common
law principle codified by the New Mexico territorial government took the ap-
propriation of Indian lands a step further, making tenancy on a parcel of land for

more than 10 years sufficient to claim ownership using the doctrine of "adverse possession." Not even a title was necessary to assume ownership of Indian land, the law protecting "non-Indian holdings within confirmed Pueblo grants on the basis of adverse possession."[54] As a result, as a Native American Silko refuses to recognize the authority of the U.S. justice system and questions the very legitimacy of Western law, suggesting the Indian experience shows it to be based on organized theft—an act that could not ever be sanctified by an ersatz title. Because of this, and because contemporary borders dividing post-Conquest nations also interrupt the flow on trade routes indigenous peoples have used for a millennium, Silko scores what she considers the illegitimacy of border authorities, who enforce what is artificial.[55] Such ideas about bi- or multi-national indigenous "territory"—rather than just the reallocation or restoration of land usurped by the state—not only challenge what have been largely sacrosanct national borders, but also defy definitions of what are strictly "internal" jurisdictions in a single nation-state. Their expression, in theory, would conceivably restrict the action of one country's authorities to deal with the problem, or even risks pitting one nation-state against another over the rights and responsibilities of its Native American citizens.

Thus the Indians' demands for greater recognition of their rights and the fact of their mobilization in ways that sometimes recall indigenous strategies tested through the centuries means that their challenge runs both broad and deep, with one eye on politics in the region's capitals and another on the boundaries and rules that guide, and confine, their daily existence. Mixtec lawyer López Bárcenas noted that, in the fight for autonomy indigenous peoples "transcend the folkloric, culturalist, and developmentalist visions that the state propagates, and many people still passively accept." By calling upon their culture and traditions in the mobilization to defend their rights, Indians are "questioning vertical political forms even as they offer horizontal forms that work for them, because they have tested them over centuries of resistance to colonialism."[56]

Elite nostalgia for a return to the former *status quo* favoring themselves is not a credible option. Classical social theories predicting "the inevitable crumbling of 'traditional' communities and cultures before the forces of modernization," including those dealing with indigenous peoples, have proven at best premature, particularly since "the rise of ethnic movements in the United States [in the 1960s] and throughout the world have demonstrated the unexpected persistence and vitality of ethnicity as a source of group identity and solidarity."[57] The concerns of indigenous peoples about their physical security and respect for their lands, cultures and natural resources today fall squarely within the purview of the mainstream human rights agenda and international organizations. What is more, a growing body of customary international law favors respect for their rights and interests on a host of issues from education, trade, environmental protection, public services and development, among others. In September 2007, the United Nations' General Assembly approved the U.N. Declaration on the Rights of Indigenous Peoples by an overwhelming vote of 143 in favor, 11 abstentions and only four countries—including the United States—against.[58]

The elite political landscape in the Hemisphere has also been redrawn along lines that increasingly acknowledge indigenous claims and power, even in those cases where they attempt to reject them. Some non-Indian elected officials, including presidents, have increasingly felt obliged to make indigenous concerns central to their own agenda. "We have a historic debt with our indigenous people," promised the incoming Guatemalan President, the non-Indian Alvaro Colom, who was elected with the overwhelming support of his country's Mayan communities. "Our government will be one with a Mayan face."[59] Upon taking office in Ecuador, the non-Indian President Rafael Correa was presented by Indian leaders a ceremonial "staff of power," and declared that his government would be "a government of the indigenous."[60] Upon taking office, one of the first acts of Paraguayan President Fernando Lugo was to appoint to a cabinet-level position—as Minister of Indigenous Affairs—an Indian woman who, as a child, had been kidnapped and sold into slavery as a domestic servant to a rich household.[61]

On the other hand, social peace in the region will require the unqualified respect of the civil rights of others, those who are non-Indian, as well. Former U.S. Ambassador to Bolivia Edwin C. Corr has noted the importance of bringing indigenous and disadvantaged minority peoples more fully into society and politics, giving them greater participation in the decisions which affect their lives and the ability to equitably share in their countries' politics, governance and economies. But this, Corr said, needs to be balanced against the importance of preserving democratic institutions and prosperous economies, while assuring the basic rights of those who once made up dominant, non-Indian social and political classes.[62] The delicate equilibrium becomes an even greater challenge in situations where distribution crises accompany those of political participation and legitimacy. Those facing losses, even relative losses of prestige and wealth in a growing economy, are likely to view Indian demands as part of a zero-sum game in which their own interests are gravely and perhaps irremediably jeopardized. In that scenario, indigenous demands for a redistribution of economic benefits and social rewards, including land rights and access to natural resources, may lead to an unpredictable distributive backlash from those classes of people historically unused to sharing power and wealth with their fellow citizens.

Chapter Three
Elite Neglect and "Rediscovery"

*Miguel Angel May May, a tall man among the Maya, handsome, now in his
40s, with a touch of gray in his hair . . . speaks Yucatecan Maya so eloquently
that when young people who have begun to lose their language and culture first
hear him, they shed tears for what has been and what can be in the Yucatán.
May May tells the story with . . . rage and pride. . . . "A Maya, of the middle
class, like me," May May said, "went into a Ford dealership here in Mérida.
He intended to buy a new pickup truck. He was well dressed, but clearly Maya.
The dealer offered him ten pesos to wash a truck." It is a common experience
for people of color in a white world. The Yucatán is not entirely a white world,
yet the Maya suffer the most severe prejudice of any large ethnic group in
Mexico. In the language of prejudice in Mexico, the Maya are said to be people
with big heads and no brains, too short, too dark and with a strange, laughable
Spanish accent.*
—Earl Shorris, in "Mad Mel and the Maya"[1]

In his classic study of nationalism, *Imagined Communities, Reflections on the
Origins and Spread of Nationalism*, Benedict Anderson offers that—contrary to
the view of his Euro-centric peers—the nationalist phenomenon first emerged in
the eighteenth century New World. There, without the existence of differences
in language or in ethnic provenance, Creole (people of unmixed European
descent born in the New World; in Spanish, *criollo*) elites sprung from new national boundaries. Their emergence in Europe's far-flung trans-Atlantic colonies
reflected both the impact of newspapers filled with new Western European economic and political doctrines, allowing them to "imagine" greater communities
with which they previously had no tangible contact, and the pattern of maturing
local administrative career structures. These early Latin nationalists—unlike
those inhabiting the same space in the early twenty-first century—were not

populists, promising what was necessary to achieve and hold power, as neither slaves nor Indians were allowed to be protagonists in their revolt, and some of these even sided with the Spanish crown. (Spain, unlike the European regimes with colonies elsewhere in the world in the twentieth century, did not develop "advanced" and "backward" ethnic groups contending for the inheritance of its colonial possessions in the Americas, nor did it leave their indigenous subjects firmly anchored to specious, haphazard and lasting ethnic or national designations.) During the Spanish colonies' war for independence,

> Far from seeking to 'induct the lower classes into political life,' one key factor initially spurring the drive for independence from Madrid, in such important cases as Venezuela, Mexico and Perú, was the *fear* of 'lower-class' political mobilizations: to wit, Indian or Negro-slave uprisings . . . It is instructive that one reason Madrid made a successful comeback in Venezuela from 1814-1816 and held remote Quito until 1820 was that she won the support of slaves in the former, and of Indians in the latter, in the struggle against insurgent Creoles.[2]

Since independence in the nineteenth century, however, there was a tendency among the *criollo* elites to embrace national Indian ancestors. This new elite appealed to an idealistic image of the noble savage as part of their political rhetoric, while rejecting indigenous peoples in their midst, including their ethnicity and sense of being. In Perú, for example, this meant Creole nationalist

> appropriation of a rhetoric glorifying the Inca past (while) exist(ing) side by side with a contemptuous appraisal of the Indians (or what the Creoles regarded as such.) This apparently contradictory situation did not, however, lack a certain logic. Appropriating and officializing a discourse that had originally belonged to the indigenous aristocracy, the Creoles neutralized whatever political connotations Indian expressions might formerly have embodied. Moreover, to appeal to the real or imagined glories of the Incas so as to defend Perú from an invasion was a way of establishing the national character as something already set or given, and of denying the Indians, the *mestizos*, and the *castas* any possibility of forging it on their own.[3]

In 1925 in Mexico, the philosopher and future presidential candidate José Vasconcelos published *La Raza Cósmica* (*The Cosmic Race*) in which he postulated, in opposition to social darwinism, the creation of a "fifth race" in the Americas composed of all the world's races and destined to create a new civilization: *Universópolis*. However, even though Mexican national identity had swathed its Indian inheritance in a glorious past, one observer noted, "despite this strand, and in certain cases even underlying it, lay a discourse that casts the Indian and the Indian culture as not truly Mexican, but rather as impediments to the unification of the nation and obstacles to its political, economic and cultural development: in short, a threat to the nation's interests."[4]

Another academic observer notes that even before the Spanish arrived to the Americas, indigenous communities' political and social structures distributed justice and regulated social rites, religious festivities and economic production:

> After the Revolution, the Mexican state declared ethnic organizations to be illegal. Indians who wished to organize themselves politically were obligated to call themselves peasants and to classify themselves in groups according to their occupations or geographic regions. . . . The policy that predominated as part of the governmental objectives . . . was to assimilate them into the modern Mexican society. Indigenist organizations were created that were sponsored by the state in order to channel or regulate the possibility of a radical agenda by the Indians. The myth of the mixed race [*mestizaje*] was disseminated specifically in order to psychologically unify Mexicans in a "Cosmic Race" of European and Indian provenance.[5]

Indians themselves often expressed their disconformities with the existing political, social and economic order through what one scholar has called a "millenarian longing for a return to Indigenous rule and a time when there was no hunger and poverty that the Europeans had brought." This sentiment

> was common in the southern Andes, and stimulated such large-scale revolts as Túpac Amaru II in 1780. More recently, in 1915, Teodomiro Gutiérrez took the name Rumi Maqui (Quechua for "Stone Hand") and led a radical separatist revolt in Puno, attempting to restore Tawantinsuyu as a state governed by Indians. Subsequently, in the 1930s in Bolivia, Eduardo Leandro Nina Qhispi assumed the presidency of the Republic of Collasuyu (the southern quarter of the old Inka empire). . . . In a 1934 peasant uprising in Chile, communist militants advocated the creation of an "Araucana Mapuche Republic."[6]

Attention to the elitist and whipsaw quality of the debate among regional leftists in the last century about the role of the "Indian Question" will repay large rewards for those interested in the relationship between indigenous peoples, non-Indian power structures (including those claiming to act on the former's behalf), and the danger of the latter falling into *vanguardismo* and paternalism, both by those representing the establishment and those who pretend to change it. The role of the Soviet Union and the Marxist thinkers who preceded its foundation is of particular interest because of the critical, if transitory, role they played in popularizing Indian nationalism during years in which the international Marxist perspective swung 360 degrees with regard to race and ethnicity: at first, race and ethnicity were unimportant, then it was heralded as the key to regional revolution, and in time, again relegated to obscurity.

Soviet policy on nationality, which received little attention before the fall of the USSR, traces its earliest beginnings to the *Manifesto* written by Karl Marx and Frederick Engels. They argued that capitalism would diminish national particularity to the point where race and ethnicity did not matter, and held that through the experience of class conflict workers would learn that their interests lay with one another. The idea helped burnish Marxism's attractiveness, and the early Bolshevik party ended up with an inordinate representation of subjugated (and thus disadvantaged) ethnic minorities. In arriving at the notion that, although their ultimate goal was universalistic, they ought to take the national question into account in the interim, the Bolsheviks also drew from the ideas of the Jewish Labor Bund, as well as the works of Austrian social democrats who sought to appeal to the working class and to preserve ethno-national cultures. First, V.I. Lenin (locked in incipient competition with Woodrow Wilson and the United States over the importance of nationality), and then Joseph Stalin picked up on a variant of this appeal by offering land, bread and self-determination for ethnic nationalities. Thus the New Soviet Man was born in various nationalist costumes. The question remained, however: Was this a strategic move or a signal of real ideological commitment to pluralism?

The policies pursued by the early Bolsheviks, "*korenizatsiia*" or "indigenization" was "a prophylactic . . . designed to defuse and prevent the development of nationalism."[7] The policy provided for the ethnic consolidation of the new Soviet Union's many peoples and specifically sought, by means of massively recruiting non-Russians as local cadre in the Communist party, to extend the effective reach of Soviet power by making it take root in non-Russian soil. Unified national languages were created. Schools, cultural and scientific institutions were established; assimilation was discouraged; and a policy of mobilization was initiated that ranged from the republics, through the oblasts, and down to individual collective farms.

Shaping and informing these policies was the so-called Piedmont principle (named after the national core upon which the modern Italian state was formed), the "ostentatious promotion of national institutions,"[8] whereby the respectful treatment of nations within the USSR was meant to provide to their co-nationals outside the Soviet borders a benign view of the communist regime. This was seen as a way of facilitating their incorporation in the future into an expanded Soviet state. However, by favoring the non-Russian nationalities, the majority Russian nation was placed at a disadvantage, with Russian chauvinism strictly punished. The strategic nature of the opening to Europe's minorities can be seen in a 1925 Politburo decree, which specifically mandated that border region minorities should have more national rights than minorities in the Soviet central regions.

Meanwhile, the Comintern, (the Communist International, also known as the Third International) an international Communist organization founded in Moscow in March 1919 to claim leadership—as the vanguard of the global revolution—of the world socialist movement, helped bring the issue of indigenous rights and the national question surrounding Indian struggles in the Americas into the non-Indian world of the Americas. In South America, the works of Lenin and Stalin placed the right to self-determination of national minorities within the context of anti-colonial struggle; the Comintern proposed the creation of an Indian Republic along the lines of the old Inka *Tawantinsuyu*. The Comintern, wrote Latin American historian Marc Becker, viewed Latin American countries as similar to multinational Russia itself, their "subordinate nationalities" living side by side with a dominant Western culture. "Oppressed nations had the right to self-determination, including the right to establish their own independent nations. Minority populations, however, had the right to the preservation and development of their languages and cultures, but not the right to secede to form separate states."[9]

The First Latin American Communist Conference held in Buenos Aires in June 1929, caused the mostly Euro-centric communist parties of the region to "discover" the Indian Question. A year earlier the Sixth Congress of the Comintern had addressed the part that racial and ethnic minorities were to play in the context of a country's revolutionary upheaval. The period, noted one scholar, "offers a unique window through which to view debates within the left over the role of ethnicity in the building of a social movement."[10] It was at the Argentine meeting that Peruvian José Carlos Mariátegui set the stage for subsequent generations of leftists to turn their backs on the indigenous (and particularly, the cultural) agenda, claiming that their oppression was due to their status in the region's class structure rather than to enduring questions of race, ethnicity or national identification.

In his extensive treatise "El problema de las razas en la America Latina" (The Problem of Race in Latin America), Mariátegui held that the Indian Question was in its essence part of a larger problem relating to the unequal distribution of land and related economic exploitation. He took issue with the Comintern's suggestion that an Indian autonomous republic be created, using class arguments to rebut the Red metropolis' proposal: "The construction of an autonomous state from the Indian race would not lead to the dictatorship of the Indian proletariat, nor much less the formation of an Indian state without classes." Eventually, he said, an "Indian bourgeois state" would be created that shared "all the internal and external contradictions of other bourgeois states." As Becker pointed out, Mariátegui's view reflected "a fundamental division between ethno-cultural and political definitions of nationalism," with the Peruvian anchored in the belief that South America's existing nation-states were already too established to call for rethinking their configuration. "At its core, Mariátegui challenged essentialist notions of nationalism. Mariátegui emphasized that Indian poverty and marginalization were fundamentally an issue of class oppression, and that the solution to Indian problems lay in ending the abusive feudalistic land tenure patterns under which Indians suffered."[11]

At bottom, the contending views of the two leftist factions in Buenos Aires shared a vanguardist orientation and, although posed as benign in its intent, the Mariátegui view actually paralleled that of more conservative *indigenistas* who promoted *indigenismo*, the assimilation of Indians rather than recognition of their cultural distinctiveness. Mariátegui held that the Indian struggle formed but part of a larger battle by workers and peasants to create a new socialist society— in essence a revolutionary class-based variant of assimilationism. In addition, the Comintern's views were extrapolations of ideas set down by Lenin and Stalin; Mariátegui himself "apparently" did not consult with Native American leaders in arriving at his own conclusions.[12] Becker points out that in Mariátegui's seminal *Seven Interpretive Essays on Peruvian Reality* he echoed Luis Valcárcel's comment that "the Indigenous proletariat awaits its Lenin" . . . implying that the movement for their liberation would come from an external source rather than from within their communities. In probing who this Lenin might be, Becker cites the words of Israeli historian Gerardo Leibner, who "contrasts the idea of a Tupac Amaru-style restoration of *Tawantinsuyu* with an urban *mestizo indigenista* leading Indians in a modernizing socialist revolution. *The first can be interpreted as a reactionary impulse* and Mariátegui opposed it, and *the second requires the intervention of outsiders such as Mariátegui.*"(Italics added).[13]

Non-Indians like Mariátegui, and their desire to subsume indigenous demands through an economic prism placed the Peruvian's position in opposition to the cultural and national demands, however inchoate or diverse, made by Indian peoples. "Mariátegui's death less than a year after the conference removed one of Latin America's intellectuals most interested in the Indigenous question," thereby depriving Central and South American militants of anything but a freeze-frame of his views on the vital issue. (Contemporary leftists, nonetheless, continue to give homage to Mariátegui as a visionary champion of indigenous peoples. Writing in the Marxist *Monthly Review,* Roxanne Dunbar-Ortiz admitted that the Peruvian "was never able to visit the Andean region and had no indigenous colleagues." However, she continued, "thanks to the guiding light and vision" of Mariátegui's work, "both communist and indigenous organizers early on were cognizant that the Indigenous peoples of the Andes are nationalities, which, in the Marxist-Leninist sense, have the right to self-determination, although Mariátegui argued against the practicality of a separate Andean state.") For its part, the Comintern appeared to lose interest in playing the indigenous card in its efforts to promote revolution in the hemisphere; it never held another continental congress and the Indian Question appeared mostly to fade from leftwing politics for several generations. However, although the Comintern's specific role in popularizing Indian nationalism in the debate ended up being short lived, the Soviet idea of encapsulating their struggle as that of "nationalities" is seen as contributing much later to indigenous demands.[14]

The retreat by the Comintern anticipated a jarring about face in Soviet ethnic politics. Between 1932 and 1941, through a "Great Retreat" that paralleled the beginnings of the centralization of the Soviet economy, Soviet power abandoned the policy of encouraging and consolidating the ethno-nationality of the minorities. Russian geopolitical insecurity about the possibility that "diaspora nationalities," such as Poles, Finns, Belorussians, Romanians and Ukrainians, were "fifth columns" for their co-nationals in neighboring states, resulted in a security driven policy of what later was called "ethnic cleansing." The sustained period of terror reasserted Russian dominance and non-Russians were subsumed into what was for all intents and purposes a new Russian Empire, disguised under the Orwellian doctrine of the "Friendship of Peoples." National institutions went into decline and suspect nationalities were deported. The 10 years between 1935 and 1945, in particular, saw greater appeals to Russian nationalism, and by the time of World War II, the focus had degenerated into anti-Semitism.

The Tatars, Chechens and Ingush were particularly difficult to sovietize because they were clan-based, Muslim mountain people. Resistant to Soviet collectivization policy, they had also been at odds with the Russians even before the revolution of 1917. Almost all Chechens and Ingush were deported to Soviet Asia, in an effort to destroy them not as individuals, but as a people. This cultural ethnocide was their punishment for being particularly recalcitrant to Sovietization. Soviet ethnic cleansing, Terry Martin wrote, was "not accompanied by overt intentional murder. However, the ethnic deportations always included many arrests that resulted in incarceration in high-mortality prison camps." The Soviet ethnic cleansing was distinctive for "the degree of its professionalization (including the professionalization of mass murder)," the extent of its commitment to total ethnic removal, and especially its practice in conditions of peace.[15] It signaled an end to efforts to woo ethnic minorities into the Soviet orbit for quite some time.

Within the "Latin" American context, the example of how Mexican leftists evolved in their thinking about the role of indigenous peoples in state formation provides an early example of the manipulation of an indigenous past and contemporary yearning. In the two decades following that Mexico's civil war, *indigenismo* became "one of the most powerful voices in explaining culture and society . . . creating a public space for the Indian in post-revolutionary Mexico . . ." and whose image was "acclaimed . . . as a model for the future of the nation." As Alexander S. Dawson has pointed out, the idealized Indian was based on those indigenous peoples who could trace their ancestry to a splendid pre-Colombian past and who emerged from this perspective "not simply a cultural icon, but at times . . . the very model of egalitarian politics, social conscience, and virtue that *Indigenistas* (and revolutionaries in general) sought to use to construct a modern revolutionary order. Far from being an 'other,' this Indian was clearly an integral member of the national community." In this context, some Indian cultural practices became in Mexico a New World equivalent to the Stakhanovian Worker—the mythic superhero of socialist realism in the Soviet Union—as a model for idealized values and specific revolutionary social reforms. Dawson notes that:

> While certain traditions, such as the use of witch doctors, represented an impediment to progress, other facets of Indian social organization, such as their

communal traditions, could serve as a model for a more equitable and 'progressive' nation. [A] "clearly . . . mythologized construction of the relationship between the Indian communal past and the agrarian reform promised by the Revolution . . . rested on an understanding that Indians possessed a deep proprietary love for the land. . . . With the advent of Cardenismo [the ideological underpinnings of the movement headed by President Lazaro Cárdenas] and the popularization of Marxist nomenclature, *Indigenistas* increasingly came to describe select Indian cultures as the equals of poor *mestizos* [people of mixed ancestry]. . . . Part of a larger current in Cardenismo which valorized the Indian as central to the nation while decrying the effects of class exploitation, this viewpoint made Indians members of a single proletariat which included the urban poor and other *campesinos.* As a class, Indians (like other rural poor) were oppressed, backward, and in need of vast amounts of financial and other assistance, but they existed clearly within a framework of a nation in which their cultural 'otherness' was really only a matter of economic problems created by their oppression.[16]

Early non-Marxist efforts to get indigenous rights on the international agenda, another scholar noted, remained curiously hobbled by "polarizing Cold War habits and sloganeering that pitted the West's focus on individual rights against the Eastern Bloc's claim that group rights were all that really mattered."[17] Even the 1948 United Nations Universal Declaration of Human Rights failed not only to not specifically designate safeguards for indigenous peoples but utterly failed to "encompass the circumstances and the worldviews of indigenous peoples . . . To put it bluntly, the plight of indigenous and minority peoples was virtually invisible as an international issue when the United Nations was founded, and remained so for twenty-five years thereafter."[18]

As little as a generation ago, in the penultimate decade of the Cold War, even social scientists regarded ethnicities as, in the words of one political scientist writing in the 1990s, "quaint residues of benighted tribal times, amorphous identities that the political socialization campaigns of modern governments were inexorably erasing. In short, the nation-state was increasingly triumphant almost everywhere."[19] Most policymakers sympathetic to "the Indian Question" in Bolivia, Ecuador, Mexico, Perú and other countries, still engaged in the largely assimilationist strategies characterized by paternalist assumptions about what to do with culturally different peoples. Throughout the twentieth century, national indigenous movements were rare, Deborah J. Yashar has noted. "It is not that real organizing did not occur among indigenous people, but people used to note that it did not occur along ethnic lines. Prior rural movements mobilized Indians to forge class, partisan, religious, and sometimes even revolutionary identities over and against indigenous ones."[20]

Since 1992, however, and the marking of the five-hundredth anniversary of the "discovery" of the Americas by Europeans, a time of remembrance for regional governments, but also of protest by Native Americans, indigenous movements have, in the words of Mixtec Indian lawyer and activist Francisco

López Bárcenas, "substantively revised their forms of political actions and their demands," ceasing to be mere ancillary organizations of rural farmer movements. "Indigenous movements demand not only rights for individuals but also for collectives, for the peoples they are a part of," he wrote. "Their demand is not limited to making state institutions fulfill their functions but also change. They demand not lands but territories. They ask not that they be allowed to exploit the natural resources in their territories, but that they are granted ownership of them. They demand that justice be administered not only according to state law, but also in recognition of their right to administer justice themselves and in accordance with their own laws."[21]

The reactivating Indian movements, López Bárcenas added, came at a time when "worker and rural farmer movements were weakening from Mesoamerica to Patagonia." With movement towards local, communal autonomies accompanied by other Indian activists who demanded, "the re-founding of nation-states based on indigenous cultures. . . . *Participants in these movements say they do not understand why, since their population is larger than the mestizos, they should adapt to the political will of minorities.*" (Italics added.) As a result, López Bárcenas said, the discourse of the indigenous movement was co-opted by a number of regional governments, who "emptied it of meaning" and began to speak of a new relationship between the state and indigenous peoples, creating "'transversal policies' with the participation of all interested parties when in reality they continue to posit the same old indigenist programs that indigenous peoples reject." A few indigenous leaders noted for their long advocacy of autonomy were brought into public view as a smokescreen, in order "to depict as change what is continuity." Thus, indigenous activism finds it is "politically destructured, affected by the politics of colonialism wielded through government entities in order to subject them to the interests of the class in power." Political gerrymandering is a concrete example and illustrative of that larger problem, López Bárcenas concluded, as "numerically larger indigenous peoples find themselves divided between various states or departments, and the smaller ones between different towns, municipalities, or mayoralties, depending on how states organize themselves."[22]

Chapter Four
Is Democracy a Zero-Sum Game?

"If the nation does not include all the people it is not really a nation at all."
—René Zavaleta Mercado, Bolivian sociologist and philosopher[1]

However arbitrary their construction, nation-states have been "probably the most salient sources of modern authority and consciousness."[2] Insights gleaned from the studies of nationalism from Europe, Asia and elsewhere today, together with examples drawn from recent indigenous experience in the Americas, allows for the critical examination of the tests this new indigenous activism pose to the concept of the nation-state itself, particularly in the Andean region. Can this activism be channeled through active, multi-cultural, multi-ethnic and pluri-national citizenship or does it portend a future of centrifugal forces tearing apart the arguably fragile consensus around democratic governance in nations until recently under authoritarian rule? How do new linguistic, religious and historical awakenings and their related definitions of group identity within a nation-state coincide with existing national boundaries, and can the latter contain them?

Much of the political analysis of why nation-states of Central and South America appear to border on the ungovernable—focusing on weak institutions and narrow party loyalties and governance—is of limited usefulness, suggesting that many observers are looking at the instability through the wrong end of the telescope, that is, from the perspective of capital elites.[3] This "wide discrepancy between theory and reality" may be explained using political scientist Walker Connor's construct, as being the confusion of symptoms with causes. "Explanations for political decay focus on interim steps, such as the weakening of 'mass parties,' rather than upon the root cause of ethnic rivalry," Connor noted.[4]

Nation-building theories much in vogue during the twentieth century, shibboleths that treated ethnic diversity as minor impediments to effective state integration, have effectively been refuted by the Indian mobilizations responsible for the overthrow of constitutional governments in both Bolivia and Ecuador, and the armed Zapatista uprising that tarnished the international luster of the neo-liberal one-party regime of Mexico's Carlos Salinas de Gortari.[5] For, as political scientist Paul Roe has noted: "Nation-building may be perceived by minority groups as a real threat to their identity. And in this respect the perception of threat can be seen as an accurate one; states require minority groups to give up all, or part, of their cultural distinctiveness if the nation-building process is to be successful."[6]

As Indian nationalists move into the fore, fundamental questions remain about who belongs to each "national" group—with decisions still to be made whether this belonging is circumscribed by the maintenance of traditional ways, or whether it pertains to genetic or some other criteria. "In contrast to Anglo North Americans who define Indians primarily on the basis of blood [which can imply racism and prejudice], for Central and South Americans cultural criteria are more important," one former U.S. ambassador to Perú and Bolivia has observed. "Once an Indian masters Spanish, adopts Western dress, acquires a certain level of education, enters the market economy, and loses his sense of being exploited, he may no longer consider himself primarily an Indian."[7] The profile of indigenous communities in the region fits within several requisites of nationalism; being "Indian" is more or less a racial category, more or less an ethnic one, and more or less determined by language. It should be noted that, in large part due to a history of forcible assimilation, Article 33 of the U.N. Declaration on the Rights of Indigenous Peoples adopted in September, 2007, specifically provides native peoples with "the right to determine their own identity or membership" in response to complaints by Native Americans about non-indigenous elites and central governments defining them in a way that denies them their own identity.

The new-found militancy of Indian peoples, whose distinguishing political characteristics were often seen by outsiders as fatalism and resignation, reflects specific harsh and adverse events that traditional peoples face. These include threats to their physical well-being and access to necessary land and resources, as well as to their cultural identity. In this context the protection of national resources, such as rich energy reserves and access to fresh water, has become a key cause for mobilization in the two predominately-Indian countries of Central and South America, Bolivia and Guatemala, as well as Ecuador.[8]

The emergence of "Latin" American Indian communities demanding fundamental changes in political, economic, social and cultural spheres offers both similarities and contrasts to theories about nationalism developed in other times and in other regions. Much of the existing literature focuses on pre-modern communities that emerged as national actors either as already dominant, or at least contending forces in their region, or as part of empires whose title to rule was not based on national criteria. During the period of the Spanish empire, Indians in largely rural populations, a vast majority of which lacked written literacy, were victims of exclusion—serving throughout the Hemisphere as slaves or peons, in arrangements that were in some cases continuations of pre-Conquest patterns established by rival tribes or peoples.[9] Today they are connected to the outside world via community radio networks, television and, perhaps most importantly, the Internet.[10]

Thus globalization appears to have replaced, at least in the Indian communities, the role of industrial society as what Ernest Gellner calls the engine that promotes "a certain kind of division of labor, one that is complex and persistently, cumulatively changing." The shortening of physical and intellectual distances caused by technology and free trade appears to in part leapfrog older limitations on agrarian society cited by Gellner as being unfavorable to nationalist principle—to the necessary preconditions of the "convergence of political and cultural units, and to the homogeneity and school-transmitted nature of culture within each political unit."[11]

The role education has played in the emergence of Native American nationalism appears to confirm Gellner's observation that, "The monopoly of legitimate education is now more important, more central than is the monopoly of legitimate violence."[12] The centrality of what he called the "school-transmitted nature of culture" can best be seen in Bolivia where, according to one authoritative source, even before Morales' election, "Indians appeared to have gone further in gaining access to higher education . . . than in any other Latin American country." Nearly half the students at Bolivia's eleven public universities are believed to be of Indian origin, with institutions in the larger cities where many indigenous people live, such as La Paz and Cochabamba, having two thirds Native American enrollments.[13]

Following a 1952 revolution led by a mixed-race leadership, public education in Bolivia was made available to indigenous children, with the first generation of Native American students enrolling in the country's mostly public universities in the 1970s. A decade later, another first generation—that of Indian scholars—began professorships at these and other institutions, although some reported "they, too, faced subtle discrimination, especially if they emphasized their ethnic origins." A small group of faculty and students also "developed research and [began] to popularize the history and culture of Bolivia's indigenous peoples—subjects until recently largely left out of both public-school curricula and the consciousness of people in the urban centers where the country is run." In 1979, San Andres University, the country's largest public institution, was the first to establish a department of native languages. Today, other than English, Aymara is the most popular language major chosen.[14]

In Bolivia, as elsewhere in the region, education was key to contemporary developments in both politics and society. As we will see later, the rise of ethnic nationalism in Bolivia required—as nationalism theorist Gellner framed it and as historically occurred in the nationalisms of Eastern, Slavic and Balkan Europe— an emerging intelligentsia of the marginalized to be the driving force behind efforts to make their "low culture" into a "high culture," one as Brendan O'Leary points out, with "an extensive vocabulary, a formal grammar, an alphabet, a literary tradition, and a capacity for context-free communication." The central "high culture" of the Bolivia's traditional ruling class was thus displaced, as Bolivia's new intellectual elite was now, like its political leadership, ethnically more consonant with the country's majority.[15]

While theorists almost exclusively have generalized based on the experiences in other lands, much Indian political and cultural activism in Mexico and Central and South America reflects Kedourie's formulation that, "In nationalist doctrine, language, race, culture and sometimes even religion, constitute different aspects of the same primordial entity, the nation." And, because "Nationalism . . . itself . . . is largely a doctrine of national self-determination . . . it has therefore been necessary to examine how self-determination came to have this central importance in ethical and political teachings."[16]

In the Latin American context, understanding the role of ultranationalist Indian perspectives is increasingly important. In a work published in Bolivia in January 2007 entitled, "Emancipation and Against Hegemony in Bolivia: Strategies to Destroy the K'hara Domination" ("k'hara" or "K'ara" is an Aymaran pejorative for Caucasians), one essayist offered a look at what Kedourie called different aspects of the same primordial entity—in an apocalyptic vision that includes the exercise of power to destroy non-Indian "domination":

> What is sought from the indigenous point of view is the destruction of the symbolic domination of the k'hara world, that is, the legitimacy of the subjective representation of what is "Bolivian" or "Western." . . . This is not, then, the social democratization of power, but rather those who were dominated before, now in power, would create a network of relationships that will allow them to govern absolutely in time. . . . It is a global operation given that it includes religious, cultural, economic, political, artistic, scientific, health, academic, international, among other, fields . . . the struggle in the "fields" of power includes all people and economic, social, political and cultural organizations, consolidating in this way a full-spectrum domination project on the national level.[17]

Warning signs abound for Indian nationalist leaders and their followers. As Conner has noted, multi-ethnic alliances do not necessarily translate into a single national consciousness, and "if one is dealing not with variations of a single culture-group, but with distinct and self-differentiating culture groups, then increased contacts . . . tend to produce disharmony rather than harmony."[18] Each indigenous person's concept of her/his identity as a Native American is passed on from the singular culture of her/his own tribe or nation. Thus efforts to unify through the organization of a pan-Indian movement means that attempting to save a people's traditions by combining diverse cultures into those of a single set of Indian customs or practices risks the "paradox" of having "to abandon their unique cultures to perpetuate them."[19]

The very diversity of Indian communities, in which members of one "nation" live side-by-side with those of one or more others, throughout Mexico and Central and South America suggests that the definition of "nation" and who belongs to it may be a point of inter-ethnic contention even as Indians move to the fore in their countries' political life. Hence the warning by a new Peruvian indigenous party, the *Movimiento al Socialismo Andino Amazonico* (MASA), of even Inca type governance under a unitarian state being a likely pretext for "low-intensity ethnic cleansing"—a hostile act, to be sure, *not* seen as being the work of erstwhile white or mestizo elites, but rather a new, emerging, leadership class within the indigenous world.

Susan Olzak offers an observation about the increased potential for ethnic conflict that speaks to the issues raised throughout indigenous America, an observation that may portend how a primarily rural struggle could be transported into ethnically segregated urban areas.

> The central argument is that increased levels of competition between two or more ethnic groups cause increases in ethnic collective action. This happens because two processes coincide. First, strongly bounded ethnic enclaves encourage high levels of ethnic identification and reaffirmation to cultural values, languages, and other characteristics [that] set members apart from others. Second, growth causes enclave communities to expand into the job, housing and other markets monopolized by the majority, causing levels of ethnic competition to rise. That is, levels of mobilization rise due to the fact that ethnic solidarity and competition are both high. It is the shifting dynamic of ethnic enclave solidarity coupled with rising levels of ethnic competition that raises the potential for ethnic conflict.[20]

The reassuring balm of the language and platform of pan-Indian solidarity needs to be assayed against the possibilities of less sanguine outcomes, even for Native Americans themselves. A nationalist ideology, Kedourie has noted, "is clearly not *ipso facto* a guarantee of prosperity or of good, honest government." The "ideological obsession" in Europe over the national question, "between 1848 and the end of World War II and its aftermath . . . could provide no remedy for the ills of alienation and oppression for which it purported to provide a cure." Nor does nationalism "make easy the relation of different groups in mixed areas . . . tend(ing) to disrupt whatever equilibrium had been reached between different groups."[21]

Chapter Five
Imagined Communities: Marxism and the Indian Nation-State

"Revolution is the extreme case of the explosion of political participation.
Without this explosion there is no revolution."
—Samuel Huntington[1]

Indian issues are not, in the main, either "leftist" or "rightist," although many non-indigenous activists try to co-opt Indian issues into their own agenda. Marxist dialectical materialism, in which social and political institutions progressively change their fundamental nature as economic developments transform material conditions, differs from capitalism in large part because of differing appreciations of the role of private property, but these European constructs are not in fact philosophical antipodes. At the most fundamental level, the indigenous agenda is one of political and economic empowerment and of cultural sovereignty, its focus field representing to varying degrees a spiritual inheritance, an environmental reverence, as well as a struggle for sustenance.

Efforts to cast native demands in the left-right dichotomy not only does a disservice to understanding the issues at hand; they frequently further marginalize those who have little voice in their own labeling. Using the leftist rhetoric of Bolivia's Evo Morales or Mexico's Zapatistas as the prism through which all or even most indigenous activism is evaluated can lead to egregious misperceptions of Indian demands and aspirations. Furthermore, careful examination of leftist claims of progress for their countries' indigenous populations under their stewardship often contradicts the public pronouncements. For example, Venezuela's mercurial President Hugo Chavez has claimed that, under his government, the country went from being the region's most backward on indigenous rights to a hemisphere leader. However, as Van Cott's research has shown, Venezuela's Indians were already well on their way to unity and political advantage before Chavez became president in 1998. Indigenous organizations and their civil society allies, she wrote, allowed them to successfully include in the 1993 state constitution in Amazona—with 43 percent of its population Native Americans the largest percentage in any Venezuelan state—"unprecedented recognition and rights, including recognition of the state as multiethnic and pluricultural." The Indians then went on to win important Supreme Court decisions in 1996, 1997, and 1998. By the time Chavez, who assumed the presidency in February 1999, convoked his controversial National Constituent Assembly that same year, Indians representing Amazonas "drew on the knowledge of Latin American constitutional law, mobilization skills, and increased political awareness and interest among the indigenous population developed during the state constitutional process." In other words, Chavez did not liberate Indians from Venezuela's backward stance; by the time he became president, Venezuela's indigenous peoples were already on their way to pulling the country into the twenty-first century.[2]

Nonetheless, the political usefulness to the new generation of regional left-wing populist politicians of Native American identity politics—including the power of victimization rhetoric—can be seen in the dispute between Chavez and King Juan Carlos of Spain. During a summit in Chile in November 2007, the monarch—who himself was under some pressure at home from right-wing factions who wanted him to resign in favor of his more conservative son—admonished Chavez, "Why don't you shut up?" after the Venezuelan accused a former Spanish Prime Minister, Jose Maria Aznar, of being a " broken-down fascist." Chavez, who claims some Indian parentage, later stated that the reason for the contretemps was that the king could not abide by indigenous peoples coming to power in the former Spanish colonies. "I think he is not used to hearing so many truths together," Chavez declared. "Latin America is changing, there is an Indian president . . . I am half Indian. We were left for many years, three hundred years of genocide, so when Indians rise up and we say the truth, it doesn't go down well. Because of that he kind of lost patience and exploded and was aggressive towards me."[3]

By appealing to a claim of Indian ancestry, Chavez appeared to successfully change the way the controversy was reported, moving the focus away from his undisputed violation of the comity typical of such international forums to stoking resentment about what he portrayed as the latest iteration of a centuries-old legacy of slights. In August 2008, the Russian media reported that Chavez had upped the rhetorical ante by proposing to rename Latin America "Indian America." Speaking to an indigenous community in Caracas, Chavez urged that the international community should "call our continent Indian America instead of Latin America," suggesting that his idea would restore "historical justice."[4]

Bolivian President Morales' embrace of leftists Fidel Castro and Hugo Chavez, indigenous peoples' opposition to free trade agreements and multinational investment, and their hostility to the international banking community, have led to a generalized and fundamental mischaracterization of the dynamics of First Nation nationalist politics. Ironically, the link between neo-Marxist populist ideology and Indian activism, while sometimes real, is based in part on a misreading of the recent and past history of indigenous peoples. Today's armed Indian movement in Chiapas, led by a Marxist non-Indian, is named after the charismatic *mestizo* peasant general Emiliano Zapata, raised in an indigenous Nahuatl-speaking community, who fought and died during the Mexican Revolution in the 1910s. The Zapatista movement in the 1910s was parochial, "fundamentally defensive, backward-looking and nostalgic," with virtually no Marxist or neo-Marxist influence, wrote Oxford historian Alan Knight.. Paul Friedrich added that it was, "a conservative reaction against economic and social changes that were proving detrimental to indigenous culture."[5] The influential Peruvian Marxist intellectual José Carlos Mariátegui, although he strongly defended indigenous peoples, in the 1920s "found himself embracing the most orthodox of Marxist positions in maintaining that the oppression of the Indian was a function of their class position and not their race, ethnicity, or national identity."[6] More recently, when faced with demands by the growing number of Indian students for programs that "both reflected and were relevant to their cultures," many of the majority leftists in Bolivia's educational institutions resisted the idea, believing social class to be more important than ethnic identity. Indian faculty members at the San Andres University who pushed for more research and academic curriculum in Native American history and culture were considered "old-fashioned and nostalgic for the past."[7]

By the end of World War I, the Left "realized that its internationalism and perceived universal class solidarity had lost its primacy to the much more powerful sentiment of particularistic nationalism."[8] Until the end of the Cold War, as Walker Connor points out also was the case in the Second World of Eastern Bloc nations, leftist scholars in the Americas largely accepted the official position of Marxist-Leninist governments that the application of Leninist national policy had solved "the national question," leading the masses to embrace proletarian internationalism. In keeping with that view, Connor writes that, "In Third World scholarship also, ethnic heterogeneity tended to be ignored or to be cavalierly dismissed as an ephemeral phenomenon." Even as late as 1990, Eric J. Hobsbawm, the doyen of academic Marxism, could expansively, if wrongly, opine that nationalism was "no longer a major vector of historical development."[9] Jennie Purnell offers that, until recently, academia had

> a much more fundamental consensus that peasant rebellions are essentially economic phenomena, explicable in terms of structural transformations and class-based interests. Political identity is a non-issue in this literature . . . Peasant rebellions that are not readily characterized as instrumental struggles for concrete material ends, usually because of their cultural or religious content,

are often dismissed as 'millenarian' in nature, a term used loosely and eclecti-
cally to designate projects and participants involved as utopian or irrational.[10]

Class-based theoretical approaches obscured the essential meaning of Native American protest, their distinct ways to view, appreciate and apprehend the
world. Within the last decade and a half, however, social scientists have begun
reevaluating their own characterization of rural populations as "peasants" driven
by class imperatives, a hoary icon with roots in pre-industrial European and colonial rural societies, a questioning that has opened up the possibility for a more
complete understanding of the emerging ethnic politics. This includes the impact
of globalization outside the community, where great numbers of rural people in
Latin America were forced to look for safety, shelter and economic well-being
during the wrenching economic and political crises of the 1980s and 1990s.
Faced with eking out a living in a transnational economy, where families struggle to subsist while forged to compete in a vortex of cultural differences, many
encountered continuity and new meaning in ethnicity. Thus in the whirlpool of
out-migration, whether to Latin American metropoles or in agribusiness and
barrios of the United States, ethnic fellowship takes on additional significance,
strengthened by the very yearning for the community and solidarity of back
home.[11]

Culture, not class, is key. Mixtec lawyer and activist Francisco López Bárcenas points to the examples of how even the most militant efforts by Indians
are sustained by images of their own history in which class takes a back seat, if
it is along for the ride at all. These include Chilean Mapuche Indians seeking to
defend their natural resources against logging interests, Bolivian Aymara mobilizing to protect water from privatizing schemes, and the Ecuadorian Kichwa,
protesting the despoliation of the rainforest by foreign oil companies.

> Instead of turning to sophisticated political theories to prepare their discourses
> [these seek to] "recover historical memory to ground their demands and politi-
> cal practices [giving] . . . the new movements a distinctive and even symbolic
> touch. Indigenous peoples in Mexico recuperate the memory of Emiliano Za-
> pata, the incorruptible general of the Army of the South during the revolution
> of 1910-1917, whose principal demand was the restitution of native lands
> usurped by the large landowners. Colombians recuperate the program and
> deeds of Manuel Quintín Lame. Andeans in Perú, Ecuador, and Bolivia make
> immediate the rebellions by Tupac Amaru, Tupac Katari, and Bartolina Sisa
> during colonization, and by Willka Pablo Zarate during the republican period.
> Local and national heroes are present again in the struggle to guide their ar-
> mies, as if they had been resting, waiting for the best time to return to the
> fight.[12]

Native peoples' own intellectual and spiritual elites are well aware of historical
and recent neo-Marxist and even "Bolivarian," hostility to their cultural agenda.
Ecuadorian investigator Fredy Rivera Velez has noted that the Marxist left has

traditionally "displaced ethno-nationalist problems to a second theoretical level since they would be solved in the new socialist society." In this way the paternalism of traditional elites is replaced by a class-based paternalism in "subtle revolutionary-proletariat camouflage."[13] Nonetheless radicalized Indian leaders such as Morales and Peru's Ollanta Humala—and other non-Indians who pretend to lead indigenous peoples, such as Venezuela's Chavez and Mexico's self-designated "subcommandante"—continue to speak as if in their name.

The legacy of left-wing antagonism to Indian causes includes memories of violence at the hands of Marxist regimes or those who sought to create them. Examples include atrocities carried out against indigenous communities by Peru's Maoist Sendero Luminoso and more recent efforts to bring Nicaragua's Sandinista President Daniel Ortega before a civilian court on charges that he led a genocide campaign against that country's Miskito, Sumo and Rama peoples during the 1980s.[14] Under Ortega, sixty five Miskito and Sumo indigenous communities were burnt to the ground; seventy thousand Miskitos and Sumos— one half the population—were forced into state and external refugee camps, with thousands subject to arbitrary arrest, jailings and torture. Soviet helicopter gunships and Sandinista elite troops attacked Indian communities whose "crime" was seeking to maintain their traditional ways of life. In his book, *Where White Men Fear to Tread,* Indian activist Russell Means—an Oglala Sioux and a vocal critic of the U.S. government, someone the *Los Angeles Times* called the most famous American Indian since Sitting Bull and Crazy Horse— recalled traveling to Nicaragua. There the Sandinistas "were trying to force the Indians to integrate with the rest of the country by using all the tools of traditional colonialism." Means said that he "learned that the Sandinistas were trying to keep the Indians from raising an army by systematically murdering young men." In one village "Sandinista helicopters had landed [and] rounded up all boys between the ages of twelve and sixteen, herded them into a local schoolhouse, and set it afire, burning them alive. . . . I heard the same story, with minor variations, in almost every village. In Wounta, soldiers had clubbed the youngsters to death. In a village near Sukupin, children had been buried alive. In several other communities, they had been machinegunned." (During this time Guatemalan indigenous activist Rigoberta Menchú, who later won the Nobel Peace Prize, publically sided with the Sandinistas: "At international forums she sang their praises, contradicted Miskito leaders denouncing human rights violations, and lectured them on their obligations to the antiimperialist cause," wrote anthropologist David Stoll. "For the enemies Rigoberta made, it was all too obvious that her first loyalty was to the Marxist International.") In negotiations with the Sandinistas Indian demands included that the Marxist government sign a formal peace treaty with both Indian and Creole nations, and recognized their territorial boundaries, and their rights to self-government and self-determination. The creation by the Sandinistas of Nicaragua's autonomous regions in 1987, while seen by López Bárcenas as "unprecedented" in Central and South America and Mexico, was done "in order to deactivate the armed opposition, and this, over time, also effectively deactivated the indigenous movement." Another commentator, an adviser to Miskito negotiators during the 1980s, pointed out that the Sandinistas used "Soviet-style autonomy laws in an effort to stamp out the peoples' wishes for self-determination." (The Sandinista operation, a reaction to a firestorm of international criticism of their treatment of indigenous peoples, began as thousands of anti-Sandinista Indians gave up the fight, angered, as the *Wall Street Journal* reported the same year, "that the Central Intelligence Agency supported only those leaders that it could control and forced them to unite with the U.S.-backed Contra rebels, who are hostile toward the Indians' traditional aspirations. . . . The CIA also didn't fully recognize that the Indians were struggling for autonomy for their region—something that both the Sandinistas and many Contra leaders oppose." The conservative newspaper quoted anti-Sandinista Miskito leader Brooklyn Rivera as saying, "The CIA cowboys want us to be their little Indians.")[15]

In Mexico, the *Ejército Zapatista de Liberación Nacional* (Zapatista Army of National Liberation, *EZLN*) rebels in Chiapas broke into international consciousness as an *Indian* phenomenon, bringing unprecedented attention from the mass media and recognition from civil society. The Zapatistas' roots, leadership and early proposals, however, were leftist rather than indigenous-oriented. Political scientist Donna Lee Van Cott noted that the Zapatistas are an anomaly among both guerrilla organizations and indigenous movements, distinguishing themselves from other Indian groups by their non-Native American organizational forms, political rhetoric, and tactics, "influenced in their formative stage by revolutionary socialism" and thus fundamentally incompatible with indigenous peoples' ethnic and cultural demands. Van Cott demonstrates that the Zapatistas emerged at a time when the electoral credibility of Mexico's long-ruling *Partido Revolucionario Institucional* (Institutional Revolutionary Party/*PRI*) was at an all-time low, when a precipitous fall in international commodity prices sent agricultural prices through the floor, particularly for goods produced without irrigation on commonly held Indian lands, and when state violence against Native communities in Chiapas was on an upswing. A proto-Zapatista movement began in the late 1970s, when "Marxist and Maoist intellectual outsiders learned the languages and organized groups of Indians in agricultural cooperatives" deep in the Lacandon tropical forest where few indigenous peoples lived. Those Indians who joined "Subcomandante" Marcos and other leftists in the new settlements were largely young people from other areas in Chiapas who "were prepared to break their ties to the cultural and ethnic communities." It wasn't until the EZLN offensive in January, 1994, when the Zapatistas "came to depend on the physical and moral support of the indigenous communities as buffers between them and the Mexican army, that [they] fully embraced the *indianista* agenda and moderated the rhetoric that characterized the socialist revolution." This, Van Cott wrote, can be demonstrated by studying both in the

EZLN official communiqués and the declarations of its leaders from before the insurrection until 1998. The group's multiethnic composition and the Marxist ideology of its leaders, she noted, led the group to initially minimize ethnicity as "divisive and irrelevant." Attention paid to the five-hundredth anniversary of Christopher Colombus' arrival to the Americas, and press attention to the rebels' Indian membership in the wake of their revolt, persuaded the Zapatistas to fly the *indigenista* banner with greater enthusiasm. At the same time Mexican peasant and indigenous organizations not linked to the rebels sought to hook up their fortunes to the Zapatistas' notoriety, while being careful not to endorse their means.

> Indianist organizations that sent out communiqués supporting the Chiapas Indians expressed their solidarity with the EZLN but roundly rejected their violent tactics, as can be seen by the words of Nahuatl leader Eustaquio Celestino de Guerrero: "We support all of its demands. We know first hand what corruption and broken promises mean. But the solution is not in weapons, but in dialogue." Both Chiapas peasant and Indian pacifist organizations forged a delicate political alliance with the Zapatistas, but at the same time continued to distance themselves from the violent tactics of the rebels. . . .
>
> The tenuous tie, a "marriage of convenience," between the Zapatistas and Mexico's indigenous organizations, was increasingly strained as negotiations with the government dragged on. A peace plan supported by both the government and the Zapatistas was rejected by more than 70 Mexican Indian organizations as not adequately spelling out the relationship between Native peoples and the state. Another group of Indian organizations rejected the rebels' modification of the term "indigenous peoples" to "ethnic minorities," a term rejected by indigenous organizations in the entire American Continent because it is considered to be derogatory and restrictive of their rights within the framework of international law. . . . The rebels had greater interest in provoking the creation of a national political movement rather than resolving the grave social deficit that afflicted Chiapas and that led to the rebellion. A great number of poor indigenous families that suffered the loss of a loved one, of their goods or scarce possessions because of the insurrection, now turned their anger and frustration against the EZLN. Nonetheless, the marriage of convenience that united the destiny of the indigenist movement with that of the rebels has benefited both sides. The incorporation of the Mayan Indians of Chiapas—supposedly the most at risk and mistreated people of Mexico—in their ranks has given the EZLN credibility in the eyes of Mexicans and of the international community. The indigenist organizations benefited from the rebellion due to the fact that they were able to attract a certain amount of attention to their demands and to the resolution of their old problems.[16]

Less than four years after they erupted into the national and international scene, Van Cott found that the Zapatistas' main contribution to Indian groups was some increase in public attention to pervasive violations of human rights in Chiapas. It was a modest harvest at best, as we shall see later on.[17]

Natividad Gutiérrez, a Mexican researcher, found the Zapatista revolt lacking in any ideological ethnic input that would credential it as an "Indian" movement. "It is led by non-Indians; claims that its principal spokesman subcommandant Marcos is only carrying out orders from a clandestine Indian committee cannot be taken seriously. Moreover, the poetic messages (some call them postmodernist critique), plans, and negotiating positions proposed by this charismatic spokesman are more likely to capture the imagination of the young, urban, educated middle sectors of society than to arouse support, identification, and trust in rural villages." Gutiérrez found that indigenous intellectuals and their ideas had been "systematically left out" of the debates and negotiations of the various phases of the Indian conflict. Instead, those roles were left to "a long list of non-Indian social scientists, civil servants, and political men and woman acting as advisers, spokespeople, and negotiators." Gutiérrez quotes a Nahua researcher, Marcos Matías:

> Myself and other colleagues have been invited to speak by the EZLN delegation and the official delegation; in both we noticed a lack of grass roots leadership. . . . They have done everything possible to isolate our voices and impede the building of a bridge among Indian peoples. . . . [A] group of us wrote our own version of a proposal of constitutional reforms for indigenous peoples. When this document was handed to Marcos, he ignored it, arguing that he already had his proposal. Indian peoples cannot be restricted to [being represented by] a non-indigenous man. This cannot be.

Such disregard for both Indian intellectuals and the grass roots of indigenous communities, Gutiérrez noted, strengthens conventional wisdom in non-Indian society, "that Indians lack means to make themselves heard, that they cannot articulate a convincing discourse, or—even more piercing—that they are susceptible to manipulation." Leftwing vanguardism, a handmaiden to manipulation, occupied a front rank in Indian concerns about the direction the Zapatistas were headed while, as Mexican researchers Araceli Burgete Cal y Mayor and Miguel Gómez Gómez found, in the aftermath of the uprising, the state of Chiapas actually lost autonomy.[18]

In Ecuador, economic anthropologist Victor Breton Solo de Zaldivar noted critically, "The ethnicization of the indigenous movement has prioritized culture and identity politics at the expense of the class-based peasant agenda still very much alive in the mid-1990s, thus hindering the formation of alliances between indigenous groups and other sectors of society."[19] Meanwhile, the elected non-Indian, left-wing populist President, Rafael Correa Delgado, who speaks Kichwa and publishes his speeches in that language as well as in Spanish, consistently invoked indigenous rights and Indian well-being as part of his governing agenda. Native leaders repeatedly complained that his emphasis on a strong central government neutralized congressional oversight, co-opted Indian social movements, and reinforced anti-democratic and "colonial and liberal ideologies that oppressed and erased the unique histories of Indigenous nationalities that emphasized control over land and natural resources." Historian Marc Becker wrote that despite the leading roles of indigenous organizations in challenging both neo-liberal economic policies and perceived violations of national sovereignty, "once Correa took office their voices were increasingly marginalized to the sidelines in favor of state-centered actions. . . . Correa's personal charisma and left-populist discourse demobilized the left, leaving popular movements in a worse situation than when he took power."[20]

Indian identity politics in Bolivia changed the national agenda, from being based almost entirely on one small group's interests (those of the non-Indian elite) to one that is—at least in part—community-based with attention to shared principles. The country's political structure changed in ways the Marxist left was never able to even approximate. Traditionally, as Bolivian anthropologist Xavier Albó has noted, because Marxist-Leninist movements in his country were mostly urban, they used Indian names, slogans and standards in order to attract rural support.[21] Nonetheless, a month after Evo Morales' election, indigenous intellectuals attending a symposium in La Paz to share perspectives on issues of identity, territory and education, openly questioned whether "Morales would be more influenced by his Aymaran traditions or by the leftwing presence around him," such as that of Chavez and Castro. Some speakers criticized the Left "for using Indian movements for their own ends."[22] Two months later, traditional Indian leaders at another indigenous conclave in La Paz recalled the Left's historic hostility to cultural demands, a critical element in contemporary Indian mobilizations. Mexico's left-of-center newspaper La Jornada reported that: "Curiously, many have a strong position against Marxism and its class concept. This can be explained because historically [the Indians] were considered 'peasants' and it has been difficult for the current movements to position themselves as indigenous."[23]

Some indigenous intellectuals even questioned the historical consistency of lining up under the "Boliviarian" standard of Venezuelan strongman Chavez, who, sharing some indigenous ancestry, regularly invokes the names of his country's Cacique (chief) Guaicaipuro and the Inca leader Tupac Katari in his speeches before Native American groups. "We disagree with the Bolivar idea," noted Pablo Mamani, the head of the sociology department at the Universidad de El Alto, Bolivia. The Liberator sought through the decrees of Trujillo and Cuzco to take away the Indians' communal lands and forced them to be individual private holders, Mamani said, which dealt them a serious blow from which many never recovered.[24]

Distrust of the Latin American Left was also much in evidence in the remarks of Argentine Mapuche activist Nilo Cayuqueo, who complained in late 1981, that leftist political parties were:

not willing to recognize the Indian people as being oppressed; they just see them as another social category. . . . Some of my brothers, some of the leaders, say that *this attitude of the left is a new form of European colonization.* Socialism is a European . . . concept because socialists want to replace the Indian communes that exist in South America with socialist organizations. So *it's a socially disruptive process because they want to destroy the organization that exists among the Indian people.* These communes, or *ayllus,* exist in all the Andean countries; they are already collective, and they don't need to become socialist. [25] (Italics added.)

The instrumentality of the Left in dealing with Indians could also be seen in the role played by the Colombian guerrilla group, the M-19, which roughly paralleled Marxist guerrilla activity in Guatemala. "Consciousness raising" activities among Indians left the peasant communities dangerously and perhaps deliberately exposed to military repression. Cayuqueo wrote that, "The problem is that M-19 is trying to gain influence with the Indians, and what they've done is gone into [the Cauca valley] and killed various landlords who have been stealing land from the Indians. . . . What happens is that then the government comes in and they kill the Indians." Left-wing guerrillas in the highlands of Guatemala, where indigenous peoples faced a U.S.-supported scorched-earth counterinsurgency campaign, also used such tactics, to disastrous effect as we will see later. [26]

The experience of Native Americans with leftwing activists in the United States, who also find in the plight of Indians a useful metaphor and tool for their own causes, is relevant here. For example, American Indian Movement (AIM) leader Russell Means, described by the *Washington Post* as "one of the biggest, baddest, meanest, angriest, most famous American Indian activists of the late twentieth century," tells a revealing story from the time the AIM carried out a seventy-one-day armed siege in 1973 at the hamlet of Wounded Knee, historic site of the last massacre of the Indian wars, at the Pine Ridge Lakota Sioux reservation. Impassioned, idealistic AIM activists from more than seventy five Indian nations converged on the spot, issuing a series of demands that included the recognition of outstanding Lakota treaty rights. Arrested by federal authorities, Means was imprisoned and seeking his freedom at the time when a friend of his overheard one of Means' lawyers, a leftist, say "the longer I stayed in jail, the better it would be for everyone. . . . He believed that if I were AIM's martyr, everyone would rally around, making it easier for us to raise money, and simpler to point out the federal government's continued oppression." More broadly, surveying the experience of tribal peoples under Marxist regimes in the Soviet Union, China and Vietnam, Means noted that, "in theory and practice Marxism demands that non-European peoples give up their values, their traditions, their cultural existence altogether." Marxism, he concluded, "is as alien to my culture as capitalism and Christianity are." [27]

Ingrid Washinawatok, a founder of the Indigenous Women's Network and an award-winning lecturer from the U.S. Menominee tribe in Wisconsin, was one of three humanitarian workers murdered in 1999 by the Colombian Revolutionary Armed Forces (FARC) in a Venezuelan field near the Colombia border. The trio was on a mission to help Colombia's Uwa tribe establish a cultural education system in order to continue its traditional way of life. According to one account, perhaps summarizing the innocence of some Native American activists attracted to left-wing promises of social justice,

American Indians now admit that they made major miscalculations in their analysis of the FARC during those eight days when Washinawatok was held captive. "We operated from the point of view—hey, we're Indians. *Ingrid had studied in Havana,* she spoke Spanish and she had worked with Indian people all over. We thought it should be OK," said Alex Ewen of the Solidarity Foundation, a New York Indian philanthropic group. *"We didn't understand that this group was different.*"[28] (Italics added.)

Chapter Six
Indian Lands, "Ungoverned Spaces," and Failing States

"A nation's existence [is] a daily plebiscite, just as an individual's existence is a perpetual affirmation of life."
—Ernest Renan[1]

Individuals and groups resorting to violence, one U.S. expert noted, "habitually find or create ways to operate with impunity or without detection. Whether for private financial gain (e.g., by narcotics and arms traffickers) or for harmful political aims (e.g., by insurgents, terrorists, and other violent extremists), these illicit operations are most successful—and most dangerous—when their perpetrators have a place or situation that can provide refuge from efforts to combat or counter them. Such places are often called *safe havens*, and potential safe havens are sometimes called *ungoverned areas.*"[2]

The fact that "Latin" America is the world's most urban region means, among other things, that both resources and state presence are often significantly skewed away from rural areas considered the homelands of indigenous peoples. These regions, "ungoverned, under-governed, misgoverned, contested and exploitable areas,"[3] together with those countries verging on the status of "failed states," are also some of the most prone to becoming safe havens for lawless groups. They include both the conflictive south of Mexico and part of the northern border with the United States; the Belize-Guatemalan border running along the Western Chiquibul Forest; the Lago Agrio area on Ecuador's border with Colombia; the Darien jungle gap between Colombia and Panama, the quarter of

Colombian land under the control of its small (barely 2 percent of the national total) Indian population,[4] and even areas in the south of Chile.

That the clandestine industrialization of narcotics enjoys safe haven in several regions of Latin America is a staple in mass media coverage. Less attention is paid to the fact that it affects the health and security of Indians, as well as frequently pollutes the lands in which they live. Cocaine production, for example, devastates the environment in and around indigenous communities. Its effects include deforestation, pesticide use, water pollution, chemical dumping, the promotion of mono-agriculture and soil erosion, and the loss of bio-diversity and traditional knowledge of plant species. Evo Morales and others point out that coca leaf cultivation has traditional medicinal, cultural and religious uses (chewing the leaf at high altitudes can help ward off hunger and fatigue) in traditional Aymara and Quechua communities dating to the time of the Inca, and therefore should not be controlled by the state. (Two Inca emperors named their wives after the venerated leaf; the honored consorts were bestowed with the plant's sacred title, Mama Coca. The only object that the emperor ever carried himself was a coca pouch, which he wore around his neck close to his heart.)

However, nearly all the coca used for chewing is grown in Las Yungas, a mountainous, semi-tropical Bolivian region where the high altitude offers an ideal climate for the high-quality crops. In places where most coca leaf is produced—Bolivia's Chapare and Peru's Upper Huallaga, both significantly lower altitudes than Las Yungas—the plant was not cultivated historically, is of much lower quality, and is almost entirely dedicated to the cocaine trade, creating staggering environmental, public safety and health challenges. Ironically, and tragically, stories abound in the sierra about how coca leaf meant for traditional consumption needs to be "exported" from Las Yungas to the Chapare for use by the coca growers.[5]

According to Colombian Vice President Francisco Santos Calderon, each year in his country three hundred thousand hectares of tropical rain forest are destroyed as the land is used for coca plants and the industrialization of cocaine. However, as falling agricultural prices and neo-liberal "reforms" increase the stress on Indian communities, some of which also face demographic explosions, so too has the U.S.-sponsored "war" against drugs meant to suppress the production by Indian farmers of coca leaf, marijuana and heroin poppy crops. Despite the palpable damage these activities can wreck on Indian lives and a revered Mother Earth, these efforts to quell the free market for illegal drug production are sometimes portrayed as the result of racially or culturally oriented repression. The public relations war was made even more difficult after the Paez Indians from Colombia's southwest region sought to market a fizzy beverage—Coca Sek—made of coca grown legally for traditional uses. The sale of the apple cider-colored drink tasting something like ginger ale, which quickly became a hip replacement for Coca-Cola among the country's urban young, was banned by the Colombian government, along with other coca-derived products, in February

2007 outside of Native American reservations, where the right to grow coca is protected by the country's constitution.[6]

Another example of the overlap of indigenous peoples, illicit groups, and "ungoverned spaces," is the Brazilian tri-border area with Venezuela and Guyana, where small indigenous communities populate the remote region; Brazilian officials point to reports that the Colombian Revolutionary Armed Forces (FARC) guerrillas are operating there. "We can't leave empty spaces," warned Col. Jose Hugo Volkmer, a former U.N. military observer in Sarajevo in the 1990s and the head of the Brazilian airmail service (Correio Aereo Nacional/CAN). "Empty spaces get occupied. If we don't occupy them, then our neighbor will."[7]

Along the U.S.-Mexican border, in a remote desert area between Phoenix and Hermosillo, members of the twenty-four-thousand strong Tohono O'odham tribe, whose members are used to traveling through informal "gates" along the frontier, now encounter violent Mexican drug and human traffickers, who force the tribe from its traditional villages, off the land and their way of life in Mexico.[8] (On the other side of the law, an elite team of U.S. Native American trackers, known as the "Shadow Wolves," is at the cutting edge of a layered border defense, patrolling the sandy expanse where the Tohono O'odham live in order to capture the criminals. They use an ancient sign-reading skill called "sign cutting"—reading and following minute clues, such as footprints, broken branches or tire tracks—in a seemingly empty landscape. The trackers are recruited from several U.S. tribes, including the Navajo, Sioux, Lakota and Apache.)[9]

> *Any map of those territories trending toward the status of "ungoverned spaces" in the region—where drug production and their distribution northward, rest areas for insurgent and terrorist groups, the proselytizing by violent Islamist groups, and other illegal or anti-democratic activities flourish—meshes largely, albeit imperfectly and not exclusively, with areas where indigenous peoples live, and where they frequently fall victim to these scourges.*

When addressing the problem of "ungoverned spaces"—real, incipient and potential—that overlap Indian lands, three problems need to be addressed. First, it is important to steer away from conceptualizing the issue as one in which the lack of central government control is synonymous with the absence of peoples and institutions—the woof and weave of society—in these outlying areas. As Princeton University scholar Deborah J. Yashar has noted:

In the agricultural highlands of Bolivia, Perú, and Ecuador as well as the rural areas of Mexico and Guatemala, the state could not assert the pervasive control that the overwhelming majority of studies of corporativism have tended to assume. To the contrary, indigenous communities managed to carve out a degree of local autonomy that remained beyond the reach of corporatist institutions. Indeed . . . Indians secured the spaces in which they could institutionalize indigenous community practices at the local level.[10]

The term "ungoverned spaces" should refer only and specifically to the lack of effective central government outreach to these areas, because they are not bereft of inhabitants, or that these have been unable to maintain their communities, using local administration, in the face of threats. Inhabitants of these areas have their own societies, methods of governance, and economic or commercial systems.

Even more basic to the dialogue on indigenous issues and ungoverned spaces is the issue of discovery. This harkens back to the early modern period of colonialism, when Europeans conquered territory from its inhabitants in the Americas, a region until then unknown to the Caucasians. These peoples were considered uncivilized—in some cases a debate raged over the nature of their humanity—and therefore subject to a civilizing and Christian enterprise.[11]

The second issue involves colonialism and its inheritance, and the potential minefields non-Indians tread in engaging in a dialogue about the lands where they live with the region's First Peoples. European powers used the international law of discovery to keep rival European states from exercising a "right" of conquest over lands they had come to occupy, thus justifying their claims over indigenous territory. Indian law activist Steven M. Tullberg explains:

> The discovery doctrine had been developed primarily by European jurists and imperial theorists to justify and regulate the competitive global trade and empire building of European powers. . . .It provided for a legal rationale for the domination over foreign lands and native peoples that Europeans asserted as they carried out their slave trading in Africa and the Americas and their colonialism around the world. The discovery doctrine was said to accomplish a guardianship or trusteeship over indigenous peoples for the beneficial spread of civilization and Christianity. . . . [It] held that the discovering European power immediately became rulers over the indigenous peoples and owners of all of the indigenous peoples' land."

In Australia, for example, a doctrine of *terra nullis*, "a variant of the discovery doctrine . . . denied property rights of Australian Aborigines through the legal fiction that their lands were uninhabited and could be taken freely by white settlers."[12] The discovery doctrine, it should be noted, was established during a time in which there was an earnest debate over the humanity of Indians and other conquered indigenous peoples—whether they could be exploited and "Christianized," which was seen as a more humane and altruistic act, and one not always practiced by conquering empires. In the United States modern Indian law originated with a doctrine that refused legal status or rights to indigenous tribal peoples because they were "heathens" and "infidels," and therefore legally presumed to lack the rational capacity necessary to assume an equal status or exercise equal rights under the Europeans' world view. "American Indian Nations have been judged, and their legal status and rights determined by alien and alienating norms derived from the European's experience of the world."[13] Remedies proposed to end lawlessness associated with ungoverned spaces must steer clear of serving as latter-day renditions of paternalistic and exploitative theories that received their legal sanction in the discovery doctrine. Any solutions based on discovery doctrine mindsets are the fruit of a poisonous tree, and their very provenance mocks modern legal standards and practices, and will likely be ineffectual in enlisting popular support from the peoples who live in these purportedly "ungoverned" areas.

Finally, because any remedy needs to avoid past errors, any solutions to problems affecting areas where indigenous peoples live must begin with those communities themselves. As one authority has noted:

> building the institutional capacity needed for the state to reassert control over an ungoverned area is not often successful. In many cases, provincial, local, tribal or autonomous governments—and in some cases, other countries, corporations, or organizations—are simply better positioned than the central government to address the local conditions that enable illicit actors to operate there. It often will be more efficient and effective to influence and enable those entities rather than—or, preferably, in addition to and with the assistance of—the host state in the short term. For diplomatic, legal, and practical reasons, the host state cannot be ignored or bypassed, but nor should it be permitted to impede progress against safe havens when other entities are positioned to help. An appropriate balance is needed.[14]

A New Search for Identity and Meaning

The historian of nationalism Elie Kedourie noted that the phenomenon "does not make easy the relations of different groups in mixed areas. Since it advocates a recasting of frontiers and a redistribution of political power to conform to the demands of a particular nationality, it tends to disrupt whatever equilibrium had been reached between different groups, to reopen settled questions and to renew strife."[15] Barry Posen, a theorist in the relationships between security dilemmas (usually associated with international relations theory) and ethnic conflict, observed in the context of Eastern Europe, that the collapse of multiethnic states, "can profitably be viewed as a problem of 'emerging anarchy.'" The failure of central government to effectively deal with security, Posen writes, signifies that it is replaced by those means available to ethnic or religious groups.[16] Thus, recent events in several nations of Central and South America recall Michael Ignatieff's warning that: "There is one type of fear more devastating in its impact than any other, the systemic fear that arises when a state begins to collapse. Ethnic hatred is the result of the terror which arises when legitimate authority disintegrates."[17] Even more benign interpretations of intentions, using the prism of security dilemmas—where the parties do not wish to harm each other but none-theless end up going to war—show how understandable clashes between two contending parties end up in anti-system *putsches*.

Rather than representing the expression of an ideological "ism," ultrana-tionalists work the rich mine of less abstract notions, such as religion and kin-ship. In this regard, it may be useful to remember George de Vos's aphorism that "the ethnic identity of a group of people consists of their subjective sym-bolic or emblematic use of any aspect of culture, in order to differentiate them-selves from other groups."[18]

The example of the indigenous peoples of El Salvador recruited into *Mundo Maya*, a well-financed Central American regional tourism initiative, suggests that the reengineering of native peoples' identity, even when portrayed in "an exoticised and commodified fashion" not reflective of their authentic past, can also arguably contribute "to fostering a social ideational climate more sympa-thetic to indigenous activism. Moreover, linking pre-Colombian and present-day indigenous cultures contradicts long-standing state-nationalist doctrine in Latin America that the Conquest represented such a profound collapse of native civili-zations that no meaningful historical connection with present-day indigenous peoples has been sustained." *Mundo Maya* not only portrayed as ersatz "Mayan" the Salvador's national identity but, political scientist Virginia Q. Tilley added, had another outcome, as it "ironically ... imports a subversive subtext, by restor-ing indigenous peoples' public profile as the region's prior sovereigns, a concept that recasts the modern state as settler-colonial, and raised the specter of indige-nous secession, autonomy claims, or at least group rights."[19]

Another example of this search for self-identity—whose uniqueness helps ratify de Vos's dictum that what is *believed*, not what objectively *was*, becomes the operative principle in the reconstruction of identity—is the recent case in-volving seven hundred Indians from Perú and Brazil. The group's ancestors in-cluded a handful of Moroccan Jewish tradesmen imported more than a century and a half ago to work in the Amazon rubber industry. "The Jewish merchants had no wives, and ended up marrying the local Indian women." In 2005, hun-dreds of these Indian descendants immigrated to Israel after reconnecting with Judaism and their Jewish heritage, which "up until twenty years ago . . . was nothing more than a distant memory . . . living through a handful of religious customs practiced by a few of the families living in the Amazon." As one author noted, the Jewish immigrants of Indian descent "prove nothing trumps the need to connect with one's heritage."[20] The Indians who identified themselves as Jew-ish qualified to emigrate to Israel under that country's Law of Return [5710-1950], which gives Jews, those of Jewish ancestry, and their spouses, the right to migrate to and settle in Israel and to gain citizenship.

Today some "imagined communities"—the concept was coined by Benedict Anderson—under construction in Indian country in Central and South America and Mexico appear to defy post-early Mesozoic geography itself, as is shown by a nascent but potentially worrisome trend towards Native American conversion to radicalized Islam (explored further below). Native peoples' growing disenchantment with Christianity, and particularly with the Roman Catholicism that has held sway in the region since the sixteenth century, in some ways parallels developments in the political sphere, in which left-wing militancy appears as perhaps merely a portal through which some Native American groups stand at the threshold of making common cause with violent non-Marxist extremist groups, including Islamic fundamentalists.[21]

"Islamic leaders are allying with South American indigenous groups, because they see this impoverished, illiterate population, as the ideal environment for starting an extremist revolution and converting them to Islam," warned José Brechner, a conservative first-generation, Bolivian politician and diplomat, in 2006. "Indigenous leaders have powerful economic and political reasons for helping these fanatics, with whom they share a common hatred for Americans and Westerners." Brechner, known for his anti-Indian writing, claimed that indigenous peoples in the region remained, without distinction, "still more animist than Christian, and their Catholic customs coexist comfortably with paganism." Employing Euro-centric racial stereotypes of Indians, he added, "People with such frail principles and scant strength of spirit are easily persuaded."[22]

Nonetheless, disaffection with a religion [Catholicism] whose origin is found in the Levant by way of Europe, and practiced overwhelmingly among indigenous peoples as a "folk" variety that leans heavily on adopted forms [ritual, symbolism], is not limited to just Morales' Bolivia. And Native American interests are likewise not limited to the religions of their indigenous forefathers, as a nascent phenomenon of conversion to Islam shows. The importance of religion in effecting political and social change is beyond the scope of this book and, in any event, may be hard to quantify; however, it is no less important. As a former Catholic missionary and director of Latin American Studies at Providence College has noted: "Religious conversion is the single greatest social process changing Latin America and the Caribbean in the twentieth and twenty-first centuries."[23]

In his study of the competition between Christian evangelicals and indigenous nationalists in highland Bolivia, sociologist Andrew Canessa took note of the fact that acceptance of the nationalists' platform grew at a time of both national and international crisis on the left. The Protestant groups, aware of the stresses of social, cultural and economic dislocation of highland Indians in the long aftermath of the *mestizo*-led nationalist revolution of 1952, had consciously exploited the Native Americans' feeling of disorientation and dislocation, offering "the most vulnerable, and the most in need . . . the support and sense of community that membership of a small and dedicated group can bring." Despite the wide gulf of creed and practice that separated them, both religious evangelism and *katarismo*—the nationalist creed of the highland Indian—offered newcomers a sense of dignity that spurred their conversion to one or the other.

Canessa suggested that eventual disenchantment with one of the options—
evangelism—led some religious converts to later embrace *katarismo*.[24]

Evangelismo and Katarismo in Highland Bolivia

Accepts Western model of modernity	Seeks to create an indigenous modernity
Rejects present for the future	Looks to past for the future
Pro-Western education	Anti-Western education
Anti-Pagan	Seeks to valorize local practice
Pro-Western	Anti-Western
Christian	Anti-Christian

Moralistic
Reject hybridity
Seek dignity for Indians
Reject cosmopolitanism
Reject cultural *mestizaje*
Undermine state ideology
Messianic figure at center
Millenarian consciousness
Waiting for a resurrection and a new order
Oppose historical homogeneous nation-state

(From: Andrew Canessa, "Contesting Hybridity: Evangelistas and Kataristas in Highland Bolivia," *Journal of Latin American Studies* 32, 2000)

Although one model looks to the past while the other focuses on the future,
Canessa found that both evangelism and *katarismo* reject the present as unsatis-
factory, and even in their differences the two movements shared striking commonalities.

> The *katarista* model of the past is moralistic and seeks to reinvigorate a demor-
> alized and decadent Indian people with the ethics of a bygone Indian golden
> age. "Don't steal; don't lie; don't be lazy" is one of the aphorisms most com-
> monly seen, and is purported to be one of the tenets of Inka moral life. *Evan-
> gelistas* also see contemporary culture as decadent and provide a moralistic
> framework . . . [P]ersonal hygiene and self-respect is something both move-
> ments stress. Most significantly they clearly agree that there is a conspicuous
> lack of pride, dignity and self-worth among Aymara Indians: they agree there is
> a moral deficit; they disagree how to fill it. . . . Both groups hold a second com-
> ing and a spiritual revolution as central tenets of their beliefs.[25]

The underlying appeal of both movements thus unites them in ways their dog-
matic offerings seem to contradict. Most of the tenets central to their common
appeal is also something they share with Islam, as can be seen in a diagram of-

fered by Canessa to compare the differences and similarities of evangelicals and *kataristas*.

In its most militant and politically radical forms, Islam shares with both the evangelicals and the *kataristas* at least seven of the ten characteristics listed by Canessa: moralistic; seek dignity; reject cosmopolitanism; reject cultural *mestizaje;* undermine state ideology; messianic figure at center; millenarian consciousness; waiting for a resurrection and a new order, and oppose historical homogeneous nation-state. There are also four other characteristics Islamists have in common to the *kataristas*: looks to past for the future; anti-Western education; and has an anti-Western and an anti-Christian worldview. The commonalities shared by two "mutually incompatible strategies for a meaningful future"—evangelism and *katarismo*—as well as their appeal to the same groups of disaffected peoples, suggests a potential reservoir of support as well for Islamist recruiters and other violent extra-hemispheric ideologies.[26]

Already in 2001, Venezuelan sociologist Gabriel Ernesto Andrade suggested that Latin America was ripe for efforts by Islamists to attract new converts from among the some 95 percent of the region's population that once practiced Catholicism. (That same year, the *Washington Post* reported that a small but growing number of Latinos in the United States were also converting to Islam, "[m]oved by what many say is a close-knit religious environment and a faith that provides a more concrete, intimate connection with God . . . part of a larger trend of American Hispanics leaving the Catholic Church, experts say.") Left-wing governments and Christian Protestant missionary activities had already weakened the Catholic Church's hold on a group whose "Latin American cultural identity has been vague and poorly defined in the majority of countries, which has triggered in many social sectors a search for new identities with profound historic roots." The fact that it can be portrayed as an antecedent both for Spanish and African (former slave) cultures upon which the Latin American identity is constructed serves Islam as an advantage in its efforts to expand into the region, Andrade noted. One group, Latin American Muslim Unity (*Unidad Musulmana Latinoamericana*), he pointed out, "emphasizes the Islamic roots of the Spanish, and calls on Latin Americans to search for their lost identity through Islam." The fact that Catholicism and its economic derivatives have not offered many Latin Americans satisfaction in their daily lives, he added, may mean that [all the more so now, with the economic downturn at the end of the first decade of the twenty-first century}:

> Islam and its belief system is very attractive to great sectors of Latin American society, who immersed in difficult social conditions can find in Islam new perspectives and moral principles about inequality, poverty, the relationship of the individual to the community, unemployment and capital . . . Faced with the problem of indebtedness and the poverty that is the product of the interest charges of banking activity in Latin America, Islam and its prohibition of 'usury' also becomes a highly attractive alternative . . .[27]

Regional oil-producing and exporting countries such as Mexico, Ecuador and Venezuela (the first two with large Indian populations) share economic interests and geopolitical perspectives with the many Islamic countries which are also petroleum exporters, Andrade noted. He warned that, with the decline of orthodox Marxism in the region due to the end of the Cold War and the resultant collapse of external support from the Soviet Union, Islam and Latin American Marxism

> agree not only in their principles based on struggle, but they also share a common enemy: the imperialism whose major exponent is the United States. Islam represents a fresh paradigm for Latin America and could come to fulfill roles that in other times were carried out by Marxism: to serve as the ideological foundation at the crossroads with imperialism. With Islam, the clash with the dominant classes and imperialism would not be a fight between the proletariat and the bourgeoisie, but rather a fight between Moslems and Infidels. *The synthesis of Marxism and Islam has already been experienced in other contexts. Palestinian guerrillas and terrorist groups (such as Hezbollah and Black September) have been based in many aspects on the Marxist paradigm in order to advance Islamic political and religious positions. . . . In Latin America, the conditions are given for an inverted synthesis: to base old Marxist notions through Islam.*[28] (Italics added.)

Andrade's portrayal of Islam as a "fresh paradigm" in the region is somewhat misleading, however, as political scientist Howard Wiarda shows in his book, *The Soul of Latin America*; in fact, a perceived kinship between indigenous peoples in the region and a proselytizing Islam could be based in part on a common history as victims of prejudice. "Latin America was founded on a feudal, oligarchic, authoritarian, and elitist basis," Wiarda noted, "the product of the Counter-Reformation, of medieval scholasticism and Catholicism, of the Inquisition, and of frankly nonegalitarian, nonpluralist and nondemocratic principles." Among the influences on Iberia was that of the Islamic Moors, who dominated the peninsula for seven centuries. "A seldom-mentioned, wholly negative factor deriving from the Moorish conquest of Iberia was the blatant racial and ethnic prejudice directed against Spain and Portugal by the rest of Europe. Spain and Portugal were often looked down upon and thought to be tainted by North African blood . . . glaring slurs bred in northern Europe a sense of superiority and in Spain and Portugal a sense of inferiority and hence resentment towards the rest of Europe that persisted into modern times."[29]

Yet Andrade's foreboding may be in the process of being proved correct in a least two countries of the region—Mexico and Venezuela—and close attention to their examples will repay important dividends in trying to determine where else violent Islamists may be successful, and why. In both countries radical Islam has already begun to make inroads in some indigenous communities. In both countries, the appeal of radical Islam, even more than Marxism, may lie in the fact that it is in essence anti-modern, and thus—like radical socialism—feeds easily on protests against an economic modernization that leaves demonstrable victims in its wake. Alastair Crooke, a former British intelligence agent known for his extensive contacts among Islamist groups across the Middle East, underscores the point in a 2009 book, *Resistance: the Essence of the Islamist Revolution*. Published by a leftwing British publishing house that prides itself on a "radical political agenda," Crooke emphasizes the metaphysical resistance to Western market-based definitions of society, and the role of the individual in it, as the core of the Islamist revolution.[30]

What is more, as de Vos has noted, sentiment—not necessarily facts—can prevail in the struggle for hearts and minds. The case of Sayyid Qutb, the Egyptian author, educator and a leader of the Muslim Brotherhood, whose writings in the 1950s and 1960s today are used as theoretical underpinnings of many Islamist groups, including al Qaeda, serves as a reminder of how cultural difference can be all important in the way something is perceived. During an extended visit to Greeley, Colorado in 1949, Qutb saw, in what most Americans would have characterized a very conservative, religious community, a town emblematic of a soulless, materialistic United States. In his book, *The America I Have Seen,* Qutb informed his Arab readers that bloody wars against the Indians were still underway in 1949, and that even before American Independence, Anglo colonists had pushed Latinos toward Central America—even though the former had not yet crossed the Mississippi. The American Revolution was "a destructive war," he wrote, led by George Washington. As for sports, the American pastime evidenced in male spectators a "primitiveness of the feeling of those who are enamored with muscular strength and desire it," while American women, even those attending church dances, were "well acquainted" with their bodies' "seductive capacity." Qutb's audience, which included the future founders of al Qaeda, was thus warned about the West and modernity, and instructed on how Islam offered deliverance. (That sentiment trumping facts is an ecumenical phenomenon can be seen in Guatemala. There, David Stoll tell us, during the 1980s the country's first evangelical dictator, General Efrain Rios Montt, a prominent member of the California-based Church of the Word, decried the moral decay of Guatemalan society in televised sermons every Sunday night, while his army committed horrendous rights violations amounting to genocide in the indigenous-dominated highlands in efforts to stamp out a guerrilla insurgency.)[31]

It is worth noting also in this context, Bolivia's decision to establish diplomatic relations with the Islamic Government of Iran—touted as promoting cooperation between the two countries in the petroleum and other sectors because, in the words of President Morales, "Iran loves Bolivia." The ties were followed up shortly afterwards by an announcement that the Iranians, with few apparent cultural linkages to the region's peoples, also planned to establish a television station in the Andean coca-growing foothills, "for all of Bolivia, for

all of Latin America, recognizing the great struggle of this peasant movement."
In October 2008, the Islamic Republic's top diplomat in Bolivia announced that
Iran would open two low-cost public health clinics in Bolivia, to be operated by
Red Crescent medical staff.[32] And in May 2009, a secret report from the Israeli
Foreign Ministry said unequivocally that Bolivia, together with Venezuela, was
supplying the Iranian nuclear program with uranium.[33] (Iran also worked closely
with Chavez and Nicaraguan President Daniel Ortega to establish a $350 million
deep-water port at Monkey Point on the Caribbean coast; the project has been
strongly resisted by Rama Indian and Creole villagers who live in the area.[34])

It is important to note that a jihadist journal, *Qaddaya Jihadyya,* predicted
in September 2008 that nationalist and Marxist resistance movements in Latin
America would soon switch to al-Qaeda, as they see the "victories of al-Qaeda,
which have never been achieved by any secular movement in the world." Murad
al-Shisani, writing in *Terrorism Focus,* noted that the jihadist prediction "raises
the pivotal question of the possibility of an alliance between Salafi-Jihadis and
radical leftist groups in Latin America, based on the common cause of confronting American imperialism and hegemony." In March 2009, a respected Israeli
counterterrorism expert interviewed by a Colombian newsmagazine charged that
both Iran and Hezbollah were seeking to use indigenous peoples as a means of
infiltrating Latin America.[35]

As useful background, it should be noted that an analysis by the Turin-
based Center for Studies on New Religions (CESNUR) maintains that Chávez,
who at times has sought to speak as the head of a movement that supposedly
benefits indigenous peoples, "has carried on a correspondence with Venezuelan
superterrorist Carlos, a Marxist convert to Islam who is serving a life sentence in
France. The President of Venezuela has expressed his appreciation for the
'Carlos doctrine,' which among other things provides for an alliance between
Islamic ultra-fundamentalism and anti-imperialist insurrectionalism, in the name
of their mutual hatred for the United States."[36]

And although Venezuela historically has been one of the Latin American
countries freest of anti-semitism, its small Jewish community being among the
oldest in the region, Chavez had been accused of anti-semitic speech by the
Simon Wiesenthal Center and others. For example, in a pre-Christmas 2005
speech by the Venezuelan leader he declared: "Some minorities, the descendants
of those who crucified Christ, have appropriated for themselves the riches of the
world."[37] "Since Mr. Chavez took the oath of office in 1999, there has been an
unprecedented surge in anti-Semitism throughout Venezuela,"one analyst noted
in *Commentary* magazine. In a speech in 2005, marking a day many non-Indians
in the Americas refer to as "Columbus Day" or *El Dia de la Raza* (The Day of
the Our Race), Chavez compared the difficulties faced by Venezuelan Indians to
that of the Palestinian Arabs. Invoking the murder "in their land" of Native
Americans by "governments, economic sectors and great landed estates,"

Chavez declared: "You were expelled from your homeland, like the heroic Palestinian people."[38]

The *Jamestown Terrorism Monitor* has noted that in Mexico: "Significantly, the majority of indigenous peoples converting to Islam are among those who previously converted to Protestantism and other sects."[39] One factor that can account for the growing attraction to radical Islamist terrorist groups in Latin America, warned Israel's authoritative International Institute for Counter-terrorism:

> could be the successful campaigns of Islamic proselytism in the heart of poor indigenous Indian tribes and populations by both Shi'a and Sunni preachers and activists. . . . Latin America is searching for its own identity and the common people are clearly looking forward to a totally different spiritual change. Proof of this is that 20 to 30 years ago, Catholicism claimed almost 90% of the total population in Latin America, whereas today the numbers are merely between 55% and 65%. Latin America is a fertile area for Islamic *dawah,* and Islamic values are already present in Latin American culture.[40]

In the south of Mexico—a nation whose more than nine million Indians give it the largest indigenous population in the Americas—rivalries between Catholic and evangelical Protestants have resulted in thousands being driven from their homes, a causal factor in the Zapatista revolt that began New Year's Eve, 1993.[41] There hundreds of Tzotzil and Tzeltal Indians who have forsaken both the region's traditional Catholicism and evangelical Christianity are converting to militant Islam, with Mayan Muslims making their first pilgrimage to Mecca in 2005.

One writer on the issue attempted

> to present aspects of Islam that are compatible with the Zapatista ideology and strategy. This is what Fausto Giudice calls 'the direct democracy,' discussing the principles of consensus, the 'shura' and the 'majlis' structure. He even asks himself if Subcomandante Marcos could be the incarnation of the Mahdi. *Marcos and his popular Zapatista movement seem to have such a symbolic importance in the eyes of the Islamists that a Turkish al-Queda publication even pretended that he has indeed converted to Islam.*[42] (Italics added.)

After more than a decade and a half, there is growing frustration and disenchantment as "Subcomandante" Marcos' classic charismatic leadership has not resulted in substantial positive change in the plight of indigenous peoples. (Even a committed American radical journalist like John Ross could, at the beginning of 2009, claim that Marcos "is singlehandedly responsible for the depreciation of the Zapatista movement as a national and international player on the Left," calling him a "vituperative, narcissistic charlatan."[43]) It is an open question whether some Chiapas and other Indians may seek alternative means of violent protest, ones that might parallel their disenchantment with Christianity and a subsequent embrace of militant Islam, in an attempt to identify a cause worth the fight. Media reports say the Indians' seemingly curious conversion to Islam is linked to a shared worldview in which Western ideas and institutions are rejected. The *Jamestown Terrorism Monitor* reported that the Sufi Murabitun Muslim present for more than a decade in Chiapas, unlike other Sufi groups, is politically radical.[44] It makes the argument that

> Catholicism represents a vestige of European imperialism that is directly responsible for the destruction of Mayan culture. Likewise, Catholicism is seen as a tool of the state that is to blame for the poverty and plight of the indigenous peoples. . . . The Murabitun discourse even emphasizes what it describes as the close cultural and ethnic links between the indigenous peoples of the region and the Muslim Moors who once ruled Spain. Therefore, *conversion to Islam represents a reversion to their original identity, essentially an assertion of cultural and ethnic identity long suppressed by European colonialism.* The Muratibun went as far as to engage "Subcomandante" Marcos and his Zapatista Army of National Liberation (EZLN), following the group's armed rebellion in Chiapas in 1994, in an effort to gain support.[45] (Italics added.)

According to *WebIslam.com*, the Murabitun effort reached out to the Zapatistas because they fought the same enemy, "that is the unjust State that should be eliminated together with all of its institutions" following a nine point Islamic program emphasizing the abolition of usury and the use of banks.[46]

In northwestern South America, a group called Hezbollah Latin America (which also calls itself Wayuu Islamic Autonomy) has emerged among the Wayuu Guajira Indians, a people who make up the largest indigenous group in Venezuela (one hundred seventy thousand) and in Colombia (one hundred thirty-five thousand). Its leader, Teodoro Darnott, is a former chief of a small Marxist group—*Projecto Movimiento Guaicaipuro por la Liberacion Nacional*—that claimed to fight for poor indigenous peasants in the Valle de Caracas region, taking as its inspiration the Zapatistas. According to one authoritative source, Darnott led the tribesmen to convert to Islam "after two previous embodiments (as affiliates of Hugo Chavez's Movimiento Quinta República and later as the Jehová Nisi) failed to secure the recognition and support he wanted for a community development project."[47] Similar to the Zapatistas' "subcomandante" Marcos, Darnott uses the name "Comandante Teodoro." The group's Web site, often disabled, has been described as emblematic of the "surprising fusion that is taking place between radical Islam and the extreme leftist discourse in Latin America." Hezbollah Latin America "denies it has any links to either Hezbollah or any other terrorist organization, although it offers its support and solidarity." The Web page also included links to other affiliated groups (*filiales*) in Argentina, Chile, Chiapas and El Salvador, although these apparently contained even less information than the Venezuelan Web page.[48] The Center for Studies on New Religions reported that:

With the blessing of President Chávez, and with the methods of an old guerrilla leader, Commander Teodoro has proclaimed Catholic missionaries "personae non grata" over a vast tribal area [for the Protestant missionaries its even worse: Chavez calls them agents of American imperialism], while proclaiming the Shi'ite Iranian missionaries very very welcome. *Estimates vary as to the result of this experiment—converts according to Teodoro and Iran come to several thousand, while anthropologists and journalists who have penetrated the area say they are fewer than a thousand—however a whole tribe, the Wayuu, has accepted the good news from Teheran.* The press of the Venezuelan regime has started printing strange photographs of veiled *Indio* women, but also of hooded militants practicing with their kalashnikovs and even their bomb-belts: not in Lebanon but in Venezuela. . . . [49] (Italics added.)

On October 23, 2006—the anniversary of the Hezbollah bombing of the U.S. Marine barracks in Beirut thirteen years before—a university student in Venezuela, José Miguel Rojas Espinosa, was arrested by police as he was about to detonate two pipe bombs, one against the U.S. embassy in Caracas, another against the Israeli diplomatic mission. According to the police, after he planted the first artifact, Rojas lost his nerve and dropped the second one outside a school, which led the police to recover the first, thus foiling the attack. Hezbollah Venezuela claimed responsibility for the attempt, its Web site hailing Rojas as "the first mujaheddin to be an example of dignity and strength in the cause of Allah, the first prisoner of war in Venezuela of the Revolutionary Islamic Movement."[50]

Growing alienation from traditional ways of life and a subsequent cultural disaggregation makes the Wayuu—like other indigenous peoples struggling against great odds to protect and transmit to future generations their traditions—increasingly likely candidates to be susceptible to recruitment by Islamist and other violent extremist groups, perhaps from outside the Americas. And, as two Israeli anti-terrorism experts noted in August 2008:

In Venezuela and other South American countries Hizbullah has been waging a long-term campaign to convert the native Indians to Shiite Islam. Teodoro Rafael Darnott, also known as 'Commander Teodoro,' recently claimed, if the United States were to attack Iran, the only country ruled by God, we would counterattack in Latin America and even inside the United States itself. We have the means and we know how to go about it. We will sabotage the transportation of oil from Latin America to the U.S. You have been warned.[51]

Analysis by the Israeli International Institute for Counter-terrorism notes that more than one hundred thirty thousand Wayuu live on the inhospitable Guajira Peninsula straddling the Colombia and Venezuelan border.

The Wayuu culture is being gradually eroded, and already many traditional skills have essentially been lost. This loss of culture is also increasingly accompanied by a lack of self-esteem, particularly among youth. The Wayuu have traditionally had a very loose social structure with few local organizations. In modern times, the clan system has become much weaker than it once was, but has not yet been replaced by alternative social structures.[52]

The Venezuela example is important for several reasons, mostly because of Hugo Chavez's self-identification with and support for nationalist Indian politics, and because his largely leftist coalition also counts on support from radical right-wing nationalist allies and Middle Eastern terrorist states. Chavez's warm relations with Iran, a country that carried out the 1994 bombing of the Argentine Jewish Mutual Association (Asociación Mutual Israelita Argentina/AMIA) that killed eighty-five people, has led the Venezuelan and President Mahmoud Ahmadinejad to create what they call an "Axis of Unity," in which several Latin American countries have been invited to join. In early 2007, Chavez introduced Ahmadinejad to Bolivia's Morales, Ecuador's Correa, and the Nicaraguan Sandinistas, including their head, Daniel Ortega.[53]

Although press attention frequently focuses on Chavez's ties to Fidel Castro and his support for belligerent status for the Colombian FARC guerrillas and Islamists everywhere, Chavez also has counted among his international followers admirers from the undemocratic right. For example, he has drawn significant support from the ultra-right-wing nationalist "Painted Faces" (carapintada) military officers loyal to the late Argentine army Col. Mohammed Ali Seineldin, who formerly worked as an advisor to Panama's dictator Manuel Noriega, and who led several coup attempts against the constitutional governments in Buenos Aires. Before he died, a former Argentine left wing guerrilla supporter and carapintada apologist, sociologist Norberto Ceresole, claimed to be Chavez's ideological guru. Ceresole, "a neo-fascist, anti-Semite, Holocaust denier, and viscerally anti-Israel," considered Iran to be "the center of resistance to Jewish aggression" and the only state that has replaced "the secular Arab resistance" in fighting Israel. Those with long memories may recall that in the early 1990s both Seineldin and Chavez were poster boys for U.S. extremist Lyndon LaRouche and were featured frequently in his publications. Almost all of these radical forces, on the left and on the right, maintain links to radical Middle Eastern regimes, rejecting liberal democracy as being controlled by "the Jews."[54]

Nationalism theorist Ernest Gellner held in his seminal work, Nations and Nationalism, that the most likely candidates for successful nation-building or secessionist movements were those communities firmly ensconced in a literate world-religion. However, nationalism today involves non-state and international actors of a kind that previously did not exist, their resources generated on the black market and their organizational and communications abilities giving them truly global reach. Mark Strauss, a senior editor at Foreign Policy magazine, offered an important insight into such globe-spanning partnerships: "The backlash against globalization unites all elements of the political spectrum through a common cause, and in doing so it sometimes fosters a common enemy . . . an anti-Semitic 'brown-green-red alliance' among ultra-nationalists, the populist green movement, and communism's fellow travelers. . . . *The far right sees national movements and indigenous rights groups as allies in the assault against the multiculturalism of the new world order.*" (Italics added.)[55]

Another foreign policy analyst, Adam Garfinkle, found that the division ran deep, with those who are upwardly mobile and who value affluence and individualism "more likely to have a positive disposition toward America and Jews by association as well." However, those who "respect traditional hierarchies, value communal or corporate identities over individual ones, and see their own social positions as vulnerable to the new global forces that have insinuated themselves into their societies, then, all else equal, they will have a more negative view of America, and of Jews along with it." By means of example, Garfinkle pointed to a curious incident in April 2008, where the Morales government "appeared to employ the Star of David as a symbol of evil" on new Bolivian ID cards. The new picture IDs, with tiny six-pointed stars within a tight circle printed on the back, "apparently were given mainly to non-indigenous peoples in eastern Santa Cruz province, the center of opposition to the Morales regime, in numbers vastly larger than the tiny Bolivian Jewish community." The government denied that the cards, part of a newly computerized national identification system, were an attempt to identify individuals or segments of the population along racial, religious or ideological lines. "But the weird facts," Garfinkle added, "speak for themselves."[56]

The plausible reach of the "brown-green-red" alliance into indigenous communities in Central and South Americas and Mexico is not without precedent. Anecdotally at least, its common language of anticolonialism even appears to straddle Latin America's borders with its neighbor to the north. In 2008, a young Navajo woman from Arizona traveled as a "peace delegate" to Iran "armed with Navajo prayer and the wisdom of the ancestors [to do] what she could to prevent the United States from declaring war" on that country. There she found that the tribal peoples of Iran had common cause with U.S. Native Americans, as they

face some of the same challenges indigenous peoples in the Americas face, poverty, lack of health services, traditional mobility, and language revitalization to name but a few. In the United States rarely do we hear about these tribes or the beauty and diversity of Iranian peoples and cultures. . . . I found a people who are in the process of striking a balance between ancient Islam and modernity. . . . I wanted Iranian people to understand the diversity of America, the idea of sovereign Native Nations, of distinct peoples, as nations within a nation. I wanted them to understand some of the realities, strengths, and challenges of indigenous peoples in the United States, most importantly not to see Navajo as a vanishing people, but as active protagonists in a long and epic battle for complete harmony and self-determination. I wanted them to know the Navajo people not only as the people who walk in beauty but also as a fierce warrior people who have fought and are still fighting for the liberation, restoration, and healing of our peoples, the earth, her resources, our culture, and our language.[57]

Similarly, Julia Good Fox, a Pawnee and a professor at the Haskell Indian Nations University in Lawrence, Kansas, participated in a "Third World Delegation" visit to Israel and Palestine in 2008. There she found also striking similarities between the plight of Palestinians and those of Indians in the United States, "Although we and the Palestinians are at different places in the politics of colonization and decolonization," she wrote in *Indian Country Today*, "as survivors of manifest destiny (and often combatants against present-day cultural practices of anti-Indianism), we immediately—and viscerally—recognize the extraordinary historic and contemporary parallels between the Palestinians and our nations and tribes." The similarities she said she found included the theft of their lands and being discouraged from speaking Arabic in public, as Native Americans have long been discouraged from speaking their own languages. Urging Indians to travel to Palestine as volunteers, Good Fox said there were other commonalities as well. Palestinian families were separated by walls imposed by another people, just as Indian communities were segregated by the border wall between the U.S. and Mexico; in both instances violating indigenous patterns of migration. Unrecognized villages in northern Palestine, she added, mirrored the manner in which some U.S. Indian nations have not been recognized by the federal government.

> Perhaps one of the most recognizable similarities that we encounter is the theft and fractionalization of Palestinian land, a process that we might know better as "removal" and "allotment." A strengthened and stabilized land-base is the basis of self-determination, and the Palestinian struggle to liberate and protect their land certainly resonates with our people. . . . Palestinians are portrayed as terrorists—modern day savages—in the mainstream media.[58]

The protection of ancestral lands, dimly understood if at all by modern urban dwellers in the global North, is nonetheless a powerful and ecumenical symbol for indigenous and traditional peoples around the world. Writing about the founding of the state of Israel, historian Hugh Seton-Watson noted that Theodor Herzl and other Zionist leaders came to clearly understand that a nation could not be created from language and religion alone; a state could only emerge when there was an unshakeable bond with a specific territory from which it could be created. Perhaps out of similar reasoning a woman who was a member of the Winnebago tribe took part in the 1969 takeover of Alcatraz Island by U.S. Indians and their sympathizers that symbolically claimed the island for indigenous peoples. There she told a journalist that she had unsuccessfully volunteered to fight for the Israelis during the 1967 Six-Day War, pointedly declaring: "I care about Zionism, because those people want a homeland, too."[59]

Pan-Indian solidarity extends far beyond both sides of the U.S.-Mexican border, offering unique challenges to governments to the north and to the south. Not only do members of the Ute-Aztecan language family extend from Idaho to Panama, with tribal variants spoken in the Great Basin of the western United States (including Hopi, Ute, Shoshone, Comanche, Papago, and Pima), through western, central and southern Mexico, into parts of Central America, including El Salvador. Classical Nahuatl, the language of the Aztecs, its modern variants spoken mainly in central Mexico, also belong to the Ute-Aztecan family. Important contacts between and among the various Indian peoples have also transcended the U.S.-Mexican border, even as it has become increasingly militarized and difficult to transit. For example, the National Association of Indigenous Salvadoreans (*Asociación Nacional de Indígenas Salvadoreños/ANIS*), the oldest indigenous organization in that country, has long counted on a small but steady stream of funds and support from U.S. tribes. Not only do Apache, Navajo and Lakota tribespeople participate in the Salvadorans' annual ceremonies and festivals, but North American Indian ceremonial practices have been incorporated into public rituals sponsored by ANIS. And, once in the United States, many of the immigrants who belong to one of some sixty Mexican Indian groups fall far outside the view of the U.S. government, even in its most benign, less threatening, forms, such as its social welfare system (as opposed to its immigration authorities).[60]

Interestingly, a translation company working with the U.S. Immigration and Naturalization Service reported a noticeable upswing in requests for translators who speak Indian languages from southern Mexico and Central America. It had to double the rate paid "since it was so difficult to find anyone who spoke English and Tzotzil Maya."[61] The *New American Media* article carrying the story also included a reader comment promoting indigenous peoples' solidarity and kinship through Mesoamerica, reconciling Indian peoples with lands alienated by U.S. laws and national borders.

The reader acknowledged that while the "vast majority" of those south of the Rio Grande were of mixed ancestry, he was a Pokomam Maya born in El Salvador. He claimed that in 1994, when the Zapatista movement appeared to gain momentum, his uncle, co-chairman of an Indian gambling casino in Arizona:

> *along with other tribes in the states, helped my people arm my Mexican Mayan brothers.* Racism in Central America and in Mexico is bad, but not as terrible as in the States. At least, in Central America and in Mexico; people know Indians exist, *in the United States, citizens believe American Indians are nonexistent.*
>
> My grandfather, a Yaqui Indian of Sonora, has family members in Arizona who speak Spanish as well as English. He remembers the time when crossing the U.S-Mexican border was no problem; now, problems abound in the border from drug smuggling and human trafficking.

What Latinos need to do is feed the good dog (Indian) not the bad (Spanish) dog to do what is right. *Latinos and Indians of the South should band together like my brothers the Zapatistas, Evo Morales, and our North American Indian brothers have done in trying to oust corrupt states and government policies.*[62] (Italics added)

The alienation of this writer is evident in several respects, all of which speak to the possibility, if not now then in the future, of an emerging pan-Indian nationalism that crosses the border from Latin America into the United States. In this rendition, Indians in the United States provide money or arms to southern Mexican Indians; all of whom are united in efforts to challenge not only "corrupt" states but also those policies they do not like. Bilingual and trilingual Native Americans move along and through a complicated U.S. southern border, elbow to elbow with traffickers of drugs and humans, and share a view of the United States that ranks the world's oldest democracy below what they think of some of the region's most troubled formal democracies. While claiming that the Indian is invisible to U.S. culture, the writer importuned readers like himself to identity with indigenous rather than "Spanish" culture and to band together, thus creating, in keeping with his vision, a pool of people outside the view and authority of non-Indian North Americans.

Should Central and South American and Mexican Indian communities ally with radical Islamists, their ensuing non-Western ideologies and programs could make co-existence in a true democracy impossible. In this regard, the significant challenges to democratic renewal posed by Evo Morales and Hugo Chavez pale by comparison to the alliances that could be formed at the margins of even the populist pretense of representative rule. To date, the evidence that such an alliance could be forged remains anecdotal, and in the experience of the United States during the inter-war period (see below) there may be a lesson about how this can be avoided. However, the possible failure of weak democratic societies and, over time, the actions of regimes such as those of Morales and Chavez, increase the possibility of an explicit 'brown-green-red alliance' among those coming together as ultra-nationalists.

Ethnic Security

Most of those responsible for national security policies in "Latin" America today come from non-indigenous (and usually non-Afro-Latino) backgrounds. With a largely urban outlook, many feel menaced by an indigenous assertiveness that in the best of circumstances seeks to destabilize the traditional status quo. Today, as in the past, military politics can thus often be analyzed as a factor, a continuation, of ethnic politics.

In the late 1970s and early 1980s, before the fall of the Berlin Wall and the resurgence of nationalities in the former Soviet Empire, before the emergence of

Native Americans as a political force in a broad swathe of Latin American countries, and before the latticework of extra-hemispheric ethnic revival ranging from Greenland to western China, a small but important body of academic literature emerged on the intersection between ethnicity and the military. U.S. political scientist Cynthia H. Enloe produced two of the most essential of these pioneering studies—*Ethnic Soldiers: State Security in Divided Societies* and *Police, Military, Ethnicity: Foundations of State Power.* Together the two works defined and highlighted the importance of military policy in determining ethnic frontiers and their prominence in unstable multi-ethnic societies.

In a wide-ranging survey across the globe, Enloe examined the extent to which military and security policies represent the elite manipulation of ethnicity. She assayed the impact of ethnic strategies in the personnel policies of the national security establishment, including the means used to ensure both ethnic group allegiance and national service. She probed the historical and contemporary influences of class, region and ethnicity on the loyalty of the military and the police. And she presented a working model for analysis about the role played by the military in the operation of the security core of the state vis-à-vis ethnic issues. This included the differentiation between the army on one hand, and the navy and air force on the other, as well as the part played by the police and the impact the relative gap in their uniformed status had in the calculations of the security establishment.

To navigate the heretofore-uncharted waters, Enloe offered what she called an "ethnic state security map" of elite expectations of various ethnic groups as well as their perceived political dependability. Such mapping, Enloe found, offered the possibility to predict political postures vis-à-vis the state, and therefore "is often an ideal design matching expectations to strategic formulas." The maps, she observed, are the mental calculation by which nation-state elites find an optimal way of securing the state by means of inter-ethnic architecture. The salient groups are "(a) ethnic groups residing along sensitive frontiers, (b) ethnic groups fulfilling strategic economic roles (exploited or privileged), (c) ethnic groups with sufficient political resources to challenge the existing political order, (d) ethnic groups with ties to potential foreign state rivals, and, finally (e) ethnic groups with the greatest access to the state structure as currently organized." In Latin America, a number of nation-states meet two or more of these criteria with regards to indigenous peoples, with the combinations suggesting in several cases the potential for future geo-strategic hecatomb. Only Bolivia is represented in the "e" category. [63]

Enloe explained how attention to an ethnic focus on security issues can repay great rewards.

First, ethnicity is a *collective* phenomenon; state elites find it more efficient deal in collectivities than in individuals when matching expectations to security strategies. Secondly, ethnicity is *cultural* and thus permits elites to base predictions not on transient interest predictions of their constituents but on more durable value orientations. Thirdly, ethnicity is *emotional*, a type of identity grounded in shared memories, which state elites presume, probably correctly, includes past experiences with the central state that foster long-term positive or negative orientations towards the state. Fourthly, in many though not all cases ethnicity has an *international* dimension as ethnic bonds extend across artificial state borders. Fourthly, in many though not all cases ethnicity has an *international* dimension as ethnic bonds extend across artificial state borders. It thus permits an elite to make predictions about how a given ethnic group will behave towards another state which figures in its security scenarios. Finally, ethnicity is selected as a basis for security 'mapping' because it frequently involves *geographic concentrations*. Those ethnic groups whose ethnicity includes regional identity can be most easily fitted into security plans. [64]

The relevance of the work of Enloe, and that of political scientist Donald L. Horowitz, and a few contemporary researchers focusing on Latin America, such as the early work of Donna Lee Van Cott and that of anthropologist Brian Selmeski and historian Cecilia Méndez G., takes on new brio as conventional elite assumptions about the armed forces' archetypal national and integrative functions are challenged by facts on the ground south of the Rio Grande. In Latin America today, the military still plays an integral role in institutionally defending the state against external foes while assuring its domination over the national population. But as Méndez points out, the armed forces play not only a political role, but also have an impact on daily life that helps define national character. In many countries in the region, a primary point of contact rural indigenous peoples have with the nation-state remains the military and the police.

As ethnic unrest continues to build in under performing democratic states, key issues are the social composition and elite direction of the legal forces arrayed to repress unrest among those groups where such instability is most likely to occur. In addition, against shibboleths about the military as a catalyst for modernization and the creation of primary group identities around the nation-state, this still-emerging literature may help fill in the blanks about the enduring appeal and relevance of ethnicity. Perceptions of a nation-state elite, and who they are, can be key in determining military-ethnic relations. As Enloe shows, the equation includes questions such as whether a particular group can be trusted based on their position on a continuum of ethnic/national identification (see Graph on page 87: "A State's Ideal Ethnic Security Group"); whether consensus or political fragmentation is a better political strategy to pursue, and the degree to which the state can forgo additional military manpower from conscription of "unreliable" ethnic groups, etc. [65]

By 2009, concern about the ways state policies place force in the hands of security custodians extended to their trustworthiness, steadfastness and definitions of citizenship during a period of increasing ethnic conflict. As we will see later on, in Chile, militant Mapuche Indian organizations have been placed on the U.S. State Department's terrorism list at a time when the country's militarized national police act as the point of the lance for state policy.

A State's Ideal Ethnic Security Map

From: Cynthia H. Enloe, *Ethnic Soldiers* (Athens: University of Georgia Press, 1980, p. 24.

In Nicaragua, the entire eastern region has been declared an independent state by a majority of that country's indigenous peoples, with a call for the creation of a new, armed ethnic force and the appointment of an Indian defense minister by the secessionists. Bolivia's self-declared Marxist-Leninist indigenous President Morales has remodeled the armed forces under his control along the lines of his ethnic re-foundation of the republic (to all lights successfully), calling for a new military-peasant pact this time led not—as in the past—by a general or a fractious colonel, but rather by indigenous people. Meanwhile Ecuador's Rafael Correa—mindful of the overthrow of two of his predecessors by Indian-led unrest—casts one eye over his shoulders, seeking to avoid their fate. And in Perú, contending national forces conduct their arm wrestling in the arena of ethnic politics, a development that has already claimed the lives of scores of poor Indians and under-resourced police, two communities that share a common status-gap with their country's ruling elite. There historically, and unlike the situation in neighboring Bolivia and Ecuador, measurable progress for indigenous peoples is identified with military governments and movements, not elected democracy.

Perhaps for that reason, when violence erupted—as it did in the Peruvian Amazon in June 2009—the non-Indian elite in Lima needed to question whether it could count on the military to loyally restore order. In each country, where ethnicity is not necessarily determinative alone in creating security challenges, these nevertheless arise when paired with the social, economic and political fault lines that modernization and market economies pose to communal societies.[66]

The Enemies of My Enemies

Lessons learned in the United States during World War I and II may be relevant here, showing how threats to national security were posed, and ultimately overcome, as a result of Native American views on citizenship. One the other hand, cultural differences—which ultimately worked to the United States' benefit during the two World Wars—could today come into play in a negative way among its southern neighbors.

During World War I, some six hundred Oklahoman Indians, mostly Choctaw and Cherokee, participated as members of the 142nd Infantry of the 36th Texas-Oklahoma National Guard Division fighting in France. Choctaw-speaking field telephone operators' quick, secure transmissions in their own language confused German soldiers on the battlefield and presaged the celebrated efforts of Navajos and other Indian "code talkers" recruited by the U.S. Marine Corps during World War II. As a result, during the inter-war period, the German Nazis sent out agents posing as anthropologists, art dealers and students to study the various Native American languages.[67] At the same time, in the 1930s, Joseph Goebbels's propaganda ministry initiated an:

> effort to lure American Indians into a favorable view of Nazism. . . . Nazi propagandists linked the communist path to which FDR ostensibly committed America with the "Jewish world plot" and racism . . . As Germany had pledged an offensive to combat the Jewish world menace, Nazis could not permit further exploitation of Indians by Jewish-controlled America. . . . To conceal the full implication of racial doctrine, propagandists veiled their ideology with the inclusion of Native Americans as Aryans . . . The explanation advanced the idea that a lost Germanic people had wandered into the New World in the distant past and bred themselves into the native population, thus building a link to German ancestry.[68]

The Nazis bet on the alienation of Indians from the United States government, which had "historically relegated" them "to extinction through warfare or federal Indian policies [while] Germany admitted some Indians to full Aryan status and viewed all Native Americans as potential bearers of German culture." One Nazi propagandist posited that if the United States and Germany were to eventually wage war against one another, "How could the American Indians think of bearing arms for their exploiters?" According to German anthropologist Colin Ross, who toured western states and Indian reservations in 1934 and 1936, a "red state" was needed to create a separate nation not controlled or interfered with by the U.S. federal government. Ross's "condemnation of poor living conditions on reservations (and) the failure of previous Indian policies" added a measure of credibility to Nazi propaganda which, for a time, created some Indian interest in domestic, pro-Nazi organizations like the German American Bund, the Silver Shirt Legion and the three thousand five-hundred-member American Indian Federation. Before a vigorous federal effort succeeded in stopping such efforts in their relative infancy, the attempts by these groups were "far more troubling and potentially more corruptive of Indian loyalty" than direct German attempts at subversion and potential recruitment.[69]

The eventually successful U.S. government action to counteract the Nazi infiltration took several forms. One of the most important was the effort by senior Bureau of Indian Affairs officials to engage Indian communities in a sincere and earnest dialogue on the absurdity and potential threat of the Nazis' racial ideas, a point by point rebuttal of pro-Nazi initiatives, both those from Berlin and the others of a homegrown variety. Official understanding of how these formed part of national and international developments and their efforts to communicate those perspectives to Indian audiences was also key to success, measured in the "magnitude of Native American support for defense mobilization" in the run-up to World War II. The fascists' efforts to convert Indians may actually have encouraged them to register for the draft in large numbers. "About 20 percent of the Indian population, eighty thousand men and women, marched off to fight in the armed forces and at the home front against Adolph Hitler, a man they called, 'he who smells his moustache.' Benito Mussolini fared little better, as the Indians called him 'Gourd Chin.'"[70]

During World War II, some forty-four thousand five hundred Indian men of a total population of less than three hundred and fifty thousand, more than 10 percent of the Native American population during the war, served in the U.S. armed forces between 1941 and 1945, in both the European and Pacific theaters. The importance of the some four hundred Marine Navajo "code talkers" was underscored by their contribution to the decisive victory achieved at Iwo Jima. Although only the Navajo language code remained unbroken by the enemy, more than a dozen tribes provided code talkers in both world wars, including the Choctaw, Cheyenne, Comanche, Creek, Cherokee, Osage, Menominee, Ojibwa [Chippewa], and Yankton Sioux.[71]

Part II: Case Studies

Chapter Seven
Bolivia: Unraveling a Present Past

"Those on the periphery actually create the center."
—Laura F. Edwards[1]

In December 2007, a group of Lakota Sioux, led by veteran Indian activist Russell Means,[2] visited the U.S. State Department and the embassies of Bolivia, Venezuela, Chile and South Africa in Washington, D.C., asking for recognition of their efforts to form a free and independent Lakota nation. Means, appealing to the imagery of Nazi collaborators in occupied France in making his denunciation, said the group had wearied of living under a government system base on colonial apartheid. "I want to emphasize we do not represent the collaborators, the Vichy Indians and those tribal governments set up by the United States of America to ensure our poverty, to ensure the theft of our land and resources." The would-be First Nation secessionists also said the new entity they sought to establish would issue its own passports and drivers licenses. The mainstream media gave scant attention to what might easily be dismissed as "guerrilla theatre" by aging activists. However, one country's envoy present clearly stated that his president did not take the declaration lightly. Gustavo Guzmán, the ponytailed Bolivian Ambassador to Washington, said that Evo Morales was "very, very interested" in the Sioux declaration of independence: "We are here because the demands of indigenous peoples of America are our demands. We have sent all the documents they presented to the embassy to our ministry of foreign affairs in Bolivia and they'll analyze everything."[3] If past is prologue, surely the presumed consanguinity gave honor to its dual meaning: a relationship by blood or by a common ancestor, and a close affinity or connection. The Lakota Sioux

declaration fell on receptive ears, as contemporary Bolivian politics are the result of a strong element of "First Nation" activism of this very kind.

The 2005 landslide election in that landlocked Andean country and the
presidency of Aymara Indian Morales, who came to power with the first outright
electoral majority not only since democracy returned to Bolivia two decades
earlier but also in the past half century, were evidence of a sea-change occurring
in the politics of several Latin democracies. Indian activism-cum-nationalism
challenged social exclusion,[4] weak governmental institutions, limited political
party identification, and, in some cases, endemic corruption..

Although different from that of other countries and their relationships to indigenous peoples, the ethnonational debate waged by Indian activists around the
redefinition of the state has nowhere been so marked or generalized as it is in
Bolivia, which has also been one of the most unequal countries in terms of opportunity and income distribution in the most unequal continent on earth. Conditions for Morales's ascent to and holding of power were especially propitious:
72 percent of the population in rural areas speak an indigenous language, as do
36 percent in urban areas; two thirds of the country's Indian population is found
among the poorest 50 percent of its overall population—in the poorest country
in Central and South America. Although on the relatively more prosperous
plains, 17 percent of the population is indigenous and 83 percent non-Indian, in
the impoverished highland and valleys 67 percent and 60 percent, respectively,
are Native Americans.[5] The contradictions are not of recent vintage: The creation of the Bolivian nation-statehood did not end in the nineteenth century, as it
had in most of the other countries in Latin America. Rather its development extended fitfully and without real completion through the twentieth century and—
although a bloody war with Paraguay (1932-1935) and the Revolution of 1952
helped consolidate notions of citizenship—the nation-state rested upon, but did
not totally dominate, the country's indigenous communities. It was against that
background that candidate Morales portrayed himself as an authentic alternative
to a broad segment of public opinion that rejected both elite-inspired neo-liberal
economic policies and corrupt traditional political leaders, while yearning for a
plausible expression of national pride.

The victory by Morales—who is counted as the third Native American
president in Latin America since the Spanish Conquest[6]—was also the recepta-
cle of the hopes and aspirations of Indians throughout the hemisphere. Admirers
say that his election enhanced the link between ethnicity and solidarity and created the impression of trust in political leaders. Tonya Frichner, founder of the
New York-based American Indian Law Alliance and a member of the Onondaga
Nation of New York, expressed a reaction typical of the pride conveyed by
many Indians across the hemisphere: Morales "is honest, he is brilliant and sincere to the cause of indigenous peoples. We know he cannot fix all that has happened in the past 500 years, but it is our responsibility to be supportive of him."[7]

Others, however, questioned whether Morales' leadership was a mere extension of what one critic, writing before his election, called a "corrupt and personalistic political party culture [that] has permeated indigenous peoples' organizations, generating divisions and diminishing the authority of traditional ethnic authorities." Under Morales, regional and ethnic tensions resulting in violence have become the worst in recent memory, while his government appeared to be de-institutionalizing, brick by brick, in a way immediately reminiscent of Chavez's Venezuela, Bolivia's already tenuous democratic public bodies. These included the judiciary, particularly the Supreme Court and Constitutional Tribunal, as well as previously independent government oversight agencies. Concern heightened in April 2009, when Morales proclaimed himself a "Marxist-Leninist," a signal to many that Bolivia's fragile liberal democracy—faced with a simultaneous vortex of ethnic, regional, social and political divisions—ultimately might be incapable of maintaining a semblance national unity, much less the rule of law.[8]

A once-poor llama herder and musician, one of three of seven children who survived beyond early childhood, Morales' own penchant for personalist politics was laid bare soon after taking office, when he had his humble adobe birthplace declared a national monument, and authorized a postage stamp adorned with his profile to be issued in his honor.[9] Even more troubling, Victor Hugo Cárdenas, a respected Aymara Indian and former vice president of Bolivia (1993-1997), complained in early 2008 that, under Morales, the official discourse had become

> entrenched in statism and centralism, with growing disregard for democratic principles and procedures. *Today, Bolivia is being led by its government toward antagonism between Indians and non-Indians, the eastern and western regions, and city and country, exacerbated by insults and actions that are acquiring an increasingly racist and ethnocentric edge.* The identity of Bolivia's indigenous peoples, who were historically excluded from political, social, and economic life, is beginning to be seen as a synonym for confrontation, violence, and ethnic aggressiveness.[10] (Italics added.)

Referring to the rapid change taking place with Morales' election, one Bolivian commentator noted that, in a country where some three dozen indigenous peoples represent more than 60 percent of the total population: "It was perhaps only ten years ago when to propose that (an Indian) would become president would be considered a joke or a provocation."[11] The change was even greater if one considered that less than a decade earlier, the ostrich-like discourse of the conservative government of retired Gen. Hugo Banzer (1997-2001) paralleled the denial of ethnic differences characteristic of traditional Marxist parties. Under the elected former dictator, there was a notable shift "from an emphasis on multiculturalism, participation, and human development to an emphasis almost exclusively on reducing poverty."[12] Even in a country where Native Americans were unquestionably the majority population, before Morales Indian issues appeared to risk disappearing from center stage.

Bolivia, noted indigenous sociologist Pablo Mamani, existed "more than five hundred years as a colony, but in the one hundred eighty years it has been a republic, we Indians have been subjects without history, subjects and actors without memory, subjects and actors without territory, without leadership, without a prospect of achieving power."[13] (What might be viewed as the reclamation of historical memory implicit in Mamani's lament might be seen by others as a pyrrhic victory. As Earl Shorris pointed out a generation ago—efforts to "reclaim" and internalize Native American history is something of a triumph for non-Indian Western Man, "the structural anthropologists hav[ing] developed a textbook definition of the difference between the two kinds of societies using the internalization of history as the salient characteristic of Western Civilization." Referring to the value of Western historicity, Thomas Benjamin noted that the venerable French social anthropologist Claude Lévi-Strauss saw "mythic thought as valuable and authentic and the European imposition of history as the obliteration of cultural difference and one more tool of human enslavement. Traditional Euro-centric analysis considered the rise of historical consciousness as part of the march of progress, while more recently [French philosopher] Jacques Derrida suggested the possibility of historical consciousness as necessary for liberation."[14])

What is certain is that in Bolivia, the Indian majority was not allowed to vote or to receive a public education until the 1952 revolution. The popular rebellion incorporated native peoples into national life, but as "junior members in a unified front" that left them systematically outside of a political and economic framework dominated by a small middle class, in a country where most of the resources in the resource-rich nation went to just 5 percent of its people.[15] The revolutionary elite based its policies on the assumption that indigenous peoples would eventually assimilate into a mixed race, predominately urban population.[16]

In the Andean context, it had been customary for Indians seeking to gain the status of being *mestizo* to forsake their own communities and reject their Native heritage. The individual who did so, however, found himself "part of a despised '*cholo*' minority in a world dominated by urban upper classes to which he cannot aspire." Despite the momentousness of the Bolivian revolution, the velocity of change apparent at the end of the twentieth century had still not made itself felt. Commentators such as Richard Patch discerned formerly Indian communities being incorporated by the 1952 Revolution's nation-building creed, in a process of authentic cultural change that was slowly, albeit fitfully, replacing the traditional language of caste (*indio*) with a class-based classification (*campesino*).

> (T)he group itself is the agency regulating the adoption of mestizo traits. The individuals within the group proceed at the same pace, with few persons stand-

ing out as "more mestizo" than the others. Neither is there strong motivation physically to leave the community nor to reject identifiably Indian behavior patterns. Rather, the individuals are participating in a true cultural change, as a group . . . There is no rush to acquire status symbols, because there is a deep sense of the ridiculousness of a person wearing a necktie, for example, when that person is unable to speak Spanish.[17]

Writing in 1968, Samuel Huntington suggested, "the stability of a modernizing political system depends on the strength of its political parties." Addressing the Bolivian case, Huntington asked, "Why, unlike the Mexican Revolution, did [the Bolivian Revolution] not also produce long-term results in terms of political stability?" Instead of consolidating itself, as did Mexico's Institutional Revolutionary Party (Partido Revolucionario Institucional/PRI), the Movimiento Nacionalista Revolutionario (National Revolutionary Movement/MNR) led by Victor Paz Estenssoro fissured and collapsed. The explanation, Huntington said, in part was due in Bolivia's case of social mobilization outstripping the pace of the development of political institutions, with "organized social forces such as the peasants and workers . . . [having] greater influence with the dominant political party in Bolivia than they did in Mexico."[18] More recently, Carlos Alberto Montaner, the Cuban social analyst and journalist who lives in Spain, noted that the Bolivian economy had grown barely 1 percent in the last fifty years, with per capita wealth "the same today as it was before the mythical revolution" led by Paz Estenssoro. Politicians were "incapable of creating a social and judicial system where enterprises could proliferate, the educational system could improve, and various ethnic groups could integrate with a greater degree of harmony. . . . You can't govern so poorly for so long . . . and not expect that a definitive catastrophe won't eventually occur."[19]

The catastrophe arrived, as Bolivia's Indians reawakened politically to their ethnic identity, and then elected Morales. "There is," Gellner noted, "one particular form of the violation of the nationalist principle to which nationalist sentiment is quite particularly sensitive: if the rulers of the political unit belong to a nation other than that of the majority of the ruled, this for nationalists, constitutes a quite outstandingly intolerable breech of political propriety."[20] Baldly put, the "nation" to which Bolivia's long-ruling elite owed allegiance was, if only tenuously, in Europe or elsewhere in the global North.

The right to vote had placed Bolivia's indigenous majority in the position to make itself heard, though their continued exclusion by a predominantly white or mixed race political, economic and social elite meant the country's elected leadership for all intents and purposes was that of "a nation other than that of the majority of the ruled." Emerging in the 1970s, Bolivia's Katarista movement sought "to increase ethnic consciousness and revitalize Amerindian traditions amongst the Aymara population of the highlands, but it promptly divided between moderate Kataristas and a radical Indianista group," noted political scientist Roberto Espindola:

The Kataristas re-emerged in the 1990s as a broader movement, including now
Quechua-speaking communities, but once again underwent several splits and
transformations that finally prompted into prominence the leader of the
Quechua coca growers of the Chapare region, a coca grower himself. Morales
went on to take control of Bolivia's peasant union confederation (Confederación Sindical Unica de Trabajadores Campesinos de Bolivia). From that
base, he led the formation of a political party, Movimiento al Socialismo
(MAS), with a left-wing redistributive program but clearly associated with a
defense of Amerindian interests and revival.[21]

For a time, Bolivia's native peoples remained too divided to form an efficient or
effective political movement. In the mid-1990s, with the passage of the Popular
Participation Law, the state recognized the "multi-ethnic and pluri-cultural" nature of Bolivian society, even as a marked radicalization within Indian groups
was occurring. The then-Vice President Victor Hugo Cárdenas, the Aymara activist who introduced nation-wide bilingual education in the country, is said to
have represented what one observer called "multicultural neo-liberalism," that is
Indian rights promoted by indigenous elites within an economic privatization
model.[22] According to Morales' Vice President, Alvaro García Linera—a non-
Indian, Catholic-educated mathematician who in 1992 was jailed for five years
for his membership in the small leftist rebel Tupak Katari Guerrilla Army (*Ejer-
cito Guerrillero Tupak Katari*, EGTK)—an alliance existed between Cárdenas
"and a series of intellectuals and activists in the indigenous movement." This
allowed the center-right government of Gonzalo Sánchez de Losada to convert
"a rhetorical recognition of the country's multicultural character into state policy, while the Law of Popular Participation created mechanisms of local upward
social mobility that could absorb the discourse and action of a good share of the
increasingly discontented indigenous intellectual milieu." However, the presidency of Sánchez de Losada, a U.S.-educated and fabulously wealthy member
of the traditional political elite, someone whose own "national" credentials were
popularly suspect in part because he even spoke Spanish with an English accent,
served only to deepen indigenous ethnic identity.[23] Sánchez de Losada's background and the popular image of his neo-liberal policies lent themselves to their
characterization as elements of what Oxford political scientist Laurence Whitehead has called the "oligarchic state," one "in which such public authority as
exist[s is] broadly defined at the service of a restricted sector of the population,
which derive[s] its coherence from the various non-state sources of social
power, such as land ownership, family lineage or a position of advantage in international trade and finance." Sánchez de Losada's truncated presidency also
confirmed Gellner's dictum about the usefulness of nationalism as "a theory of
political legitimacy, which requires that ethnic boundaries should not cut across
political ones, and, in particular, that ethnic boundaries within a given state—a

contingency already excluded by the principle in its general formulation—should not separate the power-holders from the rest."[24]

Because the country's trade union movement was in decline, peasant and indigenous groups increasingly filled the subsequent political vacuum. Before they ended up revisiting traditional forms of ethnic insurgency, historian Sinclair Thomson noted, these

> began to organize in a much more autonomous fashion; they adopted an increasingly radical ethnic discourse, an Indian discourse for self-determination, moving away from the older class discourses which were prevalent in the 1950s. When the latest cycle of insurgency happens, starting in 2000, indigenous initiatives led the way. Much of the mobilization was happening in the countryside in the form of road blockades and peasant sieges of the cities, including the capital, La Paz. *They drew upon indigenous forms of insurgent technology and organization; for example, having people do rotating turns to provide labor, to provide resources, to keep up the road blockades, to spell those protestors who have been involved for a certain period of time; to send in fresh contingents of protestors who can maintain the intensity of the blockades, of the sieges; who can provide food and fuel for protestors. These are techniques of urban siege, which have been redeployed since the eighteenth century.*[25] (Italics added.)

At the same time, Morales foe and Aymara leader Felipe Quispe, who in 1984 was an organizer of the Tupac Katari Guerrilla Army and its failed armed revolt against the government, promoted the establishment of a paramilitary group in province of Omasuyos known as the *Ponchos Rojos*, part of the re-creation of the Aymara territory (*Jach's Uma Suyu*) extending from Perú to the north of Chile. (Quispe claimed in 2006 that three years earlier, followers acting on his direct orders ambushed security forces near the town of Warisata, creating the conditions that eventually allowed for opponents of Sánchez de Losada to claim, citing the chief executive's own orders for harsh repressive measures, that the more than 120 people who died in violent clashes were victims of a government "massacre." Three years after Quispe publicly claimed credit for the ambush, some suggested that the deaths of dozens of police and Indian protesters in Bagua, Perú, appeared to have a suspiciously similar instrumentalized origin.) Bolivian sociologist Mamani noted that as a result of the collapsing legitimacy of an elitist, though elected president, Sánchez de Losada, the regional Indian militia "was able to destroy in the (indigenous) communities all the attributes of state power."[26]

The destruction of those aspects of state power came as some indigenous ideologies and groups became, as Thomson noted, more expressly confrontational and increasingly empowered politically. Former U.S. Ambassador to Bolivia Edwin C. Corr tells the story of an Aymara candidate from the *Jach'a Suya Pakajaqui* (Territory of the Red Eagle Men) political party who was campaigning for a city council seat high in the Bolivian Andes. Pascual Condori, who won the seat, grabbed the microphone and shouted, his mouth bulging with a cheekful of coca leaves: "We should not contest with one another. We should confront the K'aras." In Latin America, Corr added,

> and especially in Bolivia, to define oneself as Indian includes a rebellious sense of having been dominated and exploited for centuries, up to and including today. *Resentment and revenge against the perceived dominating class, especially traditional political elites, is part of one's Indian identity, creating an almost intractable problem.* . . . Moreover, according to Vice President Alvaro García Linera, of the Movement Toward Socialism (MAS) Party, until the advent of Evo Morales and MAS, indigenous people generally had not voted for indigenous leaders because they had not thought themselves capable of effecting the changes desired within the mestizo- and European- dominated political system.[27] (Italics added.)

The popular memory of struggles from indigenous anti-colonial revolts as well as the subsequent two centuries of Indian peasant resistance shaped and informed both Morales' election and the manner in which he took possession of the presidency. The day before taking office on January 22, 2006, Morales was crowned *Apu Mallku* (Supreme Leader) of the Aymara people in a spiritual ceremony at the pre-Colombian archaeological site of Tiwanaku, revered by the Inca as the birthplace of mankind. Aymara musicians played on reed flutes while Indians performed dances prohibited during three centuries of Spanish rule. Morales spoke amidst a sea of *wifalas*, the diagonally checkered flags of the Incas and their descendents that are today used to display ethnic pride and whose forty-nine squares in the seven colors of the rainbow serve as a symbolic representation of the original Indian nations. Clad in a bright red tunic traditionally once worn only by important pre-Incan priests, he vowed to continue "the fight to recuperate our territory and natural resources"—a message clearly directed to the Indian majority, not the non-Indian minority and their multinational allies who owned that territory and those resources. "The fight is not just for humanity, but also for planet Earth." Later, in an address before the Bolivian Congress and presidents of countries from around the region the tearful Morales compared his ascension to the presidency to the end of apartheid in South Africa.[28]

Morales' indigenous politics were viewed by Bolivians—even by many Indians themselves—as possessing greater symbolism than a narrowly indigenous appeal, a calculated electoral "neo-indigenismo." This reflected perhaps the fact that the MAS, as a coca growers association composed in large measure of a culturally and ethnically *mestizo* membership, steered clear of Indian politics until at least 2001, when Morales appeared to begin earning the notice of mostly European non-governmental organizations and radical leftist groups outside of Bolivia. Like the early Zapatistas, Morales found that his support increased as he accentuated his public identification with indigenous demands.[29] According to one analyst, for Morales' Movement Toward Socialism 'self-determination' encompasses a great deal more than simply 'indigenous self-determination.'" The MAS did "not promote a separatist ethno-national project; instead, it uses regional, national and international coalition-building to equate indigenous with non-indigenous issues through resonant political analogies that frame Bolivia's national crisis of political legitimacy in terms of indigenous rights, while making common cause with diverse urban popular sectors who, if not indigenous, recognize their cultural heritage as a crucial background to their own struggles against disenfranchisement." Nonetheless, once in power, the party retained its authoritarian and undemocratic structure, eschewing internal debate and dissent. In addition, it was largely in the control of a small group of people who, although they invoked the cause of indigenous social movements, had only come to MAS during Morales' campaign for the presidency.[30]

Having come to power at the head of a multi-class and multi-ethnic coalition, Morales—who remained at the helm of both the MAS and the coca growers union—promised a radical reconstruction of the Bolivian state, although he was initially ambiguous as to the methods he would use.[31] Once in office, he cut his salary by almost 60 percent while increasing the minimum wage by 50 percent; appointed other indigenous people to key cabinet posts, including—as non-Indian opponents gleefully pointed out—a former head of the domestic workers' union, a Quechua woman, as justice minister and, as foreign minister, an Aymara activist who upon assuming office still lacked basic knowledge of the origins of Bolivia's long-standing territorial dispute with Chile. Morales also convened a constituent assembly he said was needed to transform the country by giving more power to the native majority. He pushed both political symbolism and institutional reforms despite opposition claims of constitutional manipulation and fears that the country would be divided in two—along the fault line of highlands and lowlands geography that also roughly demarcated Indian and non-Indian regions. Morales vowed to defend Indians' traditional usage of the medicinal coca leaf by not eradicating the illicit coca plantations and by not combating narcotics production through military means. He proposed a new hydrocarbon law to guarantee that at least 50 percent of the revenue remained in Bolivia, a move that not only exacerbated tensions in the predominantly non-Indian oil-rich lowlands, but also among foreign corporations heavily invested in the industry. For their part, critics complained that Morales demonstrated his intention to impose a specific ideology, while using the rhetoric of indigenous and ethnic politics, regardless of the impact of doing so, or a claimed lack of consensus in favor of the route he chose.

At the same time, the yawning fissures in national integration meant that other identities related to ethnicity, status and regional affiliation—such as those of landowners, indigenous peoples, and coca producers, among others—became relatively more important. The country's former elites, excluded from the umbra of the Morales' presidency and outraged by the selection to high government positions of people who lacked traditional political and academic credentials, began demanding greater autonomy vis-à-vis the central government. Regional opposition from five eastern states, known collectively as the *Media Luna* (Half Moon), was at the forefront of attacks on Morales supporters (frequently laced with racial and ethnic overtones) and began to be viewed in La Paz as the focal point for concern about secessionist movements and the eventual breakup of the country.

On July 2, 2006 Bolivians endorsed Morales' plan to institutionalize his reforms and give greater power to the Indian majority by voting for a national assembly to overhaul the country's constitution. Nonetheless, Morales's supporters fell far short of the two-thirds majority required to push through proposals unopposed; in addition, four of nine states overwhelmingly voted in favor of greater political and economic autonomy from a central government they accused of siphoning off revenues in order to subsidize the highland region.[32] Perhaps as part of the need to constantly mobilize supporters in opposition to real or perceived enemies, and to sideline the only national institution that in modern times has effectively mediated and served as peacemaker in social and political conflicts, Morales also warned the Catholic Church hierarchy that some of its members were acting as if they were "in the times of the Inquisition." His education minister, an Aymara Indian, stated that Catholicism would be taught in public schools alongside other world religions, including Bolivian Indian religions.[33]

In January 2007, the government announced a new legal reform, in which the extant system based on Roman law would now co-exist with Indian traditional law based in "communitarian" or tribal justice institutions in an effort to reduce the country's legendary corruption and inefficiency. As such, decisions made by traditional Native authorities would be exempt from review by other judicial or administrative authorities.[34] In early 2008, the effort at judicial reform confronted a demand by the New York-based Human Rights Foundation that Morales "immediately cease the lynchings, tortures and immolations of people using 'communitarian justice'" practices. The challenge was not as credible as its *prima facie* argument might suggest, however. Daniel M. Goldstein, director of the Center for Latin American Studies at Rutgers University noted that the lynchings were not a result of Morales coming to power, the phenomenon having long antedated his movement's accession to the presidential *Palacio Quemado* (Burnt Palace). "Nor are lynchings examples of community justice. In its traditional form in indigenous Andean villages, community justice emphasizes reconciliation and rehabilitation. Rather than violent torture and execution, community justice promotes the 'reeducation' of community members who violate collective norms and rules, and the re-incorporation of these offenders back into the community."[35]

In December 2007, an elected constitutional assembly—composed of representatives of the major parties—voted for changes in the *magna carta,* giving special rights and privileges to those of indigenous descent, including an organic definition of Bolivia as a multi-ethnic country, and institutionalizing social reforms by using the nation's mineral resources to finance them. As late as September 2007, *The New York* Times still reported that "For all the worries that Mr. Morales' radicalism would create economic and political turmoil . . . the reality of his tenure is that the country is relatively stable." Still, suspicions remained, or even deepened, about Morales' intentions and his commitment to an indigenous agenda.[36] In fact, Indian leaders' skepticism about Morales' authenticity and real agenda predated his ascension to the presidency. Felipe Quispe, who represented an "ethnocentric, fundamentalist and Indianist" ideological current within the country's indigenous movements,[37] postulated "two Bolivias" and lampooned Bolivia's "k'aracracia" (which combines the Quechua and Aymara word for white people with the Spanish "democracia"). Quispe decried Morales' electoral ambitions before the latter's successful bid for the presidency, complaining that Morales was "in reality, a fascist disguised as an Indian." Other observers challenged Morales' authenticity by pointing to his Spanish surname, his use of Spanish as a first language, and the obvious (to many) fact that he is a *mestizo*. For some, Morales merely harnessed indigenous discontent to pursue political power and a Marxist agenda. (At the same time, some on the orthodox left faulted Morales' willingness to forge multi-class alliances).[38] However, as Connor points out, ". . . nationalism is a mass phenomenon, and the degree to which the leaders are true believers does not affect its reality. The question is not the sincerity of the propagandist, but the nature of the mass instinct to which the propagandist appeals." In this regard, Morales was undeniably successful, albeit increasingly surrounded by a chorus of oppositionist Indian voices that have, if anything, become more voluble.[39]

Less victorious was Morales' original multi-ethnic and multi-class appeal. The dividing line between his government and his party, the MAS, seemed to disappear, as both worked to increase the former's strength, to gain control of all the resorts of state power, and to silence both political critics and the independent media. Bolivians' hope for Morales, said former President Jaime Paz Zamora, the non-Indian founder of the Revolutionary Left Movement (MIR), was that he would be an Andean version of South Africa's Nelson Mandela, someone "capable of building a modern democracy in a country of indigenous origins." Instead of Mandela, Paz Zamora added that the ex-coca leader had proven to be a local version of Zimbabwe's former independence leader and later strongman Robert Mugabe. "You can feel the social breakup" based in part on Morales' lack of respect for democratic institutions and practices "out of his desire to stigmatize the past. . . . The initial euphoria with Evo is giving way to unhappiness and preventive paralysis."[40] Indian-ness became something defined by the central government, a political talisman wielded to the detriment of the country's historic indigenous leadership in both the highlands and the lowland tropics.

At the apex of a power trifecta as the head of the government, the heirarchically controlled MAS, and an important social movement (the coca growers), Morales also could count on the support of the military in what is still remembered as Latin America's most coup-prone nation. A measure of the velocity of change taking place as Morales assumed the presidency can be seen in the fact that, in a country where Indians are a clear majority, it was only in 2005 that Quechua, Aymara and Guaraní youths could attend the army's Military College, a prerequisite for later command of troops as officers. Two years later, indigenous women were also permitted to compete for positions as cadets at the military education institution, just a few years before the sole province of men.[41]

Having been an important antagonist of the security forces from his time as the coca growers' leader in the Chapare, upon assuming the presidency Morales worked hard to re-create the military according to his own needs. The membership of officer corps was drastically remodelled, with several classes of senior officers forced from their posts—particularly those Morales considered disloyal or who were critical of the influence of Venezuela's Chavez on the nation generally, and on the armed forces in particular. At the same time, Morales promoted a new officer corps comprised to a notable degree of men of indigenous background who historically had been excluded from scaling the chain of command. His efforts also extended beyond the officer ranks. As anthropologist Brian R. Selmeski has observed, the day after Morales visited the Presidential Guard's garrison for lunch, declaring himself "still 'a reserve soldier' despite holding the position of 'Captain General,' hundreds of Indian youth presented themselves voluntarily for service," in the process overcoming a "general distain for conscription [that] is particularly true for Indians." Military service, Selmeski noted, can be viewed as a win-win situation, as it "provides opportunities for *indigenas* to accept or challenge the state-idea (and concomitant notions of nation and citizenship), and the Army to resist or accommodate the contentious process of indigenous self-identification, organization, and action." With an Indian commander-in-chief, it also offers the armed forces an opportunity to redefine (and redeem) its relationship to the country's chief executive. Morales, too, went further to win uniformed hearts and minds, adopting a "nation building" model for the military promoted by his mentor Chavez, which involved the armed forces in development projects—road building and other infrastructure development, heath care, education, etc.—once the fiefdoms of civilian cabinet ministries. When the Constituent Assembly met in August 2006, thirty two Bolivian indigenous nations previously trained by the armed forces paraded in front of the president, at his request. Over time Morales' actions suggested that he understood, in the words of historian Cecilia Méndez G., the continuing cardinal importance of the military in Latin American society. Not just in terms of their much-remarked political impact, she wrote, but in daily life and socialization, where the pace of national identity itself is marked by martial parades during patriotic holidays, national hymns, flag ceremonies, and public monuments are dedicated to wars and military heroes sometimes with greater frequency than those that recall civilians. In calling for a fundamental re-foundation of Bolivian society, Morales issued his own call for a new military-peasant pact, one that this time would be lead by indigenous people and not uniformed populist *caudillos*.[42]

On January 23, 2007, Morales took his military chiefs to an indigenous peoples' rally of the *Ponchos Rojos*—paramilitary shock troops who view themselves as defenders of Aymara independence and who support him—in Omasuyos, armed for the occasion with vintage Mauser rifles. Morales, faced with increasing demands for secession among the predominantly non-Indian and relatively more prosperous lowlands, thanked the semi-official militia, saying "I urge our Armed Forces along with the 'Ponchos Rojos' to defend our unity and our territorial integrity." (Later, faced with criticism that the Ponchos Rojos had thus been given military status, Morales backtracked, seeking to disarm the Indian militia by exchanging their antiquated weapons for food.) In November 2007, Poncho Rojos leaders gathered in the town of Achachachi, where the group hung two dogs with ropes, then slit their throats while still alive. The warning offered by those gathered at the spectacle, that those who opposed Morales and the MAS, particularly the "dogs" of the lowland states in the hands of the political opposition, would face a similar fate, was seen by many as extending to all those who opposed the government.[43]

In August 2007, internal divisions within the Morales coalition spilled into the open. Four of the most radicalized unions and indigenous organizations demanded that Morales expel non-Indian "moderates" from his government, such as Vice President Alvaro García Linera and Presidential Minister Juan Ramon Quintana, neither of whom initiated their political careers with the MAS. Quintana, a former reformist army officer trained in the United States, was closely identified with Chavez's Venezuelans and served as an important interlocutor with the Iranian government. García Linera, an original founder of the Marxist-oriented experimental indigenous communities in northwest Bolivia known as *Ayllus Rojos,* a precursor of the Ponchos Rojos, had been a comrade in arms with Felipe Quispe in the Tupac Katari Guerrilla Army (EGTK), serving with him a prison term for their troubles. Despite Quintana's reputation as a first-class political analyst and a key Morales confidante, and García Linera's role as a skilled negotiator with the political opposition, their indigenous peers nonetheless saw the two as unrepresentative interlopers. Martin Condori, the leader of the indigenous Consejo Nacional de Markas y Allyus de Qollasuyu (Conamaq) declared that: "The president is all right, but those who are bothersome are . . . García Linera and Juan Ramon Quintana, because while Evo says one thing, they change it and give another message, another way of thinking. *They are outside reality.* "[44] (Italics added.)

At the same time as anti-globalization, radical restructuring of the Bolivian state was promoted by Morales, the country's relatively prosperous and largely non-Indian eastern regions pushed hard for a decentralization initiative that at times threatened to spill into an independence movement. By early 2008, passage by the elected constituent assembly of a draft constitution led to fierce opposition from the eastern region, including racially-tinged rioting. Critics advocated severing ties with the central government; regional governors declared they would unilaterally adopt "autonomy statutes" providing for greater local decisionmaking power while the government accused the opposition of plotting a coup and promoting secession. In March, opposition leaders accused Morales of taking the Andean country down the path of the ethnic maelstrom formerly known as Yugoslavia, while calling for "civil resistance" to Morales' proposed constitutional reforms. [45]

Proponents of a drastic decentralization of the state pointed out that various departments, including Santa Cruz in the tropical lowlands, were created years before the nation-state of Bolivia, which granted their claims a certain legitimacy. In July, Bolivia's first woman governor, Savina Cuellar, a Quechua Indian of humble origins, announced that she too would take the central province of Chuquisaca into the growing regional autonomy movement. Her break with Morales was perhaps emblematic of his need to convince indigenous peoples that their interests required no other protection than representation in his Movimiento al Socialismo. [46] A Bolivian indigenous publication, *Pukara*, appeared to make a point in the same direction in an article that claimed:

> Indigenous autonomy does not need a law, or political will, because it was present at the beginning (*originaria*), it is the basis and the foundation of Andean society. . . . Its legitimacy does not come from a law or from the country's political Constitution; the communities' democracy and its organization is what Bolivia can offer as its own to the world and to current modernity. . . . The party in power pretends it has discovered gunpowder in incorporating Indigenous Autonomy into the future Constitution, something that is nonsense. It is merely an attempt to constitutionalize, to recognize in the constitutional text, something that exists and is there. . . . It is necessary to incorporate that indigenous autonomy into the state structure, so that it is visible and this can be done very easily: by giving it economic resources. [47]

In the run-up to a recall election held on August 10, in which both Morales and eight provincial governors faced a vote of confidence, the president declared that "in various regions there exists a civil dictatorship." Violence broke out in several cities, including the use of racist invectives and physical violence by gangs against the Indians either individually or in groups. [48] Morales won more than 67 percent of the vote, and five of the governors also retained their offices, while three others—two opposition leaders and one pro-Morales governor—lost their seats. The president vowed to use his new mandate to press ahead for land reform, a new constitution, and the nationalization of key industries. In September, *The New York Times* reported that,

> Thousands of Mr. Morales' supporters, some wielding dynamite sticks and shotguns, marched toward Santa Cruz to press leaders [in Santa Cruz] to sign an agreement on a timetable for approving the new constitution. The marchers clashed with regional officials, beating them with sticks when they tried to persuade them to disarm, before relaxing their actions. In a veiled threat, Mr. Morales said that "peace and tranquility" would return to economically vibrant Santa Cruz if its leaders agreed in talks under way to create a framework for putting his proposed constitution to a vote.

Shortly afterward, local mobs "looted nearly every federal building, strewing offices with broken furniture and spraying walls with graffiti calling [Morales] a vassal of . . . Chavez in explicitly racist language."[49] Native American organizations from several countries declared their solidarity with Morales: the head of Ecuarunari, an association of Quechua communities in Ecuador's highlands, declaring that any coup attempt against the Bolivian leader might set off an uprising by Indians around the Andean region.[50]

As differences in political vision and ethnic divisions grew more stark, charges and countercharges took on a apocalyptic cast (even in a Latin American context). An editorial in *El País,* published in Bolivia's southern agricultural city of Tarija was entitled, "Indigenists and Separatists Destroy Bolivia." If the indigenous constitution were implemented, the newspaper warned darkly, it would "necessarily result in the total destruction of the Bolivian *indomestiza* State and nation. . . . the hard line looks to create thirty six indigenous nations with their own territory, laws and government as a substitute for our nation."[51] An ethno-nationalist, although minority, critique was increasingly leveled by non-Indian critics against Morales' *Movimiento al Socialismo*. A columnist in the Santa Cruz newspaper *El Deber* (echoing the criticism made several years earlier by Quispe against Morales, that the latter promoted a fascistoid ideology) wrote in a publication of the conservative Hispanic American Center for Economic Research that,

> I am taken by the ease with which the *Movimiento al Socialismo* accuses others of being fascists and nazis. But when we look beyond the empty accusations and look at the actual facts, we see that it is *the Movimiento al Socialismo* (MAS) the one that has an impressive number of similarities and programatic and methodological coincidences with the National Socialist (Nazi) party. . . . (B)oth are nationalist and socialist movements. Their ideology is the same: they propose a centralized and racist nationalism, Aryan in the case of the Nazis, indigenista in the case of MAS. Both parties are highly ritualistic. . . . For both parties, democracy isn't anything more than a means to take power, then to destroy it by destroying democratic institutions. . . . Both believe in armed struggle and revolutionary violence. . . . The Nazis invented the myth of the

internal enemy: the Jews, whom it accused of impoverishing the German people. Those of MAS have made the Santa Cruz non-Indian oligarchy those who it blames for the poverty of the Bolivian people. . . . Both leaders are populist speechmakers, both parties promote the cult of the leader who they exhibit as the savior of the Fatherland. . . . Both parties have former terrorists among its highest officialdom. Both have been maestros of the lie and propaganda.[52]

A Colombian analyst claimed in an article entitled "Balkan-Bolivia," that Morales's "ethnonationalism explodes the fragile equilibrium of Bolivian society. . . . If one had to blame a single factor for the violence that touched Europe during the last century, without a doubt all fingers would point to ethnic nationalism. The political mobilization on behalf of the defense of the supposed rights of a racial group, or to appropriate for itself territory, impose a culture or monopolize a government has acted as the basis for promoting some of the most lethal ideological projects in recent history." He evinced the imagery of the Turkish genocide against the Armenians during World War I, Nazi rhetoric during the Holocaust, and Serbia's Slobodan Milosevic as the poisoned fruits of such ethnic nationalism. "Seen from this perspective, it would seem clear that the absence of ethnonationalist projects has been Latin America's good fortune that mostly explains the relatively few great total wars suffered by the continent. Until now . . ." Morales' "ultranationalist regime" threatened Bolivian society in three ways, with at least one of those against the identity of an entire region of the country.

To begin with, his willingness to hand over the State to the indigenous excluded from key government posts those technocrats who were the best prepared and who were in the main white or *mestizo*. It also opened an unsalvagable fissure between the poor zones of the altiplano that are a majority Native American and the eastern plains inhabited principally by a European-origin population. . . . Finally, the Morales Administration uses its populist discourse to mask a series of measures that promise to change the ethnic equilibrium of certain regions in the country. *Thus, the agricultural reform program promoted by the Bolivian president for the east of the country includes the idea of handing over parcels of land to indigenous peoples coming from the highlands in a movement that necessarily has to be seen by santacruceños as a threat to their identity.*[53] (Italics added.)

On the other hand, the catastrophic potential for violence implicit in comparisons to the Turkish genocide, the Holocaust and the recent Balkan slaughter may be overwrought. As Bolivian political scientist George Gray Molina pointed out in 2005, despite the country's yawning social and economic inequality, "episodes of ethnic politization and changing forms of contestation, reform and revolution," among other political phenomena, the past century of Bolivian history has been one of a "harmony of inequalities. . . . In contrast to other Latin American countries of similar characteristics—Guatemala, Perú, El Salvador or Nicaragua in the 1970s and 1980s—Bolivia also stands out by the absence of large-scale social or political violence." Nevertheless, a caution Kay Warren has noted about the dilemma faced by pan-Mayan activists in Guatemala has merit here. Maya intellectuals saw ethnic "*nationalist* as a threatening label for their situation because it allows government to point to international examples of state fragmentation to justify repression in the name of national security at home," she wrote. To date, Evo Morales stands apart from other leaders in those Latin American countries with large Indian communities, in part because he dominates the state, represents an electoral majority, and has adroitly worked to ensure the loyalty of Bolivia's military—by enlisting them in his ethnonationalist remake of the country's armed institutions. Yet the rhetoric of Morales' opponents, borrowing heavily on examples from that in the former Yugoslavia and that of the Third Reich to make their point, serves to incite regional interests worried about future state fragmentation and the fragility of social order in a highly-charged atmosphere of recrimination. Any push for regional secession might well be based in large part on local concerns about "state fragmentation," justifying "repression in the name of national security" in the region where they live.[54]

The confusion accompanying Morales' efforts to re-create the Bolivian state are, if history is any guide, perhaps to be expected. "A revolution is also an interregnum," James C. Scott has written, a period between the fall of the *ancien régime* and its replacement by a new order, creating a "vacuum of sovereignty" in which local government enjoys a broad autonomy over political, social and economic affairs that comes to an end when the central state is reconstituted. "The end of the interregnum can often be conceptualized as a reconquest, sometimes peaceful, sometimes violent, of the countryside by the agents of the successor state. One purpose of such reconquist is to replace the local 'folk' variant of the revolution with the official version of the revolutionary order."[55]

The process begun in Bolivia is in some ways similar to what occured in Mexico in the 1920s, described by Jennie Purnell as including a redefinition of property rights, control over vast areas of the national economy, the establishment of new and/or resurgent cultural practices and national heroes, and novel models or standards of relations between local governments and the central government, which serve to reestablish control from the national capital. In doing so, Morales has sought to create new political institutions and a common discursive framework that—while establishing key tenets on property rights, culture and the legitimate role played by the state—attempts to normalize the means through which political struggle occurs. Those efforts generate new conflicts while exacerbating old ones among and between communities and the state, while also offering new alliances among the many political actors involving a partial realization of everyone's agendas.[56] In Bolivia, however, there is little consensus among the traditional political groupings but also, increasingly, among more ethnonationalist indigenous groups. Thus it is an open question whether Morales is confusing the undeniably successful mass mobilization against Bolivia's neo-liberal elite with sustainable support for his own program, and particularly his ability to translate that into an enduring mass organization. The personalist elements of Morales' relationship with his followers are also open to question, threatening efforts to reinforce organizational and collective structures of Indian identity.

Van Cott's description, cited earlier, of Bolivia's "corrupt and personalistic political party culture [that] has permeated indigenous peoples' organizations, generating divisions and diminishing the authority of traditional ethnic authorities" appeared to be given voice by a group of dissident Indian opinion leaders in August 2008.[57] The *irpiris del Consejo Andino de Naciones Originarias— Qullasuyu*, issued what they called the Amawtica Political Proclamation (*Proclama Politica Amawtica*),[58] reminding their readers

> during the time of the elections, that it was better to have supported the (political) project of Mallku [Indian leader] Felipe Quispe Huanca embodied in what was then the Pachakuti Indigenous Movement [Movimiento Indígena Pachakuti], for being at least a platform that was transparent, honest and revolutionary, and not a pro-system and retread project like that of the Movimiento al Socialismo (MAS), that only proposed patches and reforms that did not exit the system itself.

The *irpiris* bitterly criticized Morales as "blended-in Indian impregnated with Western principles and laws." They claimed Indian identity and the claim of an indigenous government had lost their legitimacy as "our culture is used as a folkloric weapon . . . our spirituality is manipulated politically in the crudest form . . . the values of our identity are played with so as to go to bed with the West." The lack of indigenous authenticity, they charged, thus opened the way for the Morales government to be populated with pretenders.

> Whites, *chotitos* [those wearing non-Indian clothes], mixed race and de-Indianized apples, those who are red on the outside but white on the inside, burrowed in like ticks into the current government scheme; today supposedly Indianized you see them enthroned in the Executive, in the Legislature, and in the Constituent Assembly, trying to hide their ties or trying to adapt themselves to the Indian discourse. It is curious and picturesque to listen to them speak about Indians and their rights when in reality they don't do anything but stay sheltered by the system. . . . Evo Morales' so-called group of whiteys, recycled from the political left and right, is proof of his loyalty to the system. . . . This government . . . has remained mired in its anti-U.S. imperialism, as if it was the only imperialism in the world, but it hasn't been able to go any farther. . . We don't want to 'revoke" just a president or a provincial governor [*prefecto*], it is too much a waste of time and resources for such a great effort. What we want is to revoke an entire system, rotten with corruption and theft, we want to revoke the neo-liberal reforms, we want to revoke the mandate of the *felipillos* [Indian

traitors], Serbs, Croats, Arabs, Jews, we want to revoke all the bad, big and small. Several decades of experience has taught us to by following the logic of the lesser evil, all we do is, on one hand, postpone our strategy of liberation out of fear of the overrated "coup d'tat," and on the other, give birth like rabbits to an entire generation of *felipillos* who, in government, are selling our image and irremediably provoking the freezing out of Pachakuti [cosmic upheaval] for a couple more decades.[59]

The constitution proposed by Morales was ratified on Jan. 25, 2009, the 62 percent of the vote in favor 5 percentage points less than what his August 10, 2008 referendum received. The new magna carta calls the Bolivian state "plurinational" and recognizes each of the country's thirty six indigenous languages as official state languages. Both the national and departmental governments are required to use at least one indigenous language alongside Spanish to ensure that all Bolivians can communicate accurately during judicial proceedings or other state bureaucratic processes. The document also establishes indigenous autonomy—the right to self-determination and self-government in ancestral territories, reflecting Bolivia's role as the first signatory of the 2007 U.N. Declaration on the Rights of Indigenous Peoples, which called for such a measure. Article Four of the new constitution states, "Indigenous peoples, in exercising their right to self-determination, have the right to autonomy or self-government in matters relating to their internal and local affairs, as well as ways and means for financing their autonomous functions." In autonomous indigenous areas whose existence is guaranteed by the document, Native peoples can—with some central government oversight—create governing statutes and bodies, elect their autorities using customary practices, plan their own economic development and manage the renewable resources found in their territory. The legal reform announced by the Morales government in January 2007 was also enshrined in the new national charter, giving indigenous communities the constitutional right to administer justice themselves using customary law and practices.

Despite these gains, those concerned with Bolivia's democratic governance maintained that, under Morales, the already questionable separation of state powers eroded even further, with democratic practice and procedure observed in the breach, and individual rights at risk. They pointed to the fact that while approval of a draft constitution required a two-thirds vote of the constituent assembly, when Morales and his party could not attract more than 54 percent of those voting, the president used security forces and thousands of armed partisans to impose a simple-majority rule and to bypass other legal requirements. The critics also worried about Morales's continued challenges to the country's judiciary, further evidence they said, of his willingness to treat the law with contemptuous disregard. They pointed to his hostility, and that of his supporters, to what remains of the country's independent press, and how the MAS had come to rely on a vertical structure that does not allow internal dissent. Having ridden into power on a wave of anti-corruption sentiment reaching across ethnic and political spectra, Morales' government became the target of accusations of nepotism and the sale of public offices.

Despite and perhaps because of the unprecedented regional and ethnic tensions, Morales remains the most popular politician in the county, a fact bolstered by an opposition in disarray, and without a unifying figure who can offer the electorate a credible alternative. Furthermore, as Donald L. Horowitz has noted, apropos of other regions in the developing world, less advantaged peoples are frequently willing to sacrifice even economic gain for comparative advantage, placing a premium on satisfying a collective need for self-esteem and at the same time reducing the potential for domination by a rival collectivity. In addition, Morales' deep restructuring of the military and security forces, partly along ethnic lines and buttressed by popular mobilization, makes is difficult to envision the kind of antidemocratic adventure by disgruntled elites backed by large sectors of aroused and disillusioned citizens that, as political scientists Booth and Seligson point out, is the most common form of challenge to democracies.[60]

A large part of the problem, in a country whose majority population is composed of indigenous peoples, is the racism implicit in the rhetoric and, too often, the actions of the anti-Morales opposition in the eastern Media Luna states. In particular, efforts to create an alternative national identity centered on the prosperous state of Santa Cruz appears to some to both create a racially-defined internal enemy—primarily Indians from the highlands—and a fraudulent history. To be sure, during the political violence in the late 1950s, Santa Cruz was the site of a traumatic takeover by several thousand highland peasants sent by the central government in La Paz to put down a rightwing rebellion. More recently, the province has been the engine of Bolivia's economic growth, while receiving little in the way of payments and services from the inefficient national administration. However, not only does Santa Cruz's anti-state rhetoric appear to ignore the role the Bolivian national government played in the region's economic prosperity after the 1952 Revolution, particularly the important state investment in its agro-industrial sector. It also invents "new traditions" in which the customs, symbols and even clothing of the area's historically marginalized indigenous peoples are presented as a folkloric representation of a new regional identity, one in which Indians are totally integrated into *cruzeña* society, even though they remain in fact socially, economically and politically marginalized. "If you see our natives, up until they were influenced [by outside forces], they were content living in Santa Cruz because they had their own habitat and they didn't have any problems, but the natives from the West [the highlands] have always felt more discriminated against than our own," a woman representative of the Santa Cruz civic committee claimed. The ersatz quality of the supposed equality in the eastern states could even be seen in the word the autonomy movement used to describe itself—*camba*—which was, until just a few years ago, a class-based putdown of mixed-race people of generally darker skin. The regional history offered by the separatists, "cleans up and glorifies the past" and is filled with "'Homeric feats carried out by 'white' heroes, in which indigenous peoples almost do not exist, and if they do it is as assassins or the object of white 'civilizing' missions. . . . It is thus a historic narrative that is profoundly racist, colonial and conservative," claimed Bolivian researcher Carla Espósito Guevara. Thus indigenous nationalism claiming a halcyon Inca past was countered by a regionalist rendition of history in which the eastern states were reenacting the role of a people oppressed by a Bolivian-Andean empire. This discourse, Espósito Guevara pointed out, "rests in the historical recuperation of the resistance by indigenous peoples of the lowlands against the incursion of the Inca Empire, mechanically juxtaposing that historical moment with the current political present of indigenous advancement, one that represents themselves [the autonomists] in the role" of the oppressed Indians. At the same time, those local indigenous organizations attempting to defend their lands find that representatives of the local elite threaten their leaders, often making them the objects of death threats.[61]

Some critics claimed that Morales' continued popularity is likely to wane once indigenous rights are fully institutionalized, and public attention turns to other issues. "When Morales' speech is drained dry in reference to indigenous empowerment, his power will simply crumble," said sociologist Jose Blanes. Others said that it was possible that, in the future, only indigenous candidates will become president, because the Indian majority has already begun to vote "for their own kind." The first candidate to announce that he would run against Morales was Quechua Indian René Joaquino, mayor of the southern city of Potosí and leader of the leftist Social Alliance (*Alianza Social*/AS). Former Vice President Victor Hugo Cárdenas was also mentioned as a potential candidate, deciding however in the end not to run.[62]

In April 2009, Morales promulgated a new electoral law. The election code allowed for his own reelection and included the creation of eight new rural electoral districts for those Indian peoples not belonging to the country's two major indigenous communities—Quechua and Aymara—a move seen as facilitating Morales' own permanence in power. Although the number approved was reduced from an original fourteen proposed districts, the special Indian districts, together with one for Afro-Bolivians in La Paz, sparked a firestorm of criticism from opposition political parties. Morales supporters and others rightly point out, however, that opposition leaders did not oppose the allocation of senate and parliamentary deputy seats based on geographically-determined election districts, rather than on actual population size, when it benefited them.[63]

The debate took place as Morales supporters—citing alleged customary (indigenous) law—sacked and attempted to torch the home of former Vice President Cárdenas and assaulted his wife and 24-year-old son with whips and sticks, causing them to be hospitalized for two days. Cárdenas, a leading proponent of unity in diversity who urged Bolivians to vote against the constitution successfully promoted by Morales in the January 2009 referendum, was not home at the time of the assault. Aware of the possibility of an attack, he had written to the regional police, asking for protection; during the assault lasting several hours the local police commanders did not respond to urgent calls from the family. Morales supporters accused him of "betraying his race." A few days after the attack, the president denied his government was behind the outrage, but went on to echo the attackers themselves: "The people do not tolerate or forgive traitors." Cárdenas, Morales charged, "lied about himself, about the government and about the new constitution, and these lies cause a reaction." Nearly three weeks after the attack, Morales told a group of cheering supporters: "If you are not with the official party [MAS] at this time, you are the opposition. If you are op-position, then you are right wing, of the racist-fascists, of the neo-liberals . . . It is time for definition—either you are with the MAS or you are a fascist." It was only after the brutal May 2009 whipping of Marcial Fabricano, a historic leader of the indigenous movement in the eastern Beni Department, at the hands of Morales supporters, that Justice Minister Celima Torrico said that the legal framework permitting the use of customary law would be reviewed to ensure "excesses" were not committed. A second government minister—Héctor Arce—said the way to avoid situations such as that suffered by Fabricano was to "better carry out" the constitutional principle of respect for human rights in applying communitarian justice. "We are beginning to live a strategy of fear and risking in a very dangerous way rights and citizen guarantees," claimed former Bolivian President Carlos Mesa (2003-2005) shortly after the assault on Cárdenas' wife. "Evo Morales is destroying the rule of law."[64]

Chapter Eight
Perú: The Emergence of the Unbowed "Other"

"The history that nationalists want is not the history that professional academic historians, even ideologically committed ones, ought to supply. It is retrospective mythology. . . . It is therefore more important than ever to reject the 'primordialist' theory of ethnicity, let alone of national self-determination."
—Eric J. Hobsbawm, British Marxist historian[1]

On March 3, 1982, the Maoist-inspired Shining Path *(Sendero Luminoso)* guerrillas made their first dramatic appearance in the Peruvian countryside: one hundred masked commandos wielding automatic weapons hurtled sticks of dynamite against the federal prison in Ayacucho, a provincial capital whose name in Quechua means "corner of the dead." A week later the guerrillas attacked the presidential palace in Lima, hurtling two sticks of dynamite against it with a slingshot, the latter a preferred weapon of the ancient Inca Empire. In the aftermath of the attack, a local newspaper interviewed a Shining path spokesperson who identified himself as "Comrade Pedro," a member of the group's national directorate. He declared that the guerrillas drew inspiration from Chairman Mao, but also from uniquely Peruvian sources, including eighteenth century battles against the Spanish government by Juan Santos Atahualpa and Tupac Amaru II (aka José Gabriel Condorcanqui). Comrade Pedro believed that their example showed "how easily the peasant can be brought into the revolutionary war," though he conveniently ignored the outcome of both rebellions.[2]

The Shining Path declared war on the state more than a year earlier, during a period of political liberalization replacing 12 years of military rule with a formal democracy, at a time when most leftist groups, including conspicuous former advocates of revolution, opted for electoral participation. The Shining Path's violence began with dynamite attacks against power installations and government buildings, mostly in the Andean highlands and grew in intensity with the capture of police outposts and isolated villages in Ayacucho province. Eventually the armed actions spread to the larger cities, to include the capital city of Lima. A staple in the earliest stage of the guerrilla campaign included the tactic of hanging dogs from city lampposts with banners denouncing the "running dog imperialism" of Chinese leader Deng Xiaoping and exalting the hoary regime of Albania's communist dictator Enver Hoxha. Peruvian President Fernando Belaúnde Terry tried to minimize the threat, at one point calling the attackers "naughty children." The country's chief law enforcement official, Interior Minister Gen. José Gagliardi, declared that: "The Andean man [predominantly Indian peasants] is incapable of this. The revolt must have been provoked from abroad." Others were not so sure. Historian Pablo Macera, pointing at the region's age-old ethnic divisions, looked at the detritus of the guerrillas' actions and suggested that he was "convinced that the *Sendero Luminoso* people are connected with a messianic, millenarian Andean movement, which has repeated itself, restated itself and failed from the sixteenth century onward." Macera saw the non-European culture of the Andes as potentially fertile ground for a group that used the rhetoric of both Marx and anti-imperialist revolutionaries in characterizing centuries of abuse and elite domination in a region where poverty, and extreme poverty, accounted for seven out of every ten highland residents, and four out of ten, respectively. "In Perú, like in Iran, there is a primordial experience of cultural and religious order and you could have an undetermined variable like the Ayatollah (Ruhollah Khomeini), ridiculed, but active, more active than the establishment that makes fun of it." A Uruguayan social scientist living in Lima, Amparo Menéndez Carrión, warned that: "There is a whole nation that we don't know, that we are not a part of, but which has a claim to this land they still consider valid. What we have here is an indigenous, pre-Colombian movement that rejects not only what is white, but also the mestizo. We are sitting on the top of a volcano and don't even know it."[3]

The guerrillas' social base included mostly Quechua-speaking Indians whose struggle was linked to long-time class cleavages, centuries of exploitation, and a history of resistance to non-Indian religious and military institutions. The initial attraction to the Shining Path came from its ability to exploit traditional beliefs and the promise of empowerment, both apparently enhanced by successes based primarily on both the lack of real government presence in the rural highlands and, in the infrequent case such presence did exist, the existence of corrupt and exclusionary practices. However, later studies showed that, even at this early stage, the guerrillas' main bases of support among Indian peasants came from valley communities linked both to markets and educational opportunities. Much of their attractiveness came as a result of their discourse about "reestablishing order through public punishments of peasants who flouted the communities' norms"—such as thieves, alcoholics and those guilty of corruption—and their offering a chance for revenge against a military whose indiscriminate violence had left a growing trail of dead family members and friends. Traditional communities in the highlands rejected the Shining Path's doctrine, resisting its advances in order to protect both their cultural practices and their traditional systems of authority and organization. Their fear and disdain grew with the insurgents use of the indigenous as "bait in their confrontations with the armed forces," taunting the military with showy propaganda displays near peasant communities, actions that appeared to confirm suspicions that the Indians supported the guerrillas.[4]

Belaúnde named a special commission headed by Peruvian novelist Mario Vargas Llosa to investigate the January 26, 1983 murder of eight journalists and their guide in a remote Andean village in Huanta province. The findings—attributing the deaths to villagers who mistook the group for members of the Shining Path—have been disputed; Vargas Llosa's description of the indigenous villagers at the crime scene, the mountainous rural community of Uchuraccay, as primordial, stolid and superstitious beings, reinforced the view held by many in the cosmopolitan capital city, that the Indians were savages. "They come from a Perú different from the . . . modern European Perú . . . in which I live, an ancient archaic Perú that has survived in these mountains despite centuries of isolation and adversity."[5]

With such a view prevalent among the urban elites, it was not surprising that the Peruvian armed forces killed thousands of Indian peasants in the years 1983-1986 for their real or imagined sympathies for the guerrillas. Hardline General Roberto Clemente Noel Moral, the officer in charge of the zone in which the journalists were killed in Uchuraccay, "openly advocated a scorched earth, no-prisoners policy," the *Peruvian Times* would recalled many years later. According to anthropologist Billie Jean Isbell, the guerrillas' own violent excesses—which included the use of blackmail, violence and the forced recruitment of children under twelve—led to their failure. Their messianic intolerance and coercion caused them to be identified as a new form of *naqa*, supernatural beings who, according to the belief from colonial times, killed Indians, using their body fat in religious ceremonies.[6] According to Dutch investigator Andrea Portugal, "The use of violence against the civilian population intensified over time, killing local officials and anyone considered an enemy of the party in popular trials, and restricting peasants' freedom to mobilise and trade. This was the watershed that ended the initial passive or even supportive attitude of the population and facilitated a 'collaborative' relationship between the armed forces and the rural population organized in *rondas campesinas*" (rural guards). Even though it was a "widespead and systematic practice" by Shining Path, the kidnapping and use of children by the guerrillas intensified during the years 1983-1985 and 1987-1990, with the total seizure and conscription of children amounting to more than 20 percent of all those forced to participate.[7]

In what might be seen as an interesting parallel to the Sunni Awakening alliance of tribal communities and Coalition forces against a similar brutality of al-Qaeda in Iraq, by the beginning of the 1990s, some 2,500 villages in the highland departments of Apurimac, Ayacucho, Huancavelica and Junin organized into armed peasant patrols, aided by the national armed forces, seeking to shed an image created in 1983-1983 as the architects of an indiscriminate brutality. Together they displaced the guerrillas from their mountain strongholds. Anthropologist Orin Starn points out that a national law passed in 1992 that recognized the peasant patrols to arm themselves "codif[ied] the reversal of the colonial withholding of war technology from Andean peasants."[8] An official Truth and Reconciliation Commission later reported that of the estimated sixty-nine thousand killed during the war, three quarters of the victims were Indians. Many had died at the hands of the rebels, who terrorized the indigenous communities according to Maoist insurgency doctrine, but many were killed by the armed forces because military leaders broadly suspected native peoples of supporting the *Senderistas*.[9] Thousands of Ashaninka Indians were forced to join the Shining Path guerrillas, or to provide them with economic sustenance, often by cultivating coca leaf. In the period 1989-1993 alone, some five thousand Ashaninka and Nomatsiguenga Indians were captured by Sendero Luminoso and forced into slave-like conditions, while their children were impressed into the rebels' ranks.[10] "The Shining Path killed entire communities," recalled Ashaninka leader Luzmila Chiricente.[11] According to counterinsurgency expert Tom Marks, the terror, including widespread assassinations, by the Shining Path, particularly those of Indian origin who did not trust the guerrilla group's elitist, educated and largely-mestizo cadres, served as selective incentive for recruitment that promoted the "functioning and expansion of the [group's] infrastructure." Starn points out that the guerrillas "operated through a rigid heirarchy of race and class that replicated the social order it sought to overthrow. Dark-skinned kids born of poverty filled the bottom ranks under a leadership composed mostly of light-skinned individuals."[12] Indians were, as always, relegated to a lower tier by non-indigenous Marxists who, like the Zapatistas' Subcommandante Marcos less than a decade later, pretended to speak and act in their name.

The government of President Alberto Fujimori, the son of Japanese immigrants who was a virtual unknown before he won the presidency in 1990, was able to rally Perú and crush the Sendero insurgency, though at great human cost. Fujimori had presented himself as the candidate of those who were outside Peru's traditional white and mostly Lima-based elite. Campaigning with the slogan, a "President like you," Fujimori used his Japanese ancestry to make common cause with the *mestizo* and Indian masses, pointing out that his opponents made fun of him just as they had laughed at the darker-skinned Indians.[13]

However, Fujimori's 1993 Constitution also served to weaken the legal protection offered to Indian-held lands, a tactic that in other countries of the region had been key to provoking rebellion by indigenous peoples. This is an important issue, as it provides a glimpse of what it takes to spark a revolt, as well as how much indigenous people value self-government and political rights.

In 2000, Alejandro Toledo Manrique, one of sixteen children of a family of Quechua Indian peasants, who as a young boy worked shining shoes, forged a multi-class coalition that included rural Indians, the urban lower middle class, and Lima's elite, and forced the increasingly authoritarian Fujimori into a runoff election. Educated at Harvard and Stanford universities, Toledo, a Ph.D. and a former World Bank official, had never stood for or held elective office, but nonetheless shrewdly withdrew from a runoff election, plausibly charging the government with fraud based on past practice and eventually forcing the scandal-riven Fujimori to resign in disgrace. Toledo, running on a pledge to fight corruption, to reform the administration of justice and to slash military expenditures, defeated former President Alan García in the presidential contest the following year. Toledo presided over an economic boom led by investment in mining, commerce and agribusiness sectors, which placed Peru's "country risk" ratings in international finance as among the lowest in Latin America. "For the first time in its history Perú simultaneously enjoyed economic growth, political peace, and one-person-one-vote democracy," a prominent U.S. political scientist noted. "Democratization advanced under Toledo. . . . At the top levels of government he appointed highly qualified and respected professionals." However, a newly unshackled media fighting to regain its credibility, claims of electoral chicanery by his foes, and his own controversial personal life took a toll on Toledo's popularity at a time when opponents claimed that Peru's poor had been left out of the increasing prosperity. Because violent crime was increasing, his government received little credit for the fact Sendero Luminoso, whose leadership was already decapitated during the Fujimori regime, was kept from resurrecting itself. "For years the Peruvian media had portrayed Fujimori as an austere workaholic, inaugurating one public-works project after another in remote villages. Peruvians were also measuring Toledo by their assumptions of what was appropriate for people of indigenous descent. One pundit said that if Toledo had vacationed in the southern highlands, his approval rating would have gained 30 points." Meanwhile, in neighboring Bolivia, Chavez disciple Evo Morales labeled Toledo a "traitor" to indigenous peoples.[14]

More recently, a resurgence of Indian nationalism in Perú reflects the country's weak democratic institutions and the challenge racial and ethnic exclusion poses to questions of citizenship. It also helps illustrate the importance of what historian Anderson emphasizes is the necessity for imaginings of antiquity in the creation of national consciousness, "the process of reading nationalism genealogically—as the expression of an historical tradition of serial continuity." In Europe, "the new nationalisms almost immediately began to imagine themselves as 'awakening from sleep.'"[15] The work of Walker Connor also points out the value of understanding how Indian nationalism has taken hold among numerous different peoples:

> In the final analysis, the coincidence of the customary tangible attributes of nationality, such as common language or religion, is not determinative. The prime requisite is subjective and consists of the self-identification of people with a group—its past, its present, and, what is most important, its destiny. . . . *Since the nation is a self-defined rather than an other-defined grouping, the broadly held conviction concerning the group's singular origin need not and seldom will accord with factual data.*[16] (Italics added.)

Peru's so-called ethnocacerist movement, representing an extreme nationalism whose roots lie in the vindication of the indigenous origins of the majority of Peru's population, posits both ecological and nationalist histories. Although nationalist phenomena generally should not be equated with racism or fascism, ethnocacerism highlights the presupposed superiority of Peruvians of Indian ancestry, glorifying its adherents in explicitly ethnocentric terms, and offering a pseudo-religious deification of their nation. It argues for the return to a glorious past, and proposes the abolition of modern governments, including democracy, in favor of an empire ruled by a leader who claims ownership of a demonstrated ethical authority. This mirrors Kedourie's observation, made apropos of the European context, that when nationalist history applies itself to the past, "it produces a picture of nations slowly emerging and asserting themselves in territorial sovereign states." At the same time, its appeal does not rest strictly on what was, but what is *now*; in Gellner's words: "Nationalism is not the awakening and assertion of these mythical, supposedly natural and given units. It is, on the contrary, the crystallization of new units, suitable for the conditions now prevailing, though admittedly using as their raw material the cultural, historical and other inheritances from the pre-nationalist world." In those prevailing conditions, the ethnocacerists say, Peru's "copper-colored" majority of Indians and mestizos should rule over second-class lighter-skinned Peruvians.[17]

Ethnocacerism—born in the barracks, and in some ways reminiscent of the regime of leftwing nationalist Gen. Juan Velasco Alvarado (1968-1975)— projected itself as "the flag carrier of Peruvian peasants and Indians and especially of the thousands of reservists of overwhelmingly Andean origin who fought against Sendero Luminoso, and in less proportion against Ecuador [during a 1995 border conflict], and who the State and the political parties seemed to have abandoned. . . . In effect, it was the first post-*velasquista* political movement that took an openly critical posture regarding anti-indigenous racism and neo-liberal policies, which were in other parts of the continent already being questioned." Different from the example of Ecuador, Bolivia and other countries where Indian activisms emerged from civilian popular and union movements, "in Perú, the pro-indigenous movement that would have the greatest impact had military roots, bases and ideology." That ethnocacerism appealed largely to low-ranking personnel with the military and police suggested not only the ethnic glass ceiling that is an unwritten rule in those institutions, but also the inability of Peru's national defense and public safety institutions to serve as a channel for the emergence of an Native American middle class.[18]

The founder of ethnocacerism was a well-known Marxist-Leninist lawyer who praised Hitler and said that he is a descendant of Inca royalty. His two sons, the radical mestizo ex-military officers Ollanta and Antauro Humala, educated in exclusive private schools, led two separate ultra-nationalist political parties. Both had origins in an ethnocacerist movement that does not seek "a change of government, of people or of a face, but of the state," in other words, the very foundation upon which Peru's government rests. The manner in which such ethnocacerists engage in a nationalist historiography calls to mind Kedourie's dictum that "nationalists make use of the past in order to subvert the present," offering narratives that over time become inscribed into public memory.[19] In a country where more than 45 percent of the population is Indian and an additional 37 percent are mestizo, the ultimate aim of the movement is to reunite "the three Inca republics, Bolivia, Ecuador and Perú," a *sui generis volkish* perspective that ignores the fact that the Inca empire was itself born in the brutal conquest of non-Inca native peoples. As Jorge Luís Vacaflor González, a former advisor to the Bolivian vice presidency on indigenous affairs, has noted: "The emergence of the Inca Empire and its authority was based on the denial or limitation of the autonomy and liberty of chiefdoms (*señorios;* autonomous societies in which there were permanent, centralized political hierarchies headed by chiefs) who fought against the Incas' imperial power in bloody battles. The chiefdoms fought fiercely not to surrender their liberty or autonomy. . . . Many of the chiefdoms that allied themselves with the (Spanish) conquistadores viewed it as a way of recovering their liberty and autonomy."[20] The Humalas' high card, wrote Argentine columnist Sergio Kiernan, is the "inverted racism" of their appeal. "Their anti-system, anti-capitalist and anti-bourgeois doctrine . . . rests on a concept about blood, earth and language, corporativist and messianic, that any German with a long memory will instantly recognize as the *volkism* of a certain Adolf."[21] The similarities extend to the fact Ollanta's younger brother, Antauro, published a newspaper that carried the name of his brother and which regularly denounced Jews.

In the April 2006 national legislative elections, the coalition headed by the Peruvian Nationalist Movement (MNP) and led by Ollanta (the name means "the all-observing warrior" in Quechua) came in first with 21.2 percent of the vote, his coalition garnering a plurality of forty-five seats in the congressional contests. In May former Peruvian president Alan García defeated Humala in a runoff presidential election, in which the radical Indian nationalist garnered some 45 percent of the votes. García's support came from the sprawling capital city of Lima; Humala, who talked of legalizing the cultivation of coca and commercializing its products, remained wildly popular in the highland regions, where he won all but two departments. In Ayacucho, Cusco, Huancavelica and Puno, in the southern highlands—the site of some of the worst economic, political and social exclusion for people of indigenous heritage—he won some three-fourths of the vote.

During the Peruvian campaign, one observer noted that Humala "told the world that blood is identity, that the real Peruvian is 'the Indian and the mixed-blood', that the white man is a failure, a half-Peruvian, an undesirable who should leave for things to finally get better." Postulating the superiority of the Peruvian Indian, his nationalist doctrine talked about the Peruvians, Bolivians and Indians "those of 'the mountains, jungles or coast,' a very Peruvian construction to refer to provincial groups who fight among and distrust each other, were really happy, prosperous and well-governed when they lived under the Inca's enlightened hand." [22] One problem Ollanta Humala faced is common to parties whose base is conformed through ethnocentric appeals, which can have the effect of narrowing their possible electoral constituency. Moving away from that definition of his politics may have cost Humala the election. Humala's rhetoric appealed to only one sector of the Peruvian electorate, and he found he lost some of his specific and intense attraction when he toned down that rhetoric after launching a national campaign in an attempt to garner greater popular support. Peru's escape from the type of ultranationalist leadership offered by Humala was likely based on the fact that the need to appeal to a national audience reduced the ideological danger posed by the ethnocentric, messianic leader. And as a newly constituted parliamentary bloc, Humala's supporters promptly divided into contentious factions seeking a variety of allies outside his coalition. Such a tenuous safeguard should not be counted on when a leader is not constrained by electoral considerations and is able to remain within an established power base, as was the case of Shining Path leader, Abimael Guzman, who eschewed constitutional politics for insurrection.

The initial appeal of the Humala's ideas and the subsequent efforts to recreate an ethnonationalist political agenda even as the ethnocacerists stumbled in electoral politics, can be seen in Gellner's writings:

> It is nationalism which engenders nations and not the other way around. Nationalism is not what it seems, and above all, it is not what it seems to itself. The cultures it claims to defend and revive are often its own inventions, or are modified out of all recognition. Nonetheless the nationalist principle as such, as distinct from each of its specific forms, and from the individually distinctive nonsense which it may preach, has very, very deep roots in our shared current condition, is not at all contingent, and will not be easily denied. . . .
>
> Nationalism usually conquers in the name of a putative folk culture. . . . *If the nationalism prospers* it eliminates the alien high culture, but it does not then replace it by the old local low culture; *it revives, or invents, a local high (literate, specialist-transmitted) culture of its own.* [23] (Italics added.)

In May 2007, a new indigenous party was created, the *Movimiento al Socialismo Andino Amazonico* (MASA). Its similarity to the name of the political party headed by Evo Morales' suggested an inclusive approach that may reflect awareness that some Peruvian indigenous peoples continue to identify themselves more as peasants than as members of Indian ethnic groups.[24] According to its organizers, while their ideology is "closest" to that of the Humala brothers, sharing their aim to restore a "confederal" form of government inspired by Inca tradition, MASA spokesmen said it differs with the Humalas' personalistic leadership style and their "unitarian nationalism." The latter, they claim, flies in the face of Perú being "a state of many and varied nations" and is used as a pretext for false homogenization, resulting in "low-intensity ethic cleansing," an interesting statement by one group of indigenous peoples aimed at another.[25]

The Humala chapter is but one development in the contemporary lives of Peru's indigenous peoples. Both the reach of globalization and the national identity politics across existing borders offer dynamic, if tragic, tableaus of the changes taking place. The biologically lush Peruvian Amazon region, the world's third largest tropical rainforest (after those of Brazil and the Democratic Republic of Congo) and one of the planet's most diverse ecosystems, is home to more than one thousand indigenous communities, totaling more than half a million people, including some of the world's last uncontacted peoples who live in voluntary isolation. Indigenous leaders there followed the example of the indigenous communities in Ecuador. They brought suit against the California-based Occidental Petroleum in a Los Angeles court for allegedly dumping toxic wastewater into rivers and streams during its operations in the area between 1972 and 2000. Using mapping technologies like Google Earth and an alliance with a U.S. environmental group, the suit charged that the environmental destruction wreaked on the area violated Peruvian law and industry standards, in the process putting residents' health in jeopardy.[26]

On August 22, 2008, after ten days of protests during which Indian groups shut down oil and gas operations by seizing an oil pipeline and a natural gas field and taking two policemen hostage, the Peruvian Congress moved to repeal two decrees supported by President García that had facilitated the purchase of Amazon rainforest land by foreign developers. García's initiative circumvented normal congressional legislative procedures, which the president brandished as a pretext for their unusual adoption the special powers given to him for a free-trade agreement with the United States. The measures appeared to ignore Article 66 of the Peruvian constitution, which stipulates that the right to grant land use can only be done by means of a law, not a decree. Among the oil and gas concessions leased in large blocks as a result of the legal legerdemain were those won by more than three dozen multinational corporations, whose new holdings included the most biologically diverse areas in the Peruvian Amazon. García's push for these and dozens of other decrees, many concerning natural resources, "highlighted the Indians' lack of participation in policy issues that affect them," the *Los Angeles Times* noted. A coalition of indigenous and environmental groups supported by Ollanta Humala scored the measures as weakening the Indians' land rights by favoring mining, logging and oil and gas interests. As a result, the decrees—the congressional derogation of which García refused to acknowledge—offered foreign companies the right to take vast titles of land in the region, as much as 76 percent, a large part of it already titled by indigenous communities, or the object of long-standing effort by them to do so. According to experts from Duke University, no less than fifty-eight of the sixty-four blocks the government auctioned off was superimposed on lands titled to Indians, while seventeen blocks overlay lands that have either been proposed or designated as reserved for uncontacted tribes. The measures, with their free access for extractive industries, threatened the lands, property rights and livelihoods of tens of thousands of mostly indigenous peoples. "Deforestation by loggers ruined tribal hunting grounds," the *Los Angeles Times* would later report. "An oil spill in the nearby Corrientes River diminished fishing. A ten-thousand-acre African palm plantation to produce biofuels displaced dozens of families. And a government plan to build a port facility on the Huallaga River to ease trade with Brazil stands to limit . . . people's access to the waterway. . . . The surrounding terrain of Loreto province was a rolling green moonscape that long ago had been clearcut by loggers." Outside experts lamented the fact that in Perú indigenous peoples seemed to remain largely invisible, a condition for which, observed one, it would "take two or three more generations to fix." Danish land reform expert Søren Hvalkof noted that "in the case of indigenous horticultural societies in tropical forest economies, allotment and individual titling is entirely contradictory to a sustainable indigenous production system." Implementation of García's laws, Hvalkof predicted, "will have a disastrous effect on tropical forest environments, indigenous production systems and not least lead to violent conflicts between community members and encroaching settlers, land speculators and logging entrepreneurs."[27]

The year 2008 also saw the resurgence of the Shining Path guerrillas; at one time the guerrillas' startling vision sowed terror in the Andes, but now the guerrillas were reduced to a symbiotic relationship with narcotics traffickers while they fought to survive the capture and death of several remaining leaders (and who were likely victims of betrayal from inside their own organization).[28] Ollanta Humala, who reportedly plans to run again for the presidency in 2011, joined with the head of Peru's largest labor organization in support of scores of rallies throughout 2008 demanding that a bigger share of the country's growth be given to the poor. In October, a beleaguered García, his government wracked by an oil corruption scandal that forced his entire cabinet to resign, appointed a former leftist as primer minister, Yehude Simon, in an attempt to outflank his former ultranationalist rival.[29] Meanwhile, the respected Peruvian newspaper *El Comercio* reported the formation of Aymara Indian separatist groups in and around the southern region's folkloric capital of Puno, a gateway to Lake Titi-caca, whose ethnic character drew inspiration from Aymara political movements across the border in Bolivia. Long years of alienation from Lima, indigenous activism, violent land disputes and frequent outbreaks of guerrilla warfare have resulted in Aymara Indians in the region taking law into their own hands, an-gered by corrupt local officials, including judges and policemen, several of whom have been killed. In this context, the question of "ungoverned areas," or at least, "under-governed" areas, is again important. Carlos Pereyra, of the South American Studies Center (*Centro de Estudios Suramericanos*) observed that, "The formation of political movements coming together due to their ethnic iden-tity is spilling over the border," the result of an "absent State that does not take care of citizens' needs and which doesn't even have total control of its territory." Salomon Lerner Febres, the head of the official Truth and Reconciliation Commission recalled in 2008 that an indigenous man told the group, "I hope that one day I will be a Peruvian." Lerner, who now heads the Institute of Democracy and Human Rights at the Pontifical Catholic University of Perú, noted: "Inclusion assumes a series of government policies that have not been created." Too many of the government's social programs in the rural highlands were temporary handouts, he noted. A more ambitious effort was needed, Lerner added, "so that these people feel they are Peruvians." (It was later revealed that Prime Minister Simon had reached out to the jailed Antauro Humala in search of an end to the conflict in the south. Humala had been arrested and imprisoned in January 2005, after he and several hundred armed followers occupied a rural police station in Andahuaylas, in the Apurímac region. There they demanded the resignation of President Toledo, who they accused of selling out to foreign, and particularly Chilean, investors. On the first day of the assault, four police offi-cers and one gunman died. Four years later, the jailed Humala's help was needed, Simon said, because, "in the south the ethnocaceristas are an important radical group." While Antauro's brother Ollanta was "an ambitious man who only thinks about his personal interests," Simon divined that, "Antauro is serv-ing his time and, as a way of taking responsibility, he helps. To those who want to help the country, you have to meet them halfway.")[30]

Søren Hvalkof's prediction about troubles ahead as a result of García's Amazonian land grab proved to be not far from the mark, although when it oc-curred it directly involved the Peruvian state. The threat perceived by the peo-ples of the Peruvian Amazon to their lands and ways of life had burgeoned in a short time. A map provided by the state oil company Perúpetro, in charge of the oil-permit bidding process, explained why. In 2004, only 12 percent of the Peru-vian Amazon had been conceded for hydrocarbon exploration or exploitation; by 2006, the percentage had risen to 68 percent, with estimates for 2009 ranging to as much as 76 percent. Historically reluctant to organize into a single movement, much of the Amazon native communities coalesced behind the Peru's largest Amazonian indigenous umbrella group, the Association for Inter-Ethnic Development of the Peruvian Jungle (AIDESEP), a group led by Luis Pizango, an *apu* (chief) of the Shawi people. (AIDESEP, while the most prominent indigenous alliance in the region, is not the only one, however; for example, the National Organization for the Defense and Development of Indigenous People of Perú [*Organizacion Nacional de Defensa y Desarrollo de los Pueblos Indigenas del Perú /ONDEPIP*] has been vocal in its criticism of AIDESEP and of Pizango, particularly after the events of June 2009.) AIDESEP, representing sixteen Amazon ethnic groups made up of some one thousand three-hundred communities and three hundred and fifty-thousand people, became increasingly intransigent in its demands that the government withdraw its pro-big business measures and to engage in prior consultation with Indian groups about the eventual disposition of land and resources. This, they emphasized, was required by international covenants, such at the International Labor Organization's Convention 169, to which Perú had subscribed. Indigenous peoples in Perú protested, noted Leonardo Crippa, a staff attorney with the Indian Law Resource Center in Washington, D.C.,

> because their property rights to land and natural resources under their ancestral possession is not recognized and respected by the government. They protest because the legislative decrees were not consulted with them even though they affect their land rights and interests in the Amazon region. Some of these decrees criminalize indigenous protest. . . . (This) means the reform of the existing criminal legal framework, by extending the scope of application of some torts in order to include other persons and actions into what should be considered as a crime (*delito penal*).

By early 2009, the communities felt that not only had García operated behind their backs, but that they had been misled about congressional support to overturn the president's Amazon initiative. In April, AIDESEP voted to mobilize. Painted-faced protests by indigenous tribespeople, a signal of the potential violence ahead, were ignored in Lima, where the government appeared to toss off the warriors' rite as a touch of folklore. As negotiations broke down, Pizango called for an "insurgency," a statement he later retracted. Meanwhile, García declared a state of emergency in the region, provocatively claiming that indigenous peoples were "second-class citizens." He appealed to a folk saying to challenge the Indian communities, which he provocatively compared to "garden watchdogs"—*perros hortelanos*—who defend food (i.e., Amazonian resources) that "they don't eat nor let others eat," and, by doing so, prevented foreign capital from developing the country. (One poll nonetheless showed that 92 percent of Peruvians supported the rejection the Amazon decrees by the indigenous peoples.) In public Pizango complained: "They are treating us as if we were not Peruvians, this pains our soul, we want to tell the world: our brothers give their lives in order to defend the lungs of the earth," the oxygen-generating Amazon rain forest. In May, police officials repeatedly warned of the increasing numbers of Indians pouring into the area that became the focal point of violence the next month. The reports included the amount and kinds of armaments the protestors were carrying and the fact that many were veterans of Peru's brief border war with Ecuador in 1995.[31]

In June as many as thirty thousand indigenous protestors gathered in or near the city of Bagua, 420 miles north of Lima, where they blockaded a nearby highway, which ironically was named for a deceased president who was overthrown in a 1968 coup by nationalist General Velasco Alvarado and who was returned to the presidency in time to preside over the emergence of the Shining Path guerrillas. This and other blockades of highways and waterways and interference with regional oil and gas operations had already gone on for two months, curtailing activity in the oilfields and contributing to food shortages and power outages in cities in the region. A group of protestors detained some thirty-eight police, who were under orders not to violently repel them, at a crude oil pipeline station. Then on June 5, a second police unit, numbering more than 600 officers, moved to clear the highway along a stretch called Devil's Curve of between three thousand and five thousand protestors, many carrying spears and wearing feathered crowns, a place where they encountered armed resistance. When the smoke cleared, at least three Indian protestors were killed, news that infuriated the others holding the first police contingent hostage. Nearly half of the uniformed officers were then executed by the group, which accused the government of violating a previously agreed-to non-aggression pact. (The General Intelligence Directorate, or DGI, had reportedly informed the law enforcement ministry two weeks earlier that police efforts to remove the roadblocks would cause a violent confrontation. Later, government officials publicly contradicted each other whether or not they had advanced knowledge of the plans and preparations of their indigenous adversaries, while privately suggesting the indigenous communities did have useful intelligence about the government's own plans—by means of a network of lower-ranking military and police officials sympathetic to Antauro Humalla.) As the government sought to restore order, questions arose on whether it could count on the loyalty of local military units, largely made up of area residents. Faced with charges of sedition and rebellion, Pizango fled the country. At least 34 people, including nine Indians, died in the violence.[32]

The waves of anger and shock the uprising created in Lima need to be seen in the context of the emergence of the Amazonian Indian tribes as organized political entities, willing to take up arms against a state in a country where sustained state violence was until very recently an ugly reality. With the reaction to the government's failure to consult native peoples before allotting vast tracts of their ancestral homeland to national and foreign companies, came the question of whether the non-Indian elite could count on the loyalty of the military, the lower ranks being made up to a large extent of conscripts from the rebellious region, to restore order.[33] The fact that many protestors were veterans of Peru's brief border war with Ecuador in 1995 meant that the Indians knew how to fight, using the training that many had received as army recruits. Racial and ethnic presumptions in Lima notwithstanding, the indigenous protestors upended racial and ethnic stereotypes, showing that they could organize and plan sophisticated political appeals and military strategies and that their appeal—ranging from left-ist activists to former soldiers—was broader than expected by those who mini-mized the potential reach of their protest. This combination of factors raised concerns, particularly among the Lima-based non-Indian elite, that they might soon be facing a problem even more intractable than that faced in the fight against Sendero Luminoso.[34]

In the aftermath of the tragedy, García declared a state of emergency that suspended citizens' civil rights while putting military units brought in from the country's coastal region in control. Calling the indigenous activists "death mongers," García claimed the upheaval was the work of foreign elements and phony Indian activists who conspired against his government, charging that, "Perú is living a cold war against foreign leaders." Officials specifically claimed that Bolivia's Morales and Venezuela's Chavez, together with supporters of the Humala brothers, were behind the carnage. Similarly a self-identified retired U.S. intelligence analyst, blogging under the pseudonym "Caracas Gringo," claimed Pizango and the AIDESEP received some financial support from Vene-zuela's Chavez, who also supported Ollanta Humala, while indigenous militants in Bolivia, succored by the government in La Paz, also worked clandestinely with Pizango supporters and other radical Indian groups in Perú. In addition to making the case for outside incitement of the violence, he cited a charge by Ni-cia Maldonado, Chavez's Minister of Indigenous Peoples, who accused García of perpetrating "genocide, a terrorist act," as well as the comment by Evo Morales that, "It is not possible that the most reviled (people) in Latin American history should be humiliated as we have just seen." Caracas Gringo also warned, "If the revolution cannot achieve power democratically it will seek power by triggering social, economic and political instability." The U.S. expatriate wor-ried about the potential risks to Brazilian national security should "a radical revolution rooted in the alleged defense of indigenous and environmental rights of the poor" spread to the Amazonia in western Brazil, "upsetting the national development plans of its ruling economic and political elites." Nonetheless, he warned, because the militant indigenous movement "has deep ethnic, cultural and social pillars" embraced by the nearly half the Peruvian population that claims it is of indigenous descent. While the latter may not participate in politi-cal activities, "they identify with the underlying cultural and social values de-fended by leaders like Pizango." Thus, he added ominously, "The indigenous movement cannot be contained or defeated."[35]

The Peruvian prime minister, Yehude Simon, and Interior (law enforce-ment) Minister Mercedes Cabanillas attended numerous funerals of the police victims and made other public appearances, at which they portrayed the indigenous protestors as cowardly killers or manipulated savages. Simon, who later stepped down in the face of public pressure, claimed that the reason for support for them from Bolivia and Venezuela lay in those countries' desire to weaken Peru's hydrocarbon industry so as to benefit their own. However, in an interview with *El Comercio,* Simon seemed to go "off message" when, asked about his complaint that the post-conflict public debate was filled with "hypocrisy" he replied that, "the natives are the most innocent in this regard." García's own Women's Affairs and Social Development minister resigned in protest following the televised airing of a government propaganda video that labeled the Bagua protestors "extremists." The broadcast carried images of Indians armed with spears, together with shots of the dead police with multiple spear wounds. "Their throats were cowardly slashed when they were unarmed . . . twenty-two humble policemen were furiously and savagely murdered by extremists encouraged by international forces hoping to hold back Perú," an off-camera voice intoned. "Don't let the homeland lose to their advances." The video, she said, portrayed the conflict as one of "civilization versus barbarianism and extremism." [36]

Not all indigenous leaders supported Pizango's position, either. Menancio Hualinga García, ONDEPIP regional coordinator, said that his organization wanted to work with the government and the oil companies as well as with non-governmental organizations in the search for the kind of development that would help Indian communities. Referring to the bloodshed in Bagua, Hualinga suggested AIDESEP had been shrewdly managed by non-governmental organizations that financed its operations. "Maybe for that reason brother Pizango was manipulated by them," he said, adding, "We don't trust AIDESEP and for that reason we were obligated to create our own national organization." The difference in approach between the two organizations can be seen in the role played by Irinea Bardales, a Kakataibo Indian woman and one of ONDEPIP's founders, who had been a featured speaker on a panel on "human rights and indigenous peoples" at an April 2008 conference on "Human Rights and the Petroleum and Gas Industry in Latin America," held in Buenos Aires, Argentina. The event included industry social responsibility and security experts as well as U.S. and Latin American government officials and representatives and was sponsored in part by ExxonMobil. At the meeting, Bardales lectured the group on obligations under ILO Convention 169 and the need for the prior consent of indigenous communities on projects planned on their lands. Nonetheless, one hundred days after the fighting, Peruvian police could still not return to their posts in the region as part of a reprisal action by the indigenous communities for the government's continuing arrest order against the June protest leaders. [37]

On June 18, Congress voted down the two controversial land ownership laws in a rebuff to García that gave the indigenous communities a new sense of power. But barely two weeks after the Bagua tragedy the government approved a French oil company to begin drilling in an area inhabited by an Indian community, a group that had not been consulted ahead of time. Several weeks later, during Peru's 188th Independence anniversary celebration and in the wake of appointing a new cabinet billed as one of "social inclusion and order," García announced a plan to "re-found the State" by means of "popular decentralization" in favor of the poor. For their part, Peruvian indigenous groups stressed that they wanted not only the revocation of the land laws, but also those criminalizing their protests, as well the promulgation of measures protecting their traditional knowledge and economic, social and cultural rights. Their collective property rights to land and natural resources could only be protected, they pointed out, by creating new legislation addressing these rights and by comprehensive reforms of existing laws affecting them, such as the national constitution and the civil and mining codes. They also said they wanted a domestic law that would codify the guarantees of the U.N. Declaration on the Rights of Indigenous Peoples, to which Perú was already a signatory, as well as the issuance of an amnesty for Pizango and other indigenous leaders for their involvement in the Bagua protests. They demanded the reform of congressional procedures include consultation with indigenous peoples as part of the law-making process. They expressed the concern that, having been marginalized from Peru's political and social life for so long, they were unprepared for all of the complex legal and technical issues they now faced as part of a consultative process. Past experience suggested that the indigenous organizations needed to remain on guard against outside political actors ravenous for resources and impatient for any consultations to reach their end. If forced into precipitous action, the communities themselves might find their own interests betrayed by those indigenous groups eager to cut a deal on the myriad critical issues that needed to be understood in their complexity, before they could be negotiated.[38]

Chapter Nine
Ecuador:
A Populist Test of Plurinationalism

"When society fails, the nation appears as the ultimate guarantee."
—Miroslav Hroch[1]

"Just as intriguing as the MAS's rise in Bolivia is the rapid disintegration in Ecuador of what five years ago was Latin America's most successful indigenous movement," wrote political scientist Donna Lee Van Cott in February 2009, shortly before she died. "The movement's troubles provide important lessons to indigenous movements in those Latin American countries—that is, most of them—where the indigenous constitute a minority." Part of the reason, she wrote, was that the United Plurinational Pachakutick Movement, a dynamic amalgam of Ecuadorian Indian and popular organizations and urban intellectuals that grew out of the Confederation of Indigenous Nationalist of Ecuador (*Confederación de Nacionalidades Indígenas del Ecuador*/CONAIE), proved to be susceptible to cooptation and fragmentation at a level below its national leadership, in large part due to non-Indian efforts at patronage to local communities. The movement was also, Van Cott noted, a "victim of its own success."

Pachakutik had delivered on promises "such as recognition of indigenous territories, bilingual education, and political inclusion." Its willingness to enter into electoral and governing alliances left it open to charges that it was becoming more like the traditional political parties many Ecuadorians, including many indigenous Ecuadorians, abhorred. Personal rivalries, regional divisions and an inability to regenerate leadership cadres, together with the movement's past history of using coercive protest measures such as roadblocks—thus giving it a popular image as politically radical and lacking in democratic credentials—

added to its difficulties, she noted. So, too, did its 2003 choice of focusing on an indigenous agenda and identity. "The new ethnocentric strategy meant there was less space in the party for nonindigenous militants," Van Cott wrote. "Prominent mestizos abandoned Pachakutik, costing the party representation in urban areas. Important organizations—peasant, urban, and Afro-Ecuadorian—left the alliance in 2005; they cited as their reason an increasing emphasis on indigenous candidates."[2]

Van Cott's declaration was all the more striking for the context in which it was made. On September 28, 2008, in a vote in which nearly two-thirds of voters supported the adoption of its twentieth constitution since becoming a republic in 1830, Ecuador became the first country in Latin America to recognize its status as a plurinational and multicultural state. Chapter Four of the new magna carta recognized the collective rights of "communities, peoples and nationalities." Article 57 of that chapter recognized and guaranteed "Indigenous *comunas*, communities, peoples and nationalities in conformity with the constitution and agreements, conventions and declarations and other international human rights instruments for the protection of collective rights." These include "the unfettered maintenance, development and strengthening of (native peoples') identity, sense of belonging, ancestral traditions and forms of social organization," the protection of natural resources, and the holding of communal territories.[3]

That Ecuador adopted rights greater than the cultural and collective guarantees in the constitutions of Colombia (1991), Perú (1993) and Bolivia (1994) is due in part to the fact that the history of the once politically powerful, well-articulated Ecuadorian indigenous movement had differed in important ways from those of other neighboring countries. Since the 1920s, an important segment of non-Indian Ecuadorians embraced the idea of indigenous peoples as a nationality, so that as indigenous movements surfaced throughout the continent eighty years later, nationality became the discursive vehicle for Ecuadorian Indians' alternative democratic project that encompassed civil society, rather than the clientelistic dynamics of party politics that dominated other countries in the region. Latin American historian Marc Becker has observed that the Ecuadorians' "long, rich, previous tradition that can be traced back to Comintern proposals in the 1920s . . . subsequently contributed to a strong Indigenous movement" in that country. In 1933, even as Soviet policy vis-à-vis the nationality question in Europe was doing a *volte face*, a Comintern document referred to African and indigenous peoples as "oppressed nationalities," calling for greater organization by "Indian and Negro peasant masses" as a means of ushering in a revolutionary process. That same year, an Ecuadorian worker-peasant bloc coalesced behind Communist presidential standardbearer Ricardo Paredes who ran as the "candidate of workers, peasants, Indians and soldiers." His platform included the demand for the defense of "Indians and Blacks, not only as exploited and oppressed classes, but also as oppressed nationalities," and became the first published political reference to Indian peoples as a nationality.[4] Two years later, indigenous leaders participating in a Conference of Indigenous Leaders at a left-wing labor headquarters in Quito issued instructions in the Indian newspaper *Ñucanchic Allpa* for the unification and organization of indigenous peoples in defense of both their class interest and as "oppressed nationalities." They noted that

> the Indian workers have something else that differentiates them from the other white, *mestizo*, black and mulatto workers and peasants: the Indians have languages that only they speak (Kichwa, Cayapa, Cofan, etc.), they have their own clothes and customs, they belong to their own races and nationalities or peoples that have lived free for more than four hundred years without being subjected as today to whites and *mestizos*. It is for this reason that Indians have been for more than four centuries subjected to a great oppression of their people or nationality, rejected as if they were an inferior race.[5]

At the beginning of the 1990s, Ecuadorian Indians—today estimated at between 10 to 45 percent of the population, emerged as truly key actors in the country's political drama. Many of these had lived virtually as serfs on large landholdings (*haciendas*) owned by the country's Hispanicized elite as recently as the 1970s. In the view of the non-Indian elite

> Ecuador is not a country inhabited by white folk, for as an ethnic minority they only add up to scarcely one-tenth of the total population. Neither is it a country of Indians, for in that case its history would be one of regression, or else, of stratification . . . the nation is *Mestizo*. . . . Once the Indians enter civilized life . . . the *Mestizo* part of the population will be more homogeneous.[6]

A pan-American indigenous conference held in Quito in 1990 served as a catalyst for an unprecedented uprising that June that united Amazonian and highland Indians in a transportation strike that paralyzed the country and established Indians as such as a permanent factor in national politics. A decision by the government of center-right Sixto Duran Ballen (1992-1996) two years into his presidency to reverse a promised agrarian reform and end the break-up of large landed estates was seen by the indigenous movement as "a blatant attack against the hopes of agrarian equity [which] deepened its mobilization and radicalized its outlook." Major revolts blockaded Ecuador's critical highways and non-violent crowds occupied and disrupted larger cities with clockwork regularity from mid-1990 onward, creating the conditions for the ouster of elected President Abdala Bucaram in 1997, and that of an elected successor, Jamil Mahuad, in 2000. The overthrow of Mahuad marked the debut of a new power combination on the turbulent Ecuadorian scene, for as anthropologist Brian R. Selmeski has noted, as it was the first time the armed forces—which for the preceding decade had jettisoned the promotion of *mestizaje*, or integration through acculturation, in favor of "multicultural nationalism"—and important indigenous groups allied themselves as openly and collaborated so closely.[7]

The constitution was amended in 1998, declaring that the country was a multi-ethnic and pluricultural society, which required the state to consult with Indian communities on those decisions that affected their territories, prohibited the alienability of communal lands, and recognized traditional (customary) law. In addition, new government offices were created to assist Indians in bilingual education, health care and rural development, and more than one million hectares of land was returned to indigenous communities in the Amazon region. After Mahuad's departure from office, an indigenous representative briefly became a member of an ephemeral triumvirate that assumed power following an indigenous uprising supported by rebellious military officers.

CONAIE then created a political party, *Pachakutik*, which in the past decade has won significant representation in parliament, elected provincial governors and heads of municipalities. In 2002, as a result of an electoral alliance with Lucio Gutierrez, a former army lieutenant colonel who had been a partner in the coup against Mahuad, Pachakutik representatives were placed at the head of the foreign affairs and agricultural ministries and several other government portfolios, an arrangement that ended when CONAIE demanded that they resign from an administration it felt had reneged on their common agenda. Specifically CONAIE felt betrayed over agreements for negotiations with the International Monetary Fund on structural adjustment, closer ties with the United States and Colombia, and a pact with the rightist Social Christian Party. Despite the withdrawal of its support, however, the Indian confederation did not support the overthrow of their erstwhile ally in 2005. An interim president was successfully pressured to expel the California multinational, Occidental Petroleum, as a means to calm unrest in the indigenous community resulting from accusations of massive environmental spoilage.

Throughout this period, as a political scientist Thomas C. Bruneau has argued, the central government remained saddled with "a set of economic and political compromises and understandings that has ultimately resulted in the weakening of the capacity of the central government to govern." This turbulent panorama meant that Ecuador "embodie[d] all" of the problems faced by the region's governments, such as "consolidating and deepening democratic institutions, the cultivation or transit of illegal drugs, uncontrolled spaces inviting establishment of terrorist networks, and problematic relations between the armed forces and civilian government."[8]

Because of their previous experience in Gutierrez's government, seen as having cut off the indigenous movement's leadership off from its base, Pachakutic offered as its presidential standard-bearer in the 2006 presidential elections a founder of CONAIE, the Kichwa leader and intellectual Luis Macas Ambuludí. By participating in co-governments, especially that of Lucio Gutierrez, "important leaders made commitments with the government and followed their policies, leaving behind the leadership of Indigenous nationalities and peoples for other interests," recalled Marlon Santi, who was elected CONAIE president in January 2008. "This significantly hurt the Indigenous movement."[9] Kenneth J. Mijeski, a political scientist, and Scott H. Beck, a sociologist, added that, despite contemptuous criticisms of the country's traditional parties and its declared goal of profoundly changing Ecuadorian politics, Pachakutik had "simply become another maligned party whose interest in patronage outweighs its commitment to social justice."[10]

The choice to field Macas' candidacy resulted in greater internal dissention within the Indian movement itself, eventually dividing in two: part of the organization stayed with Macas, and others allied themselves with leftwing populist Rafael Correa, the former dean of Quito's most elite private university. The two men's platforms were nearly identical—rejecting "imperialism," trade agreements with the United States, and Plan Colombia, and supporting calls for a constituent assembly and an extensive program of agrarian reform. The similarities also caused an unusual split between Bolivia's Morales and Venezuela's Chavez, as the former endorsed Macas while the latter expressed his support for Correa, who combined traditional populist appeals with a broad pan-ethnic appeal.[11] Macas' support evaporated before the first round vote was held and Correa went on to beat his archconservative rival; *Pachakutick* won only 6 percent of the seats in Congress.

In supporting Correa's demand that Congress approve a Constitutional Assembly, the president of one important indigenous group warned that "if they try to stop it, and an indigenous rebellion is necessary, we'll do it." Amazonian Indian leaders also met and reminded Correa of the need to include indigenous leaders in the new deliberative body, and asked for greater control over Amazonian lands.[12] Indian leaders openly questioned Correa's commitment to their agenda, wondering if he—like a long line of other non-Indian presidents who ran as leftwing populists but governed along traditional lines—would also jettison them when their support was no longer needed. *Pachakutik* National Constituent Assembly delegate Ramssés Torres observed that Correa's emphasis on executive privilege indicated that he sought a "submissive and obsequious congress that would not monitor his government." Becker expressed similar concerns, noting that

> Correa was more sophisticated than Gutiérrez in manipulating movements, and activists feared that spaces were closing for social movements. Strengthening the executive meant coopting social movments. Increasingly, many leaders argued that they could organize most effectively as a social movement outside of the government rather than by joining Correa's project.[13]

It is important to note that Ecuadorian indigenous organizations have not sought nation-state affiliation from outside the existing system; that is, they have always worked within the country's rough-hewn political process. Just as significantly, the traditional or cultural practice of cultivating and chewing coca leaves for religious and medicinal purposes in Perú and Bolivia is virtually unknown among the Kichwauichua and other Indian peoples of Ecuador.[14] Security issues, however, loom as a problem: In early 2008 news reports suggested that various Indian communities in Imbabura province may have been infiltrated by Colombian guerrillas, who used indigenous residents, including children as young as twelve, to transport guns and other military supplies across the country's porous border.[15]

In September 2008, Ecuador became the fourth country in the Western Hemisphere to include indigenous languages as official languages. The National Constituent Assembly had originally only listed Spanish as an official language, but spokespersons from Ecuarunari, an association of highland Kichwa communities, and the CONAIE, called the decision "racist," pointing out that to recognize only Spanish violated the concept of Ecuador as a plurinational state. The assembly capitulated and included Quechua and Shuar as official languages, on a ninety-to-forty vote, approving legislative language that read: "Spanish is the official language of Ecuador; Spanish, Quechua and Shuar are official languages of intercultural relation. The rest of the ancestral languages are of official use for the indigenous peoples in the zones where they live and in terms fixed by the law. The state will respect this and their conservation and use." The measure was ratified in the September 28 referendum in which the new constitution was approved overwhelming at the ballot box, recognizing ethnic diversity and expanding social and environmental rights, including becoming the first in the world to recognize legally enforceable Rights of Nature, or ecosystem rights. Missing from the document, however, was a guarantee of the right to "previous informed consent" for the exploitation of natural resources on Indian lands, a key demand in indigenous peoples' quest for real self-determination.[16]

The gap between Correa's rhetoric and the reality faced by Ecuador's indigenous peoples became even clearer in 2009. On April 26, after a constitutional reform allowing for reelection, he was returned to office in a first-round landslide. As he prepared to be inaugurated once again, Correa promised that his government would "deepen democracy," vowing, "We are going to radicalize this revolution." Just a month before making that pledge, on the day Indians and Peruvian security forces engaged in a deadly clash in Bagua over land and resource rights in the Amazon, Correa announced his government had signed an agreement with Chile's state-owned copper company, Codelco, to explore and develop mining concessions in the southern Ecuadorian Amazon. While Correa said he would discuss the potential environmental impact with anyone concerned about it, he would not meet with "fundamentalists." In language reminiscent of that of his Peruvian presidential colleague, Alan García, Correa declared: "We cannot live like beggars sitting on a bag of gold." Those who recalled a televised address he had made just a week before were flummoxed. Then he had offered the international community the opportunity to pay Ecuador $5.2 billion in order for his government to leave untouched a large crude oil deposit in the country's northern Amazon, on the Yasuni biosphere reserve and national park. Apparently, for a price, sitting on a bag of gold was open for negotiation. The Confederation of Indigenous Nationalities of the Ecuadorian Amazon (*CON-FENIAE*) denounced Correa's "arrogant and dictatorial political regime . . . (which) violates the precepts of Constitutional Rights of the Republic, the principles of the ILO Convention 169, and the rights affirmed in the United Nations Declaration on the Rights of Indigenous Peoples." The Correa government, it declared, "is provoking political and social disorder in the Amazon region disregarding Ancestral Territorial Rights of Indigenous Nationalities and Peoples, by the intrusion of military forces and surrender to the national and transnational oil and mining companies of our territories, with a clear plan to create the looting, subjugation and misery of our communities." In September, Humberto Cholango, the president of Ecuarunari, the association of highland Kichwa communities, strongly criticized the Water Law being debated by the National Assembly as well as the creation of a new National Water Secretariat, saying indigenous groups worried about the unequal distribution of the liquid under the government's plan could lead another indigenous uprising. Asked about the guarantees to give priority to irrigation and alimentary needs and to avoid water privatization supposedly offered by the new water secretariat, Cholango replied flatly that those were not being carried out: "Here there is a real Ecuador and an Ecuador constructed from paper."[17]

On the eve of his second inauguration, cloaked in a red poncho, with head bowed and eyes closed, Correa participated in an indigenous cleansing ceremony forty miles outside Quito flanked by fellow leftists Evo Morales, the first Indian president of Bolivia, and Guatemalan Nobel peace prize laureate Rigoberta Menchú. As incense bellowed from a large bowl, the newly reelected leader was tapped with a holy stick and shadowed by the rattling of clumps of herbs. Correa he promised far-reaching social reforms to aid his country's poor and indigenous peoples. He said that the new government, about which he called on indigenous peoples to help him "radicalize," would emphasize a "preferential option for the poor, the young and ancestral peoples . . . for whom justice has been too long delayed." Perhaps thinking of the Indian activists and communities who were at the forefront of toppling two of his predecessors within the last decade, including as part of an unprecedented alliance with the armed forces, he called on the Indian community to eschew "bullets and boots." Although during the ceremony Correa accepted a ceremonial staff of knotted wood symbolizing command, it was clear that longstanding collaboration between Ecuador's urban leftists and its indigenous communities, a singular and fruitful relationship in the context of Latin America and its Native peoples, had entered an uncertain and perilous stage.[18]

Chapter Ten
Guatemala: Many Nations within a Single Nation-State

The distinction between the races is in Spanish America a distinction of rank or class rather than color. . . . [Indians] are not actively hostile to the white people, and indeed, get on better with their landlords than some European peasantries have done with theirs. But they live apart, inside the nation, but not of it.
—Lord Bryce (1912)[1]

In Guatemala, where until today no indigenous candidates have ever been elected to national office in a country with an estimated 66 percent Indian population, leftwing guerrillas battled the central government inconclusively from at least 1962 until hostilities ended in the mid-1990s. The mismatched civil war proved to be one of the bloodiest confrontations in the region since the wars for independence from Spanish rule. As one U.S. political scientist noted, the military-controlled government's attitude toward the majority of the Maya population reflected the growing national security concerns that indigenous peoples constituted a potential communist threat. The idea that communism would spring from the rural population emerged from worries about the menace of Bolshevism in the 1920s, bolstered by the Salvadoran rural rebellion in 1932, ascribing both communism and revolt to native peoples.[2] Leftwing strategists who saw the chance to mine Indian discontent subsequently fueled such worries. For example, in the late 1960s and early 1970s, a number of Mayan peasants in the Guatemalan region of Quiché gave up their folkloric Maya-Catholic identity to embrace a more orthodox Catholicism, with some splintering off to join the guerrillas.[3] Significant evidence exists as well that the overwhelmingly non-Indian Marxist guerrilla leaders often maneuvered Indian peasants into confront-

ing the Guatemalan army, in an attempt to stiffen anti-government popular resolve and collaboration in the countryside. According to Guatemalan journalist
Mario Roberto Morales, the military's counterinsurgency campaign was assisted
by "a strategic error of the guerrillas . . . in which their leaders left the civilian
population defenseless when the Army carried out its punitive 'scorched earth"
incursions, and didn't mobilize nor arm them or offer them means to escape or
to resist. A good part of the indigenous population thus felt betrayed by the
guerrillas . . . ."[4]

The long and bloody civil war culminated in brutal repression of the country's Mayan peoples—particularly during a racially- and culturally-based
scorched-earth military counterinsurgency campaign in the late 1970s and
1980s. The three-decade-long conflict resulted in the deaths of more than two
hundred thousand people, mostly Native Americans. In total, some 626 villages
were destroyed, 1.5 million were displaced in the violence, and more than one
hundred and fifty thousand were forced to seek refuge in Mexico. Although not
an ethnic war, per se, a report by the United Nations Historical Clarification
Commission (CEH) documented that Indians bore the brunt of the 93 percent of
the human rights abuses that were investigated and were committed either by the
army or by paramilitary groups operating with government acquiescence.
Agents of the Guatemalan state, the CEH reported, "committed acts of genocide
against groups of Maya people . . . all these acts were committed 'with intent to
destroy [them] in whole or in part.' [The] massacres . . . obeyed a higher, strate-
gically planned policy." A CIA document (later declassified) from 1982, a year
the counterinsurgency reach a peak, stated bluntly that in the Ixil Triangle, an
indigenous area where the rebels were believed to be strongest: "When an army
patrol meets resistance and takes fire from a town or a village it is assumed that
the entire town is hostile and it is subsequently destroyed." The carnage, however, far outstripped the real threat, as the CIA itself reported: "the army has yet
to encounter any guerrilla force in the area," its "successes to date appear to be
limited to the destruction of several "(guerrilla)-controlled-towns" and "the killing of Indian collaborators and sympathizers." Like the Guatemalan army, however, the CIA appeared to conflate ethnic identity with alleged sympathy for the
guerrillas: "The well documented belief by the army that the entire Ixil Indian
population is pro-(guerrilla) has created a situation in which the army can be
expected to give no quarter to combatants and non-combatants alike." (The
United States supported the counterinsurgency effort for most of its duration, but
with a noticeable distancing during the Carter Administration from the Guatemalan military regime, which considered U.S. human rights policy during that
period [1977-1981] an anathema. It was during the time that the U.S. was either
absent or its aid strictly conditioned by the U.S. Congress that Israel stepped in
to offer the military counter insurgency techniques and weapons and other assistance during the worst years of the genocide.)[5]

A non-Indian guerrilla vanguard, acting in the name of Guatemalan indigenous communities and their interests, brought in their wake a hellish repression. As anthropologist David Stoll has noted, "revolution came from outside, with less reference to the Ixil experience and aspirations than has often been assumed . . . the local population became involved mainly because of the polarizing effect of guerrilla actions and government reprisals." To identify "the revolutionary movement with ethnic aspirations also ignores the many (indigenous people) who decided that they were betrayed by the guerrillas, a position voiced increasingly by Mayan intellectuals," Stoll observed. Caught up in violence, Indian communities had been pitted against each other; pro-regime "civil self-defense patrols" comprised of local people exercised surveillance of the countryside, reported back to the army and engaged in atrocities. Native American army recruits were compelled to participate in the selective assassinations of other Indians. An Indian villager, referring to local Mayan youth forcibly impressed into service who were then indoctrinated for service in the dirty war, recalled: "They leave as Indians, but they don't come back Indian."[6]

The guerrillas, eventually unified under the *Unidad Revolucionaria Nacional Guatemalteca* (The Guatemalan National Revolutionary Unity/*URNG*), were a mostly mixed-race (*ladino*) Marxist movement with a platform oriented almost exclusively on class-based demands. It did not promote or advocate the ethnic or cultural claims of the Mayan majority. Nonetheless, as shown above, government suspicions about indigenous organizations' allegiance led the military to single out the Mayan communities, causing thousands of Mayas to join the guerrillas, among other causes, either to escape the subjugation or avoid being forced into local paramilitary civil patrols. Later, as peace negotiations got underway, Maya organizations demanded that they represent themselves, seeking to prevent either the government or the guerrillas from co-opting their agenda or ignoring or misrepresenting their interests. An effort by the former battlefield enemies to exclude the Indians even on the subject of "the identity and the rights of indigenous populations" led Maya-Caqchiquel writer Estuardo Zapeta to bitterly complain that the peace talks were a monologue taken up by two *ladino* minorities who maintained the same colonial discourse. In a lament that might have extended the length and breadth of Latin America, indigenous leader Demetrio Cojtí Cuxil observed, "We have to admit that until now the problem of nationalities has not been resolved by any revolution or counterrevolution, by any reform or counterreform, by any independence or annexation, by a coup or countercoup."[7]

The URNG guerillas used indigenous rights during the peace process as a way of both guaranteeing its immediate political viability and gaining credibility in civil society. Having lived through the many leftist betrayals on the battlefield they called home, indigenous groups strongly criticized the guerrillas for agreeing with the government to neither investigate nor seek to sanction past violations of human rights atrocities.[8] The military and its allies in the country's con-

servative elite vigorously contested Indian demands for territorial autonomy,
claiming such an accord would create states within the nation-state and thus
threaten to the existence of the Guatemalan "nation." In response, the Mayan
movement demanded, and brought into the national discourse, recognition of
Guatemala as a "multi-ethnic, culturally plural, and multilingual" country.[9]

The Accord on Identity and Rights of Indigenous Peoples (Saqb'ichil-
COPMAGUA) which was signed by the civilian government, the military and
the guerrilla high command on March 31, 1995, was included as part of the final
document at the conclusion of the peace process a year later. The accord committed the government to:

- Recognize Guatemala's indigenous people as descendants of an ancient
  people with diverse historically related languages and sharing distinctive
  cultures and cosmology. (The Non-Maya Xinca and Garifuna communities were given equivalent status.)
- Recognize the legitimacy of the use of indigenous languages in schools,
  social services, official communications, and court proceedings.
- Recognize and protect Maya spirituality and spiritual guides, as well as the
  conservation as indigenous heritage of ceremonial centers and archaeological sites, and the involvement of Mayas in their administration.
- Undertake education reform, specifically the integration into the curriculum of Maya materials and educational methods, the involvement of families in all areas of education, and the promotion of children's intercultural
  programs.
- Include indigenous representation in administrative bodies on all levels,
  regionalize government structures, and recognize local customary law and
  community decision-making powers in education, health, and economic
  development.[10]

As the long-running war wound down, the *movimiento maya* "pursued
scholarly and educational routes to social change and nation building, in contrast
to the mass mobilizations of the popular Left (or the troubled Zapatista rebellion
in neighboring Chiapas)." Out of this struggle an indigenous consciousness
emerged that helped to anchor Guatemala's precarious democratic rule, increasing the significance of citizen participation at the local level, although the relatively low level of ethnic political activism—when compared to Bolivia and
Ecuador, for example—may be in part a legacy of the traumas suffered during
the civil war. The self-expression of Mayan identity in Guatemala is itself poles
apart from the type of iconic cultural renaissance promoted by Indian nationalists such the Humala brothers in Perú. As John Watanabe cogently argues, reflecting on the interface of his own profession with Guatemala's indigenous
communities, "Rather than objectifying culture as essential traits that endure or
erode, anthropologists have come to treat Maya cultures in Guatemala as strategic self-expressions of Maya identity, motivated—and thus presumably more

appropriately authenticated—by Maya propensities and possibilities in the present rather than by pre-Hispanic primordialisms." Thus, the current movement of indigenous peoples, concentrated in eleven of Guatemala's twenty-two departments, focuses on a pan-Maya revitalization emphasizing Indian languages, Mayan history and expanding indigenous education. This Indian renaissance reflects a conscious decision to contest the purposeful exclusion by the non-Indian elite and virtual segregation by *Kaxlan* (the Mayan word for non-indigenous) Marxists both in academia and in the guerrilla elite responsible for those massacres they either led or helped to provoke.[11]

The choice has not been without costs as critics of the pan-Mayanists are accused of seeking refuge in "strategic essentialism" in order to gain international support. "Critics have expressed fears that the movement would lead to Balkanization or separatism that could provoke further violence and destroy the state," noted sociologist Beverly Nagel. "Political activists from the left have criticized the pan-Mayanists for breaking with their 'natural' allies, the popular, or broad class-based movement, and ignoring class exploitation. Even sympathetic Western scholars betray discomfort with the pan-Mayanists' ethnic nationalism." Mayanist insistence on an ethnicity-based argument, Nagel argued, cut across class boundaries while focusing on two "essential" goals: "They reframe who is accountable to social criticism to include poor Ladinos and the popular, as well as elites; and by valorizing their culture, they give Mayans, including urban professionals, a continuing stake in their home communities."[12]

The identity politics embraced by the Mayan nationalists has its limits, as seen in Guatemala's national elections in September of 2007. The decisive defeat of Nobel laureate and Indian activist Rigoberta Menchú's leftwing presidential bid, a stinging personal defeat to an international figure who ran a lackluster campaign, in part reflected the difficulty faced by any indigenous candidate trying to unite myriad Mayan groups behind a single ethnic candidate. Not only was Menchú's Quiché Mayan language unintelligible to many Indian groups, but traditional rivalries among them meant that in important respects, Menchú was as much an outsider to other Indians as were non-Indian candidates. She earned only 3 percent of the vote, despite a poll released by the newspaper *Prensa Libre* a year earlier that indicated as many as 71 percent of Guatemalan voters liked the idea of an indigenous presidential candidate, and despite much stronger showings in the September primaries by Indian candidates at district and municipal levels.[13]

Important lessons can be learned in the difference between the vote for Menchú and that of indigenous candidates running for more local offices. Of the country's 332 municipalities, an estimated 129 were won by indigenous mayoral candidates in the September 2007 elections, up from 123 in those of 2003; including four out of seventeen elected in the department of Guatemala, which does not have an majority indigenous population.[14] In other words, while the indigenous vote went to local politicians identified as part of local voters' ethnic blocs, national politics required affinities and political platforms that spanned specific Indian as well as other ethnic identifications. At the national level, elections—like revolution, counterrevolution, coups and countercoups—had yet to provide an answer to the problem of nationalities.

Chapter Eleven
Chile: Contesting the Lands of the "People of the Earth"

"How is it possible to have 37 episodes (of violence) to then continue sending in the Carabineros (militarized police), thinking that the Carabineros will solve the problem?"
—Francisco Huenchumilla, a Mapuche leader and former secretary-general of the presidency

A majority of the native peoples of Chile are Mapuche and number between six hundred thousand and one million people, 4 to 7 percent of the country's population. The Chilean Mapuche territory, in a large area in the central part of the country, is more densely populated than where their relatives, the Argentine Mapuche, live—the same people sharing a common ancestral home—the latter numbering approximately one hundred and thirty thousand and who reside in a vast area encompassing the Patagonian provinces of Neuquen, Rio Negro, Chubut and Santa Cruz. The very name, Mapuche, which means "people of the Earth," underscores the fact, as one Mapuche leader himself noted, that "indigenous thought does not distinguish the environment from the self." Although more Mapuche today find work in Chile's urban areas than in rural precincts, land remains an indispensable part of the spiritual and economic elements of the Indians' culture and way of life, helping them maintain a strong cultural identity.[1] Today more than three thousand Mapuche communities in Chile in the country's southern region are home to numerous ethnic and emerging ethno-nationalist organizations, giving impetus to a "national" Mapuche project, united in demands for constitutional recognition of their identity, culture and rights, together with ownership of their traditional lands. Momentum has rapidly in-creased as their ancestral territory has been steadily eroded by claims by multi-national corporations, land barons and even non-Indian farmers. Because of this, some Mapuche seek a legal status similar to that of the *Rapa Nui* (Polynesian) people of Easter Island, to which the government in Santiago has conceded a relatively self-governing autonomy as a "special territory."[2] However, the geo-graphic isolation of Easter Island makes autonomy an easier political decision; the geography of the Mapuche does not lend itself to a straightforward decision.

In 1961 anthropologist Louis C. Faron noted that the Mapuche—"one of the largest functioning Indian societies in South America" and known pejoratively as "Araucanians"—have historically been viewed by non-indigenous Chileans as

> hopelessly ignorant, shiftless, and lazy. This situation is aggravated by the fact that Mapuche reservations occupy some of the most desirable farming and cat-tle-raising land in this part of Chile—land coveted by white settlers, who com-plain that the reservations surround them like a "ring of iron," preventing their expansion. . . . The government is desirous that the land be exploited by the best agricultural methods, and regards the Mapuche as a stumbling block to the improvements strategic white colonization would bring. These attitudes are translated into "pressures" on Mapuche society.[3]

Because they halted the advance of the Incas at the Rio Maule in the fifteenth century, their foes at that time called the Mapuche "Promaucae"—a deformation of the Quechua word "purum auca," meaning "rebellious people; " their title was reaffirmed when the Chilean Indians became the only indigenous people in Central and South America to successfully avoid conquest by the Spanish. They signed a treaty in 1641 formally recognizing their territorial independence and autonomy. "There was a moment when the advancing Spanish army declared a truce with the Mapuches," recalled Steven M. Tullberg, the former Washington, D.C. office director of the Indian Law Resource Center. "Regularly afterwards, there was a formal meeting between government officials and Mapuche leaders at the site of that agreement to commemorate it. Indigenous rights lawyers in Chile have been collecting the documentary history of those events and what is, in effect, a treaty."[4]

After the Mapuche sided with the Spanish and received recognition of their status as an independent nation during the Independence War (1803 to 1818), they were demeaned and dehumanized by the eventual victors, who after the war was over pushed the Indians ever more south.[5] The Mapuche were definitively beaten by the Chilean state in 1881, more than six decades after national inde-pendence was declared. It took the simultaneous effort by the Chilean and Ar-gentine nations to defeat the Mapuche, warring, on both sides of the Andes dur-ing the same decade and ending almost the same year. In Argentina, General Julio Argentino Roca directed the Conquest of the Desert, the campaign ending the Indian wars in 1879, securing the southern and western Pampas and the northern reaches of Patagonia for European settlement. Upon assuming the presidency a year later, Roca appeared to concede the joint interests of Santiago and Buenos Aires in the bloody repression: "I have always thought that Chile and the Argentine Republic, instead of being bad neighbors ought to reach out to one another, not only to combat together and in a single effort, the savage tribes, but also to influence, with vigor and together, South America's great ends toward progress."[6]

Even in the twentieth century the physical mistreatment of the Mapuches in Chile continued, with reports of Indians having their ears sliced off and being branded by the same instruments used on cattle.[7] One authoritative author in the early 1960s wrote that the Mapuches stood apart from other indigenous communities in Latin America, their

> final defeat in the 1880s (leading) to their placement on reservations rather than to enslavement or forced incorporation into haciendas as laborers. The turning point, and . . . the significant cultural base line . . . is the beginning of the reservation period in 1884. This history is more like that of North American Indians than other South American Indians, who were deeply influenced by the Spaniards at a very early time. Like the Hopi, Zuni, Navajo, and others, whose reservations have retarded the impact of European culture, the Araucanians have remained in comparative cultural isolation. . . . the Araucanian culture, although now a sub-culture of Chile, continues to be a very distinctive ethnic identity.[8]

When Marxist Salvador Allende Gossens gained the Chilean presidency in 1970 many thought his administration would improve how the government treated the Mapuche, although this help was framed as owing to their membership in the "proletariat." An Institute of Indian Development was created to improve the economic conditions of indigenous peoples, recognizing their unique status as Indians. The overthrow of Allende in a military coup led by Captain General Augusto Pinochet in 1973 put an end to the experiment. Because the Indians had been identified with the rule of the deposed elected leftwing populist, many were singled out for repression. Pinochet's regime allowed corporations to encroach even further onto Indian lands and the law according special status to the Indian reservations was abolished. "In this situation, the Mapuches, deprived of government sympathy or support, were left to survive in a free-market society in which they lacked the main ingredients for success: economic power, high levels of education, and a mentality favorable to individual entrepreneurship."[9]

The return of democracy to Chile in 1990 meant small but significant improvements along with continued problems associated with elected authorities' decisions to maintain the regime's economic policies virtually intact, despite its markedly unequal distribution of wealth. (Chile ranks higher than such countries as Mexico in terms of economic inequality.) Law 19.253, passed in 1993 and entitled, "Protection, Promotion and Development of Indigenous People," established a National Corporation for Indigenous Development (CONADI), affirmed the right of Native Americans to bilingual education and freedom from discrimination, and developed a network of protected communities in which the Mapuche could defend their cultural and archeological traditions. A bilingual education initiative is credited with expanding educational opportunities for the Chile's indigenous peoples.

Problems continued, however. President Eduardo Frei (1994-2000), supported a dam project on the Biobio River, even inaugurating its operation, displacing the Pehuenche Mapuche from their ancestral homes to mountainous terrain covered much of the year by snow. Frei was accused of having a conflict of interest, since he previously served as a partner with the Sigdo Koppers consulting firm that helped build the first Endesa dam on the river, a fact that highlighted the narrow confines in which the Indian rights debate took place.[10] Not only were the Mapuche not consulted; two Indian representatives on the planning committee were dismissed because of their opposition. Conflicts with the government over land use are not limited to hydroelectric projects, either. "For the Mapuche, the timber expansion signals their death as a people," claimed one sympathetic observer. "Each year the borders of the timber companies grow by one hundred twenty-five thousand acres. . . . A study by the Central Bank shows that in 25 years, Chile will be without native forests. They conclude, nonetheless, that the expansion of the timber companies is unstoppable."[11]

After nearly two decades of democratic rule, vigorous debate continues over whether the Mapuche should be integrated into Chilean society with the status of indigenous peoples, or merely assimilated as Chilean citizens. With President Michelle Bachelet's election in 2006, the perception continued to be of a government hostile and/or indifferent to the plight of the Indians. Her inaugural speech ignored entirely any mention of indigenous peoples, despite the strong presence of their agenda during the national election campaign. Bachelet's promise to incorporate indigenous rights into the national constitution, and to ensure consultation in areas in which they were affected led to complaints that indigenous representatives had not been fully consulted on the proposal and that the proposed constitutional reforms "actually conspired against Indians being granted the status of a collective people." As the *Rapa Nui* moved toward a "special territory" status on Easter Island, Mapuche leaders questioned why a similar treatment was not accorded to them.

> If what is promised is carried out, it would be a historic step for the autonomous aspirations of the Rapa-Nui people. However, this willingness to authorize a Special Statute contrasts with the government and the distinct branches of the state in general to even debate the possibility for a similar solution in the case of the Mapuche. An Autonomous Statute for the Mapuche region? Impossible one hears from La Moneda [presidential palace] and the armed forces command, worried—according to what they say—about national security and

the "territorial integrity of the State." How then can the government concession to the Rapa-Nui people be explained?[12]

In April 2007, Bachelet offered a new set of proposals, including "new mechanisms for the autonomous and representative participation of the indigenous peoples in society and state," and an amendment to the constitution "recognizing the multicultural character of the Chilean nation, the existence of the original peoples and the exercise of their rights." In June 2008, she proposed the creation of an Undersecretary of Indigenous Affairs, and ordered each regional government ministry to create specific units to deal with indigenous issues. Bachelet also announced the return of twenty-eight thousand hectares of land in the Atacama Desert to the indigenous Talabre community. Three months later, the Chilean government ratified the International Labor Organization's Convention 169 (which had already been given constitutional status in neighboring Argentina) establishing a system of special protection for indigenous groups and mechanisms for consulting with them on laws, economic projects and policies that affect them and the areas where they live. However, the decision by the Bachelet government to add an "interpretive declaration" to the ratification instrument, seeking to limit its application, was both rejected by the ILO and fiercely criticized by Mapuche leaders. (Government footdragging on indigenous questions can be seen, too, in their approach to health care. In an attempt to integrate Mapuche traditions, in the southern region of the country, "machis"—Mapuche women healers—work in state-owned medical centers. The innovation came only after Mapuche pharmacies sprung up in Santiago at the beginning of the twenty-first century.)[13]

Meanwhile a new indigenous political party, *Wallmapuwen* (*Tierra Mapuche)* was recognized by the Chilean Electoral Service. Organized around a proposal to create a new self-governing nation in the *Wallmapu,* extending from the Andes into Chile and Argentina to the east, this area included the "restitution" of Puelmapu, the easternmost Mapuche territory in Argentina. The group received the explicit support of the European Free Alliance, which describes itself as "a European Political Party which unites progressive, nationalist, regionalist and autonomist parties in the European Union." *Wallmapuwen* President Pedro Gustavo Quillaqueo, pointing to the autonomous regions of Spain, openly recognized the importance of the European precedent when he asked, "If inside Spain there exists a Basque country or Cataluña, and no one in Chile seems to get worked up about it, why can't a Mapuche country exist in Chile?"[14] Or, some ask, why can't the Mapuche at least receive the same treatment as that now extended to *Rapa Nui?*

Mapuche activism today appears to transcend that of an "ethnic" group, taking shape in a "Mapuche-nationalist" movement whose five characteristics, identified by Hernandez, define its transformative ethno-nationalist character:

- The demand for recognition as a people (*pueblo*);
- The demand for territory, not just land;
- The demand for political autonomy;
- The emergence of a nationalist intellectual class, and
- The emergence of "national sentiment" among the Mapuche. [15]

Beginning in 1997, Mapuche activists began to set fire to forestry plantations as a tactic aimed at recovering their traditional lands, as their demands went from increasing land ownership to creating autonomous territory. They have fought in courts against charges of setting fire to non-Mapuche houses and farmland on property they say belongs to the community, justifying such action by claiming to defend their communal property from the predations of outsiders. They have engaged in civil disobedience and acts of sabotage against non-Indian companies' property and machinery, including several arson attacks against forestry companies, to protest the encroachment by transnational hydroelectric plants and foreign-owned logging companies on their land and the use of their resources. *The Patagonian Times* recently noted that the Mapuches'

> latest enemy comes . . . in the form of forestry companies who are exploiting Mapuche land to feed the booming Chilean lumber trade. A recent Pricewater-houseCooper study ranked two Chilean businesses, ARAUCO and CMPC . . . as the largest forestry companies in Latin America, and they look on course to keep growing.

Detained protestors faced laws (The Antiterrorism Law and the Law of Internal State Security) first established in 1984 under the Pinochet military dictatorship. These treat those crimes as national security threats on the same level as terrorism, severely limiting the basic legal defense rights of the accused. Human Rights Watch noted in a 2004 report, "Undue Process: Terrorism Trials, Military Courts and the Mapuche in Southern Chile," that the anti-terrorism statute "doubles the normal sentences for some offenses, makes pre-trial release more difficult, enables the prosecution to withhold evidence from the defense for up to six months, and allows defendants to be convicted on testimony given by anonymous witnesses. These witnesses appear in court behind screens so that the defendants and the public cannot see them." The measures meant, for example, that some one hundred witnesses were allowed to "conceal their identity while testifying" against Mapuche activists and community leaders. Local and international human rights groups said the sentences handed down were "far out of proportion to the activists' actions," arguing that "protests by Mapuche people for the protection of their traditional lands and in defense of the environment are not acts of terrorism." [16]

In late 2007, an arson attack by a group of eight to ten people—wearing ski masks and military-style camouflage uniforms and armed with shotguns and rifles—against two logging camps was believed to have been committed by the most radical Mapuche organization, the *Coordinadora Arauco-Malleco* (CAM), most of whose leaders accused of participation were already in jail. Government officials claimed the group, which has acted in the name of Indian rights for a decade, was linked to the Basque separatist organization ETA.[17] A CAM communiqué declared that "because there has been no sign from the government that it will withdraw the repressive forces from the [Mapuche] communities and the continuous advance of capitalist investments in our territory, we have given freedom of action to the organs of Mapuche resistance to act against capitalist interests [so] the Coordinadora Arauco-Malleco assumes full responsibility for the recent actions carried out by the *weichafe* [warriors] against forestry interests in the area of Malleco."[18]

Early in 2008, a clash between police and Mapuche activists occupying a ranch in the Araucania region resulted in the death of one Mapuche university student, Matías Catrileo, who was shot in the back, and a call by two senators from Bachelet's ruling coalition to the Organization of American States for mediation. (On a tape-recording later made public, a police special forces officer could be heard urging a colleague to shoot the Indians: "Fire at them.") Although the government continued to declare its willingness to resolve the situation, the regional police were reinforced and complaints about rights abuses continued. In September, a consortium of international and Chilean human rights and other non-governmental organizations issued a report that claimed,

> The violent eruption of the uniformed police in the [indigenous] communities has become a frequent phenomenon . . . (including) racist insults, assaults and threats with firearms against children. . . . Police violence against the Mapuche population is one of the most grave and unpunished, as it takes place in the context of the historical discrimination this First Nation population has suffered and a permissive governmental policy that, together with the criminalization of Mapuche demands, tolerates and justifies the police against the communities.[19]

In June 2008, CAM Director Hector Llaitul was found innocent by a three-judge court in Temuco of charges of arson, the possession of illegal arms and receiving stolen property. However, the 2009 U.S. State Department report on world terrorism characterized the CAM as "a violent Mapuche group that has burned farms and attacked police in lands that they claim as theirs," showing "improved planning" in its activities and a more "professional use of arms." It also took note of Chilean claims that the Mapuche militants were working with the Basque terrorist group ETA. The U.S. government report was issued as human rights organizations criticized what they said was a pattern of government harassment of the mass media —including the detention on terrorism charges of reporters and documentary filmmakers covering the Mapuche conflict. "People's belief in the recovery of these lands is very powerful, not because of wickedness nor out of wishing to create a problem for the state, but because there is a permanent sense of injustice," said Francisco Huenchumilla, a Mapuche who was secretary-general of the presidency under Bachelet's predecessor Ricardo Lagos (2000-2006). The Chilean political class ignored the dimensions of the conflict and the fact that its solution was necessarily political, Huenchumilla added. "How is it possible to have 37 episodes (of violence) to then continue sending in the *Carabineros* (militarized police), thinking that the *Carabineros* will solve the problem?"[20]

Meanwhile, the underlying dynamics of Mapuche discontent entered a new stage, propelled by poverty, the continued corporate encroachment on Mapuche lands, and the actions of a state that appeared unwilling to involve itself in the righting of a historic injustice that continued to fester. Dam projects in the Patagonian wilderness proposed by a private Chilean-Spanish energy company would require moving Mapuche families out of their homes, which they acquired after being relocated a decade ago prior the construction of another hydroelectric dam—two moves in a decade. Aucan Huilcamán, leader of the Mapuche Council of All Lands (*Consejo de Todas las Tierras*), warned that some of Chile's most important planned energy and mining projects—such as the mammoth HidroAysén hydroelectric project that is also strongly opposed by environmentalists—were likely to come into conflict with ILO Convention 169 and a new Code of Responsible Conduct (CCR) slated to come into effect in late 2009. The CCR stipulated that businesses must carry out reports on the impact of their activities on indigenous rights, and to have their enterprises reevaluated every three years. In addition to the prior consultation requirements included in both Convention 169 and the CCR, profit sharing and other benefits were also required, with compensation for those indigenous people who were displaced as a result of the economic activity. If the impact of a project was significant, Huilcamán said, "It will be necessary to take more radical measures in order to slow the project down."[21]

The bi-national character of demands by the Mapuche people—a population that straddles the common Chilean-Argentine border in an ancestral area they claim as theirs—may receive additional attention in 2010, as both Chile and Argentina celebrate their independence bicentennials. It may also create significant cross-border problems for both countries as they seek to address Native American demands. Article 32 of ILO Convention 169, signed by both nations, addresses "Contacts and Co-Operation Across Borders," stipulating that: "Governments shall take appropriate measures, including by means of international agreements, to facilitate contacts and co-operation between indigenous and tribal peoples across borders, including activities in the economic, social, cultural, spiritual and environmental fields."

Although both countries are now at peace, it was just three decades ago that festering border disputes brought them to the brink of a major military conflict.[22] Every proposed solution to the Mapuche question in their respective territories carries with it the potential of renewed conflict, particularly given the national security cast in which Chilean politicians and private analysts have usually framed the Indian question. In October 2008, the president of the powerful Confederation of Production and Commerce (*Confederación de la Produccion y el Comercio/CPC*) called on the government to employ a heavy hand in dealing with violence linked to the Mapuche question. "The acts of violence are not 'isolated incidents. The citizenry has been witness to the level of complexity, organization and increase in scale that has recently become worse." It was, the business group complained, "part of a long-term plan with ideological connotations of a terrorist kind."[23] Such warnings had been foreshadowed already in May 2004, when designated senator and retired army general Julio Canessa declared that the creation of a new, largely Penhuenche-Mapuche community in the Upper Bio-Bio in the 8th Region brought with it important security questions:

> The Upper Bio-Bio is a frontier zone that is very important to national defense and, as such, of great geopolitical significance. Because of this, it would have been prudent that the Committee on Government, Decentralization and Regionalization call, in order to hear their views, the [military high command], which would have given us a correct opinion, from the perspective of the country's security, about whether what is under consideration is proper.[24]

Canessa's desire to place the Indians' demands under a national security perspective echoed an essay written five years earlier by military analyst Captain Paula Videla del Real, who found that

> Despite the measures adopted by the government, meant to alleviate the situation, these have proven to be insufficient and ineffective regarding the Mapuche claims. . . . *In effect, the Mapuche conflict tends to escalate and could become a perturbing element that could even affect national security . . . a situation that the Armed Forces, given their constitutional mandate of being essential for national security and guarantee of the Republic's institutional order, should not ignore, if abominable outcomes are to be prevented.* Taking into account that historically claims, such as in this case, are followed as an example by other social groups, when the lack of effective solutions impedes the definitive solution of the problem. . . . What is more, *in their effort to obtain their demands, the Mapuche communities have found support in national and international organizations for the protection of minorities, from whom they have received support and guidance. These influences, which have inserted into the Chilean situation foreign socio-cultural elements, have only contributed to the distortion of the true reality of the indigenous communities in our country. . . . The result of the ethnic mobilizations have been a rebellion against the current juridical regime, promoted and underwritten by the aforementioned organizations and infiltrated by anti-system groups, such as the Frente Manuel Rodríguez [Manuel Rodríguez Front/FMR] and the Movimiento de Izquierda Revolucionario [Revolutionary Left Movement/MIR.],* which together have found in ethnic demands the mechanism by which to obtain propaganda objectives and concrete actions by the government faced with a critical situation that

affects part of the national community lashed by the results of the current world economic crisis.[25] (Italics added.)

Unlike the other indigenous peoples who attribute their defeat to Spanish armies during the Conquest, the fact the Mapuche were vanquished little more than a century and a quarter ago means the relatively fresh wounds might serve to strengthen nationalist feeling among the group. Although that feeling may be attenuated by the fact that they are relatively non-hierarchical in their social structure and political organization, it should be noted that the large number of Mapuche scholars and activists make them one of the most articulate and vocal of the hemisphere's indigenous peoples.[26] The intellectual and community resources of the Mapuche have nevertheless not translated into acceptance in the Chilean nation-state, even before the upswing in violence further complicated the possibility of pluralistic respect. A 2005 study by the Chilean Ministry of Planning and Cooperation showed that Chileans of indigenous descent are paid approximately 26 percent less that non-Indian Chileans occupying similar jobs, while a UNICEF study the previous year showed that some 50 percent of Chilean students said they thought that Chile was superior to other nations in the region because their country's population included fewer native peoples. "'Chileans consider the Mapuche to be ungrateful, because they do not want to integrate after all these years," one community development expert noted, echoing the findings of Faron nearly five decades earlier. "They think that they are lazy, drunkards and thieves."[27]

By 2009, *The Santiago Times* noted, in Chile's conflicted south, "uprisings between members of the country's largest indigenous group (the Mapuche) and government authorities are almost a daily occurrence." Press reports suggested that an anti-Mapuche paramilitary group, el Comando Trizano, had reappeared to threaten Mapuche leaders. "The most important Mapuche leaders are going to disappear from the world, after we put two dynamite sticks in their belts if they continue their demands for land," one member of the group was quoted as saying. On July 16, a year after he was found innocent on arson charges, CAM Director Llaitul was again detained, charged this time with leading an 2008 attack in which a military prosecutor was wounded. The same month, some one hundred Mapuche leaders traveled some 360 miles to Santiago to meet with Bachelet or her representative to speak about Indian issues, but were not only not received by them, but were dispersed in front of La Moneda government palace by anti-riot personnel. On August 5th, Luis Trancal Quidel, Llaitul's successor at the militant Mapuche organization, was also arrested on charges of arson and attempting to kill policemen. Media reports claimed that Trancal had received military training from Colombia's narco-guerrillas, the Revolutionary Armed Forces (FARC), between July 2005 and July 2006, (The same week Trancal was detained the Carabineros announced that six policemen, including four who were fired, were being investigated for stealing wood from a forestry company located in southern Chile, a crime for which Mapuche groups had previously been blamed.) On August 12, another Mapuche, Jaime Mendoza, a one-time army conscript, was killed under circumstances—an attempt, with some fifty other Mapuches, to occupy a farm over which they claimed ancestral owner-ship—similar to that surrounding the death of Matías Catrileo, the Indian stu-dent, the year before. Police said that they shot Mendoza—the third Mapuche to die at the hands of the militarized force in six years—in "self-defense" after be-ing ambushed, but community leaders said the victim had been shot in the back and was armed only with a stick. (The Spanish Basque separatist group, *Askap-ena*, linked to the political wing of the ETA, publicly lamented Mendoza's death and condemned the Chilean government for "robbing lands and committing in-justice against the Mapuche.") The police killing of the young Mapuche activist, *The Patagonia Times* reported, "has once again pushed age-old tensions be-tween the indigenous group and Chilean authorities beyond the breaking point."[28]

Three days after Mendoza was killed, more than 60 Indian communities formed the Mapuche Territorial Alliance as a means to fight for political auton-omy. Juan Catrillanca, at the head of the combative Teumcuicui community and an activist in the land seizure campaign, took distance from the CAM but de-clared in the newspaper *El Mercurio*: "We do not want more bread crumbs. We want to reclaim our original territory, but the government does not listen to us. For that reason we were united." Manuel Calfiu, head of the Mapuche commu-nity Meli Wixan Mapu, said the group would forcefully confront the Santiago government with their demands for poverty alleviation. "The government does not want to hear us, so there is no other option than to 'strike the table' to be heard," Calfiu told the *Associated Press*.[29]

As Chile prepared for December 2009 national elections, conservative presidential candidate Sebastián Piñera called for the application of the Pino-chet-era antiterrorism laws against the Mapuche. *Ex-pinochetistas* even made the claim that the Chilean Indians were better off during the dictatorship than they had been in two decades of democracy. Rightwing Senator Víctor Pérez charged that the government "should have been thinking about the indigenous issue a long time ago and not waited until it has gotten to this point, where the violence is out of control." For the past twenty years, Pérez claimed, "Mapuche communities have continued to be mired in poverty, and that is just the breeding groups extremists need to sow terror in the region." The day before, a UN com-mission investigating racial discrimination expressed its concern about the use of the Pinochet-era anti-terrorism statutes against the Mapuche. One panel member asked pointedly if, "those masked people who violently oppose Mapuche demands have also been judged by the anti-terrorism law?"[30]

Chapter Twelve
Colombia: Special Rights
Within a Context of Lawlessness

Colombia, South America's fourth largest country, has some eight hundred thousand indigenous people from eighty-four ethnic groups who speak sixty-four languages and three hundred dialects and live in thirty-two departments (provinces). They are also among the poorest of its forty million people. At the same time, Colombia has been until recently the country in South America that has done the most, at least in theory, to accommodate indigenous claims on the state and to provide a measure of legal protection for these peoples' persons, cultures and access to natural resources. Indians have been elected to the national Congress, departmental assemblies, as mayors and as members of municipal councils. Their two political parties—the Indigenous Social Alliance (ASI) and the Indigenous Authorities of Colombia (AICO)—are

> strong competitors in local and regional races and, in alliances, have captured departmental governorships. ASI recognizes its minority status and so reaches out to non-indigenous organizations and voters as part of a strategy to expand its political support nationally. Indigenous parties have a clear advantage to offer voters: Their elected officials are not under investigation for connections with drug traffickers or armed groups. This is a claim that many Colombian parties cannot make.

Indians have rights over some quarter of the national territory; most of the land is held collectively in 408 *resguardos*, a right upheld by a provision in the Constitution of 1991 confirming the inalienable nature of the collective holdings. Indigenous languages and dialects have been designated official languages in the areas in which they are spoken, bilingual and intercultural education are considered a right, and dual citizenship is provided for those living in border regions. In addition, Indian communities have the right to limited judicial autonomy, recognizing the existence of indigenous criminal justice systems for the first time, and the disbursement of state monies directly to the council authorities of the *resguardos*. (Tax money is collected by the central government and divided and distributed to Departments, Territories, cities and *resguardos* directly, with no strings attached. This disbursement of the monies to the *resguardos* is an example of the state treating Indians as regular citizens while respecting their cultural traditions of governance.) Nonetheless, in January 2009, Colombia's Constitutional Court ordered the government to protect the country's indigenous peoples, charging that they "were in danger of cultural and physical extermination."[1]

According to Brett Troyan, an historian with SUNY Cortland in New York, even before the indigenous agenda began moving into public consciousness in the 1980s the Colombian state in two different time periods had actively promoted the formation of Indian identity, becoming a principled and consistent national and international advocate of indigenous rights. During the seventeen years prior to the eruption of the now six-decade-long period of violence, "the Liberal state began to construct an ethnic indigenous identity based on collective landholding and to value indigenous culture." The leader of the Conservative Party, Laureano Gómez, characterized Indians and Afro-Colombians as indolent lesser peoples who contributed to the country's backwardness. In contrast, the Liberal party leadership, worried about Marxist penetration into the Colombian countryside, incorporated *indigenismo*—"the attempt to value indigenous peoples and their culture in the context of a national culture that had esteemed its Spanish character above all else"—into the party's political agenda. In the political calculus of the time, the Indians' relatively small numbers were compensated in part by their relatively larger size in the crucial Cauca department and by their political activism. One of the main organizations that promoted both nationalism and the new valorization of Indian peoples was the artistic and literary *Bachué* group, which took its name from the Chibcha language and meaning "the one with the naked breast," the goddess of the Muisca Confederation the Spanish encountered at the time of Conquest believed to be the mother of Man. The aim of the *Bachué* group was to "create an authentic and nationalistic culture while avoiding the pitfalls of European fascism" by examining Colombian national identity from a variety of perspectives. The second pivotal period, Troyan noted, came from 1958 to 1962, when the national government "legitimized the claims of indigenous communities based on ethnic identity, thereby creating a political space that indigenous activists would use to mobilize and negotiate their claims." The national government's susceptibility to those claims meant that they were later on "adopted, transformed and fully consented to precisely because the Colombian state had not been in a strong position."[2] "Colombia established more than 200 Indian reserves between 1960 and 1990, then in 1989 made history by declaring approximately half of its Amazonian area a protected zone—including special rights for Indian residents," another observer has noted, "(W)hile the government claims it preemptively granted participation rights, indigenous movements assert that twenty years of mobilization promoted their standing"[3]

Critics, however, claim the multiethnic and multicultural advances enshrined in the Colombian *magna carta* "have never amounted to more than paper," and complain that their closer proximity to the Colombian political elite has meant internal dissention in the Indians' ranks, and the corruption and cooptation of indigenous leaders. State funding earmarked for indigenous communities dropped to about 13 percent of what it was just a decade ago, although it is unclear to what extent this reflects the war's impact on state finances. Indians also face increasing access to their lands by squatters, who take advantage of their relative defenselessness, and multinational corporations challenging the right to land considered to be key to their continued survival as separate peoples. Political and criminal violence also pose significant threats to the Colombian indigenous communities, particularly the most vulnerable in terms of their size, suffering—as do other Colombians—at the hands of leftwing guerrillas, rightwing paramilitary forces and narcotics traffickers associated with either of the first two or acting alone. Much of the violence is carried out on Indian lands, with the foundation of the appeal of the narco-Marxist Revolutionary Armed Forces of Colombia (*Fuerzas Armadas Revolucionarias de Colombia/FARC*) based on its holding out an "'emancipatory ideal' to people in areas with little state presence," particularly among those "whose ethnic or racial background, or gender, severely constricts their opportunities" for a better life. However, once a part of the guerrilla ranks, both indigenous and Afro-Colombian women are passed over for delicate and coveted assignments, such as intelligence work, because they "are considered less attractive and lacking in persuasive skills." Upon leaving the FARC rural indigenous guerrilla recruits often find that their reinsertion into indigenous society is fraught with difficulties, as they are "considered tainted by interaction with non-indigenous society, and are welcomed back in their communities only after they have undergone lengthy purification rituals, 'which pisses them off, so they leave,'" In 2007, a representative of the United Nations High Commissioner for Refugees said that in the previous five years, due to the violence some two thousand Colombian Indians had to seek refuge in Brazil. The National Indigenous Organization of Colombia (*Organizacion Nacional Indígena de Colombia/ONIC* also complained that 1,226 Indians had been killed since 2002; "75 percent under the responsibility of the paramilitary and the government," with another three hundred missing and one thousand six-hundred in prison.[4]

In October 2008, tens of thousands of Colombian Indians and their supporters marched on the southern city of Cali demanding protection from corporate encroachments on their ancestral land, as well as more land and better education and health care. At least four people were killed in associated clashes between the indigenous groups and government security forces. President Alvaro Uribe was compelled to admit that, although his government promised that it would not fire on the protestors, some policemen had indeed fired. At the same time, Uribe remained the only Latin American president who refused to sign the Declaration on the Rights of Indigenous Peoples approved by the United Nations in September, 2007.

Colombia enlists indigenous communities to protect the environment

The territorial overlap between "ungoverned" areas, indigenous communities and what remains pristine environment in the region is significant. The Colombian government headed by President Álvaro Uribe Vélez began a important, though controversial, effort to enlist that country's Indian communities in state-sponsored efforts to protect the environment while aiding in the fight against coca and heroin poppy cultivation. A number of Indian reservations (*resguardos*) have enlisted in the government's Family Forest Ranger (*Familias Guardabosques*) program, in which protection of the country's forests is seen as part of a larger effort to conserve Colombia's watersheds, as well as its animal and plant life, seeking to increase the monetary and social capital of some of the poorest families. The United Nations Office on Drugs and Crime has found that in several of the reservations surveyed, the illegal cultivation of drug-related plants has dwindled to virtually nothing.[5]

In February 2009, eight Awá Indians accused of being government informants by the FARC were tortured and killed by the guerrillas, part of at least twenty seven Awas killed by the leftwing insurgents in southwest Colombia that month. ONIC leader Luis Andrade reported that two of victims were pregnant women, whose stomachs were cut open and the fetuses removed. In March, the Colombian Constitutional Court ruled that indigenous peoples could refuse to serve in the military. Luis Fernando Arias, ONIC secretary-general, pointed out that the Indian communities were aware of their patriotic duties and, for that reason, were trying to make government officials aware of the work being done in the *resguardos* by indigenous self-policing units called *guardias nativas.* The government, Arias said, "ought to recognize that indigenous authority and self-policing by these peoples is comparable to military service." In the department of Cauca in the country's southwest, the same month the FARC committed the Awá massacre, Nasa Indians announced that they were expelling the FARC, as well as those operating drug-production laboratories, from their territory using non-violent methods. These included setting up control posts on mountain roads and rescuing youths forcibly recruited by the guerrillas. Within four months, three community leaders at the forefront of the effort were murdered in reprisal. Asked by a visiting journalist if the presence of fifty heavily-armed Colombian police made the community feel any safer, one Nasa teacher responded with worldly disdain: "We're the ones that protect them."[6]

Part III

Chapter Thirteen
Toward a New American Identity

"(W)hen they took the bus to Mérida [Mexico] . . . they were afraid to speak
Maya, because people would think them stupid Indians (Mayeros). . . . The Maya
have internalized their recent history. And like all people who live in the violent
mirror of racial and ethnic hatred, they suffer for their suffering. It is the bitterest
irony of colonialism."
—Earl Shorris[1]

Senator Romeo Dallaire: *"We have heard about the Aboriginal Day of Action.*
Is the internal security risk rising as the youth see themselves more and more
disenfranchised? In fact, if they ever coalesced, could they not bring this coun-
try to a standstill?"

The Right Honourable Paul Martin: *"My answer, and the only one we all have,*
is we would hope not."
—Canadian Senate Committee on Aboriginal Peoples
Ottawa, April 8, 2008

As this book has shown, socio-political progress for indigenous peoples within
the context of democratic consolidation and respect for human rights goes beyond the mere accession by native peoples to power. The challenge of ensuring
that indigenous groups' rights will be respected within a democratic framework
requires finding ways that their conceptions of sovereignty and security can
function in concert with those of nation-states and the organizations of the international community. The search includes finding ways in which co-management
and traditional self-government can reinforce national citizenship but also offer
to indigenous peoples a greater control over their lands and their lives, including

the ability to preserve their way of life and revitalize their languages, as well as a continuing voice over just what sovereignty and security can and do mean. As the last vestiges of colonialism recede, issues with strong internal, domestic dynamics surge to the fore and demand attention—modernization, globalization, sectarianism, ethnonationalism, and fundamentalism, as well as questions about sovereignty, the rule of law, and the importance of environmental and human security, the latter two which need to be translated into and elevated—at the tribal, national and international levels—to the category of basic sovereign rights. All this poses new challenges, including questions about what means might be used to resolve crises collaboratively. What is more, patience and good will, sometimes the scarcest political commodities, will be needed because, in the best of circumstances, what lies ahead is surely the beginning of a complex, evolving process. Fortunately, as political scientist Donald L. Horowitz has noted in reference to other parts of the developing world, although "ethnic problems are intractable . . . they are not altogether without hope." Viable democracies, he added, can and should be forged through cultural pluralism.[2]

The following chapter will examine some innovative ways indigenous peoples, nation-states, and international and non-governmental organizations are seeking to confront current challenges and to provide solutions. In particular, it focuses on the critical issue of land and what it means to Native peoples; offers a clear-eyed look at indigenous peoples' possibilities and limitations regarding the natural environment and its protection, and examines U.S. tribal administration of justice and other issues as points of comparison for future democratic development. The chapter will also include a look at the example provided by Canada's Inuit, the native people of the far north. Observers such as Barry Scott Zellen offer the context of the peaceful and overwhelmingly successful struggles of the Inuit—the native people of the Arctic—and new international arrangements based on a forward-thinking suite of concepts and ideas about political inclusion, accountability and mutual respect, that might fill the vacuum left by the evanescent international structures of the Cold War era.[3]

As Zellen has noted, within the last generation the Inuit have made "tremendous gains" in increasing their autonomy and broadening their political power. Now governing partners, indigenous leaders and organizations share in the assessment of environmental risks, mitigating development's effects on traditional subsistence, and participating in economic windfalls in resource royalties, education and training, and jobs. In part due to a "shrewd and powerful" tribal political elite, and in part due to "the tolerance and encouragement and support of the Canadian government," he wrote, the Inuit today enjoy "greater autonomy, greater wealth, greater political power, and greater environmental control than any comparable indigenous minority group worldwide." Or, as historian Shelagh D. Grant noted: "Considering that less than a half-century ago the Inuit were still denied the basic right of citizenship—the right to vote—their progress in regaining control over their lives, culture, lands and resources has been no less than phenomenal." More prosaically, John Amagoalik, an Inuit activist and chairman of the committee overseeing the creation of new territory of Nunavut across the eastern half of Canada's rugged north, expressed a decade ago the practical import of the decision to create the first full-fledged political region in North America governed by Native Americans, declaring: "It won't solve all our problems overnight. But people will have a government they can relate to—a government that speaks and understands their language."[4]

The Westphalian nation-state system—territorially organized states operating in anarchic surroundings—bound nations and tribes together into single polities whose geographic reach and permanence was made seemingly immutable by the cement of Cold War imperatives. However, that very system limited the franchise for organizing power and curbed the ability to organize regionally, which is important for Indian and other tribal and indigenous national communities that span nation-state borders, from the Banks Island in Canada to Punta Arenas in Chile. As legal expert Ernst-Ulrich Petersmann has noted: "The Westphalian system of international law among sovereign states—based on internal sovereignty (as defined by constitutional law) and external sovereignty (as defined by state-centered international law)—was power-oriented and lacked democratic legitimacy, as illustrated by colonialism and imperial wars."[5] At the same time, that arrangement has been inadequate to task of meeting the security challenges now faced by those same nation-states. Douglas C. Lovelace, Jr., director of the Strategic Studies Institute, has noted: "Unprotected borders are a serious threat to the security of a number of states around the globe. Indeed, the combination of weak states, ungoverned space, terrorism, and international criminal networks make a mockery of the Westphalian system of international order."[6]

Particularly in the Third World, for most of the twentieth century the Westphalian system served as the organizing principle that marshaled the exclusive authority to govern within defined borders; but its myriad contraventions were largely obscured during the Cold War by the logic of superpower-enforced bipolarity. Now, two decades after the fall of the Berlin Wall, globalization has meant that national governments have lost part of their authority and prestige to both sub-national and international institutions, those "spheres of authority" that include professional societies, advocacy groups, non-governmental organizations, and corporate networks.[7]

Even on the Old Continent, where the Westphalian paradigm originated, the European Union is leading the way in offering more dynamic approaches to accommodating diversity, Belgium and Switzerland already, like Canada, time-tested counterpoints to the call for "one culture, one polity." The trend is now away from centralized national governments in favor of a model of "multi-level governance [that] allows decision makers to adjust the scale of governance to reflect heterogeneity," i.e., new types of organizations such as consociations, federalisms and condominiums that do not require sameness as a price of effective admission. National federations, each having its own government, laws, territory and cultural space have come into their own, serving as a beacon for some in lands across the Atlantic, and holding out the possibility of democracy revitalized through institution building. The changes, cloaked in high-minded rhetoric, reflect baseline realism. As two University of North Carolina at Chapel Hill political scientists have noted, jurisdictions that span large territories "have the virtue of exploiting economies of scale in the provision of public goods, internalizing policy externalities, allowing for more efficient taxation, facilitating more efficient redistribution, and enlarging the territorial scope of security and market exchange. Large jurisdictions are bad when they impose a single policy on diverse ecological systems or territorially heterogeneous populations."[8]

In an article on the independence of Kosovo and the liberation of "a small, poor, landlocked territory of two million people, riven by ethnic hatreds and memories of atrocities," *The New York Times* pointed to the examples of Estonia, Slovenia and Slovakia, as well as Ireland, as small states living in the "shadow of ethnic rivals" but thriving. "These successes showed that if its members relinquished some sovereignty to a continent-wide authority that could nurture and shield even small nations, Europe might finally have a way to extract the poison of regional conflict and allow the small to co-exist confidently alongside the large," it noted. "Now comes Kosovo, even more frail, and so the idea goes a step further: that Europe's identification as a continent has become strong enough to rewrite the definition of nationhood itself. Now, perhaps, the continent as a whole can protect at least the self-governance of national groups too small and weak to form self-sufficient states of their own."[9]

The example of the European Union, and in particular, the efforts made in the Balkans, where in the 1990s bitter conflict showed how nationalism was still not definitively or even necessarily contained within states, offers a useful point of comparison when addressing real and potential ethno-national conflict in Central and South America and Mexico. The debate in Europe over challenges to Westphalian notions of statehood resonates even more strongly in nation-states located even farther—and not just geographically—from older, European political ideals. New ideas about federalism, how governments interrelate at various levels, and what should be the most advantageous distribution of authority for each, are questions today are being played out, for good or for ill, across the Americas. At the bottom are interrelated questions of sovereignty, security, democratic legitimacy and citizenship.

Today Mexico, Central and South America are increasingly faced with a number of "intermestic" issues, those with both international and domestic characteristics. These challenges require policymakers to "think outside the box" in ways that include the possibility of more robust roles for both sub-national and international bodies. At the same time, political realism is also required, a condition that in the European context Dr. Rowan Williams, the archbishop of Canterbury, seemed to ignore when he suggested that *sharia*, or Islamic law, be recognized in Britain.[10]

The new challenges make it important to keep in mind what Colombian indigenous rights pioneer Gregorio Hernandez de Alba noted at the close of World War II: "When telling what is Indian, we express what is American. When looking down on what is Indian, we scorn what should be uniting our countries."[11] More recently, Mixtec Indian lawyer Francisco López Bárcenas wrote:

> The struggle for the installation of autonomous indigenous governments represents an effort by indigenous peoples themselves to construct political regimes different from the current ones, where they and the communities that form them can organize their own governments, with specific faculties and competencies regarding their internal life. The decentralization we are talking about, the one that indigenous peoples and communities advancing toward autonomy are showing us, includes the creation of paralegal forms to exercise power that are different from government entities, where communities can strengthen themselves and make their own decisions.[12]

The emergence of indigenous consciousness in the mid-1970s, and its demand for new political, economic, religious, cultural and territorial possibilities, carries with it the possibility of avoiding the dark legacy of centuries, providing the prospect of a new compact between races, cultures and nations in the Americas. This opportunity, in the words of behavioral scientist William Dean Rudoy, requires "an evolution of thinking and acting, rather than the curse of a revolution of repetitive historical forms of oppression-resistance-oppression" while eschewing "seductive ideologies that exploit the hopes and dreams of impoverished people by making deceitful promises of liberation from the tyranny of imperial enemies."[13]

After more than a decade of participation in electoral democracy, Native peoples have seen the possibilities offered, particularly at the local level. However authoritarian political traditions and clientelistic practices still limit democratic potential. The example of Ecuador, cited previously, shows the perils of offering increasing powers to central government as a solution. As many native peoples in Ecuador have realized, strong governments without checks and balances, and the politics of cooptation by those who claim to act on their behalf, have often not worked to their benefit: rather the indigenous movement has been left weaker, disoriented, and without the luster of its initial promise.[14] At the same time, the writings of Danish development expert Søren Hvalkof and others suggest that critical land reform that recognizes communal tenure requires a strong central government "with well functioning and attendant institutions, and certainly not its withdrawal and substitution with the moral indifference of savage market mechanisms."[15]

Although one possibility is for indigenous peoples to remain at the margins of political parties, experience shows that Indian communities can also be divided and their fundamental demands ignored. Thus while there are dangers both to Indian unity and purpose in participating in electoral politics, there are also dangers in not participating. As was shown at the end of the chapter on Perú, where indigenous peoples seek to devise a strategy to protect their lands, resources and cultures in the wake of the tragedy of Bagua, new concerns have arisen about the need for transparency and the adherence to a common purpose. History is replete with examples of those who—on their own, despite social sanction—seek to win the best accommodation they can for personal purposes or narrowly sectarian needs.

Careful study of the indigenous agenda, and positive examples of Indian survival if not prosperity, suggest that the prospect of unremitting ethnic conflict can best be avoided by recognition of the plurinational character of the state and recognition of group rights and effective citizenship. (On the latter, human rights activist Steven M. Tullberg has noted, "Don't forget that Romansch is one of the four official languages of Switzerland. Respecting the language of a small minority is not a crazy idea.")[16] Such rights, it should be pointed out, do not necessarily challenge nation-state sovereignty, but opposition to them often does mean the continued effective absence of the state; this absence is related to what Dirk Kruijt and Kees Kooning call "governance voids" or the continued erosion of the ability and desire of state officials to abide by the rule of law themselves.[17] The urgency is just not one pertaining to the collective fate of a single or particular nation-state, but also—to the extent that the current lack of rights adds to the extreme out-migration in several countries of impoverished Indian peoples looking for work—it poses important threats to regional stability and economic well-being as well. The warning by economists José G. Montalvo and Marta Reynal-Querol, noted earlier, may well extend beyond nation-state borders: "Business as usual is not possible in a society with a high level of potential ethnic conflict, since this situation affects all levels of economic activity."[18]

The search for new and more effective forms of incorporation of indigenous peoples in nation-states is necessarily circumscribed by adherence to democratic practice and the standards of international human rights. However, those who vocally oppose these efforts might temper their indignation by employing perspective, historical and otherwise. (The illiberal rants against Bolivia's Indians by Michael S. Radu, a Romanian-born American political scientist and journalist, included a December 26, 2005 piece in *FrontPageMagazine.com* entitled "The End of Bolivia." In it he literally credited all of the country's advancement as the work of its non-Indian elites while blaming long-suffering indigenous peoples for mob action and political radicalism. After calling for draconian international measures against the Morales government, Radu declared: "If this leads to the end of Bolivia as we know it, so be it.") Historian Marc Becker usefully reminds that Ecuadorian Indians "gained strength by organizing on a corporatist model that emphasized their group rights" because the exercise of their rights was effectively limited in other areas, including the fact that until 1978 the Ecuadorian constitution denied them citizenship:

> Beginning with the 1929 constitution, the concerns of the 'Indigenous race' were to be represented in congress by an unelected 'functional representation.' The rights of various groups to representation in congress were maintained throughout most of the twentieth century. *Although there were battles over who would have the rights to this representation, on occasion indigenous activists could manipulate it to their benefit.* (Italics added.)[19]

Thus, while others might conveniently forget, from that convoluted history Ecuadorian Indians and other Native Americans might logically draw the conclusions that dominant society changes the rules of the nation-state game as a means of attempting to maintain their dominance. And also, that much-debated group rights as defined by international declarations and other instruments, and already admitted in other countries, have their own precedent in Ecuadorian models.

The challenges posed to the effective incorporation of indigenous peoples also reflect more than a century of conflict between what historian Robert Whitney calls the contrast between "the evolving theoretical ideas of liberal democracy with the political reality of mass mobilization." Although Whitney chronicled the clash between "liberal democratic discourse" and the "need to promote capitalist relations of production" in Europe and in his study of pre-Castro Cuba, a nexus exists with today's Indian question, as now, like then, "the problem was that the subordinate classes did not always wait to be 'liberated' by those who claimed to speak on their behalf." Indeed, both the urgency and the substance of the demand for respect by and for native peoples require understanding that paternalistic and vanguard attitudes by non-Indians are necessarily unwelcome and unwise.

Whitney's characterization of the elite attitudes of imperial Europe and oligarchic Cuba ring true as the type of paternalism heard even now, from once-unchallenged non-Indian elites as well as the populist and leftwing politicians who claim to act in the interests of Native Americans: "The 'masses' . . . could not be relied upon to be responsible citizens, at least in the short term. The people needed the firm hand of the state to guide them, willingly or not, into the modern world"[20]

The bar for the realization of constructive engagement by nation-states and their native peoples is high, in no small part because once subordinate indigenous peoples are no longer waiting to be "liberated" by others. It is also a difficult test of democratic will because the requirements for real pluralism demand fundamental change. In her analysis of efforts to implement constitutionally mandated legal pluralism in Bolivia and Colombia, political scientist Van Cott found the practical realization of those regimes shared important possible impediments. These included "the capacity of the political system, the legal tradition and society to tolerate normative diversity; the geographic isolation and cultural alienation of indigenous communities; the degree of internal division within indigenous communities and movements regarding legal pluralism in general and in specific cases that have arisen, and the availability of effective legal mechanisms to indigenous communities seeking to protect those rights."[21]

Respect for diversity is key, as Mexican sociologist Héctor Díaz Polanco, reminds, because it means the co-existence of different cultural systems, but also "the necessary living side by side of various comprehensive doctrinal views (philosophical, religious, political, etc.) that permit individuals to construct (not withstanding their belonging to a same cultural system, i.e., "Western civilization") different world views, the reasons for being alive and, in short, conceptions about what 'the good life' means for them."[22]

The costs of working together to achieve such changes are not insignificant, and the road to their realization is not measured in a few steps now, but many extending over a lifetime or more. However, failure to address these changes can be even more costly while, in the last analysis, such positive feats can be achieved because similar odysseys already have. The essential commonality of the rights and demands of indigenous peoples today is one with those of other peoples in history, as Zellen himself realized two decades ago in his first trip to the Arctic and the land of the Inuit, the journey of "a wandering Jew in a magical, and in so many ways, promised land." There he found "the first peoples of the North to be in a state similar to my own people earlier in the century, in conflict with a dominant European culture that largely viewed tribes as anachronisms, primitive and obsolete in a modern age, and thus in need of rapid modernization, assimilation, and integration into mainstream society."

Careful attention to Zellen's recollections about what he found then in Canada will repay generous dividends now, when considering "Latin" America:

> My people had been nearly exterminated by the hatred of the Nazis, and earlier in history brutally oppressed by the Spanish Inquisition and repeated European pogroms intended to displace us, and to clear European soil of our presence.
>
> My people almost lost their Old Law and their old ways, and by almost forgetting their traditional knowledge, they came close to cultural extinction. But they held on, and when they could, they fought back, reasserting their traditions, reclaiming their heritage and identity.
>
> I saw the first people of the Far North at a similar crossroads, with many seeds planted for a cultural renewal, intermixed with the painful legacy of the long erosion of their traditional ways after more than a century of contact.
>
> The fate of the first peoples of the North seemed to be hanging in an unsteady equilibrium, much as my own people's had before their own national rebirth.[23]

Land

The struggle for land rights is one of the biggest challenges Indian peoples face today and remains one of the most important roots of conflict in Latin America. Although a simplification of a much richer and more complex phenomenon, contending forces throughout the region can be seen as arraying into two camps—those of greed and those of grievance, the "loot seeking" and the "justice seeking"—which in the worst of all cases can result in serious violence, or even civil war. As events in Perú, Chile, Ecuador, Nicaragua and Mexico show, tenure issues remain the principle cause of violence between indigenous peoples and their neighbors.[24] The legal gray area shrouding land and resources where indigenous people live, and have lived for centuries, still contributes to an anxious atmosphere where two or more sides often seek immediate gain because, it is feared, access may be foreclosed in the future. The economic crisis suffered around the resource-hungry region at the end of the first decade of the twenty-first century adds to the pressures, putting indigenous peoples' holdings at even greater risk.

At issue are not only the concept of land, or property, and its value, but also its usefulness, cultural as well as group and individual rights, and ultimately, who is in control. Ethicist Burke A. Hendrix found fundamental, and for that reason difficult, moral issues underlying legal strategies designed to return land expropriated from indigenous peoples. In addition to recovering properties where original ownership has not been overtaken by events, and to aid in the survival of endangered cultures, legal strategies should include challenging and rectifying fallacious historical narratives held by often racist dominant society. The concern, Hendrix adds, is that "attacks on Native claims will be specific and easily remembered by members of the majority culture, while attacks on the accuracy of their national narratives may simply be shrugged off as the words of malcontents."[25]

Respect for traditional land tenure is a key element of respect for cultural diversity. For most Native Americans access to and ownership of land is not limited to its use as a commodity to be leased or sold but rather as an inheritance that forms part of their cultural identity. It is no accident the name Mapuche, the Native community in Chile and Argentina, means "people of the Earth," signifying the unity of humans with the environment—land and life are synonymous. Communal ownership and community management of natural resources are common, and often preferred. This in turn sparks criticism from those for whom common tenancy and enterprise suggests socialism, or at very least violates the concept of private property as understood by many non-Indians, whose nation-states and corporate entities nevertheless themselves hold land and other property in "communal" trust.

For centuries, racial and ethnic discrimination paired with a lack of understanding of and respect for indigenous land tenure systems to produce laws and

policies designed to take Indian property, force native peoples towards assimilation and eradicate their way of life. More recently, however, this land and resource larceny has given way to new constitutions and laws throughout Latin
America that, on paper at least, recognize the pluricultural nature of the nation-
states, with much of the land still under indigenous control recognized, again on
paper, as inalienable territories under their collective ownership. Nonetheless,
throughout the region, Indians face important obstacles to the effective recognition of their land rights. Cases of indigenous communities enjoying the most
secure land tenure and the greatest access and control of its natural resources are
juxtaposed with those in which external forces—often with corporate headquarters outside the region—not only despoil the environment and plunder its
wealth, but also have left far too many Indians dead for trying to defend their
territories, in some cases putting whole tribes and peoples at risk. In a region
where the lack of protection of private property is seen by many analysts as a
key to continued economic underdevelopment, a lack of political will, ineffective enforcement of laws and agreements about Indian lands, as well as poor
administration—sometimes by indigenous peoples themselves—mean those
lands and natural resources, together with the cultures they support, remain part
of the problem, rather than part of a lasting solution. The problem is exacerbated
as well when outside economic nostrums come from people without ties to Native communities and their welfare, are largely untested, and are usually promoted by outside groups interested either in access to indigenous peoples' lands
and resources or in reducing the financial and other costs of what state protection there is for Native peoples.

Danish development specialist Søren Hvalkof noted that, as well, "there are
significant contradictions between indigenous communal land arrangements and
tenure systems, and the market-based land and agricultural policy reforms being
promoted by the multilateral donor agencies. In the conventional economic development discourse land tenure security is considered a prerequisite for economic growth." However, "in relation to indigenous communities the question
of tenure security is much more complex and closely related to the security of
social reproduction, safeguarding of communal control and of the communal
decision-making authority." Available evidence, he added, shows that privatization and individualization of land tenure based on neo-liberal paradigms emerging from the shadows of the 1990s Washington Consensus *per se* did not generate the expected results. "Land tenure regularization models in the region had
not seriously taken customary land tenure practices into account, which were
merely seen as static systems, relics of feudal regimes that were now standing in
the way of modernization and liberal agricultural development." Surveying Peruvian legislation on the land tenure of indigenous people a year before the violent irruption at Bagua, Hvalkof found it put local communities in an Orwellian
dilemma,

a kind of either-or condition . . . where it is possible to privatize the peasant communities or parts thereof, and put them for sale on the market, but the indigenous community members themselves are not allowed to buy their own privatized land, as long as they are members of the community. They must renounce their community membership first (as if it were a sports club). On the other hand, if the community decides to go along with an allotment of communal lands, there is no problem in selling it to third party mestizos or whichever outsider may be interested. The message of this perverted legislation is that if you want to participate in the national economy and receive support, you must give up being indigenous. Such a mechanism of ethnically defined exclusion is highly discriminatory, bordering on racism. . . . [26]

What successful land demarcation and titling can mean to indigenous peoples can be seen in the example of the Shuar Federation in eastern Ecuador, one of the oldest Indian organizations in Latin America. The Shuar successfully petitioned the central government in the late 1960s and 1970s for collective title for the land inhabited by its widely dispersed communities. The land campaign itself helped the Shuar to establish the bonds that permitted the tribes to implement a number of spin-off programs, including a bilingual distance-learning effort as well as an effort to curb cattle farming so as to stem deforestation. Today, firmly anchored in their own ancestral territory, the Shaur remain an important actor in the national politics of their country. [27]

One of the key stumbling blocks to successful protection of Indian lands and natural resources is the very remoteness of many indigenous communities, whose distance from national capitals puts them at greater risk from illegal activities ranging from logging, mining and ranching, to guerrilla insurgency and narco-terrorism. Another is the insistence by nation-states that Native peoples must register with the government as a legal entity before juridical demarcation and titling occur. Procedural requirements such as these rest uneasily on peoples frequently not overly familiar with bureaucratic regulation or, in many cases, the technical legerdemain that is wielded against them, threatening the long-term security of their title.

The promotion of indigenous land tenure in national plans and policies is a key element to successful demarcation and titling, and goes beyond them. These plans and policies need to include greater participatory roles in project planning, training and technical assistance in areas running from the law to the possibilities of profitable interface in market economies. (Remembering always, as Pope Benedict XVI acknowledged in his recent encyclical, *Caritas in Veritate*— Charity in Truth—that the market is itself shaped by culture.) Like their non-Indian countrymen, indigenous peoples need to be liberated from the Kafkaesque bureaucratic requirements that are legendary in nearly every Latin American country, an inheritance dating back to Spanish colonialism. In keeping with international law and convention, the right of Native peoples to set their own development priorities needs to be protected, their land claims expediently resolved, and access to natural resources respected, as well as—something particularly important in cases of mining and other extractive industries—to be consulted about the exercise of sub-surface rights held by the nation-state.

Since the beginning of the twenty-first century two cases in Latin America have helped create international legal precedents that have implications for indigenous peoples around the world. The Awas Tingni, one of many Sumo indigenous communities on the Atlantic Coast region in Nicaragua, sought the peaceful title of their traditional lands. *The Case of the Mayagna (Sumo) Awas Tingni Community v. Nicaragua*, decided on August 31, 2001, by the Inter-American Court of Human Rights (IACHR), was the first legally binding decision by a recognized international tribunal to uphold indigenous peoples' collective land and resource rights when a state failed to do so. The court found that the international human right of enjoyment of property benefits, as affirmed in the American Convention on Human Rights, included the right of indigenous peoples to the protection of their customary land and the tenure of their resources. The court found further that the State of Nicaragua was in violation by granting a logging concession to a foreign company with the community's traditional lands, and by otherwise failing to offer adequate acknowledgement and protection of its customary tenure. The court said that it was insufficient that the Nicaraguan constitution and laws offered general recognition of the rights of Native peoples to land they traditionally used and live on. It rebuked Nicaragua, saying that the state must secure the effective enjoyment of those rights—something it had not done for the vast majority of indigenous communities on the Atlantic Coast, who like the Awas Tingni did not have specific government recognition of their traditional lands in the form of a land title or another official document. Absent such specific government recognition, Nicaraguan authorities went on to treat substantial untitled traditional indigenous lands as state lands, and thus granted concessions for logging. The Court ordered Nicaragua to demarcate and title the Awas Tingni's traditional lands in accord with their customary land and resource tenure patterns. It also told them to refrain from any action that might undermine community interests in those lands, and to establish an adequate mechanism to secure the land rights of all of the country's native communities. (It was only in late 2008 that the Sandinista government finally granted communal land title in compliance with the ruling.)

A second case, decided in 2007 by the IACHR, involved the Saramaka, a group of Maroons—descendants of fugitive slaves—living in central Suriname who protested military-supported Chinese logging companies that sought in the late 1990s to use their lands without the tribe's permission. Already nearly half of their lands had been inundated in the 1960s, when a hydroelectric dam was built to power an aluminum factory. Fearing that the logging companies not only threatened individual villages but all of the Saramaka nation, they formed an association to represent some thirty thousand Saramaka living in sixty-three villages, and used Global Positioning System technology to document the timber poachers on their lands, even though they were threatened by imprisonment if they disrupted the outsiders' work. After the association filed a petition with the IACHR in 2000, the body requested the Surinamese government to suspend all development activities on the communities' lands pending an investigation. Nonetheless, some $11 million in tropical hardwoods were cut down and exported.

A unique people and culture, the Saramaka feared that, by losing more territory, they were at substantial risk of irreparable harm to both their persons, their survival as a people, and their cultural integrity. The IACHR in November 2007 ruled that Suriname had "violated, to the detriment of the members of the Saramaka people, the right to property" and ordered the government to modify the logging concessions to preserve their survival. The court also demanded that Suriname grant the Saramaka "free informed, and prior consent" for any future development or investment projects affecting their territory, which would also trigger the provision of reasonable benefit sharing and proper environmental and social impact assessments. Although the decision was the first international ruling to hold that a non-indigenous minority group has legal rights to the natural resources within their territory—a precedent that may persuade other regional bodies or national courts considering similar land disputes, the ruling will help indigenous peoples as well. The court's ruling underscored the fact that land is not only a physical asset with economic and financial value, but an intrinsic dimension and part of peoples' lives and belief systems. It found that a people's identity had been developed specifically in relation to a specific territory, whose culture was held to be shaped and informed by it, and that they could not maintain that their cultural character if they were moved to another site. In April 2009, two Saramaka community organizers were awarded the prestigious Goldman Environmental Prize. In making the announcement, the Goldman committee noted that because the case had been settled by the binding judgment of the IACHR, the activists "changed international jurisprudence so that free, prior and informed consent will be required for major development projects throughout the Americas. They saved not only their communities' nine-thousand square-kilometers of forest, but strengthened the possibility of saving countless more."[28]

Environment

Not only do indigenous peoples seek recognition of their collective rights over ancestral lands, including territorial and political autonomy; they also seek to harmonize use of that land with their own sense of stewardship of the earth. However, nearly two decades after Japanese sociologist Kinhide Mushakoji scored the "developmental racism" of some developing countries, a governmental practice allowing for the environment of indigenous peoples to be despoiled in order to promote national development in the name of an allegedly greater good, Indian peoples around Latin America continue to suffer from such discrimination. The practice remains based on biases that in practice mean Indians are entitled to fewer rights and have less protection; in short, they are citizens in name only. International corporate interests have borne the brunt of indigenous protests about use of these lands, and news reports have shown how foreign companies have often engaged in destructive practices that have not only despoiled the land, but also poisoned those living on it. In Perú, Indians in the Andean region have joined those from that of the Amazon to protest and to protect communities devastated by natural resource extractive companies that have contaminated the environment where they live, including illegal mahogany logging that has put the very existence of small tribes at risk. Looking behind conventional views about the Zapatista rebellion, a "close study of the ecological history of Chiapas reveals that the process of ecological marginalization also plays a significant causal role. The rioting, protesting, human rights violations, and electoral fraud of the past fifty years has often been over land tenure issues and the manipulation of property rights, factors stemming from and complicated by rapid population growth, soil erosion in the Central Highlands, and deforestation in the Eastern Lowlands."[29]

Leftwing populists such as Ecuador's Correa and Venezuela's Chavez, seeking to exploit the land for mining, resource extraction and the construction of oil pipelines as well, have been bitterly criticized by indigenous peoples, often working in tandem with environmental and other social activist organizations. In response, Correa has even employed heavy-handed military techniques, such as arresting scores of Indians protesting oil extraction and having them charged with sabotage and terrorism. These very tactics are repudiated by Correa's own supporters, it should be noted, when conducted by conservative governments.[30]

Key to the creation of a new compact for the peoples of the Americas is a common forward approach that recognizes both rights and mutual obligations. The near-perfect overlay of maps showing where Indians live and where the hemisphere's last unexploited natural resources are roughly parallels the track between Native American communities and what capital-based elites call "ungoverned areas." As Jose del Val, director of the Mexico Multicultural Nation University Program (PUMC) and a former director of the Inter-American Indigenous Institute, noted:

If we compare a map of the region that shows where indigenous people live with another that shows the planet's last unexploited natural resources, it turns out that they fully coincide. That is the reality—and the tragedy. . . . What should happen over the next decade is recognition of the fact that the resources found in indigenous territories belonging to the indigenous people. Thus, if the state and transnational corporations want to do business, they have to become partners with the indigenous communities. But this isn't happening anywhere.[31] (Italics added.)

One idea that has been given increasing currency is that of engaging indigenous peoples in efforts to protect the environment, on terms that safeguard their own rights. There has been some resistance to the idea of Native Americans as "innate" stewards of forest and other natural resources both by non-Indians and Indians alike, with the former frequently poking fun at the idea and the latter worrying about the hidden designs of non-Indians, who might be trying to use the environmental issue as a way of continuing to have a say about Indian lands. "A recurring idea about indigenous peoples (American, in this case) is to see them as the protectors of Nature," noted an article in *Pukara*, an online publication in Spanish dedicated to the "culture, society and politics of original peoples."

A closer look reveals the paternalism of such a concept and the green-tinted neo-colonial strategies that are at work underneath. . . . The indigenous, in general, are seen as groups who—frozen in a kind of Eden—live in harmony with their natural and cultural environs and that, aware of their knowledge and their fragility, fight for the defense of such surroundings. . . . The figure of the indigenous as good savages is erected as an icon whose supposed almost natural wisdom converts him into a guardian of the ancestral, both natural and cultural. . . . To consider the indigenous to be guardians of the ecosystem is to charge them with a responsibility that gives modern society a rope to grab onto to delay eco-cide. . . . *In times past, they tried to domesticate the Indian by means of religion, work or indigenista ideologies; now the green doctrine can be the alibi for a new neo-colonialism.* (Italics added.)[32]

It is true that not all Indian communities practice the same stewardship over the environment. For example, although coca grower Morales justifies—as many of his indigenous peers in Ecuador do not—the production of the coca leaf on spiritual grounds dating to the period of pre-Conquest, it is also a fact that cocaine production devastates the environment, particularly in areas where indigenous peoples live. As noted earlier, the process of manufacture includes such noxious effects as deforestation, pesticide use, water pollution, the dumping of precursor chemicals, the promotion of soil erosion and mono-agriculture, and the loss of traditional knowledge of plant species and bio-diversity.

At the same time, environmental concern is present in most of the traditional cultures that remain in the Americas, and was most recently enshrined in the new Ecuadorian magna carta, with specific acknowledgment about the cosmovision of indigenous peoples:

The constitution also recognizes the nature of *Pacha Mama*, the Goddess whose name in Quechua signifies "Mother Earth" and is venerated by Andean indigenous groups, as a subject of rights defendable by law. In addition, *sumac kawsay*, which translates as "the balanced living concept," is now a term supported in the very wording of the constitution. *Sumac kawsay*, among other things, defends nature's right to maintain and to regenerate vital cycles, protects national diversity, and prohibits the privatization of natural resources such as water.[33]

Morales supported a declaration issued by representatives of indigenous communities from five continents that called for a national and international effort to protect the planet from environmental destruction. (In a September 2008 address to the United Nations, Morales promised to "respect Pachamama," and claimed that Bolivia's newly drafted constitution "is to support a new pact with all humanity and Pachamama, from the heart of the Andes, from the South, for all the world.")[34] Without exalting indigenous peoples in the region as "ecologically noble savages," a phrase used by one academic skeptic to lampoon the presumption of indigenous respect for the planet, it is important to note some concrete examples of just what that reverence means. By way of illustration, in Ecuador, "recent trends in Shaur land use suggest that even when Amerindians become more acculturated, they still maintain more biologically diverse landscapes than their mestizo neighbors." And the way the Mapuche of Chile and Argentina think "does not distinguish the environment from the self."[35]

As part of the effort to increase cooperation across ethnic, state and regional lines, a number of concrete steps can be taken to mainstream indigenous knowledge and innovation in order to integrate cultural diversity with biological diversity and to roll back environmental devastation. There needs to be increased access to funding and capacity building for indigenous peoples both in the Americas and around the world for their environment and conservation efforts; international organizations need to implement biocultural diversity impact assessments that go beyond social impact and environmental assessment, and Native American traditional knowledge should be recognized and promoted as potentially innovative ways to confront current environmental and climate crises, both in the hemisphere and globally.[36] That knowledge, it should be pointed out, is built on experience and fact, not gauzy romanticism. Some indigenous peoples, noted one follower of anthropologist Claude Levi-Strauss, recognize "vast numbers of flora: two hundred and fifty are recognized by a single Seminole, three hundred and fifty by the Hopi, and more than five hundred by a Navajo. (Levi-Strauss) finds the Navajo able to recognize fifteen different parts of a stalk of corn; and with amusement he tells of the anthropologist who could not learn a certain aboriginal language because the people attempted to teach her the names of various plants they recognized, and while she was able to repeat their words, her powers of observation were not sufficiently acute to differentiate among the various plants."[37]

The synergy created among security interests, environmental protection and the effective incorporation of indigenous rights within the framework of democratic empowerment can potentially generate new ideas and new frameworks that offer significant benefit in the pursuit of all three.

The U.S. Model of Tribal Justice

The ability of the (U.S.) tribal court to interpret law to the Indian people and to interpret Indian culture to other legal institutions may be the most important of all assets flowing from the tribal court system. In the absence of an Indian court system, the remaining vestiges of tribal culture and values might soon disappear, being swallowed up by the ever-encroaching norms and procedures of the dominant (white) majority within the country.
—Vine Deloria, Jr. and Clifford Lytle, *American Indians, American Justice*[38]

The U.S. model of federal-tribal relations, although far from perfect,[39] has emerged as a key element in successful efforts by U.S. tribes to use tribal courts and tribal law to establish effective means of modern self-government, finding in the recovery and use of tribal values the means to address contemporary legal issues. It offers critical lessons regarding vital issues ranging from self-determination and sovereignty and the struggle for cultural survival (including the safeguarding of spirituality and identity for future generations), to the protection of native lands and resources. In an age when policymakers focus on the need to drain "swamps" of neglect and despair around the globe that are potential breeding grounds for terrorists and their supporters, those areas of disaffection and radicalization can be contained, at least in part, in the words of Indian rights lawyer Steven M. Tullberg, "by offering the poorest and most neglected people access to legal systems that recognize their human rights under the rule of law." [40]

A legitimate question might be raised about why, in those countries of the region in which Native Americans are either an outright majority or a demographically significant minority, the U.S. experience, with its "small numbers, remote geography [and] unique history"[41] is, to whatever degree, instructive. At the same time, it is no less certain that U.S. Indians share with others in the region not dissimilar aspirations for cultural survival, economic prosperity, security and justice on their own terms, and that there have been watershed improvements in the United States in a number of respects in the last four decades. Or, as a Guatemalan ambassador to the United Nations remarked after visiting the Meskwaki tribal settlement in Iowa in October 2007, "It is an eye-opener to find indigenous peoples in a different state of social and political development."[42]

For Fergus M. Bordewich, author of *Killing the White Man's Indian; Reinventing Native Americans at the End of the Twentieth Century,* published in 1996, what was happening on the U.S. reservations was "an upheaval of epic proportions . . . a revolution that had gone unnoticed by a public that still sees

Indians mainly through the mythic veil of mingled racism and romance." The sea change, he said,

> encompassed almost every aspect of Indian life, from the resuscitation of mori-
> bund tribal cultures and the resurgence of traditional religions, to the develop-
> ment of aggressive tribal governments determined to remake the entire relation-
> ship between Indians and the United States. In almost every respect, it was
> challenging the worn-out theology of Indians as losers and victims and was
> transforming tribes into powers to be reckoned with for a long time to come.
> For the first time in generations, Indians were shaping their own destinies
> largely beyond the control of whites. . . . Inspired individuals were reinventing
> Indian education, rewriting tribal histories, helping to bring about a remarkable
> resurgence of traditional religions, and coming to grips with the alcoholism and
> social pathologies that blight reservation communities.[43]

At minimum, the U.S. experience offers perspectives on how Indians attempt in a variety of ways to interact with mainstream American culture while maintaining a distinctive identity, even while many criticize their own tribal governments as too rooted in the values and ideas of the dominant society. Most U.S. Indian tribes have in the last half century successfully resisted federal government efforts to force them to accept assimilation, while some have developed strategies for "turning the tables on the oppressors" within a democratic context and maintaining a sense of nationhood, largely through education and the maintenance of oral traditions.[44] A recent study on the future of Navajo nationalism notes that,

> The tribal governance standards of the past are not obsolete. They are appropri-
> ate and have stood the test of time. They were focused on maintaining the
> health and wellness of every member of the community. Safety, health, well-
> ness, and protection were facilitated, not by dominance, confrontation, conflict
> and coercion, but by ethics, communication, cooperation, and reverence for the
> creator and the laws of nature.[45]

Human rights activist Tullberg has noted that the Indian Self-Determination Act adopted during Richard M. Nixon's presidency "offered . . . . from 1970 to the present—is the longest sustained period in 200 years during which the official U.S. Indian policy has not been designed to inflict systematic human rights abuses on Indians by denying their collective rights as nations and tribes."[46] The sea-change the Nixon era legislation signified was underlined by President Nixon himself, who declared: "The time has come to break decisively with the past and to create the conditions for a new era in which the Indian future is determined by Indian acts and Indian decisions."[47]

This is important for the discussion today in Central and South America and Mexico, because although a growing number of indigenous movements "do not demand autonomies but the re-founding of nation-states based on indigenous cultures,"[48] clearly the "vast majority is demanding self-determination and autonomous self-government in their indigenous territories within legal and political frameworks of the states where they now live. . . . The march for indigenous rights in the United States and elsewhere is under the banner of self-determination."[49]

On U.S. Indian reservations, a unique system of tribal justice helps indigenous peoples in their effort to protect and sustain their cultures while seeking to provide effective, if occasionally controversial justice for both Indians and non-Indians alike; this thus provides a possible model for discussion by and engagement with indigenous peoples around the region. In so doing, such an effort could promote cultural understanding and enhance regional collaboration on defense and security, in general as well as in so-called "ungoverned spaces," and particularly in Bolivia (already embarked on its own disputed path), Chile, Ecuador, Guatemala, Mexico, Nicaragua, Panama and Perú.

As Indians seek to exercise constitutionally guaranteed sovereignty and self-rule, the role of tribal courts and tribal police forces in the United States has become increasingly significant,. What many Latin American indigenous peoples aspire to—meaningful inclusion in their country's legal framework, protecting their rights and their communities, and giving them the chance to preserve their own cultures—is already in place, to varying degrees, on U.S. reservations. Already, a quarter of a century ago, Indian legal experts Vine Deloria, Jr., and Clifford M. Lytle, could write that the benefits offered by the U.S. tribal court system included an increasingly dedicated tribal judiciary; relatively speedy access to a fair forum, and the ability to bridge the gap between law and Indian culture, as well as deference by federal courts, and growing support from federal agencies, tribal leaders, and organizations. More recently, Raymond D. Austin, who served for 16 years as a justice on the Navajo Nation Supreme Court, noted in this book, *Navajo Courts and Navajo Common Law, A Tradition of Tribal Self-Governance,* that the leading role played by his tribe in this legal revolution places it in a unique position to help indigenous peoples around the world as they seek to retain their cultures, languages, and spiritual traditions.[50]

In the United States, the broad deference federal courts give to tribal courts includes, where appropriate, being given the first opportunity to determine whether the tribal court has the power to exercise jurisdiction over non-Indians.[51] Although there are a wide variety of approaches to tribal justice among the more than five hundred federally recognized tribes who survive in the United States, certain fundamental rules and similarities exist among all of them. In the last four decades, a number of tribes, one of the most successful of which has been the Navajo Nation, have sought to codify their traditional law (in Spanish, *derecho consuetudinario*) into positive law. This in itself has helped to fortify tribal identity and self-determination, while at the same time extending the effective reach of the national justice system. As then Attorney General Janet Reno observed:

> While the federal government has a significant responsibility for law enforcement in much of Indian country, tribal justice systems are ultimately the most appropriate institutions for maintaining order in tribal communities. *They are local institutions, closest to the people they serve. With adequate resources and training, they are most capable of crime prevention and peacekeeping.* . . . Tribal courts are essential mechanisms for resolving civil disputes that arise on the reservation or otherwise affect the interests of the tribe or its members.[52] (Italics added.)

In his seminal work, *Handbook of Federal Indian Law,* Felix Cohen described the nature of Indian tribal powers. Judicial decision on the nature of tribal powers, he wrote, is "marked by three fundamental principles:

> (1) An Indian tribe possesses, in the first instance, all the powers of any sovereign state.
> (2) Conquest renders the tribe subject to the legislative power of the United States and, in substance, terminates the *external* powers of sovereignty of the tribe, e.g., its power to enter into treaties with foreign nations, but does not by itself affect the *internal* sovereignty of the tribe, i.e., its power of local government.
> (3) These powers are subject to qualification by treaties and by express legislation of Congress, but, save as thus expressly qualified, full powers of internal sovereignty are vested in the Indian tribes and in their duly constituted organs of government.[53]

The administration of justice on Indian reservations is guided by the Major Crimes Act (Stat. 362, 285), which originally was made law by the U.S. Congress in 1885 and in effect took from Indian tribes their jurisdiction over major offenses. Thus, major felonies involving an Indian, whether as victim or accused, are matters for federal prosecution and on most of the nearly three hundred Indian reservations, the federal government retains the sole authority to prosecute felony crime. The Supreme Court has ruled that, like all other federal regulation of Indian affairs, the Major Crimes Act is not based on racial classification, but rather "is rooted in the unique status of Indians as 'a separate people' with their own political institutions. Federal regulation of Indian tribes, therefore, is governance of once-sovereign political communities; it is not to be viewed as legislation of a 'racial' group consisting of Indians."[54] Initially, the act covered seven felonies (crimes which carry a maximum penalty of more than one year imprisonment); today, their number stands at sixteen. The amended act reads:

> Any Indian who commits against the person or property of another Indian or other person any of the following offenses, namely murder, manslaughter, kidnapping, rape, carnal knowledge of any female, not his wife, who has not attained the age of 16 years, assault with a dangerous weapon, assault resulting in serious bodily injury, arson, burglary, robbery, and larceny within the Indian

country, shall be subjected to the same laws and penalties as all other persons committing any of the above offenses, with the exclusive jurisdiction of the United States.

Crimes committed on Indian lands and not covered by the U.S. Code are within the jurisdiction of the Indian court system, a principle reinforced by the landmark decision by the U.S. Supreme Court, *Williams v. Lee*, which in 1959 affirmed tribal court authority in reservation-based claims. The investigation of major crimes, it should be noted, is not without serious difficulties, with lines of responsibility and authority often unclear or jumbled, and efforts to resolve problems underfunded, or unfunded. Instead, as one journalistic investigation recently noted, "With several agencies potentially involved—both tribal and federal—major investigations offer an opportunity for broad mutual support. Instead, they are hampered by cross-cutting jurisdictional lines, poor communication, thin resources and a vast lack of accountability."[55]

Generally, U.S. tribal courts resemble in some important respects those of the Anglo-American judicial system found at the local, state and federal levels.[56] As Deloria and Lytle noted, "Judges sometimes wear robes, witnesses are called to testify, attempts are made to keep testimony relevant, the litigants are permitted to have judicial advocates, and tribal court decisions are subject to appeal."[57] However, many Indian judges are not lawyers and, because there is usually no professional counsel present, take an active role in hearings and trials. Tribal courts are not usually courts of record and rarely are written opinions handed down. Many tribal judges act in a manner more akin to the head of a family trying to mediate a dispute, with the desired outcome one in which the entire community is seen to benefit rather than one in which an individual offender is punished.

The goal of adversarial law in the Anglo-American tradition, noted Robert Yazzie, Chief Justice of the Navajo Nation Court from 1992-2003, "is to punish wrongdoers and teach them a lesson. Adversarial law and adjudication offer only a win-lose solution; it is a zero-sum game. Navajo justice prefers a win-win solution." He added:

Navajos do not think of equality as treating people as equal *before* the law; they are equal *in* the law. Again, our Navajo language points this out in practical terms: When a Navajo is charged with a crime, in the vertical system of justice the judge asks (in English), "Are you guilty or not guilty?" A Navajo cannot respond because there is no precise term for "guilty" in the Navajo language. The word "guilt" implies a moral fault, which demands punishment. It is a nonsense word in Navajo law because of the focus on healing, integration with the group, and the end goal of nourishing ongoing relationships with the immediate and extended family, relatives, neighbors, and community.[58]

Although in the United States the selection process varies from tribe to tribe, judges are frequently people appointed by the tribal council due to the respect with which they are held in the community. Other selection methods include being chosen by community religious leaders or through a general election in which all tribal members participate. In the Navajo Nation, which has the world's largest tribal court system, judges are appointed for a life term and, after completing a probationary period, can be removed only for cause. While formal education in non-Indian law is not a requirement—providing as it does neither an understanding of, nor an appreciation for, Indian customs and traditions— familiarity with tribal custom is considered an essential prerequisite for being selected. The informality of tribal courts helps to reassure tribal members that they are being offered a forum for the resolution of disputes among tribal members in accordance with their traditions, with the primary goal being mediation and consensual restitution, rather than ascertaining guilt then inflicting punishment upon the offender.

The emphasis on mediation and resolution of disputes rather than the adversarial system of the Anglo-American justice means that tribal hearings are often convened not to determine guilt or innocence, but to negotiate some appropriate form of restitution. (Technical guilt or innocence is not considered sufficient in Indian communities; if an offender is declared innocent in an Anglo-American court because of a technical violation, he or she will nonetheless be shunned by the tribe since the transgressor has neither paid for nor reflected upon his/her actions.) Not only is the offender involved in the tribal court process, but also the victim, the "elders" and/or family members. Working together, these determine what punishment is appropriate and allows for both restitution and rehabilitation. "Cleansing ceremonies" are frequently held once restitution has been made and punishment/reconciliation effected.

Law enforcement in Indian country can be carried out by any one of four types of state agents, including tribal police, the Bureau of Indian Affairs (BIA) through its Division of Law Enforcement Services, other federal law enforcement, and state and local law agencies, or a combination of any of the above. Enforcement is handled by many tribal governments through the use of police officers contracted with federal funds under the Indian Self-Determination Act of 1975 and with appropriated funds from the tribe itself.[59]

The administration of justice on tribal lands in the United States does, to be sure, have many imperfections, as a six-month-long investigation by the *Denver Post* conducted in 2007 showed; and many of these imperfections are related to continuing problems in the relationship the tribes have with the federal government. In "some of the most violent and impoverished places in America," where drug-related crimes are on the upswing, the *Post* found that "Indian reservations are also plagued by a systematic breakdown in the delivery of justice." The series cited U.S. attorneys and FBI investigators who faced "huge challenges" in the fight against reservation crime. Seen as outsiders not to be trusted, they work in remote locations where alcohol abuse is high among witnesses, as well as victims and suspects, making serious crimes "very difficult to prove." At the same time, "institutional resistance to using the high-powered federal judicial machine to prosecute run-of-the-mill violent crime" accompanies on-going budget shortfalls and competing federal priorities. Efforts to increase the number of federal agents and magistrate judges dealing with reservation crimes ran into opposition from some tribes worried that such measures would enhance federal power. And because felony crime is the province of the federal government, with the nearest prosecutorial offices sometimes hundreds of miles away, as many as 65 percent of all felony cases are declined for prosecution. Vernon Roanhorse, a Navajo tribal prosecutor interviewed by the newspaper said of the federal justice system flatly: "They've created a lawless land."[60]

Nonetheless, tribal administration of justice has worked to strengthen the cultural identity and self-determination of Indian peoples in the United States. U.S. Indian leaders, and their counterparts within the federal government, can make an important contribution to hemispheric security and democratization by pro-actively sharing that knowledge with those Native peoples in Latin America desirous of protecting their lands, access to resources and cultural inheritance through a fully representative democratic franchise.

The Example of the Inuit People

Another example of particular relevance to indigenous peoples in "Latin" America is the case of the Inuit people of northern Canada. There the evolution of land claims policy—a constant in the efforts of Canada's Native peoples to maintain their heritage—also allowed the Inuit to become politically empowered for the first time in the modern era. They became stakeholders with voice and vote in a region whose modernization suddenly moved into overdrive with the thawing of frozen lands associated with an international rush to claim land, water and resources in a territory that is rich with all three. In two recent works— *Breaking the Ice: From Land Claims to Tribal Sovereignty in the Arctic* and *On Thin Ice: The Inuit, the State, and the Challenge of Arctic Sovereignty*—Zellen has shown the ways in which the Inuit example offers a striking contrast to the declamatory and divisive goals of Latin American populists, all the more so because in the Canadian case they have been so successful. There security issues were broadly defined—taking advantage of Canada's long-standing view that environmental protection was also a national security question—to incorporate local and indigenous perspectives that reflected their rights and values. The arrangement forged between the Inuit and the national government not only allows for remediation and compensation when activities such as oil drilling and mining scar the land or leave the environment contaminated, "itself a big win for the Native peoples who not too long ago were neither consulted nor compensated," Zellen points out. But in addition,

With the real political gains of land claims and the various self-government processes, Natives are positioned to reap huge rewards from the coming wave of development. They own most of the coastal land, have significant regulatory powers and various co-management regimes that will ensure numerous benefits, from training and employment, including indigenous hiring and tendering preferences, to royalties, compensation, and remediation guarantees. The Inuit will find themselves in a central role not unlike that now enjoyed by the Saudi royal family.[61]

The process, of course, has not solved all the Inuit's problems. The Arctic people still wrestle with steep learning curves in capitalism, the ways and means of interfacing with modernity and globalization, as well as with their limited management experience. Crushing social problems remain—such as poor housing and education, high suicide, infant mortality and alcoholism rates, and low life expectancy; political accountability mechanisms remain weak and, in large measure a result of this, cronyism and other corruptions accompany large cash settlements past, present and—perhaps—future. But few other Native peoples in the world embark on this new journey with as many things in their favor as the Inuit. "The Nunavut experiment, blending an historic, comprehensive land claim settlement with the creation of a new, predominantly Inuit territorial government, could fail, despite its structural innovations and paradigm-shifting advances in self-government," Zellen noted. "Success will require closer, and more continuous attention, by Ottawa, and more time, experience, training, and education will be required by the Inuit."

It should be noted here that other, more numerous, indigenous peoples in Canada do not share the Inuit's current and prospective good fortune. "Canadians are largely ignorant of the extent to which we experience paternalism, absurd irony and very real oppression," H. Freddy Sweetgrass, a Toronto-based Ojibwa writer wrote recently. "The Indian Affairs Minister and staff are never Indian. And yet they, as part of an immigrant government, decide who is and who is not indigenous to the land, granting 'status' where 'applicable.' . . . The Indian Act . . . [t]his Draconian and discriminatory piece of legislation treats natives as wards of the state, as children, controlling nearly every aspect of their lives. It has allowed the theft of Indian lands that were too close to populous towns, the deposing of traditional governments in place of corrupt band councils and their exclusion from economic life . . ." Noted Phil Fontaine, national chief of the Assembly of First Nations: "Poverty among Canada's first nations peoples rivals Third World conditions. It's this country's dirty little secret." And in late 2008, two Canadian Marxists, surveying the high rates of substance abuse, violence and poverty faced by First Peoples in that country, created a firestorm when they published a book provocatively entitled *Disrobing the Aboriginal Industry; The Deception Behind Indigenous Cultural Preservation.* In it, they claimed the policies proposed by the government to address indigenous needs—

land claims and self-government—were the very measures contributing to the fortification of their dependency. For his part Zellen underscores "the emergence of a shrewd and powerful political elite that has helped the Inuit make huge political gains, particularly in comparison with the much larger Indian population to their south, who in many respects suffered more, and yet have won far fewer concessions from the state." [62]

The fate of the Inuit might have been different had native land rights not moved into the national spotlight in a way not too different from myriad experiences in Latin America. By the late 1980s, both the promise and the abject failure to redeem Canada's relationship with its indigenous peoples could be heard in the complaint voiced by one Indian representative: "We have lived up to our side of the treaties, but the rights promised to us have been neglected. . . . To us a treaty is an international document signed by two nations." In 1990, the small town of Oka was the site of a violent showdown between Native peoples—in this case the Mohawk—the Canadian police and, later, the Canadian army. A Québec police officer charging the barricades erected by a militant Mohawk faction during a 78-day armed standoff was shot and killed. The specter of indigenous armed conflict, Zellen wrote, "paralyzed the nation, and hinted at the dangers that would ensue should the path of militancy and armed resistance, and an armed response by the state, be chosen." [63]

Not only did the crisis help to increase the public awareness of the concerns of Canada's indigenous citizens, who rode a wave of public sympathy from Anglo-Canadians. It also led to a highly visible Royal Commission that in 1996 issued a lengthy report on its findings. For the Canadian government, the violence assured it would honor the Nunavut Land Claims Agreement of 1993, which set the stage for the creation of the largest and newest federal territory in Canada, seven hundred seventy thousand square miles in all, the home to the country's thirty thousand Inuit. The land claims negotiations, an elaborate process of negotiation between non-Indians and Inuit, created both corporate structures and co-management systems that enabled the Inuit to enjoy an unusual degree of self-government allowing the Native people more than a semblance of control not only of their lands, but also the terrain upon which indigenous culture interfaced with myriad forms of modernity and globalization. The talks, conducted in a democratic framework of mutual respect, helped both sides understand the countervailing interests within their own forces, adding to the impetus for a successful conclusion to the negotiations. "By letting go, central authorities were in fact strengthening their hand, gaining greater political legitimacy through their new collaboration, co-management, and devolutionary policies," Zellen noted. The settlement of land claims, he added, has allowed the Inuit to move on to those challenges having to do with restoring self-government. Their relative control over the environmental impact on their homeland of external development efforts have given the Inuit a potential "hammer" to assert their values; the environmental assessments becoming "extremely important" as a way for the indigenous group "to stand at the crossroads of the ongoing debate between development and conservation." Such independence is important not only vis-à-vis the federal government. As historian Shelagh D. Grant observed: "Most environmental activists thought their efforts to halt further development in the Arctic would be welcomed, failing to understand that a pristine wilderness could not provide a viable economy sufficient to sustain the Inuit people."[64]

Across the nation-state border, in the United States, respect for democratic rules and procedures have also resulted in positive results. "Even in places like Alaska, where strong state interests have been pitted against the Native community in a long battle over who controls the resource wealth extracted from the land, the situation between state and tribe is far more harmonious than between state and tribe in other parts of the world, where ethnic violence and civil warfare have erupted in response to the same centrifugal forces," Zellen said. The blending by the tribe and the state of contemporary constitutional, economic and political institutions, he added, "defines the very essence of neotribalism—neither a surrender to the forces of assimilation, colonialism, or even imperial occupation; nor a rejection of the modern state outright. . . . The transformation of the land claims model from being a tool of assimilation, wielded by state against peripheral and interior tribes, into a tool of empowerment wielded by the tribe against those very forces of assimilation induced by the continued penetration of the modern state into its frontier region . . . suggests the potential for a synthesis to the long conflict between state and tribe since the modern era of nation-states began." The Canadian example stands in stark contrast to that of Perú, where the government of Alan Garcia stubbornly holds to the idea that Amazonian tribes control only the surface rights of their lands, to which his government can, without consultation, lease subsoil mineral rights to outside companies, a stance mirrored by Ecuador's leftwing populist Correa.[65]

The Canadian case, in particular, provides an important contrast to the country with the Hemisphere's largest indigenous communities—Mexico. There the Mexican state continues to be embarked on efforts to enforce sovereignty, rather than making it more attractive, the latter approach the focus from Ottawa.

In an important work, Mexican researchers Araceli Burgete Cal y Mayor and Miguel Gómez Gómez show how, in the aftermath of the Zapatista revolt and under their assumed tutelage, with indigenous mobilization waning, the Mexican state has reestablished its hegemony under the guise of a purported multiculturalism, enforcing a universal local government model that ignores the sociocultural diversity of indigenous political organization. In fact, Burgete Cal y Mayor and Gómez Gómez point out, today the state of Chiapas actually enjoys less autonomy than it did before the Zapatista uprising. Despite the agreement reached at San Andrés Larráinzar, where talks began in January of 1996 to discuss the subject of indigenous rights and culture, and after the—for Mexico—novel phenomenon of political party alternation in the presidential palace, the constitutional reform of 2001 did not result in promised autonomy and the right of self-determination for indigenous Mexicans, but rather the return of heteronymous relations, those in which Indians are once again subject to external laws or domination. "One can say that today there is not a single indigenous state policy to address the ethnic-national question in the country," Burgete Cal y Mayor and Gómez Gómez added. "The differing links are left at the mercy of the specific dynamics in which various indigenous regions insert themselves into (the process of) globalization." Although the constitutional reform formally recognizes autonomy and self-determination, the means under which they are to be implemented make the putting into practices of such guarantees "empty" gestures, incapable of being put into effect.

> By means of a strategy of recognizing "empty rights," the State again takes hold of the prerogative of deciding which institutions, what indigenous cultural practices and characteristics 'are recognized," which rights, institutions and practices ought to be protected and strengthened, and which ought to be eliminated and eventually criminalized and persecuted . . . . Those that are not "recognized" remain outside the law. . . . The gravest issue is the prerogative assumed by the Nation-State to decide what are "autonomous" indigenous institutions. . . . It is important to underline the fact that in this indigenous rights and policies of recognition have been subordinated, placed as a screen that justifies the new state reengineering that reconstructs a new State hegemony in indigenous zones, in the post-1994 Chiapas.[66]

As Subcomandante Marcos and his armed followers lose their profile and their relevance to even some of their leftist colleagues, the Mexican state has carefully re-created its authority vis-à-vis indigenous communities. The 2001 reforms strengthened the federal executive, legislative and judicial powers in what Burgete Cal y Mayor and Gómez Gómez called an effort to reconstruct state hegemony over indigenous territories, much of which was done without consultation of Indian peoples themselves. It also increased state jurisdiction over Native communities by refining and increasing its presence and opportunities to intervene in local affairs. Customary law, although mentioned in the statutes, was not given the status of a "right," making any efforts to create local indigenous tribunals necessarily subordinate to state and federal judicial bodies. "As occurred in the 1970s with the creation of the National Council of Indian Peoples (CNPI)," Burgete Cal y Mayor and Gómez Gómez noted, "the recognition of 'self government' that promotes indigenous representation was fenced in by institutions that the government could homogenize and corporatize as moldable counterparts." In the ten years following the armed conflict, they added, "Chiapas Indians lost their autonomy and have seen their autonomous openings weakened."[67] In the context of a nation-state weakened by organized crime and other rampant lawlessness, it is difficult to see how such a welter of legal exclusion and marginalization helps Mexico functionally protect its own sovereignty, particularly when traditional communities, too, operate within a system of laws and values.

As this book was being sent to the publisher, the author received an e-mail from a young Canadian undergraduate student, She was preparing a senior honors project for her college involving a comparative study of the experiences of First Nations in British Colombia and indigenous peoples of Mexico seeking to, in her words, "exert their identity and reclaim their autonomy." The woman grew up in a coastal community in British Colombia, home to one of the largest Indian tribes in the province, a geographically beautiful place with what she remembers as an "unspoken rule of division and racism." Growing up she wondered how Indians could "live in such poverty, suffer from alcoholism, mental illness, drug addiction and health problems despite receiving so much 'help' from the government." In 2009, the woman traveled to Mexico on a study abroad program; from the eyes of those new to this world, clarity. "While I am aware that the situation of indigenous peoples in Mexico is very diverse, there, in the Zapatista movement, I saw for the first time indigenous people who were strong, proud and demanding that their voice be heard," she wrote. This contrasted with what she recalled as the failure of a state dependency system back home and the apparent despondency and depression of the Natives peoples she knew while growing up. "I know the comparison is not so black and white," she added. "There are many movements of empowered First Nations people in British Colombia and many impoverished indigenous peoples in Mexico." These complexities, she concluded, were what she hoped to explore in her own research.

Hers is a subject that should concern us all.

Chapter Fourteen
Conclusions

"My American Indian policy begins with creating a bond between an Obama administration and the tribal nations all across this country. We need more than just a government-to-government relationship; we need a nation-to-nation relationship, and I will make sure that tribal nations have a voice in the White House."
—U.S. presidential candidate Barack Obama[1]

"It's time to quit being loyal Canadians? . . . We don't need the white man's money. We need a share of our own wealth . . . . There are only two ways of dealing with the white man: Either you pick up a gun or you stand between him and his money."
—Terrance Nelson, Chief
Roseau River First Nation, Manitoba
CTV News, May 15, 2007

"The time of islands is over. Insularity is now the province of madmen and doomed societies."
—Earl Shorris, *The Death of the Great Spirit* (1968)

The emergence of Indian nationalism within the context of increased activism by some of the Western hemisphere's poorest and historically marginalized peoples, and the ethnonationalist reaction from some of the descendants of those who arrived in the hemisphere after Christopher Colombus, raise fundamental questions about democratic governance in Latin America. From international relations theory, the question of security dilemmas—occurring when two parties end up going to war, even when neither wishes to harm the other—looms in the background, as ethnic communities extending even beyond those of pre-1492 indigenous peoples, such as the Maroons, Garifuna and others, vie to wrest enough power and autonomy to enjoy "the attributes of sovereignty."[2]

Today in several countries in "Latin" America, Felix Cohen's observation that treatment of Indians reflects the rise and fall of a people's democratic faith is being put to the test, in others his dictum is in some ways in danger of being turned on its head. Will the just empowerment of Native peoples and real respect for not just their "symbolic" rights of within the nation-state, the respect for their customs, traditions, and forms of political organization, but also effective recognition of their claims to lands and access to natural resources, be fairly balanced against the equally immutable rights and dignity of the sons and daughters, or great grandsons and great granddaughters, of those who once repressed them?

Writing about the United States, author Earl Shorris points out that in the 1960s both politically militant and traditionalist Indians made the false assumption "that an Indian oppressor would not be an oppressor because he is an Indian . . . the linking of race and culture, the absurd trap baited with identity, goi[ng] the next step and defin[ing] the essence of the individual prior to action."[3] And, as cited earlier, an important warning is offered by political scientists Joshua S. Goldstein and Jon C. Pevehouse, that when conflicts take on an ethnic cast, they become harder to resolve, "because they are not about 'who gets what' but about 'I don't like you.' . . . Almost all the means of leverage used in such conflicts are negative, and bargains are very hard to reach. So ethnic conflicts tend to drag on without resolution for generations."[4] Of course, Native Americans might reasonably point out that it was just such conflicts that have stripped from them their rights and resources from the arrival of Columbus onward; those familiar with hemispheric pre-history might counter that such clashes stretched back even earlier.

Even as hemispheric politics continue to experience the tectonic shifts of current ethnic pride and nationalism, questions still remain as to where the high-water mark of indigenous rights and community and national organization will be found, or, as political scientist Donna Lee Van Cott seemed to somewhat gloomily suggest just before her death, has it been reached already? Can the various Indian communities always be counted on to vote, in their common interest, as a bloc? The experience of Rigoberta Menchú in majority Indian Guatemala offers a suggestive "no" to that question. If the emerging indigenous agenda lacks programmatic cohesion, a dose of pragmatism and a shared identity and vision, will the inclusion of Indians into the governments of nation-states merely mean the number of normally fractious national political parties will go from, say, a half dozen to twenty or more? Or perhaps will the potential for social transformation sometimes offered by the Native American critique of the modern society, and thus a fount of their multicultural attractiveness as an alternative way of doing politics, fully fade, as clientelistic, populist and corrupt figures acting in their name come to dominate their democratic franchise, as has already been the experience with non-Indian elites around the region? Can the necessary decentralization that comes with real autonomy for peoples work effectively, so that the governmental efficiency of states already under scrutiny is not questioned even further?

What role will religion and education play in reconstructing the national or pluri-national character of existing states? And what role will Indians who practice European-centered religions have in any new nation-states and regional order, a question that in today's Bolivia acquires a certain urgency. How do Indians decide where the appropriate balance is in being part of the state apparatus and the larger political society, when their very participation can be seen as potentially threatening to the political and cultural autonomy that forms key elements of the Indian agenda?

Throughout the Hemisphere, recorded history is replete with examples of Indians who sided with European colonizers against other indigenous peoples precisely because they wanted to get back at other indigenous peoples who had oppressed them, as occurred when Spanish conqueror Hernán Cortéz took Mexico. In countries such as Argentina, Bolivia, Ecuador, Guatemala and Mexico, where the history of those pre-Conquest empires was also one of subjugation and exploitation, will the descendants of the less fortunate living in the Americas before the arrival of Christopher Colombus agree to a "national" identity taken from a dominant, though indigenous, rival group?

Will the new embrace of national Indian ancestors form the sustaining myth necessary to either cause a "nation" within an existing state to press for secession or to seek to force the combination of two or more existing nation-states to recapture the imperial splendor of a pre-Conquest past, even as anthropologists and other social scientists struggle to "avoid the trap" of presenting the contemporary cultures of indigenous peoples as "the ossified artifacts of a bygone epoch"?[5] (Care needs to be taken, lest even those of best intentions, seeking democratic empowerment and the remediation of historical wrongs, as well as those on the other side, fall into the kind of distortions that have received purchase, among others, by the many admirers of ancient Rome, as those in Mussolini's Italy, and in the aftermath of the U.S. Civil War, the defeated true believers who elevated the memory of the antebellum South, not only minimizing the effects of slavery, but promoting it as a benign institution. As historian David W. Blight has noted in the latter case, the white South's "Lost Cause" ideology sought to enshrine the Old South as "America's classical past, a terrible and fascinating civilization that multitudes wished to redeem and admire because it was lost." These and other examples were a siren's song particularly attractive to those whose present condition left them nostalgic for previous privilege.)[6]

Or will the pan-Mayan vision found in Guatemala, "the scholarly and educational routes to social change and nation building," find purchase among peoples whose needs are many, including the need to survive, endure and eventually prosper.

And, who will have the deciding voice in the distribution, when not redistribution, of resources coming from the land itself?

In early 2009, *The New York Times* headlined: "In Bolivia, Untapped Bounty Meets Nationalism," referring to the fact of gathering storm clouds in the country that held almost half the world's lithium deposits, a key mineral for producing more fuel efficient cars that countries need to escape their dependence on foreign oil. The Morales government, it reported, favored "closely controlling the lithium itself and keeping foreigners at bay." However, local indigenous groups in the desert region where the mineral is found have their own ideas, demanding a share of future rewards. "We know that Bolivia can become the Saudi Arabia of lithium," a leader of salt gatherers and quinoa grain producers told *The Times*. "We are poor, but we are not stupid peasants. The lithium may be Bolivia's, but it is also our property." Caught between nationalist plans and local ethnic claims, how will Morales, and others like him or who profess similar ideas, react in the future? If the harvesters of Bolivian salt, like the Inuit sitting on vast petroleum reserves in the thawing north of Canada, already see themselves as possibly the local equivalents of the Bedouin potentates that emerged from the deserts of the Middle East, how will they react to demands for solidarity, including material support, from other peoples and tribes? What might happen if local authorities quote Morales' slogan—that he seeks "not bosses, but partners"—back to him?[7]

Finally, is the emergence of Native American peoples as principal protagonists in their own countries' history the harbinger of the expanded democratic franchise, or the beginning of the kind of internecine strife which, as in case of Eastern Europe, wound its way into the swamp of classes of undesired peoples forced into exile, privation, or worse? Will a legacy of aggrandizing, neocolonial ethnic cleansing be repaid with the self-assertion of those historically, and in some cases even contemporaneously, the victims of devalued citizenship, or worse?

The first option has given Indian militancy legitimacy in international forums; the writings of Kedourie, Gellner, and others, including the former Aymara vice president of Bolivia, Victor Hugo Cárdenas, suggest the latter is a possibility. Native American experience may thus resemble in unexpected and undesired ways the fate of Kosovo, Kenya,[8] China, and other countries wracked outside the region by ethnic strife.

In a worst case scenario, Indian ultra-nationalism could result in the trading of one case of historic domination for another, the latter extending not only to non-Indians but also those indigenous peoples with less political or economic clout, or those seen not to share a common vision of the past. Posen, who writes on security dilemmas and ethnic conflict, has noted that in a non-American context, when groups need to arrive at judgments of others' intentions, "[t]he main mechanism they will use is history, how did the other group behave the last time..."[9]

Writing about the run-up to the U.S. Civil War, David M. Potter traced the dynamic that ended up tearing the still-young nation-state apart. In isolation from each other, in both North and South realities were replaced by stereotypes, the to-and-fro of politics became inescapable points of principle, and political action was transformed "from a process of accommodation to a mode of combat." And in that way, politics was replaced by war.[10]

It is important to realize that the resurgence of ethnonationalism south of the U.S. border will require a tectonic shift in perspectives in the north, to a wider scope in viewing regional history. Historian Jerry Z. Muller explains that people in the United States (and surely policymakers in Washington) find "ethnonationalism discomfiting both intellectually and morally," perhaps an enduring inheritance of Tocqueville's observation that the country was loath to "derive its belief from a proper study of the past." As Muller explained:

> Social scientists go to great lengths to demonstrate that it is a product not of nature but of culture, often deliberately constructed. And ethicists scorn value systems based on narrow group identities rather than cosmopolitanism. But none of this will make ethnonationalism go away. Immigrants to the United States usually arrive with a willingness to fit into their new country and reshape their identities accordingly. But for those who remain behind in lands where their ancestors have lived for generations, if not centuries, political identities often take ethnic form, producing competing communal claims to political power. The creation of a peaceful regional order of nation-states has usually been the product of a violent process of ethnic separation.[11]

The creation of an orderly legal basis for restoring and respecting indigenous rights and a framework for adjudicating the righting of past wrongs, the work of many indigenous advocates and international organizations, is a positive contribution to the shaping and informing of modern law. Such efforts will help to make democracy real for millions of people still outside the arc of its benefits, address the unfinished business of decolonization in the hemisphere, and offer a broad assurance that the clock will not be turned back on Indian progress. As we have seen, expanded concepts of property rights, including acceptance of communal and ancestral lands and the need for the prior consent of their inhabitants, is key to future progress.

At the same time, Indians in Latin America remain one group in a vast majority in Latin America who do not have either voice nor effective vote in the politics, economies and—for those and related reasons—in the futures of their own countries. Indian demands need necessarily be part of the region's adoption of a democratic governing system that allows all to participate fully, not just as tenuous clients and peripheral shareholders during elections. If Indian rights are, as Cohen eloquently suggested, the miner's canary of democracy, then it is important to remember that others beside the songbird are at risk when toxic airs are present.

The opponents of a morally mandated and democratically required rebirth of indigenous rights often engage in heated, hate-tinged rearguard actions that put them outside the mainstream of the world debate. Yet one point with which even they might agree is worth heeding.

To judge earlier times by today's ethical and behavioral standards risks holding peoples from those eras responsible for not viewing the world then as we do today. By ignoring the idea of the evolution of all societies and of historic change, the end game could be the denial of any good in everything that happened since a long-gone glorious moment that beckons in memory, but perhaps less in fact. The result then would not be a new accommodation based on respect, but rather an increase in miserly commonalties that reflect enduring hurt and mutual recrimination.

In that case, the outcome is likely to be a cycle of vengeance and violence between races and cultures that have not learned, and which would have continued to refuse to learn, to abide by the rules of multi-ethnic and multi-cultural democracy, to which all contesting parties have much to contribute.[12]

Appendices
U.S. State Department Annual Human Rights Country Reports 2008

Sections on Indigenous Peoples

Bolivia

In the 2001 census, approximately 62 percent of the population over 15 years of age identified themselves as indigenous, primarily from the Quechua and Aymara groups. The IACHR reported that 70 percent of these indigenous people lived in poverty or extreme poverty, with little access to education or to minimal services to support human health, such as clean drinking water and sanitation systems.

Indigenous lands are not demarcated fully, and land reform remained a central political issue. Historically, a majority of indigenous people shared lands collectively under the "ayllu" system, a system that was not legally recognized during the transition to private property laws. Despite laws mandating reallocation and titling of lands, recognition and demarcation of indigenous lands have not been resolved. Indigenous people protested the government's failure to provide them with title to all of their claimed territories; they also objected to outside exploitation of their resources. Indigenous peasants illegally occupied several private properties, often with the backing of the Landless Movement.

Indigenous groups used the Popular Participation Law to form municipalities that offered them greater opportunities for self-determination. Several political parties, citizens' groups, and NGOs actively promoted the rights of indigenous people, although progress was minimal. Indigenous people continued to be underrepresented in government and politics, and indigenous groups bore a disproportionate share of poverty and unemployment. Government educational and health services remained unavailable to many indigenous groups living in remote areas. The government tried to improve the situation with the delivery of pensions to the elderly and funding for youth to attend school.

Discrimination against indigenous groups was extensive. On May 24, large opposition gangs, encouraged by local civic leaders from Sucre, captured and humiliated a progovernment group of approximately two dozen indigenous workers and leaders, who journeyed to Sucre to ensure President Morales could enter the city. A mob took the group prisoner, beat several of them, and forced many of the men to take off their shirts and march several miles to the central plaza, where they were forced to kneel and shout antigovernment slogans.

Chile

The law gives indigenous people (approximately 5 percent of the total population) the right to participate in decisions affecting their lands, cultures, and traditions and provides for bilingual education in schools with indigenous populations. Approximately one-half of the self-identified indigenous population remained separated from the rest of society, largely due to historical, cultural, educational, and geographical factors. Both internal factors and governmental policies limited the participation of indigenous people in governmental decisions affecting their lands, cultures, traditions, and the allocation of natural resources. Indigenous people also experienced some societal discrimination and reported incidents in which they were attacked and harassed. According to the 2006 Socioeconomic Characteristics Survey, the indigenous population's poverty rate dropped 10 percent since 2003, and the gap between indigenous and nonindigenous poverty narrowed more than 5 percent.

The National Corporation for Indigenous Development (CONADI), which included directly elected indigenous representatives, advised and directed government programs to assist the economic development of indigenous people. According to CONADI, in 2007 approximately 40,000 acres were transferred and registered as indigenous lands, benefiting approximately 1,000 Mapuche families. During the year the Ministry of Education and CONADI provided scholarships to nearly 44,000 indigenous elementary, high school, and college students, compared with approximately 42,000 in 2007. Indigenous groups noted, however, that the scholarships were actually small stipends to cover living expenses and did not cover tuition costs.

There were isolated instances of violent confrontations between indigenous Mapuche groups and landowners, logging companies, and local government authorities in the southern part of the country. The actions normally took the form of protests. Instances of rock throwing, land occupations, and burning crops, buildings, or vehicles occurred occasionally. The Coordinadora Arauco Malleco (CAM), an indigenous group that has been accused of domestic terrorist acts, reportedly initiated many of these actions.

There were reports of police abuse against Mapuche individuals and communities and harassment of NGOs associated with the promotion of indigenous rights. On January 3, police shot and killed 22-year-old Matias Catrileo while he and approximately 30 other Mapuche individuals occupied private land and destroyed crops in Vilcun. A military court indicted Corporal Walter Ramirez for the shooting, but he remained free and on active duty with the case pending at year's end.

The Observatory of Indigenous People's Rights (OIPR) reported incidents of police searches of indigenous homes without a warrant, arrest and release of indigenous individuals without a detention control hearing, and police use of intimidation and discriminatory statements against indigenous individuals including minors. The OIPR also reported that individuals and organizations that defend indigenous rights were subject to threats.

On November 3, a court absolved alleged CAM member Avelino Menaco of involvement in an October 2007 arson fire. The Prosecutor's Office filed an appeal that was pending at year's end. Also pending at year's end were investigations regarding the 2007 arrests of two other Mapuche CAM members under charges of arms possession or arson.

Colombia

The constitution and laws give special recognition to the fundamental rights of indigenous people, who comprised approximately 2 percent of the population, and require that the government consult beforehand with indigenous groups regarding governmental actions that could affect them.

By law indigenous groups have perpetual rights to their ancestral lands. Traditional indigenous authorities operated approximately 545 reservations—accounting for 30 percent of the country's territory—as municipal entities, with officials selected according to indigenous traditions. However, many indigenous communities had no legal title to lands they claimed, and illegal armed groups often violently contested indigenous land ownership. The National Agrarian Reform Institute administered a program to buy lands declared to belong to indigenous communities and return those lands to them.

The law provides for special criminal and civil jurisdictions within indigenous territories based on traditional community laws. Proceedings in these jurisdictions were subject to manipulation and often rendered punishments that *were more lenient than those imposed by regular civilian courts. The law permits indigenous communities to educate their children in traditional dialects and in the observance of cultural and religious customs. Indigenous men are not subject to the national military draft.*

Indigenous leaders complained about the occasional presence of government security forces on indigenous reservations and asked that the government consult with indigenous authorities prior to taking military action against illegal armed groups and guerrillas operating in or around such areas. The government stated that for security reasons it could not provide advance notice of most military operations and that it consulted with indigenous leaders when possible before accessing land held by the communities. The law permits the presence of government security forces on lands of indigenous communities; however, Ministry of Defense directives instructed security forces to respect the integrity of indigenous communities, particularly during military and police operations.

The Ministry of Interior and Justice, through its Office of Indigenous Affairs, is responsible for protecting the territorial, cultural, and traditional rights of indigenous people. Ministry representatives resided in all regions of the country and worked with other governmental human rights organizations and NGOs to promote indigenous interests and investigate violations of indigenous rights.

Despite special legal protections and government assistance programs, indigenous people continued to suffer discrimination and often lived on the margins of society. Parties in the internal armed conflict continued to victimize members of indigenous communities. In March UNHCHR reported that ethnic groups, particularly indigenous and Afro-Colombian populations, were increasingly vulnerable as a result of the internal armed conflict. ONIC reported that violence during the year killed 43 indigenous persons and displaced 7,190 others.

The Presidential Program on Human Rights reported a reduction in homicides (28 percent), kidnappings (25 percent), displacement (54 percent), and forced migration of indigenous peoples in the first eight months of the year. Investigations continued at year's end into allegations that, in February and March 2006, military officials beat Wayuu indigenous community members, Roberto Solano Uriana and Lorenzo Rafael Solano.

In August 2006 hooded gunmen in Ricaurte, Narino, killed five members of the Awa indigenous community, including a former governor of the Chinbuza indigenous reserve. An investigation by the Prosecutor General's Office identified 11 suspects, of whom six were military officers and five were civilians. Authorities detained seven of the suspects and were searching for the remaining four.

The UNHCHR continued to criticize threats and violence against indigenous communities, characterized government investigations of human rights violations against indigenous groups as inadequate, and appealed to the government to do more to protect indigenous people.

Ecuador

Estimates of those who maintained their indigenous cultural identity and lived in indigenous communities varied between 7 and 20 percent of the population. The vast majority of indigenous citizens resided in rural areas, including the highlands and the Amazonian provinces. Despite their political influence and the advocacy efforts of grassroots community groups, indigenous people continued to suffer discrimination at many levels of society and, with few exceptions, were at the bottom of the socioeconomic scale.

Arable land was scarce in the more heavily populated highland areas, where high infant mortality, malnutrition, and epidemic disease were common among the indigenous population. Electricity and potable water often were unavailable. Although the rural education system was seriously deficient, many indigenous groups participated with the Ministry of Education in the development of the bilingual education program used in rural public schools.

The 2008 constitution strengthens rights of indigenous peoples; it declares the state plurinational, recognizing Kichwa and Shuar as "official languages of intercultural relations," and specifically recognizes indigenous justice. Existing law also recognizes the rights of indigenous communities to hold property communally, to administer traditional community justice in certain cases, and to be consulted before natural resources are exploited in community territories. Indigenous people also have the same civil and political rights as other citizens.

The former and new constitutions grant indigenous peoples the right to participate in decisions about the exploitation of non-renewable resources that are located in their lands and that could affect their culture or environment. They allow indigenous people to participate in the benefits the projects may bring and to receive compensation for the damage that could result. The 2008 constitution mandates, in the case of environmental damage, immediate corrective government action and full restitution from the responsible company. However, some indigenous organizations asserted a lack of consultation and remedial action.

Indigenous groups lobbied the government, enlisted the help of foreign and domestic NGOs, and mounted protests in attempts to win a greater share of oil revenues and a greater voice in natural resource and development decisions. Colonists, drug traffickers, and loggers illegally encroached into indigenous territory. Corrupt local officials, a lack of political will, and divisions among and within indigenous communities undermined indigenous efforts to stop the flow of illegally harvested timber. Widespread environmental damage, in part due to deforestation and petroleum production, constituted another serious problem.

The ombudsman's office had representatives in indigenous communities throughout the country. These had responsibility for promoting human and in-

digenous rights among indigenous communities and providing specific advisory services to these groups.

Guatemala

Indigenous persons from 22 ethnic groups constituted an estimated 43 percent of the population. In addition to the many Mayan communities, there were also the Garifuna, descendents of Africans brought to the Caribbean region as slaves who intermarried with Amerindians, and the indigenous Xinca community. The law provides for equal rights for indigenous persons and obliges the government to recognize, respect, and promote their lifestyles, customs, traditions, social organization, and manner of dress.

Although some indigenous persons attained high positions as judges and government officials, they generally were underrepresented in politics and remained largely outside the country's political, economic, social, and cultural mainstream due to limited educational opportunities, poverty, lack of awareness of their rights, and pervasive discrimination. While the indigenous population increased its political participation, some civil society representatives questioned whether such participation had resulted in greater influence in the national political party structure.

The NGO Human Rights First noted a tendency to criminalize social movements, especially community mobilizations against large-scale industrial projects that would negatively impact the livelihood of their community. Several indigenous community members of San Juan Sacatepequez have been arrested over the past few years because of their opposition to the construction of a cement factory. In July authorities issued arrest warrants for eight individuals as a result of a dispute between a landowner and a mining company, the second time in 18 months that residents opposed to the mine were targeted for arrest. At year's end there were no new developments in the case.

According to INE's 2006 ENCOVI report, 51 percent of the population lived in poverty. Of those living in poverty, 56 percent were indigenous.

Rural indigenous persons had limited educational opportunities and fewer employment opportunities. Many of the indigenous were illiterate, and approximately 29 percent did not speak Spanish, according to INE's 2006 ENCOVI report. More than 50 percent of indigenous women over the age of 15 were illiterate, and a disproportionate number of indigenous girls did not attend school. According to the Ministry of Education, 76,232 preschool- and kindergarten-age indigenous children were enrolled in Spanish-indigenous language bilingual education programs.

The Department of Indigenous People in the Ministry of Labor, tasked with investigating cases of discrimination and representing indigenous rights, counseled indigenous persons on their rights. This department had a budget of

40,000 quetzales ($5,175), only four employees, and insufficient resources to investigate discrimination claims.

Legally mandated court interpreters for criminal proceedings were rarely available, placing indigenous persons arrested for crimes at a disadvantage due to their sometimes limited comprehension of Spanish. There was one indigenous supreme court judge, and there were 114 judges who spoke Mayan languages among the 561 tribunals in the country. There were 84 court interpreters, including 44 bilingual Mayan speakers, and the Supreme Court of Justice reported that the judicial system had 907 employees who spoke indigenous languages. However, in many instances bilingual judicial personnel continued to be assigned to areas where their second language was not spoken.

Mexico

The indigenous population has long been marginalized and subject to discrimination, particularly in the central and southern regions where indigenous people sometimes represent more than one-third of the total state populations. Indigenous communities remained largely outside the political and economic mainstream, due to longstanding patterns of social and economic marginalization. In many cases their ability to participate in decisions affecting their lands, cultural traditions, and allocation of natural resources was negligible. More than 130 NGOs were dedicated to the promotion and protection of indigenous rights.

Indigenous people did not live on autonomous reservations, although some indigenous communities exercised considerable local control over economic, political, and social matters. In the state of Oaxaca, for example, 70 percent of the 570 municipalities were governed according to the indigenous regime of "usages and customs" law, which did not follow democratic norms such as the secret ballot, universal suffrage, and political affiliation. These communities applied traditional practices to resolve disputes and choose local officials. While such practices allowed communities to elect officials according to their traditions, "usages and customs" laws tended to exclude women from the political process and often infringed on other rights of women.

The government generally showed respect for the desire of indigenous people to retain elements of their traditional culture. The law provides protections for indigenous people, and the government provided support for indigenous communities through social and economic assistance programs, legal provisions, and social welfare programs. Budget constraints, however, prevented these measures from meeting the needs of most indigenous communities, as severe shortages in basic infrastructure as well as health and education services persisted.

The law provides that educational instruction shall be conducted in the national language, Spanish, without prejudice to the protection and promotion of indigenous languages. However, many indigenous children spoke only their native languages, and the government did not provide a sufficient number of native language or bilingual teachers.

Some groups claimed that the security forces used the war on drugs as a pretext to occasionally harass indigenous groups. During the year the CNDH received 161 complaints about human rights violations of the indigenous population. By year's end it had concluded an investigation into 119 of these complaints; 42 remained under investigation.

Panama

The law affords indigenous people the same political and legal rights as other citizens, protects their ethnic identity and native languages, and requires the government to provide bilingual literacy programs in indigenous communities. Indigenous people, comprising approximately 10 percent of the population, have the legal right to take part in decisions affecting their lands, cultures, traditions, and the allocation of natural resources. There were legally designated comarcas (provincial-level indigenous regions) governed by traditional community leaders for five of the country's seven indigenous groups, including the Embera-Wounaan, Ngobe-Bugle, and Kuna. The government did not recognize comarcas for the Bri-Bri and Naso communities.

The Ministry of Government and Justice maintained an Office of Indigenous Policy. Although federal law is the ultimate authority on indigenous reserves, local groups maintained considerable autonomy. The government recognized traditional Kuna marriage rites as the equivalent of a civil ceremony. Indigenous workers had greater health problems and mortality rates, suffered from lack of educational and health services, had lower life expectancy, and experienced higher levels of malnutrition compared to nonindigenous workers. The International Fund for Agricultural Development estimated the poverty rate among the indigenous population at 95 percent. Although indigenous people represented only 10 percent of the population, they accounted for 19 percent of those considered poor and 34 percent of those in extreme poverty.

Many indigenous people misunderstood their rights and failed to employ legal channels when threatened because they did not have an adequate command of Spanish. The government did not provide legal tribunals in indigenous areas and failed to address specific indigenous property and resource use rights problems. Outside settler encroachment threatened the comarca of the Ngobe-Bugle, while the Embera-Wounaan struggled to protect their intellectual property rights concerning medicinal plants.

Social and employment discrimination against indigenous people was widespread. The ILO reported that employers paid indigenous workers 32 percent

less than nonindigenous workers. Employers frequently did not afford indige-
nous workers basic rights provided by the labor laws such as a minimum wage,
social security benefits, termination pay, and job security. Indigenous laborers
in the country's sugar, coffee, and banana plantations continued to work under
worse conditions than their nonindigenous counterparts. Employers were less
likely to provide quality housing or food to indigenous migrant laborers, and the
children of these workers were much more likely to work long hours of heavy
farm labor than nonindigenous children. A 2006 ILO report, the most recent
available, estimated that 14 percent of indigenous children ages 5 to 17 per-
formed some type of child labor.

Perú

The law prohibits discrimination based on race and provides for the right of all
citizens to speak their native language. Spanish and Quechua are the official
languages; the government also recognizes 49 other indigenous languages. The
government did not provide sufficient resources to protect effectively the civil
and political rights of indigenous persons.

Most indigenous persons and those with indigenous features faced societal
discrimination and prejudice. They were often the victims of derogatory com-
ments and subjected to illegal discrimination in restaurants and clubs.

Language barriers and inadequate infrastructure in indigenous communi-
ties impeded the full participation of indigenous persons in the political process.
Many indigenous persons lacked identity documents and could not exercise ba-
sic rights.

The geographic isolation of highland and Amazon jungle communities con-
tributed to their social, economic, and political marginalization. The UN Chil-
dren's Fund reported that indigenous persons in rural areas often did not have
access to public services, particularly health care and education. Ninety percent
lived in poverty, and only 39 percent had completed primary school. Child mor-
tality rates were higher in indigenous areas, and only 20 percent of births took
place in public health centers.

While the constitution recognizes that indigenous persons have the right to
communal land ownership, indigenous groups often lacked legal title to demar-
cate the boundaries of their lands, making it difficult to resist encroachment by
outsiders. By law local communities retain the right of unassignability to pre-
vent the reassignment of indigenous land titles to nonindigenous tenants. How-
ever, some members of indigenous communities sold land to outsiders without
the consent of the majority of their community. Mineral or other subsoil rights
belong to the state, a situation that often caused conflict between mining inter-
ests and indigenous communities. The International Labor Organization (ILO)
Committee of Experts 2008 (ILO COE) observations asked the government to
provide information on measures adopted, in consultation with and the partici-

pation of indigenous persons, to determine to what extent indigenous community interests would be affected before undertaking or authorizing programs for prospecting or utilizing subsurface natural resources in indigenous lands and territories.

On August 9, indigenous communities in the provinces of Loreto, Cusco, and Amazonas blocked roads, surrounded hydrocarbon installations, and threatened to halt the flow of energy resources in a move to protect indigenous lands against alleged incursions by outside investors. The protesters demanded that the government annul decrees that reduced from two-thirds to a simple majority of local community members required to approve changes in communal land ownership. In response to the protests, the government declared a state of emergency in the three provinces. On August 22, Congress overturned the decrees.

The constitution provides that all citizens have the right to use their own language before any authority by means of an interpreter. In Congress native speakers of Quechua conducted some debate in Quechua (translators were available for non-Quechua speakers). The National Program of Mobilization for Literacy continued teaching basic literacy and mathematics to poor men and women throughout the country.

In May MIMDES restored the status of the National Institute of Development of Andean, Amazonian, and Afro-Peruvians (INDEPA) as an autonomous government entity. INDEPA's board had 23 members including four Andean, three Amazonian, and two Afro-Peruvian representatives elected by popular vote in their respective communities. INDEPA's mission is to formulate and adopt national development policies, programs, and projects for Andean, Amazonian, and Afro-Peruvian communities. During the year INDEPA lacked a separate budget and was ineffective.

Notes

Acknowledgments

1. Paul A. W. Wallace, "People of the Long House," *American Heritage Magazine,* February 1955, Vol. 6, Issue 2 online at: http://www.americanheritage.com/articles/magazine/ah/1955/2/1955_2_26.shtml, and Bruce E. Johansen, *Forgotten Fathers, Benjamin Franklin, the Iroquois and the Rationale for the American Revolution*; Jimmy Carter, "Obama's Human Rights Opportunity," *The Washington Post,* December 10, 2008. See also, http://www.jefflindsay.com/Oneida.shtml.

Chapter One

1. Anecdote obtained at http://www.ilhawaii.net/~stony/shawnee.html.

2. Mabel Azcui, "Bolivia excluye el pasado criollo en el bicentenario de la independencia," *ElPaís.com,* July 15, 2009.

3. Van Cott, "Indigenous Movements Lose Momentum," *Current History,* February 2009, p. 83.

4. Steve J. Stern, ed., *Resistance, Rebellion, and Consciousness in the Andean Peasant World, 18th to 20th Centuries*, p. 11.

5. Steven M. Tullberg, "Securing Human Rights of American Indians and Other Indigenous Peoples Under International Law," in Cynthia Soohoo, Catherine Albisa, and Martha F. Davis, eds. *Bringing Human Rights Home, Volume 3, Portraits of the Movement*, p. 55; Cánepa, "The Fluidity of Ethnic Identities in Peru," CRISE Working Paper No. 46, June 2008.

6. Anderson, *Imagined Communities, Reflections on the Origin and Spread of Nationalism (Revised Edition)*, pp. 14-15; Craig Calhoun, "Nationalism and Ethnicity,"

Annual Review of Sociology, Vol. 19, 1993, p. 211-212; Horowitz, *Ethnic Groups in Conflict*, p. 90..

7. Central Intelligence Agency, *Mapping the Global Future*, pp. 5-7, online at: http://www.cia.gov/nic/NIC_globaltrend2020_s3.html.

8. Cojtí Cuxil, *Ri Maya' Moloj pa Iximulew: El Movimiento Maya*, p. 78.

9. Edward F. Fischer and Peter Benson, *Broccoli and Desire: Global Connections and Maya Struggles in Postwar Guatemala*; the authors argue that, as a new export crop broccoli has allowed Maya producers to hold onto their lands and to make a livable wage.

10. See, for example, Tina Rosenberg, "Why Mexico's Small Corn Farmers Go Hungry," *The New York Times*, March 23, 2003, and George A. Collier, *Basta!: Land and the Zapatista Rebellion in Chiapas, Third Edition*.

11. "Se hace poco contra la corrupción en el país," *Peru21.pe*, June 2, 2009.

12. Becker, "Ecuador: Indigenous Struggles and the Ambiguities of State Power," in *The Resurgence of Latin American Radicalism: Between Cracks in the Empire and an Izquierda Permitida*; Becker's paper was presented at the Midwest Association of Latin American Studies (MALAS) annual conference in San Juan, Puerto Rico, November 18, 2008; Søren Hvalkof, "Privatization of Land and Indigenous Communities in Latin America: Tenure Security or Social Security," Danish Institute for International Studies (DIIS) *Working Paper No. 2008/21*, p. 8, online at www.diss.dk; Kay B. Warren, *Indigenous Movements and Their Critics: Pan-Mayan Activism in Guatemala*, p. 4.

13. Tilley, "New Help or New Hegemony? The Transnational Indigenous Peoples' Movement and 'Being Indian' in El Salvador," *Journal of Latin American Studies*, Vol. 34, No. 3, August 2002, p. 526; Kikuchi, "¡Ojo con el Malon!" *Nuevo Encuentro*, October 26, 2009.

14. The 2007 Failed States Index (FSI) ranked 177 countries on the social, economic, and political pressures they face. The Index is arrived at by using the Fund for Peace's Conflict Assessment System Tool (CAST) "used to assess violent internal conflicts and measure the impact of mitigating strategies. In addition to the risk of state failure and violent conflict, it assesses the capacities of core state institutions and analyzes trends in state instability." Available online at: http://www.fundforpeace.org/web/index.php?option=com_content&task=view&id=99&Itemid=140.

15. Seligson and Booth, "Predicting Coups? Democratic Vulnerabilities, the AmericasBarometer and the 2009 Honduran Crisis," *AmericasBarometer Insights 2009;* for a more in-depth view of the risks of instability, see Booth and Seligson, *The Legitimacy Puzzle in Latin America: Democracy and Political Support in Eight Nations*; Rogers Brubaker, *Nationalism Reframed: Nationhood and the National Question in the New Europe;* Montalvo and Reynal-Querol, "Ethnic Polarization, Potential Conflict, and Civil Wars," *The American Economic Review*, Vol. 95, No. 3 (June, 2005), pp. 796-797.

16. Kruijt and Kooning, *Armed Actors*.

17. Goldstein and Pevehouse, *International Relations*, pp. 163, 174.

18. Van Cott, "Las poblaciones indígenas y la política de seguridad en America Latina," available online at: htpp://www.airpower.maxwell.af.mil/apjinternational/apj-s/1997/4trimes97/ vancott. htm.

19. Alexei Barrionuevo, "A Tribe in Brazil Struggles at the Intersection of Drugs and Cultures," *The New York Times*, December 6, 2008; "Narcos mexicanos controlan cierta zonas en Guatemala," *EFE Spanish News Agency*, December 13, 2008,

http://www.elnuevoherald.com/noticias/america_latina/story/338952.html;   Sarah
Granger, "Guatemala Drug Trade Leaves Trail of Local Addicts," *Reuters,* August 26,
2009.

20. Angel Rabasa, et al., *Ungoverned Territories; Understanding and Reducing Terrorism Risks,* pp. xviii-xix.

21. Zellen, *On Thin Ice,* pp. 53, 151.

22. Diego Cevallos, "Mexican Indians Suffer Brunt of Drug Trafficking, Illegal
Logging," *Inter   Press   Service,*   June   5,   2003,   online   at   http://
www.sierramadrealliance.org/coloradas/Inter   Press   Service-english.shtml;   Statement
submitted author to the Western Hemisphere Subcommittee of the House Committee on
Foreign Affairs, February 2, 1994, *Federal Document Clearing House Congressional
Testimony.*

23. "Correa acusa a movimiento de indígenas ecuatorianos," *EFE Spanish News
Agency,*   November   16,   2008,   available   online   at
http://www.elnuevoherald.com/noticias/america_latina/story/322996.html;   Van   Cott,
"Indigenous Movements Lose Momentum," op. cit., p. 87.

24. Peter H. Smith, *Argentina and the Failure of Democracy, Conflict among Political Elites, 1904-1955,* p. 89.

25. Jerry Z. Muller, "Muller Replies," in "Is Ethnic Conflict Inevitable: Parting
Ways Over Nationalism and Separatism," *Foreign Affairs,* July/August 2008; see also,
Chaim Kaufmann, "Possible and Impossible Solutions to Ethnic Civil Wars," Interna-
tional Security vol. 20 no. 4 (Spring 1996), pp 136-75; and Kaufmann, "When All Else
Fails: Ethnic Population Transfers and Partitions in the Twentieth Century," International
Security vol. 23 no. 2, Fall 1998, pp. 120-56.

26. James D. Fearon and David D. Laitin, "Explaining Interethnic Cooperation,"
American Political Science Review, 1996, p. 717.

27. Warren, op. cit., p. 198.

28. Tim Rodgers, "Separatists Declare Nation of Moskitia," *Nica Times,* May 1,
2009, http://www.nicatimes.net/nicaarchive/2009_05/0501091.htm; Rogers, "Mosquito
Coast Bites Nicaragua's Ortega," *Time,* May 1, 2009, available online at:
http://www.time.com/time/world/article/0,8599,1894376,00.html?xid=rss-world-cnn.

29. Juan Forero, "In Deeply Split Honduran Society, a Potentially Combusible
Situation," *The Washington Post,* July 15, 2009; Rick Kearns, "Indigenous leaders call
for President Zelaya's return," *Indian Country Today,* July 13, 2009, online at
http://www.indiancountrytoday.com/home/content/50466647.html; Dan Kovalik, "Honduran Coup Government Continues Attack on the Poor with Plan to Seize Indigenous
Hospital," *Huffington Post,* August 7, 2009; Wellington C. Ramos, "Commentary: Honduras government takes over the only Garifuna hospital in the country," *Caribbean Net
News,* August 19, 2009; "Defacto Honduran Regime Threatens Takeover of Indigenous
Garifuna Community Hospital," Medical Education Cooperation with Cuba, August 11,
2009, online at: http://www.medicc.org/ns/index.php?s=20.

30. Sábato, *El otro rostro del peronismo: Carta abierta a Mario Amadeo,* p. 40.

31. Roeder, "Who Gets a State of Their Own," *Where Nation-States Come From,*
pp. 4-5.

32. Anderson, *Imagined Communities,* op. cit.

33. Earl Shorris, *The Death of the Great Spirit,* p. 66.

34. Harold Olmos, "South American Indians Seek New Nation," *Associated Press*, February 7, 2006.

35. Laura Rivera and Jorge Barreno, "Acusan a los Mapuches de relacionarse con los terroristas de ETA y las FARC," *El Mundo*, September 5, 2009; Goldstein and Pevehouse, op. cit, p. 176.

36. Michael Astor, "Brazilian Supreme Court Warns of Civil War in Part of Amazon Region," *The Associated Press*, August 5, 2008, available online at: http://www.huffingtonpost.com/2008/08/05/ brazilian-supreme-court-w_n_116981.html.

37. Tilley, "New Help or New Hegemony?" pp. 537; 536-542.

38. Bland, *Outbreak,* Toronto: Blue Butterfly Book Publishing Inc., 2009; the promotional material can be read online at: http://www.bluebutterflybooks.ca/titles/uprising.html and also at: http://www.bluebutterflybooks.ca/titles/uprising_about.html; Bland's novelized warnings came more than a decade and a half after those raised by Barry Scott Zellen in "500 Years after Columbus: The Liberation of Native Peoples," *The Sourdough,* December 31, 1992. "The dynamic of guerrilla war can work in the North," Zellen wrote. "Industrial developments are scattered and isolated, vulnerable to sabotage. A few well placed explosives could destroy a pipeline, remove a bridge from a haul road, and shut down the extraction of resources from the Native homeland."

39. Whitney, *State and Revolution in Cuba; Mass Mobilization and Political Change, 1920-1940*, pp. 9-10.

40. Stern, *Resistance, Rebellion,* op. cit.

41. Xavier Albó, "From MNRistas to Kataristas to Katari," in Stern, ed., *Resistance, Rebellion, and Consciousness in the Andean Peasant World,* op. cit., pp. 379-380, 412-413.

42. Earl Shorris, "Mad Mel and the Maya," *The Nation,* December 18, 2006.

43. Migdal, "The State in Society," in Migdal, Atul Kohli and Vivienne Shue, ed., *State Power and Social Forces: Domination and Transformation in the Third Worlds*, p. 15.

44. Crawford Young, *The Politics of Cultural Pluralism,* p. 457; Political scientist Roberto Espindola observes that the exception to this void of ethnic politics "had been some former European colonies that became independent in the 1960s and 1970s, particularly Belize, Guyana, Suriname, and Trinidad-Tobago, where ethnic-related parties have developed since the pre-independence period." Espindola, "New Politics, New Parties?" in Richard Millett, et al., eds., *Latin American Democracy: Emerging Reality or Endangered Species*, p. 153.

45. It is useful to note here Espindola's observation that Morales is not the first Latin American president from an Amerindian ethnic background. What makes Morales different, Espindola observes, is that fact he comes from outside the elite that has ruled their societies. Espindola, op. cit., p. 142.

46. Mailer, "Superman Comes to the Supermarket," *Esquire,* November, 1960.

47. Knight, *The Mexican Revolution: Vol. 1, Porfirians, Liberals, and Peasants*, p. 84.

Chapter Two

1. Cited in Elie Kedourie, *Nationalism, Fourth, Expanded Edition*, p. 125.

2. 62 *Yale Law Journal*, 1953, pp. 348, 390.

3. "So That Men Are Free," (1962), Director: Willard van Dyke, Production Company: CBS, Distribution: McGraw-Hill Films, available online at: http://course.cit.cornell.edu/vicosperu/ vicos-site/cornellperu_page_1.htm#stmaf; the comment was made to the author by Dobyns in the spring semester of 1975; see also, Dobyns, Doughty, and Lasswell, eds., *Peasants, Power, and Applied Social Change: Vicos as a model.*

4. "So That Men Are Free," op. cit.

5. Tullberg, op. cit., p. 87.

6. The definition by Martinez Cobo can be found online on the Web site of the International Work Group for Indigenous Affairs, at: http://www.iwgia.org/sw310.asp.

7. Brett Troyan, "Gregorio Hernandez de Alba (1904-1973): The Legimitization of Indigenous Ethnic Politics in Colombia," *European Review of Latin American and Caribbean Studies*, Vol. 82, April 2007, pp. 93-94.

8. According to the University of Minnesota Human Right Center's *Study Guide: The Rights of Indigenous Peoples* (2003): "In many countries, Indigenous Peoples rank highest on such underdevelopment indicators as the proportion of people in jail, the illiteracy rate, unemployment rate, etc. They face discrimination in schools and are exploited in the workplace. In many countries, they are not even allowed to study their own languages in schools. Sacred lands and objects are plundered from them through unjust treaties. National governments continue to deny Indigenous Peoples the right to live in and manage their traditional lands; often implementing policies to exploit the lands that have sustained them for centuries. In some cases, governments have even enforced policies of forced assimilation in efforts to eradicate Indigenous Peoples, cultures, and traditions. Over and over, governments around the world have displayed an utter lack of respect for Indigenous values, traditions and human rights."

9. CEPAL Comunicado de Prensa, 2000, "Situacion de indígenas y afro americanos en America Latina y el Caríbe," July 18, 2000.

10. López Bárcenas, "Indigenous Movements in the Americas: From Demand for Recognition to Building Autonomies," translated from "Autonomías Indígenas en America: de la demanda de reconocimiento a su construcción," Center for International Policy, February 26, 2008.

11. For example, a study by the medical journal, *Lancet,* shows that the health of indigenous peoples in Latin America, like that of their peers in Asia and Africa, is much worse off than other poor people, online at: http://www.thelancet.com/collections/series/indigenous_health. Indigenous populations, which make up 5.4 percent of the total residents of Chile, Latin America's economic success case, make up the majority living in extreme poverty there. "Discrimination against Chile's indigenous people continues," *Santiago Times,* November 29, 2005. In December 2006, the first time the Economic Commission for Latin America and the Caribbean (ECLAC) included a chapter on indigenous peoples in its annual Social Panorama report, the UN agency urged recognition of Native Americans' individual and collective rights, including self-determination. Ecuador's new constitution officially describes the country as a multiethnic state and par-

ticipatory democracy; between 1987 and 1999, Argentina, Brazil, Guatemala, Mexico, Nicaragua, Paraguay and Venezuela have all passed constitutional reforms meant to improve Indians' political and social standing.

12. Daniela Estrada, "Latin America: Indigenous Peoples Gaining Ground (On Paper)," *Inter Press Service,* December 5, 2006; "Brazil investigating use of Indians in military exercises," *Associated Press,* January 10, 2006; Frank Bajak, "Fighting the odds to keep Indian tongues alive," *Associated Press,* November 7, 2009..

13. "More than 80 Percent of Indigenous People Live in Extreme Poverty, According to World Bank," March 1, 2007 http://www.stwr.org/poverty-inequality/more-than-80-percent-of-indigenous-people-live-in-extreme-poverty-according-to-world-bank.html; "Malnutrition in Guatemala; A National Shame," *The Economist,* August 27, 2009.

14. Roberto Andolina, "The Sovereign and its Shadow: Constituent Assembly and Indigenous Movement in Ecuador," *Journal of Latin American Studies, 35,* pp. 721.

15. On how international interest in indigenous rights has helped Central and South American Indians in their claims to political, economic and social rights, see for example Alison Brysk, *From Tribal Village to Global Village, Indian Rights and International Relations in Latin America.*

16. Rick Kearns, "Protection of indigenous media sought at the UN," *Indian Country Today,* May 19, 2008.

17. Maivan Clech Lam, *At the End of the State: Indigenous Peoples and Self-Determination,* p. 166.

18. Stratfor, *Geopolitical Diary: Geography and Conflict in South America,* March 6, 2008.

19. According to political scientist Phil Kelly, geopolitical factors "have played their part to bring peace to the area, and I maintain they have done so for the past two-hundred years, for a geopolitical presence has provided South America with a structure of peace that has and will persist," with six geopolitical factors that he sees having "created a structural foundation that provides a 'long peace' to the republics of South America," in "South America as a 'Zone of Peace'; Facilitating a Geopolitical Model," a paper presented at the Midwest Association of Latin American Studies (MALAS) annual conference in St. Louis, November 3, 2006.

20. Stratfor, *Annual Forecast 2008: Beyond the Jihadist War,* p. 27. "On one side is Morales and his efforts to seize economic control of the country; Morales boasts the support of a cohesive military and Venezuelan President Hugo Chavez. Opposing him is the wealth of the lowlands, which might be able to bring in outside support, particularly from the power with the strongest economic interest in the lowlands: Brazil. Such Brazilian involvement is likely to be informal and political, unless Chavez sends paramilitary forces in to assist the highlanders."

21. Brad Haynes, "Chile: United Nations Investigates Mapuche Police Violence," *The Santiago Times,* November 2, 2009.

22. Nilo Cayuqueo, "Guest Column," *Indian Country Today,* August 10, 2005; Rick Kearns, "Seeking justice, Latin indigenous leaders come to testify," *Indian Country Today,* April 6, 2009; Gustavo González, "Latin America: 'War on Terror' Has Indigenous People in Its Sights," Inter Press News Service Agency, June 6, 2002; see also, Coordinadora Andina de Organizaciones Indígenas, *Preso por defender a la Madre Tierra, Criminalización del Ejercicio de Derechos de los Pueblos Indígenas,* 2008.

23. "Fundamentalist" here refers to creeds composed of those who believe in the manifestations of the Holy Spirit as seen in the first century Christian Church, such as miracles, prophecy, and speaking in other tongues or languages.

24. José Brechner, "Bolivia, Israel, and the Muslims," March 2, 2009.

25. Foner, *Reconstruction: America's Unfinished Revolution, 1863-1877*, pp. 104, 410; On the ethnic consciousness-raising that can come with migration away from one's homeland, see Michael Kearney, *Reconceptualizing the Peasantry: Anthropology in Global Perspective*; Writing about "the smaller, more all-of-one-piece countries" in Europe, Irish political scientist Tom Garvin wrote that those countries "which sometimes can be characterized as suffering from what amounts to a surfeit of national identity: religion, language, geography, statehood, and 'history' all conspire to tell Swedes they are Swedish, Danes they are Danish, and Portuguese they are Portuguese. Japan, the Scandinavian countries, the Baltic states, Greece, Portugal, and Iceland share this surfeit of identity—national identity being reinforced to the point of immovability by other identities which are not necessarily connected with the concept of 'citizenship'; a Greek is a Greek is a Greek, in a way no Canadian can ever be a Canadian or Belgian a Belgian." In "Ethnic Markers, Modern Nationalisms, and the Nightmare of History," in Peter Kruger, *Ethnicity and Nationalism: Case Studies in Their Intrinsic Tension and Political Dynamics*, p. 65.

26. Kedourie, *Nationalism*, op. cit., pp. 110-111.

27. Chua, *Worlds on Fire*, p. 51.

28. See, for example, Donna Lee Van Cott, *The Friendly Liquidation of the Past: The Politics of Diversity in Latin America*.

29. "Self-determination" is the term recognized as a right in Article 3 of the U.N. Declaration on the Rights of Indigenous Peoples that was approved, over the objection of the United States, in 2007.

30. CONAIE, *Las nacionalidades indígenas y sus derechos colectivos en la Constitución*, p. 52.

31. Yale H. Ferguson, "Ethnicity, National and Polities Great and Small," *Mershon International Studies Review*, 1994, Vol. 38, p. 244.

32. Andolina, "The Sovereign and its Shadow," op. cit., p. 724.

33. Andersen, "The Robespierre of the Andes," *The Washington Times*, September 2, 1999.

34. John Harwood, "A Lot Like Home; Campaign Strategists Give Foreign Elections That American Cachet; They Arrive From the U.S. With Slick TV Ads and Centrist Platforms," *The Wall Street Journal*, March 24, 1999.

35. James Habyarimana, et al., "Is Ethnic Conflict Inevitable? Parting Ways Over Nationalism and Separatism." *Foreign Affairs*, July/August 2008.

36. González, "Latin America: 'War on Terror' Has Indigenous People in Its Sights," op. cit.

37. Florencia Mallon, *Peasant and Nation: The Making of Postcolonial Mexico and Peru*, p. 4.

38. A. J. Rossmiller, *Still Broken; A Recruit's Inside Account of Intelligence Failures, from Baghdad to the Pentagon*, p. 146.

39. Espindola, "New Politics, New Parties," op. cit., p. 154.

40. Zamosc, *The Indian Movement and Political Democracy in Ecuador*, *Latin American Politics & Society*, Volume 49, Number 3, Fall 2007, pp. 1-34.

41. Ernesto Laclau, *Politics and Ideology in Marxist Theory*, p. 167.

42. "Attempting to shape regionwide policies," *Latin American Special Report*, July 2007, SR-03-07, p. 15. "Listed were the Quechua, the largest indigenous group in Bolivia and Peru, also present in Argentina and Chile; the Kichwa, the largest group in Chile; and the Mapuche, the largest group in Chile, also present in Argentina. The only Colombian group mentioned was that of the Guambiano people, which rank eighth in size. Absent from the list were the Amazonian peoples of Bolivia, Peru and Ecuador (though in the latter the Amazonian Kichwa are the third-largest group). Included, on the other hand, were a number of minor groups from Bolivia (Chuwi, Larecaja, Kallawaya, K'ana, Killaka, Uru), Ecuador (Cayambi, Sarapuro) and a Mapuche subgroup (the Lafquenche) that straddles the border between Chile and Argentina."

43. Harold Olmos, "South American Indians," op. cit.

44. "Mapuche party born as legislative battle rages," *Latin American Special Report*, July 2007, p. 11.

45. Daniel Gonzalez, "A man of the (indigenous) people," *The Arizona Republic*, January 26, 2008.

46. Gonzalez, op. cit.

47. David Escobar, "The invisible Indians of California," *El Tecolote*, June 17, 2006, available online at: http://news.eltecolote.org/news.view_article.html?article_id=2342993089c251a1e2660d592a979721; see also Robert A. and Beverly H. Hackenberg, "Notes Toward a New Future: Applied Anthropology in Century XXII," *Human Organization*, Winter 2004.

48. William Langewiesche, "The Border (Part I)" *The Atlantic Monthly,*" May 1992, www.theatlantic.com/issues/92may/border.htm.

49. Brenda Norrell, "Censorship and the US brand of terrorism at the border," *Narconews*, February 25, 2009.

50. The letter was signed by the following Members of the U.S. Congress: Raul Grijalva, Solomon P. Ortiz, Silvestre Reyes, Ruben Hinojosa, Bob Filner, Henry Cuellar, Susan Davis, and Ciro D. Rodriguez.

51. Beach played two legendary U.S. Marine figures, Ira Hayes in Clint Eastwood's *Flags of Our Fathers* (2006), a movie about the U.S. invasion of the Japanese-held island of Iwo Jima and in another as one of the Native American linguists in *Windtalkers* (2002), a film about Navajo Marines who used their native language as an unbreakable radio cipher in the Pacific theatre struggle against Japan.

52. Bob Strauss, "Adam Beach," *The Toronto Globe and Mail*, October 20, 2006, p. R35.

53. The treaty ended the Mexican-American War (1846-1848) by ceding 525,000 square miles to the United States, while recognizing pre-existing property rights of Mexican citizens in the transferred territories; Silko, *Almanac of the Dead*, p. 213 see also, David A. Reichard, "'Justice is God's Law,' The Struggle to Control Social Conflict and U.S. Colonialization of New Mexico, 1846-1912," Ph.D. dissertation, Temple University, 1996.

54. G. Emlen Hall, "The Pueblo Land Grant Labyrinth," in Charles L. Briggs and John R. Van Ness, eds., *Land, Water, and Culture: New Perspectives on Hispanic Land Grants*, p. 100.

55. Silko, *Almanac*, op. cit., pp. 133, 216.

56. López Bárcenas, "Indigenous Movements in the Americas: From Demand for Recognition to Building Autonomies," op. cit.

57. Kathleen Neils Conzen and David A. Gerber, "The invention of ethnicity: A perspective from the U.S.A.," *Journal of American Ethnic History*, Fall 1992, Vol. 12, Issue 1, p. 3.

58. On U.S. hostility to the indigenous agenda, and some of the domestic politics driving the hostility, see Tullberg, op. cit., esp. pp. 83-86.

59. Hector Tobar, "Guatemala's new president will assume great burden," *Los Angeles Times*, November 6, 2007.

60. Lisa Garrigues, "Ecuadorian Native movements turn up the heat," *Indian Country Today*, February 19, 2007.

61. Rick Kearns, "From slavery to government; The rise of Ache Guayaki Chief Margarita Mbywangi of Paraguay, *Indian Country Today*, October 3, 2008.

62. Corr, "Whither Bolivia: The ethnic, cultural and political divide," *World Literature Today*, March-April 2006, p. 34.

Chapter Three

1. *The Nation*, December 18, 2006.

2. Anderson, op. cit., pp. 47-50. The authoritative study of Spanish colonial America, the *Anuario de Estudios Americanos XXXVI* offers eloquent testimony of how mistreatment of Indians assigned to forced labor (*encomiendas*) in the Spanish colony, with the complicity of the local governor, led to a complaint by a bishop being elevated to the Crown in 1710 denouncing the mistreatment, p. 591-592.

3. Cecilia Mendez G., "'Incas Sí, Indios No.' Notes on Peruvian Creole Nationalism and Its Contemporary Crisis," *Journal of Latin American Studies*, Vol. 28, No. 1, February 1996, p. 222.

4. Stephen D. Morris, "Reforming the Nation: Mexican Nationalism in Context," *Journal of Latin American Studies*, Vol. 31, No. 2, May 1999, p. 374.

5. Donna Lee Van Cott, "Matrimonio de Conveniencia: El movimiento indigenista mexicano y la rebelión Zapatista."

6. Becker, "Mariátegui, the Comintern, and the Indigenous Question in Latin America," *Science & Society*, Vol. 70, No. 4, October 2006., p. 472.

7. Terry Martin, *The Affirmative Action Empire; Nations and Nationalism in the Soviet Union*, p. 126.

8. Martin, "The Origins of Soviet Ethnic Cleansing," *The Journal of Modern History*, Vol. 70, No. 4 , Dec., 1998, p. 832.

9. Becker, "Mariátegui," op. cit., p. 464.

10. Francisca da Gamma, "La Internacional Comunista, Mariátegui y el 'descubrimiento' del indígena," *Anuario Mariateguiano*, Vol. 9. No. 9, 1997, p. 53.

11. Becker, "Mariátegui," op. cit., pp. 458, 452.

12. Becker, op. cit., p. 471.

13. Gerardo Leibner, *El mito del socialismo indígena de Mariátegui*, p. 155; Becker, "Mariátegui," op. cit., p. 471

14. Melina Selverston-Scher, *Ethnopolitics in Ecuador: Indigenous Rights and the Strengthening of Democracy*, p. 23; Becker, "Mariátegui," op. cit., p. 473; Dunbar-Ortiz,

"Indigenous Resistance in the Americas and the Legacy of Mariátegui," *Monthly Review,* September, 2009.

15. Martin, "The Origins of Soviet Ethnic Cleansing," op. cit., pp. 823, 822.

16. Alexander S. Dawson, "From Models for the Nation to Model Citizens: *Indigenismo* and the 'Revindication' of the Mexican Indian, 1920-40," *Journal of Latin American Studies,* Vol. 30, No. 2 (May 1998), pp. 280, 282-284, 288-289, 294-295.

17. Tullberg, op. cit., p. 56.

18. Richard A. Falk, *Human Rights Horizons: The Pursuit of Justice in a Globalizing World,* pp. 51, 131.

19. Ferguson, "Ethnicity, National and Polities Great and Small," op. cit., p. 241.

20. "Bolivia's New President Inspires Region's Indigenous Leaders," *VOA English Service,* January 26, 2006; Deborah J. Yashar, *Contesting Citizenship in Latin America, The Rise of Indigenous Movements and the Postliberal Challenge,* p. 63.

21. López Bárcenas, "Indigenous Movements in the Americas," op. cit.

22. López Bárcenas, op. cit.

Chapter Four

1. Quoted in George Hutchinson and Anthony D. Smith, *Nationalism: Critical Concepts in Political Science, Volume 4,* p. 1267.

2. George M. Frederickson, quoted in Kevin Kenny, "Diaspora and Comparison: The Global Irish as a Case Study," *The Journal of American History,* June 2003, p. 146; it was Kenny who, citing Frederickson, made reference to the possible arbitrariness of the nation-state's construction.

3. Typical example of this kind of analysis, which is also characteristic of mainstream news analyses, can be seen in "Final week for Ecuador's presidential race," *Mercosur Press,* Oct. 9, 2006 (see "Marxist Thought Online," on the Web site *politicalaffairs.net,* online at: http://www.politicalaffairs.net/article/view/4214/1/213), which attributes 15 years of political instability in that country on "weak institutions (and) limited party fidelities and governance." Obviously, it is beyond the scope of this paper to survey other possible root causes of democratic instability, such as economic mismanagement.

4. Walker Connor, *Ethnonationalism, The Quest for Understanding,* p. 70.

5. This point is extensively documented in Connor, *Ethnonationalism,* op. cit, esp. *Chapter Two, American Scholarship in the Post-World War II Era ("Nation-Building or Nation-Destroying?").*

6. Roe, "The Intrastate Security Dilemma: Ethnic Conflict as a 'Tragedy.'?" *Journal of Peace Research,* Vol. 36, No. 2, March 1999, p. 198.

7. Edwin G. Corr, "Whither Bolivia: The ethnic, cultural and political divide," *World Literature Today,* March-April 2006, p. 35.

8. Jill Replogle, "Indigenous Taking Note of Morales' Rise to Power," *The Miami Herald,* October 8, 2006; In Mexico, Indian peasants in Chiapas, whose livelihood was threatened by the free market and open trade reforms of the Carlos Salinas de Gortari administration, rose in arms on New Year's 1993. In Bolivia, popular anxieties over access to water being restricted by multinational corporations and foreign participation in the sale of natural gas foreshadowed Morales' sweeping electoral victory. And in Ecua-

dor, contamination of the rainforest homes of Amazon Indians by foreign oil companies, with devastating consequences to their communities' physical health, together with unrelenting inflation and concern that a free-trade agreement would spell doom for small-scale Native farmers faced with competing with cheap imports from the United States, helped keep tens of thousands of Indians mobilized on a seemingly indefinite basis. In May 2006, the position of the Ecuadorian, Guatemalan and Bolivian Indian protestors regarding extractive industries was strengthened when the UN Permanent Forum on Indigenous Issues announced it endorsed without reservation Native peoples' demands that States must recognize both their right to self-determination and to respect the principle of "free, prior and informed consent" regarding development activities taking place on their land and resources." "UN Forum urges inclusion of indigenous peoples' concerns in global anti-poverty goals," *United Nations News Center* (www.un.org), May 26, 2006. (An "informed consent" clause is contained in Article 28 of the U.N. Declaration on the Rights of Indigenous Peoples adopted in September 2007.)

9. Yashar, *Contesting Citizenship,* op. cit., p. 63.

10. In his revised classic *Imagined Communities*, Benedict Anderson offered a caveat to his argument about the centrality of print communication in the birth of national consciousness, making it relevant to today's Indian communities, when he added the caveat: "Invented in only 1895, radio made it possible to bypass print and summons into being an aural representation of the imagined community where the printed page scarcely penetrated. Its role ... generally in mid-twentieth century nationalisms, has been much underestimated and understudied." *Imagined Communities*, op. cit., p. 54.

11. Ernest Gellner, *Nations and Nationalism*, pp. 8-9, 24, 39.

12. Gellner, op. cit., p. 34.

13. Burton Bollag, "Bolivia's Indian Majority Goes to College," *The Chronicle of Higher Education*, Vol. 52, No. 45, June 14, 2006, p. 36.

14. Bollag, "Bolivia's Indian Majority," op. cit.

15. O'Leary, "On the Nature of Nationalism: An Appraisal of Ernest Gellner's Writings on Nationalism," *British Journal of Political Science*, Vol. 27, No. 2, April 1997, p. 211.

16. Kedourie, *Nationalism,* op. cit., pp. 67, 23.

17. The anonymous 15-page treatise was posted on January 16, 2007 on the Qollasuyu-Ivi Iyambae-Bolivia Web site and can be found online at: www.bolivia.indymedia.org/es/ 2007/01/38984.shtml; the translation of "full-spectrum domination project" was originally in Spanish "un proyecto de dominación de espectro global."

18. Connor, *Ethnonationalism,* op. cit, pp. 51-52.

19. Shorris, *The Death of the Great Spirit*, p. 103.

20. Susan Olzak, "Ethnic Collective Action and the Dynamics of Ethnic Enclaves,' unpublished paper, Department of Sociology, Cornell University, p. 3, cited in Charles Tilly, "Transplanted Networks," in Virginia Yans-McLaughlin, ed., *Immigration Reconsidered*, p. 91.

21. Kedourie, *Nationalism,* op. cit. pp. XVI-XVII, 110-111.

Chapter Five

1. Huntington, *Political Order in Changing Societies*, p. 266.

2. Statement submitted by the author to the Western Hemisphere Subcommittee of the House Committee on Foreign Affairs, February 2, 1994, *Federal Document Clearing House Congressional Testimony*; a useful picture of the disconnect between leftist groups and ideology and the Native American agenda in the United States during the turbulent 1960s can be found in Shorris, *The Death of the Great Spirit*, particularly chapters 8, "Crazy Horse is Alive in San Francisco," and 11, "Welcome to the Proletariat."; Van Cott, "Andean Indigenous Movements and Constitutional Transformation: Venezuela in Comparative Perspective," *Latin American Perspectives*, Vol. 30, no. 1, Indigenous Transformational Movements in Contemporary Latin America, January 2003, pp. 52-53.

3. "Spain's king can't handle Indians in power, says Chavez," *Reuters*, November 21, 2007.

4. "Chavez proposes renaming Latin America to Indian America," *RIA Novosti*, August 12, 2008 http://en.rian.ru/world/20080812/115976867.html.

5. Knight, *The Mexican Revolution*, op. cit., p. 310; Friedrich, *Agrarian Revolt in a Mexican Village*, p. 53.

6. Marc Becker, "Mariátegui," op. cit., p. 450.

7. Bollag, "Bolivia's Indian Majority Goes to College," op. cit.

8. Andrei S. Markovits, "The European and American Left since 1945," *Dissent*, Winter 2005, Vol. 52, Issue 1.

9. Connor, *Ethnonationalism*, op. cit, p. 68; Hobsbawm, *Nations and Nationalism since 1780: Programme, Myth, Reality*, p. 163.

10. Purnell, *Popular Movements and State Formation in Revolutionary Mexico; The Agraristas and Cristeros of Michoacan*, p. 16.

11. See, for example, Michael Kearney, *Reconceptualizing the Peasantry*, op. cit., especially Chapter 14, "Class and Identity,: The Jujitsu of Domination and Resistance in Oaxacalifornia."

12. López Bárcenas, "Indigenous Movements in the Americas," op. cit.

13. Rivera Velez, "Los indigenismos en Ecuador: de paternalismos y otras representaciones," *America Latina Hoy*, Julio, 1998, vol. 19, Universidad de Salamanca, pp. 61-59.

14. Tim Rodgers, "A tale of genocide in a year of politics," *Miami Herald*, June 19, 2006; on Ortega's potential pending date with the justice system, see also: John Corry, "On 13, Sandinistas vs. Miskitos," *The New York Times*, July 29, 1986; "Ortega Acusado de Genocidio Contra Miskitos," *EFE Spanish News Agency*, June 8, 2006.

15. Bernard Nietschmann, *The Unknown War: The Miskito Nation, Nicaragua and the United States*, pp. 62-65; Roger Miranda and William Ratliff, *The Civil War in Nicaragua*, pp. 253-254; Means and Marvin J. Wolf, *Where White Men Fear to Tread; The Autobiography of Russell Means*, pp. 468-469; David Stoll, *Rigoberta Menchú and the Story of All Poor Guatemalans*, p. 214; López Bárcenas, "Indigenous Movements in the Americas," op. cit.; Nicaragua's indigenous peoples were the first to embrace armed rebellion against Sandinista rule, their numbers swelling to more than 100,000 by 1983 and offering, as *The Wall Street Journal* noted, the "most promising anti-Sandinista

front." In Frederick Kempe and Clifford Krauss, "Flawed Approach; U.S. Policy on Indians in Nicaragua Damages Anti-Sandinista Effort," March 2, 1987.

16. Van Cott, "Matrimonio de Conveniencia," op. cit.

17. Van Cott, op. cit.

18. Gutíerrez, *Nationalist Myths and Ethnic Identities; Indigenous Intellectuals and the Mexican State*, pp. 195-197; Araceli Burgete Cal y Mayor and Miguel Gómez Gómez, "Multiculturalismo y gobierno permitido en San Juan Cancuc, Chiapas: tensiones intracomunitarias por el reconocimiento de 'autoridades tradicionales,'" in Xochitl Leyva, et al., eds., *Gobernar (en) la diversidad: experiencias indígenas desde América Latina. Hacia la investigación de co-labor*, pp. 362-366.

19. Victor Breton Solo de Zaldivar, "From Agrarian Reform to Ethnodevelopment in the Highlands of Ecuador," *Journal of Agrarian Change 8*, no. 4, October 2008, cited in Becker, "Ecuador: Indigenous Struggles and the Ambiguities of State Power," op. cit., p. 41.

20. Becker, "Ecuador: Indigenous Struggles and the Ambiguities of State Power," op. cit., pp. 10, 23, 25, 26, 51, 54.

21. See Albó, "And from Kataristas to MNRistas?, The Surprising and Bold Alliance Between Aymaras and Neoliberals in Bolivia, " in Donna Lee Van Cott, ed., *Indigenous Peoples and Democracy in Latin America*, pp. 55—82.

22. Lisa Garrigues, "Morales' victory brings indigenous leaders to Bolivia," *Indian Country Today*, February 10, 2006.

23. Magdalena Gomez, "Bolivia: tequio del pensamiento," *La Jornada*, March 28, 2006.

24. Mamani, "Las estrategias del poder indígena en Bolivia," *Rebellion*, April 24, 2006.

25. "Interview with Nilo Cayuqueo," *Latin American Perspectives*, Vol. 9, No. 2, Minorities in the Americas, Spring 1982, pp. 101, 103-104.

26. "Cayuqueo, op. cit, p. 106.

27. Means and Marvin J. Wolf, *Where White Men Fear to Tread*, op. cit., pp. 290-291, 550-551, 554.

28. Ana Arana, "Murder in Colombia: American Indians seek to avenge the murder of one of their leaders by leftist rebels," *Salon*, December 14, 1999.

Chapter Six

1. Renan, "Qu'est-ce qu'un de nation?" delivered at the Sorbonne, cited in Homi K. Bhabha ed., *Nation and Narration*.

2. David Spencer, *Reexamining the Relevance of Maoist Principles to Post-Modern Insurgency and Terrorism*, unpublished manuscript 2007; A groundbreaking analysis of this phenomenon is found in Robert D. Lamb, "Ungoverned Areas and Threats from Safe Havens; Final Report of the Ungoverned Areas Project," prepared for the Office of the Under Secretary of Defense for Policy, U.S. Department of Defense, 2008; The strategic relevance of ungoverned spaces is discussed in Angel Rabasa, et al., *Ungoverned Territories: Understanding and Reducing Terrorism Risks*.

3. Lamb, op. cit.

4. It is interesting to note that the Colombian Constitution of 1991 recognizes the existence of indigenous criminal systems, with Articles 246 and 330 giving Native American authorities the right to exercise judicial functions within *resguardos* (Indian reserves), in keeping with their own rules and custom, provided that these do not contravene either the Constitution or ordinary Colombian law. (On this point, see, Juanita Chaves, "Criminal Justice and Indigenous People in Colombia," *Indigenous Law Bulletin*, online at: www.austlii.edu.au/au/journals/LIB/1999/73.html; A penetrating look at Colombia's indigenous movements is found in Joanne Rappaport, *Intercultural Utopias: Public Intellectuals, Cultural Experimentation and Ethnic Pluralism in Colombia.*

5. William Golden Mortimer, *Peru: History of coca, "The divine plant" of the Incas*; Douglas Farah, "Into the Abyss: Bolivia under Evo Morales and the MAS," International Assessment and Strategy Center, June 17, 2009, pp. 15-16, online at http://www.strategycenter.net/docLib/20090618_IASCIntoTheAbyss061709.pdf.; confidential interview with a Bolivian human rights activist.

6. See, for example, Marcelo Ballvé, "'Mother Coca' Wins in Bolivia—Can Evo Morales Foster World Coca Market?" *New American Media*, December 21, 2005; Jessicah Curtis, "Colombia Calls Cocaine Users 'Predators of the Rain Forest,'" *The Huffington Post*, December 8, 2008; Sibylla Brodzinsky, "Colombia's Indians bank on coca drink becoming the real thing," *The Guardian*, December 14, 2005; Sergio de Leon, "Coca-Cola Vs. Coca-Sek in Colombia," *The Associated Press*, May 10, 2007.

7. Tom Phillips, "Healed by the Amazon angels," *Guardian Unlimited*, December 21, 2007.

8. Tim Gaynor, "Mexico drug gangs muscle border tribe out of homes," *Reuters*, December 2, 2007.

9. "Native American Trackers to Hunt bin Laden," March 12, 2007, online at: http://www.theaustralian.news.com.au/story/0,20867,21364526-2703,00.html; "Shadow Wolves," November 9, 2007, available online at: http://www.kold.com/global/story.asp?s=7337853&ClientType; A number of the trackers have extensive law enforcement experience and have been called upon to train border guards and other security officials in countries around the world. They have also been sent to join the hunt for terrorists crossing Afghanistan's borders and to train local border units in Uzbekistan and Tajikistan.

10. Yashar, *Contesting Citizenship*, op. cit., p. 63.

11. Interview with Latin American colonial historian James L. Zackrison, Washington, D.C., February 26, 2000.

12. Tullberg, op. cit., pp. 57, 59, 60, 67.

13. Robert A. Williams, Jr., "The Algebra of Federal Indian Law: The Hard Trail of Decolonizing and Americanizing the White Man's Jurisprudence," *Wisconsin Law Review 219* (March 1986), pp. 290-291.

14. Lamb, "Ungoverned areas," op. cit., p. 5.

15. Kedourie, *Nationalism*, op. cit, pp. 110-111.

16. Posen, "The Security Dilemma and Ethnic Conflict," *Survival*, 35(1), 1993, p. 27.

17. Ignatieff, *Blood and Belonging*, p. 16.

18. De Vos, "Ethnic Pluralism: Conflict and Accommodation," *Ethnic Identity: Cultural Continuities and Change*, George de Vos and Lola Romanucci-Ross, eds., p. 13.

19. Tilley, "New Help or New Hegemony?" op. cit, pp. 536-537; Anthropologist Jean E. Jackson offered a different twist on Tilley's important insight about identity in her own study of the indigenous Tukanoans in the Amazonian Vaupés region in southeast Colombia. There Jackson found that *the Tukanoans were "in effect, learning about their Indian culture and identity from non-Tukanoans—a process of 'becoming Indian' as well as 'being Indian.'"* These riverine people, she added, had "undergone extensive changes since the beginning of the 1970s, primarily as a result of their increasing incorporation into the Colombian state." In the process they "mobilized around notions of recapturing and preserving culture as they work to recover land, maintain language, and protect traditional healing systems. Indeed, preserving culture is sometimes the main goal of projects for which funds are requested from state agencies and nongovernmental organizations (NGOs)," in Jackson, "Culture, Genuine and Spurious: The Politics of Indianness in the Vaupés, Colombia," p. 3. (Italics added.)

20. Moshe Ronen, "Indian Summer; From the jungles of Peru to Ramla, Jewish immigrants of Indian descent prove nothing trumps need to connect with one's heritage," *Israel Jewish Scene,* March 30, 2008, online at: http://www.ynet.co.il/ english/articles/ 0,7340,L-3522812,00.html.

21. An interesting example of the relationship between religious praxis, ethnic identity and a shift to violent political action, in this case Mayan peasants who gave up their folk Maya-Catholic beliefs for more orthodox Catholicism, only to later splinter into an important pool of recruits for Guatemala's left-wing guerrillas, is contained in Ricardo Falla, *Quiché Rebelde: Religious Conversion, Politics, and Ethnic Identity in Guatemala.*

22. Brechner, "Latin America - waiting for Allah," September 19, 2006.

23. Indira A.R. Lakshmanan, "Evangelism is luring Latin America's Catholics; Charismatic sects focus on earthly rewards," *The Boston Globe,* May 8, 2005, found online at: www.rickross.com/ reference/fundamentalists/fund161.html.

24. Canessa, "Contesting Hybridity: *Evangelistas* and *Kataristas* in Highland Bolivia," *Journal of Latin American Studies,* 32, 2000, pp. 127, 132, 141.

25. Canessa, op. cit., p. 142.

26. Canessa, op. cit., pp. 142-143.

27. Andrade, "Posibilidades de Crecimiento del Islam en América Latina: Oportunidades y Dificultades," *Opción,* Vol. 17, Número 035, Universidad de Zulia, Maracaibo, Venezuela, pp. 120-126; It should be noted that the Islamic prohibition of "usury" is currently less uniformly supported in the Middle East where, according to a National Public Radio Marketplace report: 'Bonds called sukuks, designed to conform to Islamic rules forbidding interest on loans, have been popular investments the past few years. But now a leading scholar has cast doubt on whether the bonds are truly Islamic, prompting fears of a subprime-like meltdown." Recording of "Sanctity of Islamic bonds questioned," March 20, 2008, found at http://marketplace.publicradio.org/display/web/2008/03/20/sukuk/; Chris L. Jenkins, "Islam Luring More Latinos; Prays Offer a More Intimate Link to God, Some Say, *The Washington Post,* January 7, 2001.

28. Andrade, "Posibilidades de Crecimiento," op. cit.

29. Wiarda, *The Soul of Latin America,* pp. 52-54.

30. Crooke, *Resistance: The Essence of the Islamist Revolution*; The Pluto Press Website is at: http://www.plutobooks.com/shtml/aboutpluto.shtml.

31. Robert Siegel, "Sayyid Qutb's America," *National Public Radio*, January 4, 2009; see the chapter, "The New Jerusalem in the Americas, in Stoll, *Is Latin America Turning Protestant? The Politics of Evangelical Growth.*

32. "El gobierno de Evo Morales oficializa relaciones diplomáticas con Iran," *EFE Spanish News Agency*, September 11, 2007; "Morales: Iran to start TV channel in Bolivian coca country," *The Associated Press*, February 19, 2008, reproduced in *The Jerusalem Post;* "Iran to open 2 health clinics in Bolivia" *The Associated Press, October 10, 2008,* reproduced by *Forbes.com* online at: http://www.forbes.com/feeds/ap/2008/10/10/ap5537649.html.

33. Mark Lavie, "Israeli document: Venezuela sends uranium to Iran," *The Associated Press*, May 25, 2009.

34. Todd Bensman, "Iran making push into Nicaragua," December 16, 2007; According to Adam Garfinkel, "In April 2008 the Bolivian government, seemingly under the influence of Cuban and Nicaraguan advisers, appeared to employ the Star of David as a symbol of evil on new government ID cards. The new cards apparently were given mainly to non-indigenous peoples in eastern Santa Cruz province, the center of opposition to the Morales regime, in numbers vastly larger than the tiny Bolivian Jewish community. Attempts to get to the bottom of this incident have been inconclusive—the government denies all. But the weird facts speak for themselves," in Garfinkle, "Autumn Note: The Future of Jewcentricity," *The American Interest*, September-October 2009.

35. Hamed Bin Hasan al-Qahtani, "Seven Years After September: Has al-Qaeda Achieved its Goals?," *Qaddaya Jihadyya*, Issue 2, September, 2008, cited in Murad al-Shisani, "Is al-Qaeda Seeking Allies in Latin America?" *Terrorism Focus*, Vol. 5, Issue 37, October 30, 2008; "'Hezbolá usa indígenas para penetrar en Latinoamérica', dice experto en antiterrorismo," *Cámbio*, March 30, 2009; see also, "Islamic institutions in Latin America: Inciting radicalization?" *Latinnews.com Strategic Insights Papers*, December 2008, and Ely Karmon, "Iran and its Proxy Hezbollah: Strategic Penetration in Latin America," Elcano Royal Institute, Madrid, Spain, April 8, 2009.

36. Massimo Introvigne, "Chávez and the Strange Story of the Shi'ite Indios in Venezuela," *il Domenicale. Settimanale di cultura*, March 24, 2007, online at: http://www. cesnur.org/2007/mi_03_24_en.htm; In June 2006, Chavez referred to the Venezuelan-born international terrorist Carlos Ilich Ramirez, jailed in France and known more commonly as "The Jackal," as his "friend" during a meeting of OPEC countries hosted in Caracas. See Ely Karmon, "Hezbollah America Latina: Strange Group or Real Threat?" p. 7, available online at: http://www.instituteforcounterterrorism.org/var/119/35195Hezbollah%20iin%20LatinAmerica_Dr%20Karmon.pdf.

37. "Chavez, acusado de antisemitismo," *La Nación* (Argentina), January 6, 2006.

38. Travis Pantin, "Hugo Chavez's Jewish Problem," *Commentary*, July/August 2008 issue, 2, at http://www.commentarymagazine.com/viewarticle.cfm/hugo-ch-vez-s-jewish-problem-11455.

39. Chris Zambelis, "Islamic Radicalism in Mexico: The Threat from South of the Border," *Jamestown Terrorism Monitor*, Volume 4, Issue 11, June 2, 2006.

40. Karmon, "Iran and its Proxy," op. cit., p. 8.

41. Ioan Grillo, "Zapatista leader touring Mexico," *The Associated Press*, January 3, 2006.

42. Karmon, "Iran and its Proxy," op. cit., p. 8.

43. John Ross, "Commodifying the Revolution: Zapatista Villages Become Hot Tourist Destinations," *Counterpunch,* February 12, 2009.

44. Also rendered in Spanish as "Morabitum."

45. Chris Zambelis, "Islamic Radicalism," op. cit.

46. Cynthia Hernandez Gonzalez, "El Islam de Chiapas," *WebIslam,* September 13, 2006 http://www.webislam.com/noticiatema_imp.asp?idt=5719.

47. "Islamic institutions in Latin America: Inciting radicalization?" op. cit.; "The Americas Report," Menges Hemispheric Security Project, Center for Security Policy, Vol. 3, Issue 11, March 28, 2007.The group's Web site, written in Spanish and Chapateka—a combination of Wayuu and Spanish—can be viewed online at: http://groups.msn.com/AutonomiaIslamicaWayuu.

48. Manual R. Torres Soriano, "La Fascinación por el Exito: El Caso de Hezbollah en America Latina," *Jihad Monitor Occasional Paper No. 1,* Universidad Pablo de Olavide, Sevilla, Spain; see also, Gustavo Coronel, "The Hezbollah Venezuelan Metastasis," *Venezuelatoday,* September 4, 2006.

49. Introvigne, "Chávez and the Strange Story," op. cit.

50. Introvigne, op. cit; see also a news report that claimed Darnott was taken into the custody of the Venezuelan Dirección de los Servicios de Inteligencia y Prevención (DISIP), who was "presumably involved in the placing of a pipe bomb (*niple*)" at the United States embassy, in "Detenido presunto 'niplero' en Zulia," *ElUniversal.com,* Nov. 18, 2006, online at: http://buscador.eluniversal.com/2006/11/18/sucgc_art_73446.shtml, and Clinton W. Taylor, "Hezbollah in Latin America," *The American Spectator,* November 30, 2006.

51. Jonathan D. Halevi and Ashley Perry, "Hizbullah's global reach; Shiite group's reach extends far beyond Lebanon, poses global threat," online at: http://www.ynet.co.il/english/articles/0,7340,L-3580047,00.html.

52. Karmon, "Iran and its Proxy," op. cit., p. 16.

53. Sam Logan, "Iran courts Latin America," *ISN Security Watch,* January 22, 2007.

54. Martin Edwin Andersen, "The Robespierre of the Andes," *Washington Times,* September 2, 1999; Karmon, "Hezbollah America Latina," pp. 4, 7.

55. Strauss, "Antiglobalism's Jewish Problem," *Foreign Policy,* Nov./Dec. 2003, pp. 60, 65-66. In *Uncouth Nation: Why Europe Dislikes America,* author Andrei S. Markovits provides a view of the origins of an "increasingly strong overlap between anti-Americanism and anti-Semitism" that also mirrors the outlook held by Chavez and his regional and Islamist allies. In the late nineteenth century, Markovits says: "It was the fear and critique of capitalist modernity that brought these two resentments together. America and the Jews were seen as paragons of modernity: money-driven, profit-hungry, urban, universalistic, individualistic, mobile, rootless, and hostile to established traditions and values." Quoted in Jonathan Yardley, "Exploring the roots of anti-Americanism among European elites," *The Washington Post,* March 4, 2007.

56. Adam Garfinkle, "Autumn Note," op. cit.; "Bolivia raises hackles with ID," *Washington Times,* April 10, 2008.

57. Brenda Norell, "Navajo youth peacemaker to Iran," *The Narcosphere,* August 1, 2008, http://narcosphere.narconews.com/notebook/brenda-norrell/2008/08/navajo-youth-peacemaker-iran; see also, Navajo peacemaker Michelle Cook's full report from Iran, "Navajo peacemaker, walking in beauty in Iran," online at: http://bsnorrell.blogspot.com/2008/07/navajo-peacemaker-walking-in-beauty-in.html.

58. Good Fox, "Palestine: Stop the re-creation of 'Indian country' in the Holy Land," *Indian Country Today*, January 13, 2009.

59. Hugh Seton-Watson, *Nations and States; An Inquiry into the Origins of Nations and the Politics of Nationalism*, pp. 394-406; Shorris, *The Death of the Great Spirit*, op. cit., p. 190.

60. Tilley, "New Help or New Hegemony?" op. cit., pp. 538, 545; Juliana Barbassa Madera, "Immigrants from Mexico's indigenous groups work to preserve traditional health care," *The Associated Press*, December 29, 2005.

61. Louis E.V. Nevaer, "The Return of the Native Americans as Immigrants," *New American Media*, October 24, 2007.

62. The comment by Walter Morales, posted on Nov 10, 2007 at 21:57:48, was the first one listed at the end of Nevaer, "The Return of the Native Americans," op. cit.

63. Cynthia H. Enloe, *Ethnic Soldiers*, pp. 15, 17.

64. Enloe, op. cit, pp. 14-16.

65. Cecilia Méndez G., "Populismo militar y etnicidad en los Andes," *Iconos, Revista de Ciencias Sociales No. 26*, Facultad Latinoamericana de Ciencias Sociales (Flacso), Sede Quito, September 2006, p. 14.

66. The existence of speculation by the military high command about the ultimate loyalty of troops stationed in the Amazon, many of who were from that region, particularly in the lower ranks, was provided to the author by Peruvian defense and security expert Luis Giacoma Macchiavello.

67. Adam Jevec, "Semper Fidelis, Code Talkers," *Prologue Magazine*, The U.S. National Archives & Records Administration, Winter 2001, Vol. 33, No. 4.

68. Kenneth William Townsend, *World War II and the American Indian*, pp. 31-33.

69. Townsend, op. cit., pp. 38-60.

70. Townsend, op. cit., pp. 56-60.

71. American Indian Heritage Month, "American Indians in World War II," http://www.defenselink.mil/specials/nativeamerican01/wwii.html; "In their 'twilight years,' Navajo Code Talkers called into service to help save endangered native languages," *U.S. Newswire*, November 13, 2006.

Chapter Seven

1. Edwards, *Gendered Strife and Confusion; The Political Culture of Reconstruction*, p. 17, paraphrasing the work of Chandra Talpade Mohanty.

2. Like many other indigenous peoples from around the Americas, Means, it should be noted, defies easy left-right Eurocentric political categorization common in the United States outside of Indian reservations. In 1972 Means participated in the violent take-over of the Bureau of Indian Affairs offices in Washington, D.C., and a year later in the armed occupation of Wounded Knee, South Dakota, for 71 days while the U.S. Marshals Service laid siege. In 1986 he traveled to Nicaragua to express his support for the Miskito Indians allied with the US-funded Contra guerillas against Nicaragua's Sandinista government. A year later, he sought the presidential nomination of the Libertarian Party, but lost the contest to Rep. Ron Paul.

3. "Russell Means Challenging 150 Years of Broken Treaties" online at: http://thirdpartywatch.com/2007.12/20/russell-means-challenging-50-years-of-

brokentreaties/; Faith Bremner, "Lakota group pushes for new nation," Argus Leader, December 20, 2007; Tabitha Fleming, *Associated Content*, "Lakota Indians Declare Sovereign Nation Status." Interestingly a blogger responding to the thirdpartywatch article, Omar Zaid, maybe united by an anti-colonial argument, or maybe signifying something else taking place, wrote: "To All Concerned With The New Imperialism, Assalaamualaikum. As an American ex-pat (living in Kuala Lumpur, Malaysia) and convert to Islam, I support this historic turn of events. Indeed, those of us who recognize the Autonomy of our Creator, The Great Spirit, stand in solidarity with the Lakota People. ... May Allah increase the right hand and arm of the Lakota." Chavez has also made direct overtures to U.S. Indian tribes, providing tribal governments with discounted heating oil. David Sharp, "Venezuela deal with Indians could be prelude to big announcement," *Associated Press*, January 7, 2006. Jim Sappier, chief of the Penobscot Nation, one of the Indian tribes accepting Chavez's largess, told a reporter that he did not understand critics of the Venezuelan: "I don't know why people are talking that way. Helping poor people really should be a priority."

4. "Exclusion is part of life" in Bolivia, wrote aid official William Powers, in "Poor Little Rich Country," in the June 11, 2005 *New York Times*, before Morales' election. "Indians are barred from swimming pools at some clubs for example ... In La Paz, I was walking through the fashionable South Zone beside an Aymara woman, Fatima, when another Bolivian viciously pushed her off the sidewalk. She wasn't shocked by the sentiment, but she was amazed that the man had been willing to touch her."

5. World Bank, "Peoples, Poverty and Human Development in Latin America, 1994-2004," cited in *Latin American Weekly Report*, May 24, 2005.

6. The two prior Indian presidents were Mexico's Benito Juarez (1861-1872), born to an indigenous family in San Pablo Guelatao, Oaxaca, and Peru's Alejandro Toledo (2001-2006), one of sixteen children of a family of indigenous rural workers from the town of Cabana, Pallasca Province, Ancash Department. A case can also be made that the infamous Mexican revolutionary and president Victoriano Huerta, "a career soldier with a sanguinary record . . . the son of a mestizo *campesino* and Huichol Indian mother (which, for some, explained by his stoic virtues and brutal vices)" was also Native American. See Knight, *The Mexican Revolution*, op.cit, pp. 262, 323-324.

7. Haider Rizvi Tierramerica, "N. American tribal leaders energized by Morales meet," *Inter Press Service/GIN*, October 23, 2006; Connor, op. cit., p. 42., tells us that the essence of the nation "is not tangible. It is psychological, a matter of attitude rather than of fact. ... A prerequisite of nationhood is a popularly held awareness or belief that one's own group is unique in a most vital sense. In the absence of such a popularly held conviction, there is only an ethnic group." the Onondaga Nation belongs to the Haudenosaunee, or Iroquois Confederacy.

8. Van Cott, *The Friendly Liquidation*, op. cit., p. 186; "Bolivia: Country Report," *Freedom in the World, 2009 Edition*, online at: http://www.freedomhouse. org/ template.cfm?page=22&year=2009&country=7570; "Morales Moves Against the Judiciary," *Andean Group Report/Latin American Newsletters*, May 29, 2009; "El Presidente se Declaró Marxista-Leninista y Rechaza Discriminación de Cuba en la OEA," *La Razón*, April 28, 2009.

9. Hinde Pomeraniec, "Evo Morales, de pastor de llamas y sindicalista, a presidente de Bolivia, *Clarín*, January 23, 2006; Cordova-Claure, "Cuidado con el latente fundamentalismo indígena," *BIP*, September 14, 2006.

10. Cárdenas, "View: Bolivia divided," *Daily Times* (Pakistan), January 30, 2008.

11. Edwin Tapia Frontanilla, in *Opinion*, January 7, 2006.

12. Van Cott, *The Friendly Liquidation*, op. cit., p. 509.

13. Mamani, "Las estrategias del poder," op. cit.

14. Shorris, *The Death of the Great Spirit*, op. cit., p. 107; Thomas Benjamin, "A Time of Reconquest: History, the Maya Revival, and the Zapatista Rebellion in Chiapas," *The American Historical Review*, Vol. 105, No. 2, April, 2000, p. 418.

15. Rick Kearns, "News Analysis on indigenous Latin America," *Indian Country Today*, March 3, 2006.

16. On this point, see Silvia Rivera, "La Raiz: colonizadores y colonizados," in Xavier Albó and Raúl Barrios, eds., *Violencias encubiertas en Bolivia*, pp. 27-139, "Bolivian Horizons: An Interview with Historian Sinclair Thomson," *ZNet*, Nov. 7, 2007, http://www.zmag.org/content/print_article.cfm?itemID=14221&sectionID=52, and Brooke Larson, *Cochabamba, 1550-1900: Colonialism and Agrarian Transformation in Bolivia, 2nd. Ed.*

17. Richard Patch, "Bolivia: The Restrained Revolution," *The Annual of the American Academy of Political and Social Sciences*, 334:130, 1961.

18. Huntington, *Political Order*, op. cit., p. 408.

19. Bolivia: Failure of a Nation," www.firmaspress.com, posted Nov. 29, 2005.

20. Gellner, *Nations*, op. cit., p. 1; this perception, and the fact that the last elected president before Morales took office was the failed Gonzalo Sánchez de Losada, allowed Morales to be the first presidential candidate in recent memory to be chosen by a majority of voters.

21. Espindola, "New Politics, New Parties?" op. cit., p. 155.

22. The characterization of Cárdenas by Ricardo Calla, former Bolivian minister of ethnic and indigenous affairs, is cited in Albó, "And from Kataristas to MNRistas?" p. 449.

23. Alvaro García Linera, "Indianismo and Marxism: The mismatch of two revolutionary rationales," *Atlantic Free Press*, January 30, 2008.

24. Whitehead, "State Organization In Latin America since 1930," In Leslie Bethell ed., *The Cambridge History of Latin America*, Volume 6, p. 9; Gellner, op. cit, p. 1.

25. "Bolivian Horizons: an Interview with Historian Sinclair Thomson," *ZNet*, op. cit.; Thomson's mention of nineteenth century urban siege techniques recalls Bolivian linguistic anthropologist Xavier Albó's tracing of the collective memory linking the rebellion by Tupaj Katari in 1781 in La Paz by Aymara Indians to the emergence of a powerful peasant movement in the early 1980s, cited in the Introduction to this book.

26. Mabel Azcui, "La milicia indígena de Morales," *El País*, February 19, 2007; Abdel Padilla, "Yo ordené la emboscada de Warisata," *Semanario Pulso*, May 28, 2006; "Bolivia: Country Report," Freedom House, op. cit.

27. Corr, "Whither Bolivia," op. cit., p. 32.

28. Lisa Garrigues, "La Paz hosts continental indigenous encounter," *Indian Country Today*, October 27, 2006; Monte Reel, "For Bolivian Majority, A New Promise," *The Washington Post*, January 23, 2006.

29. See, for example, "Editorial: ¿Qué filosofía política tiene el gobierno en Bolivia?" *Pukara*, No. 17 March 7-April 7, 2007; "Editorial: 'Sabios indígenas' y el peligro del neo indigenismo, *Pukara*, No. 19, May 7-June 7, 2007, and Ramiro Reynaga, "La Ropa de Evo Morales: Incongruencia entre vestimenta, palabra, y acción, " *Pukara*, Nº

20, June 7-July 7, 2007; The observation made by Rogers Brubaker and David D. Laitin, who note the waning post-Cold War incentives for using grand ideological constructions to frame conflicts, may provide a useful context here: "Even without direct positive incentives to frame conflicts in ethnic terms, this has led to a marked ethnicization of violent challenger-incumbent contests as the major non-ethnic framing for such contests has become less plausible and profitable. . . . a thickening web of international and nongovernmental organizations has provided greater international legitimacy, visibility, and support for ethnic group claims (normatively buttressed by culturalist extensions and transformations of the initially strongly individualist human rights language that prevailed in the decades immediately following World War II.) ... Ethnicity is not the ultimate, irreducible source of violent conflict in such cases. Rather, conflicts driven by struggles for power between challengers and incumbents are newly ethnicized, newly framed in ethnic terms," in Brubaker and Laitin, "Ethnic and Nationalist Violence," pp. 425.

30. Roberto Albro, "The Indigenous in the Plural in Bolivian Oppositional Politics," *The Bulletin of Latin American Research,* Vol. 24, No. 4, pp. 433, 445; Farah, "Into the Abyss," op. cit., p. 8.

31. A useful study in this regard is Forrest Hylton and Sinclair Thomson, *Revolutionary Horizons: Past and Present in Bolivian Politics.*

32. Fiona Smith, "Bolivians Elect Assembly to Revise Constitution; Morales Wins Only Narrow Majority for Plan Touted as Step Toward Equality," *The Associated Press,* July 3, 2006.

33. "Morales: Catholic leaders acting like 'Inquisition,'" *The Associated Press,* July 26, 2006. Morales' own religious beliefs are unclear. Veteran Bolivian journalist Ted Cordova-Claure noted that, before heading the coca growers union, Morales was a musician in a charismatic Catholic Indian band in the "Diablada" in the Oruro carnival, in which dancing and alcohol consumption were featured attractions. Cordova-Claure, "Cuidado con el latente," op. cit.

34. "Morales dará à Justiça indígena valor de Justiça comum," *EFE Spanish News Agency,* January 4, 2007.

35. "A propuesta de Evo Morales, daran latigazos a los delincuentes en Bolivia," *Diario Exterior,* April 17, 2007; Goldstein noted: "Typically, the last resort for this kind of community justice would be to exile offenders, prohibiting their return to the community where their family, lands, and all other signs of their social existence are located," Goldstein writes. "Such punishment has a powerful deterrent effect on would-be criminals, such that extreme forms of violent punishment are rarely required. Punishments under this system are not decided upon in anger, but are the result of a deliberative process in which elected elders of the community participate and pronounce judgment. Lynchings like those described in the report—from Ayo Ayo to El Alto to the Cochabamba valley—obey no form of adjudicative process, but proceed from the rage and vulnerability that poor, indigenous people feel in the face of almost continual and uncontrolled crime in their communities. Unable to rely on the state justice system or the national police—which are underfunded, understaffed, and inaccessible to the majority of poor and marginal people—community residents resort to violence as the only possible means that they can imagine to control crime and punish the accused. Lynch mobs frequently misidentify the perpetrators of crimes, and end up punishing the innocent." In "Response to the Human Rights Foundation" Don't mistake lynching and other forms of

vigilante violence for community justice," *Andean Information Network,* January 28, 2008; see also, Helene Risør, "Twenty Hanging Dolls and a Lynching: Living Insecurity and Recognizing Dangerousness in the Margins of the Bolivian State," paper presented at the 2009 Latin American Studies Association Congress in Rio de Janeiro, June 6, 2009.

36. Simon Romero, "A Radical Gives Bolivia Some Stability," *The New York Times,* September 18, 2007.

37. The characterization of Quispe is also by Ricardo Calla, cited in Albro, op. cit., p. 449.

38. As late as 2005, a writer in the Marxist *Monthly Review* accused Morales, who had just announced a preliminary agreement on a united electoral front with the more moderate La Paz Mayor, Juan del Granado, of "committing political suicide and attempting to take the lives of all left cadres with him;" in Jeffery R. Webber, "Left-Indigenous Struggles in Bolivia: Searching for Revolutionary Democracy," Volume 57, Number 4, September 2005.

39. Eduardo Febbro, "Felipe Quispe habla de Evo Morales," *Pagina/12,* Nov. 16, 2003; Cordova-Claure, op. cit., stresses Morales' mixed race heritage; Connor, *Ethnonationalism,* op. cit, p. 76.

40. "Entrevista a Jaime Paz Zamora: No se puede construir el futuro desde el rencor," *El País,* October 28, 2006.

41. Edwin Alvarez, "Inaudito: Por primera vez en su historia el ejército boliviano recibe indígenas en sus filas," *El Tiempo,* August 8, 2005; Daniel Espinosa, "El 2007 mujeres indígenas podrán entrar al ejército," *Bolivia.com,* June 10, 2006.

42. Brian R. Selmeski, "Multicultural Citizens, Monocultural Men: Indigeneity, Masculinity, and Conscription in Ecuador," Doctoral Dissertation, Anthropology, Graduate School of Syracuse University, December 2007, p. 10; Farah, "Into the Abyss," op. cit., pp. 33-36; Cecilia Méndez G., "Populismo militar y etnicidad," op. cit., p. 14; Pablo Stefanoni, "Arranca en Bolivia la Constituyente," *Página/12* (Argentina), August 6, 2006.

43. Azcui, "La milicia indígena de Morales," op. cit.; Max Seitz, "Ponchos Rojos, Milicia Indígena?" *BBC Mundo.com,* January 24, 2009; Farah, "Into the Abyss," op. cit., pp. 20-27; "Ponchos Rojos Matan Perros Para Amenazar," *La Razón,* November 23, 2007, online at: http://www.la-razon.com/versiones/.../nota_249_510475.htm.

44. Farah, op. cit., pp. 20-24, 27-28; "Bolivia: Indigenistas y sindicatos exigent a Evo Morales que expulse a los moderados," *Infolatam,* August 14, 2007. The original Spanish italicized was "No estan en la realidad."

45. Monte Reel, "South America's Constitutional Battles," *Washington Post,* January 18, 2008; "Bolivia back at brink of institutional breakdown," Latin American Newsletters *Latin America Security and Strategic Review,* December 2007, p. 1; Human Rights Foundation, "La Human Rights Foundation pide al gobierno de Evo Morales el cese inmediato de los linchamientos, torturas y quemas vivas de personas por las practicas de 'justicia   comunitaria,'"   January   8,   2008,   available   online   at: http://www.lahrf.com/media/BolReportJan08.html; "Opposition compares Bolivian situation   to   Yugoslavia,"   *Mercopress*   (Uruguay),   March   2,   2008,   online   at: http://www.mercopress.com/vernoticia.do?id_12789&formato=HTML.

46. Ana Maria Fabbri and Eduardo García, "Interview-New Bolivian governor to press for autonomy," *Reuters,* July 11, 2008.

47. Jorge Luís Vacaflor González, "Reformas de Estado y esencia de las autonomies indígenas," *Pukara,* No. 36, October 7–November 7, 2008.

48. See, for example, Franz Chavez, "Bolivia" Indigenous leaders beaten and publicly humiliated," *Green Left Weekly,* Issue # 753, June 4, 2008.

49. Simon Romero, "Fears of Turmoil Persist as Powerful President Reshapes Bitterly Divided Bolivia," *The New York Times,* September 28, 2008.

50. Kintto Lucas, "Latin America: Native Groups Express Solidarity with Bolivian Leader," *Inter Press Service,* September 23, 2008.

51. *El País,* September 11, 2008.

52. Javier Paz García, "Bolivia: Nacional Socialismo y Movimiento al Socialismo," *HACER; Hispanic American Center for Economic Research,* September 29, 2008.

53. Roman D. Ortiz, "Balkan-Bolivia," *HACER; Hispanic American Center for Economic Research,* September 29, 2008. Ortiz is the coordinator for the Security and Defense Studies Area of the Colombian business think tank, La Fundación Ideas para la Paz (FIP).

54. George Gray Molina, "Ethnic Politics in Bolivia: 'Harmony of Inequalities,' 1900-2000," paper prepared under auspices of the Center for Inequality, Human Security and Ethnicity (CRISE) and presented at the Third Forum for Human Development, Paris, January 17-19, 2005; Warren, *Indigenous Movements and Their Critics,* op. cit, p. 209.

55. In Forward to Gilbert M. Joseph and Daniel Nugent, eds., *Everyday Forms of State Formation: Revolution and the Negotiation of Rule in Modern Mexico,* p. ix

56. Purnell, *Popular Movements and State Formation,* op. cit., p. 12.

57. Van Cott, *The Friendly Liquidation of the Past,* op. cit., p. 186.

58. *Amautas* were Inca wise men.

59. "El mejor sistema es el Amawtico: Proclama Politica Amawtica," distributed August 9, 2008 by e-mail by Editora Pachakuti; Amawta are wise men and spiritual guides in Aymara culture.

60. Horowitz, *Ethnic Groups in Conflict,* op. cit., p. 175; Booth and Seligson, "Predicting Coups?" op. cit.

61. See, for example, Carla Espósito Guevara, "El discurso del movimiento Autonomista," *BolPress.com,* September 4, 2008.

62. Raul Penaranda, "Is there a shift toward indigenous leaders in Bolivia," *Global Post,* February 24, 2009; *EFE Spanish News Agency,* "Un alcalde indígena es el primer rival de Evo Morales a la presidencia," *El País* (Spain), May 3, 2009.

63. "El congreso de Bolivia aprueba la nueva ley electoral," *El País* (Spain), April 14, 2009; Mabel Azcui, "Evo Morales promulga una nueva ley electoral para los comicios de diciembre," *El País,* April 14, 2009; Xavier Albó, "La circunscripciones especiales indígenas," *La Razón,* April 6, 2009.

64. "El Gobierno Justifica las Acciones Contra Cárdenas," *La Razón,* March 10, 2009; "La oposicion de Bolivia denuncia un clima de acoso," *El País* (Spain), March 18, 2009; Paola Flores and Carlos Váldez, "Indians Challenging Morales in Bolivia Face Dangers," *Associated Press,* March 18, 2009; "Bolivia: Unequivocally Condemn Mob Violence: Politically Motivated Attacks Threaten Rule of Law," Human Rights Watch, March 12, 2009; "Oficialistas piden poner limites a la justicia comunitaria," *La Razón,* May 13, 2009.

Chapter Eight

1. Speech before the 1991 American Anthropological Association annual meeting, whose theme was "Nationalism, ethnicity, race and racism," cited in *Anthropology Today*, Vol. 8, No. 1, February 1992, pp. 3, 5.

2. Martin Edwin Andersen, "Peruvian officials are shaken by terrorist attacks," *Miami Herald*, March 11, 1983; Andersen, "Little-known Peru group gains public attention," *The Associated Press*, April 3, 1982

3. Andersen, "Peruvian officials are shaken," op. cit.; Andersen, "Little-known Peru group," op. cit.; the reaction of Belaúnde was provided to the author by Nestor Ikeda, a Peruvian correspondent for the *Associated Press*, in a November 19, 2008 e-mail. Ikeda said Belaúnde's reaction was based on the mistaken "indication that he believed that the phenomenon originated with immature people and would have a short life;" see also, Gonzalo Portocarrero, *Razones de Sangre. Aproximaciones a la violencia política*, p. 85.

4. See, for example, José Coronel, "Violencia política and respuestas campesinas en Huanta," in Carlos Iván Degregori, et al., eds., *Las Rondas Campesinas. La Derrota de Sendero Luminoso*, p. 102; Andrea Portugal, "Voices from the War: Exploring the Motivation of Sendero Luminoso Militants," CRISE Working Paper No. 57, October 2008, pp. 14, 33-39, 65.

5. Vargas Llosa, "The story of a massacre," *Granta 9*, 1983, pp. 69, 82; see also, Enrique Mayer, "Peru in Deep Trouble: Mario Vargas Llosa's 'Inquest in the Andes' Reexamined," in George E. Marcus ed., *Rereading Cultural Anthropology*.

6. Isbell, "Shining Path and Peasant Responses in Rural Ayacucho," in David Scott Palmer ed., *The Shining Path of Peru*, pp. 71-74.

7. "Tribute: Peru journalists remember fallen colleagues on 26th anniversary of Uchuraccay massacre," *Peruvian Times*, January 28, 2009; Portugal, "Voices from the War," op. cit, pp. 41, 56.

8. The interesting parallel to tribal rejection of al-Qaeda was brought to the author's attention by Barry Scott Zellen; Orin Starn, "To Revolt against the Revolution: War and Resistance in Peru's Andes," Cultural Anthropology, Vol. 10, No. 4, November 1995, pp. 548, 552, 554.

9. Juan Forero, "Peru Report Says 69,000 Died in 20 Years of Rebel War," *The New York Times*, August 29, 2003; according to "Special Focus: Reassessing the Sendero Luminoso threat," Latin American Newsletters, *Latin American Security and Strategic Review*, December 2007, p. 6, while the rebels were "undisputedly brutal, the high toll of Peru's internal conflict was also due to the no-holds-barred strategy adopted to combat it."

10. Milagros Salazar, "Peru: Indigenous People, Ignored Even by the Statistics," *Inter Press Service*, October 10, 2006.

11. "Luzmilla Chiricente: Lucharé porque los ashaninkas sean también reparados y se acabe con la discriminación," *Ideeleradio*, transmitted October 25, 2006, and found at: http://www.ideeleradio.org.pe/look/Ideeleradio/article.tpl?IdLanguage=13&IdPublication=7&NrIssue=32&NrSection=30&NrArticle=12099.

12. Marks, "Making Revolution with Shining Path," in David Scott Palmer ed., *Shining Path of Peru*, p. 219-220; Starn, op. cit., p. 551. Also, David Spencer, *Reexamin-*

ing the Relevance of Maoist Principles to Post-Modern Insurgency and Terrorism, unpublished manuscript, 2007.

13. Among the outside observers who presciently reported on Fujimori's ability to tap into smoldering racial and ethnic resentments was the *Washington Post's* Eugene Robinson; see, for example, his "Economic Hardship. Sharpens the Racial Schism in Peru," *Washington Post,* February 25, 1990.

14. Cynthia McClintock, "An Unlikely Comeback in Peru," in Larry Diamond et al., eds., *Latin America's Struggle for Democracy*, pp. 155-157, 163.

15. Anderson, *Imagined Communities,* op. cit, final chapter, "Memory and Forgetting," especially p. 195.

16. Connor, *Ethnonationalism,* op. cit., pp. 4, 94.

17. Kedourie, *Nationalism,* op. cit, pp. 71-72; Gellner, op. cit., p. 49.

18. Cecilia Méndez G., "Populismo militar y etnicidad," pp. 13-14; Manuel Piqueras Luna, "Etnicidad, Ejército y Policia en el Perú: Una aproximación," undated, online at: http://blog.pucp.edu.pe/item/44822.

19. Kedourie, op. cit., p. 70.

20. Jorge Luís Vacaflor González, "Reformas de Estado y esencia de las autonomías indígenas," *Pukara,* No. 36, October 7–November 7, 2008; Antauro Humalla's platform can be seen online at: http://mnp.pe.tripod.com/.

21. Sergio Kiernan, "El IncaPaz," *Pagina/12,* February 20, 2005; CIA, "The World Factbook—Peru," https://www.cia.gov/cia/publications/factbook/geos/pe.html.

22. Kiernan, "'Mi Lucha, versión andina," *Pagina/12,* January 29, 2006.

23. Gellner, op. cit., pp. 55-57.

24. See, for example, Ladislao Landa's work, cited in "Indians & politics in Latin America—after Evo Morales," *Latin America Special Report,* July 2007, p. 1.

25. Edith Casafranca Tinoco, "Finalizó Primer Congreso Politico Indígena Peruano," May 5, 2007, available online at http://www.nodo50.org/pachakuti/ textos/campanas/indígenas/nace_masa.html.

26. Kelly Hearn, "For Peru's Indians, Lawsuit Against Big Oil Reflects a New Era," *The Washington Post,* January 14, 2008; Matt Bostock, "Indigenous Rights Bloodily Suppressed for Oil and Gas Returns," *The Santiago Times,* June 18, 2009.

27. Søren Hvalkof, "Privatization of Land and Indigenous Communities," op. cit, pp. 5, 8; Amazon Watch, "Peru Indigenous Mobilizations Issue Brief," May 18, 2009; Chris Kraul, "Peru's indigenous people win one round over developers," *Los Angeles Times,* June 25, 2009; Bostock, "Indigenous Rights," op. cit.

28. "Special Focus: Reassessing the Sendero Luminoso threat," *Latin American Security and Strategic Review,* op. cit., pp. 3-6.

29. Dana Ford, "Peruvian prime minister asks the left for a truce," Reuters, October 17, 2008; "Peru's PM vows to stamp out terrorism," Reuters, online at: http://tvnz.co.nz/view/ page/536641/2210427.

30. Nelly Luna Amancio, "Grupos politicos radicalizan un discurso étnico aimara en Puno," *El Comercio,* January 13, 2008; Barbara J. Fraser, "Work remains in struggle to repair human rights violations in Peru," *Catholic News Service,* August 22, 2008; "Yehude Simon, "Ollanta es ambicioso y Antauro me ayudó y le regalé libro," *Peru.com,* July 16, 2009; Daniel Yovera, "Antauro Humala: 'Simon me pidió interceder,'" *Perú21.pe,* July 16, 2009.

31. Raúl Sohr, "Peru and the law of the jungle," *The Santiago Times,* June 18, 2009; Bostock, "Indigenous Rights," op. cit.; personal communication with Crippa, August 15, 2009; Rocio Otoya, "Disturbios en la Amazonía revelan fractura social en Perú," *EFE Spanish News Agency,* June 6, 2009; Paola Ugaz, "Indígenas peruanos, en guardia contra Alan García," *Terra Magazine,* May 12, 2009; Kristina Aiello, "Peru's Cold War against Indigenous People," *Worldpress.org,* July 19, 2009; "Inteligencia para ciegos," Instituto de Defensa Legal, August 26, 2009.

32. Sohr, "Peru and the law of the jungle," op. cit.; Bostock, "Indigenous Rights," op. cit.; "García's development plans trigger bloody clashes in Peru's Amazon," *Latin News.com Weekly Report,* June 11, 2009 (WR-09-23); Doris Aguirre, "¿Quién dió la orden de desalojar a indígenas sin prevenir represalias?" *LaRepublica.pe,* June 12, 2009; "Editorial: Renuncia, diálogo y pacificación nacional," *ElComercio.com.pe,* June 8, 2009, online at: http://www. elcomercio.com.pe/impresa/notas/renuncia-dialogo-pacificacion-nacional/ 20090608/297631; information about the use of the informal Antauro Humalla extended network to spy on the government was obtained in a confidential interview with the author.

33. Author interview with Peruvian defense and security expert Luis Giacoma Macchiavello, July 30, 2009.

34. "Policías de Bagua no pueden volver a sus comisarías," *ElComercio.com.pe,* September 13, 2009, online at: http://www.elcomercio.com.pe/impresa/notas/policias-bagua-no-pueden-volver-sus-comisarias/20090913/341449; "Inteligencia para ciegos," Instituto de Defensa Legal, August 26, 2009, online at: www.seguridadidl.org.pe/.../26.../inteligencia-para-ciegos.htm; The author is indebted to James Zackrison and Giacoma Macchiavello for their insights into the underlying significance of the Bagua violence.

35. Aiello, "Peru's Cold War," op. cit; James Suggett, "Venezuelan Government Responds to Massacre of Indigenous Protestors in Peruvian Amazon,"*Venezuelanalysis.com,* June 10, 2009; Caracas Gringo, "Bolivarian Revolution in Peru," June 16, 2009, available online at http://caracasgringo. wordpress.com/2009/06/16/bolivarian-revolution-in-peru/. On his Web site, "Caracas Gringo," claimed to have "lived and worked in Latin America over 38 years," and that his "past lives include U.S. Marine Corps, journalist, intelligence analyst, think tank policy wonk, Spanish TV political talk show pundit, security consultant, small business owner, and guest lecturer on US-Latin American issues at US and other government entities."

36. Mariella Balbi, "Entrevista: Yehude Simon; Renunciar sería desleal al país," *El Comercio.com.pe,* June 14, 2009; Renzo Pipoli, "García denies massacre and keeps laws; forces Native chief out," *Indian Country Today,* June 15, 2009.

37. "Buscamos trabajar con las empresas petroleras y ONG," *La Región; Diario Judicial de Loreto,* July 11, 2009, available online at: www.diariolaregion.com/index.php?option=com_content&task=view&id=16914; information about the conference in Buenos Aires can be found online at: www.ipieca.org/activities/social/downloads/.../apr.../programme.pdf; "Policías de Bagua," *ElComercio.com.pe,* op. cit.

38. Aiello, "Peru's Cold War," op. cit; Pipoli, "García denies massacre," op. cit., July 20, 2009 e-mail to author from Crippa, staff attorney at the Indian Law Resource Center, who visited Bagua in the aftermath of June confrontation and shared a two-page assessment from his after-action report.

Chapter Nine

1. Cited in Eric J. Hobsbawm, "Ethnicity and nationalism in Europe today," *Anthropology Today,* Vol. 8., No. 1, February 1992, p. 6. .

2. Donna Lee Van Cott, "Indigenous Movements Lose Momentum," op. cit.

3. Republica del Ecuador, "Constitución de 2008," http://pdba.georgetown.edu/Constitutions/Ecuador/ecuador08.html.

4. An important new work that was published after this book was written is Becker's *Indians and Leftists in the Making of Ecuador's Modern Indigenous Movements.*

5. Cited in Marc Becker, "From Oppressed Nationalities to Ethno-Nationalists: Historicizing Ecuador's Indigenous Movement," online at: www.yachana.org/research/confs/aha08andean.pdf.

6. Cited in Norman E. Whitten, "Jungle Quechua ethnicity; an Ecuadorian case study," in Leo A. Despres ed., *Ethnicity and Resource Competition n Plural Societies,* p. 58.

7. Julio F. Carrion, "The Persistent Attraction of Populism," in Richard Millett, et al., eds., *Latin American Democracy: Emerging Reality or Endangered Species* (New York: Routledge, 2008), p. 239; Selmeski, "Multicultural Citizens, Monocultural Men," op. cit., pp. 2-3.

8. Bruneau, "Ecuador: The Continuing Challenges of Democratic Consolidation and Civil-Military Relations," *Strategic Insights,* Volume V, Issue 2, February 2006, p. 1.

9. Patricio Zhingri T., "Interview with Marlon Santi, new president of Ecuador's indigenous confederation," January 15, 2008.

10. Beck and Mijeski, "The Electoral Fortunes of Ecuador's Pachakutik Party: The Fracaso of the 2006 Presidential Election," *The Latin Americanist 52.* No. 2, June 2008, p. 54.

11. Maurice Lemoine, "Ecuador's unknown president," *Le Monde Diplomatique,* January 20, 2007.

12. Lisa Garrigues, "Ecuadorian Native movements turn up the heat," *Indian Country Today,* February 19, 2007.

13. "Constituent Assembly to supercede Congress," *Andean Group Report* RA-07-07 (July 2007), p. 6; Becker, "Ecuador: Indigenous Struggles and the Ambiguities of State Power," op. cit., pp. 24-25, 27.

14. Information on the Ecuadorian Quichua's abstemiousness as far as coca products is concerned was provided in a "Face-to-Face" discussion with Ecuadorian Defense Minister Wellington Sandoval on January 25, 2008 at the Center for Hemispheric Defense Studies (CHDS). Sandoval's observation might lead to the question of why Peruvian and Bolivian indigenous leaders claim coca leaf production as a religious/spiritual right when their Ecuadorian ethnic peers do not. The associated cocaine industry not only wreaks havoc on the environment, but is has become a serious public health problem for Indians youths who obtain cheap semi-refined cocaine products, as well as a security issue for Indians all the way up to and including the United States—the region's biggest consumer of the illegal product.

15. "Indígenas en las FARC?" *Vistazo,* February 14, 2008.

16. Rick Kearns, "Indigenous languages added to new Ecuadorian constitution," *Indian Country Today,* August 22 and September 10, 2008; Haroon Siddique, "Ecuador referendum endorses new socialist constitution," *Guardian,* September 29, 2008; Van Cott, "Indigenous Movements Lose," op. cit.

17. "Correa se muestra decidido a radicalizar su revolución," *The Associated Press,* July 22, 2009; "Ecuador: Correa's Codelco accord risks upsetting Shuar," *LatinNews.com Weekly Report,* June 11, 2009 (WR-09-23); "CONFENIAE condemns Decree 1780 and the militarization of their territories," CONFENIAE press release, July 9, 2009; "Ley de Aguas: Indígenas instan al regimen a considerar su postura," *Vistazo,* September 14, 2009.

18. Walker Simon, "Ecuador's Correa: New term will favor poor, Indians," *The Associated Press,* August 10, 2009.

Chapter Ten

1. James Bryce, *South America*, pp. 471-474.

2. Van Cott, "Las poblaciones indígenas y la politica de seguridad," op. cit.

3. See Ricardo Falla, *Quiché Rebelde: Religious Conversion, Politics, and Ethnic Identity in Guatemala*; "Guatemala: Autoritarismo e Interculturalidad (III)", *Cuadernos de Bakeaz* (Spain), December 2003; Internet edition *La Insignia.* (Guatemala), May 2004, http://www.lainsignia.org/2004/mayo/dial_005.htm.

4. Falla, op. cit.; according to Guatemalan journalist Mario Roberto Morales, the military's counterinsurgency strategy was helped by "a strategic error of the guerrillas ... in which their leaders left the civilian population defenseless when the Army carried out its punitive 'scorched earth" incursions, and didn't mobilize nor arm them or offer them means to escape or to resist. A good part of the indigenous population thus felt betrayed by the guerrillas ..." In "Guatemala: Autoritarismo e Interculturalidad (III)", *Cuadernos de Bakeaz* (Spain), December 2003; Internet edition *La Insignia.* (Guatemala), May 2004, http://www.lainsignia.org/2004/mayo/dial_005.htm; On guerrilla manipulation to put Indians in harm's way, see Paul Hans Robert Kobrak, "Village Troubles: the civil patrols in Aguacatán, Guatemala," Ph.D dissertation, University of Michigan, 1997, pp. 111-112, and David Stoll, *Between Two Armies in the Ixil Towns of Guatemala*, pp. 118, 126, 154. According to Stoll, peasant survivors of the violence often blamed the guerrillas for "putting victims in harm's way," p. 126.

5. *Guatemala, Memory of Silence: Conclusions and Recommendations*, pp. 40-41; Central Intelligence Agency, "Document Secret G5-41," February 1982 (declassified February 1998), p. 1-3; U.S. Defense Intelligence Agency, *Military Intelligence Summary (MIS), Volume VIII: Latin America* [extract], secret summary, November 1979, p. 5, online at: http://www.gwu.edu/~nsarchiv/NSAEBB/NSAEBB32/16-09.htm; A useful study of the counterinsurgency campaign and its consequences is Jennifer Schirmer, *The Guatemalan Military Project: A Violence Called Democracy.*

6. Stoll, op. cit., pp. 113-117, 308, 312; Linda Green, *Fear as a Way of Life: Mayan Widows in Guatemala*, p. 64.

7. Zapeta, "Guatemala Peace Talks: Are Maya Rights Negotiable?" *Abya Yala News* Vol. 8; No. 4 (Winter 1994), pp. 26, 37, http://abyayala.nativeweb.org/maya/zapeta.html; Cojtí Cuxil *Configuración del Pensamiento Político del Pueblo Maya*, p. 13.

8. "Guatemala: Peace Talks on the Rocks," *Central American Report,* February 3, 1995, pp. 7-8.

9. "The Maya vision of a new Guatemala: Beyond the peace talks, a package of thorny demands," *Latin American Weekly Report,* March 9, 1994, p. 534.

10. Saqb'ichil-COPMAGUA (Coordination de Organizations del Pueblo Maya de Guatemala). *Acuerdo sobre Identidad y Derechos de los Pueblos Indígenas.* Punto 3 del Acuerdo de Paz Firme y Duradera. Suscrito en la Ciudad de México por el Gobierno de la República de Guatemala y la Unidad Revolucionaria Nacional Guatemalteca.

11. Warren, *Indigenous Movements and Their Critics,* op. cit., p. 4; Watanabe, John, "Mayas and Anthropologists in the Highlands of Guatemala since the 1960s," in, John Monaghan, ed., *Supplement to the Handbook of Middle American Indians.* Vol. 6. *Ethnology,* p. 4.

12. Nagel, "Indigenous Movements and Their Critics: Pan-Maya Activism in Guatemala," *Latin American Politics and Society,* Spring 2002.

13. Marc Lacey, "Complex defeat for Nobel Winner in Guatemala," *The New York Times,* September 11, 2007; Alejandro Varela, "Escrutinio electoral expone el fracaso de Menchú," *ElNuevoHerald.com,* September 11, 2007; Luis Enrique Perez, "Error y arrogancia de Rigoberta Menchú," *Siglo XXI,* September 19, 2007; Ronald Alvarez, "¿Rigoberta Menchú para presidenta?" *Tiempos del Mundo,* July 2006.

14. Wendy Ruano, "Indígenas logran poder local," *PrensaLibre.com,* September 13, 2007.

Chapter Eleven

1. "Mapuche Put Earth First: An Interview with Floriano Cariqueo Colpihueque," *Multinational Monitor,* November 1995, Vol. 15, No. 11. http://multinationalmonitor.org/hyper/mm1195.09.html.

2. Lorenz Gonschor, "Rapa Nui," *The Contemporary Pacific* , Volume 20, Number 1, Spring 2008, pp. 238-244; Comisión Política—Wallmapuwen, "El Reparto del Territorio," http://www.wallmapuwen.cl/tr_3b.htm; Kolectivo Lientur, "Sobre la autonomía del Pueblo Rapa-Nui," July 23, 2003 http://alainet.org/active/show_text.php3?key=4197.

3. L.C. Faron, *Mapuche Social Structure: Institutional Reintegration in a Patrilineal Society of Central Chile,* p. 11.

4. Personal communication with the author, March 1, 2006.

5. On the "State-to-State" relations maintained by the Spanish Crown and the Mapuche tribes, available online at: http://biblioteca.serindígena.org/libros_digitales/cvhynt/v_iii/t_ii/v3_t2_c2-_-6.html.

6. Isabel Hernandez, *Autonomia o ciudadanía incompleta: El pueblo mapuche en Chile y Argentina,* p. 127.

7. Mario Sznajder, "Ethnodevelopment and Democratic Consolidation in Chile: The Mapuche Question," in Erick D. Langer and Elena Munoz, eds., *Contemporary Indigenous Movements in Latin America,* pp. 21-22.

8. Julian H. Steward, "Forward," in L.C. Faron, *Mapuche Social Structure, op. cit.,* p. viii-ix.

9. Sznajder, "Ethnodevelopment and Democratic Consolidation," op. cit., p. 26.

10. "Chile dam plan: Death of a culture?" November 6, 2002, *Mapuche International Link*, available online at: http://www.mapuche-nation.org/english/html/environmental/enviro-26.htm.

11. Sznajder, "Ethnodevelopment and Democratic Consolidation," op. cit., p. 31; R. Marhikewun, "Indigenous Leaders Speak Out: R. Marhikewun of Chile," in Erick D. Langer and Elena Munoz, eds., *Contemporary Indigenous Movements in Latin America*, pp. 213-214; "The Mapuche People of South America," Indigenous Peoples' Human Rights Initiative (a collaboration of the International Indian Treaty Council and the University of Minnesota Human Rights Center, available online at http://www.hrusa.org/indig/reports/sami.shtm); Raul Zibechi, "The Mapuche in Chile; What their resistance can teach us," *Znet*, August 1, 2007.

12. Commission Política—Wallmapuwen, "El Reparto del Territorio," op. cit.

13. "Gobierno chi leno artifice Convention 169 per insisted con 'tetra chic," September 24, 2008, www.mapuexpress.net/?act=news&id=3285; author communication with Chilean development specialist Caroline Koch, August 15, 2009.

14. Daniela Estrada, "Mapuche Land Conflict Stained with Blood," *Inter Press Service*, January 3, 2008; "El lobby mapuche en Europa," *El Mercurio*, February 11, 2008; information about the European Free Alliance can be found online at: http://www.e-f-a.org/whatsefa.php.

15. Hernandez, *Autonomic o ciudadania*, op. cit., p. 181.

16. Estrada, "Mapuche Land Conflict," op. cit.

17. Interestingly, Mikel Garikoitz Aspiazu Rubina, the military head of the ETA, appeared to admire Native American warrior prowess. Arrested in November 2008 near the Catholic shrine of Lourdes, he used the alias "Txeroki" (Cherokee); see, for example, Fiona Govan, "ETA leader arrested in France," *Telegraph.co.uk*, November 17, 2008 http://www.telegraph.co.uk/news/worldnews/europe/spain/3472076/Eta-leader-arrested-in-France.html.

18. Natalie Hart, "Born Guilty—Chile's Hidden War Against the Mapuche," *The Patagonian Times*, August 25, 2008; "Mapuche radicals return to torching logging firms," Latin America Newsletters, *Latin American Security and Strategic Review*, December 2007, p. 13.

19. "Chilean Cop Caught on Tape Telling Comrade to Shoot at Indians," *Latin American Herald Tribune*, July 6, 2009; "Mapuche Conflict: Chile Gov't flip flops as abuses continue," *Santiago Times*, February 14, 2008; "Alto Ahi!! La violencia policial en Chile," http://www.altoahi.cl/; see also, Thomas Rothe, "Mapuche Girl Seeks Political Asylum in Switzerland," *The Patagonia News*, October 21, 2008. According to the report, "Ten-year-old Relmutray Cadin Calfunao has been arrested and interrogated by Chile's Carabinero uniformed police force. She barely survived a mysterious arson attack on her house in 2005 and has repeatedly seen police beat her parents and brothers."

20. Elaine Ramirez, "Chilean Mapuche Leader Acquitted," *The Patagonian Times*, June 16, 2008; Cathal Sheerin, "Chile: U.S. Government Keeping Tabs on Mapuche 'Terrorists,'" *The Patagonia Times*, June 17, 2009; "Chile: Government 'oversteps the mark" on Mapuche conflict," *LatinNews.com Security & Strategic Review*, June 2009; "Conflicto con Mapuches no se soluciona con más repression," *Ansalatina.com*, July 28, 2009.

21. "Mapuche: Opposition to Power Plants," *Inter Press Service,* December 22, 2008 http://www.unpo.org/content/view/9042/127/; Marine Comte-Trotet, "Mapuche: Codes of Conduct to Face Their First Test," *Santiago Times,* June 1, 2009.

22. An interesting perspective on the prospect of confrontation is contained in Javier Saez Paiva, *La crítica mapuche a la frontera chileno-argentina: antesala a una crisis binacional? Tesis Magister en Seguridad y Defensa, Academia Nacional de Estudios Políticos y Estratégicos* de Chile (ANEPE), Fall 2008.

23. Ivan Fredes, "Empresarios piden al Gobierno aplicar 'mano dura' por los atentados mapuches en el sur," *El Mercurio,* October 22, 2008.

24. Speech given by Canessa on May 18, 2004 in the Chilean Senate, which can be found www.senado.cl.; Canessa also published an article on the subject, "El dilema mapuche: Integrar o segregar," in the *Revista UNOFAR,* No. 8, pp. 4-9. The magazine is published by the pro-Pinochet *Movimiento 10 de Septiembre,* group of retired military officers who promote the "ideals" of the 1973 coup in that country, online at: http://www.movimiento10deseptiembre.cl/index.php?action=fullnews&id=977.

25. Videla del Real, "El Conflicto Mapuche y su Impacto en la Seguridad Nacional;" originally published by the Centro de Estudios e Investigaciones Militares (CESIM), the paper can be found http://www.mapuche.info/fakta/cesim1999.html.; the rightwing Fundación Libertad y Desarrollo published a work in 2003 by Andres Benavente and Jorge Jaraquemada, "Conexiones políticas de las agrupaciones mapuches," in a book, *La cuestión mapuche: aportes para el debate,* in which the authors claimed Mapuche activists, inspired by the Zapatista insurrection in Chiapas, Mexico, sought to create a situation of ungovernability and the creation of armed groups.

26. A useful Web site containing the Indians' agenda is the Mapuche Documentation Center (http://www.mapuche.info/); the site also includes a January 7, 2008 Al Jazeera video "Chile's Mapuches fight for their land."

27. Caroline Koch communication, op, cit.; "Discrimination Against Chile's Indigenous Peoples Continues," *The Santiago Times,* November 29, 2005.

28. Guillermo Chávez, "Aparece vocero de 'Comando Trizano' y amenaza con 'hacer volar' a dirigentes y lonkos indígenas," *El Austral,* July 30, 2009; "El Comando Trizano cuenta con dinamíta... para hacerlos volar de una vez y con ello daremos termino al problema o conflicto mapuche..." *Kilapan,* July 29, 2009, online at: http:// www.kilapan.entodaspartes.net/spip.php?article331; Eva Vergara, "Mapuches chilenos dialogarán sólo con la presidenta Bachelet," *The Associated Press,* August 25, 2009.; "Carabineros de La Reina detiene a nuevo jefe operativo de la CAM," *El Mercurio,* August 5, 2009, online at: http://www.emol.com/noticias/nacional/detalle/detallenoticias. asp?idnoticia=370343; Silke Steiml, "Fugitive Mapuche Activist Caught," *The Santiago Times,* August 7, 2009; Iván Fredes, "Nueva unión de grupos mapuches impulsa estrategia de tomas para presionar por tierras," *El Mercurio; The Patagonia Times,* "Chile: More violence in wake of Mapuche death," August 13, 2009.

29. Fredes, "Nueva unión de grupos mapuches," op. cit.; Eva Vergara, "Chile's Mapuches announce alliance to push fight," *The Associated Press,* August 15, 2009.

30. "Conflicto indígena vuelve a enfrentar al Gobierno y la oposición," *El Mercurio,* August 15, 2009, online at: http://www.emol.com/noticias/nacional/detalle/ detallenoticias.asp?idnoticia=371754; "ONU preocupada por aplicación de Ley Antiterrorista a mapuches," *ElMostrador.cl,* August 14, 2009, online at: http://www.elmostrador.cl/ index.php?/noticias/articulo/onu-preocupada-por-conflicto-mapuches/.

Chapter Twelve

1. Gloria Helena Rey, "Colombia: Indians neither museum exhibits nor tourist attractions," *Inter Press Service News Agency,* December 17, 2007; Troyan, "Gregorio Hernandez de Alba (1904-1973)," op. cit., p. 89; Van Cott, "Indigenous Movements Lose Momentum," op. cit.; Roberto Pineda Camacho, "Pueblos Indígenas de Colombia: una aproximación a su historia, economía y sociedad," in Jaime Arocha and Nina S. Friedemann, eds., *Un siglo de investigación social: antropología en Colombia,* p. 13; Juanita Chaves, "Criminal Justice and Indigenous People in Colombia," online at: *Indigenous Law Bulletin* http://www.austlii.edu.au/au/journals/ILB/1999/73.html.

2. Troyan, op. cit., pp. 89-91, 102; an interesting discussion of how the Soviet-led Comintern promoted the possibility of a revolution in Colombia as early as the late 1920s is contained in Klaus Meschkat, "Helpful Intervention? The Impact of the Comintern on Early Colombian Communism," *Latin America Perspectives,* Issue 159, Vol. 35, No. 2., March 2008.

3. Brysk, *Tribal Village to Global Village,* op. cit. p. 267.

4. Rey, op. cit., p. 102; Van Cott, *The Friendly Liquidation of the Past,* op. cit., pp. 94, 110; "Colombian conflict driving Indians to seek refuge in Brazil," *International Herald Tribune,* December 13, 2007; Natalia Herrera and Douglas Porch, "'Like going to a fiesta'—the role of female fighters in Colombia's FARC-EP," *Small Wars and Insurgencies,* December 1, 2008, pp. 614, 621, 626-627.

5. Presentación del libro: "SEMBRAMOS Y AHORA RECOGEMOS: Somos Familias Guardabosques," discurso del Sr. Sandro Calvani, representante UNODC Colombia www.unodc.org/pdf/colombia/discursos/DISCURSO%20libro.pdf; "$500 milliones recibirán primeras familias guardabosques indígenas de Nariño," February 22, 2004, http://www.presidencia.gov.co/prensa_new/sne/2004/febrero/23/09232004.htm; "Uribe sugiere indígenas ciuden selva para evitar siembra de coca," *EFE Spanish News Agency,* December 21, 2006; Alexander Vaca, "Servicios ambientales: Un proyecto productivo y un proyecto de vida," *El Bosque, Publicación del Programa Familias Guardabosques y del Programa Proyectos Productivos,* November 2007-January 2008, p. 4.

6. "Colombian president to meet with Indian protest leaders," *CNN.com,* Oct. 24, 2008, www.cnn.com/2008/WORLD/americas/10/24/colombia.indian.protests/index.html; "Mass Indian protest seen as 'infiltrated' by Farc," *Latin American Security & Strategic Review,* October 2008, pp. 9-10; "Indígenas colombianos denuncian que FARC torturó y abrió vientre de mujeres,"*Hoy.com.ec,* April 2, 2009; "U.N. agency to investigate Indian massacre in Colombia," *CNN.com,* August 27, 2009; Marce Rojas, "Indígenas pueden rehusarse a prestar servicio militar," *Generación Invisible,* April 27, 2009; Lorenzo Morales, "Los indígenas desafían al narcotráfico," *La Semana,* July 21, 2009.

Chapter Thirteen

1. Earl Shorris, "Mad Mel and the Maya," *The Nation,* November 30, 2006.

2. Horowitz, op. cit., p. 600.

3. Zellen, op. cit, pp. 15-16.

4. Zellen, op. cit, pp. 46-47, 50; David Crary, "Countdown begins for Canada's new territory," *Associated Press/Juneau Empire Online,* March 29, 1998.

5. Ernst-Ulrich Petersmann, "State Sovereignty, Popular, Sovereignty and Individual Sovereignty: from Constitutional Nationalism to Multilevel Constitutionalism in International Economic Law?" *EUI Working Papers, Law No. 2006/45,* European University Institute.

6. In Gabriel Marcella, "War Without Borders: The Colombia-Ecuador Crisis of 2008," Strategic Studies Institute, December 2008.

7. See James Rosenau, *Along the Domestic-Foreign Frontier. Exploring Governance in a Turbulent World.*

8. Warren, *Indigenous Movements and their Critics,* op. cit., pp. 199, 205; Liesbet Hooghe, Gary Marks, "Unraveling the Central State, but How? Types of Multi-Level Governance," *The American Political Science Review,* Vol. 97, No. 2., May, 2003, p. 236.

9. Graham Bowley, "Declaring Something a Lot Like Dependence," *The New York Times,* March 2, 2008.

10. "Bishops' backlash as Archbishop of Canterbury defends calls for sharia law," *ThisisLondon,* February 8, 2008; see also, Geneive Abdo, "Islamic Democracy; Two law professors offer very different assessments of sharia," *The Washington Post,* July 27, 2008; The resulting outcry from fellow clergymen led Williams to beat a hasty retreat, claiming he had just wanted to "tease out some of the broader issues around the rights of religious groups within a secular state" by using *sharia* as an example. The road to political hell is paved with good intentions; It might useful, as a reality check about the "out-of-the-box" viability of, and ultimate loyalties generated by, alternatives to existing nation-state structures to recall the observation made by U.S. political scientists Goldstein and Pevehouse about multinational corporations, whose power exceeds that of many poorer nation-states. "The head of Dow Chemical once said he dreamed of buying an island beyond any state's territory and putting Dow's world headquarters there. In such a view, (multinational corporations) act globally in the interests of their (international) stockholders and low loyalty to no state," in Goldstein and Pevehouse, op. cit., p. 338.

11. Troyan, "Gregorio Hernandez de Alba (1904-1973)," op. cit., p. 95.

12. López Bárcenas, op. cit.

13. Personal communication to author by Dr. Wm. Dean Rudoy, secretary of the board of directors of the Robert F. Kennedy Memorial, December 10, 2008.

14. Becker, "Ecuador: Indigenous Struggles and the Ambiguities of State Power," op. cit., pp. 2, 23, 25, 27. "Because of the strong power of social movements, conservatives cloaked themselves in a progressive discourse in order to win elections, but only to rule on behalf of the oligarchy once in office," Becker observed. "Abadala Bucaram (1996-1997), Jamil Mahuad (1998-2000), and Lucio Gutierrez (2003-2005) had all campaigned with the support of grassroots movements before turning on their bases after they had won an election"; Van Cott, "Indigenous Movements Lose Momentum," op. cit., pp. 85-88.

15. Hvalkof, "Privatization of Land and Indigenous Communities," op. cit, p. 19.

16. Personal communication with the author, March 1, 2006.

17. Kruijt and Kooning, *Armed Actors.*

18. See Becker, "Ecuador: Indigenous Struggles and the Ambiguities of State Power," op. cit., pp. 24, 28; Margarita Nolasco and Miguel Ángel Rubio, "La Migración

Indígena: Causas y Efectos en la Cultura, en la Economía y en la Población," online at: www.etnografia.inah.gob.mx/pdf/Linea5.pdf; Alicia Vacacela, La migración indígena, *Boletín ICCI-ARY Rimay*, Año 4, No. 41, August 2002. Montalvo and Reynal-Querol, "Ethnic Polarization," op. cit., p. 797.

19. See Becker, "Ecuador: Indigenous Struggles and the Ambiguities of State Power," op. cit., pp. 2, 26.

20. Whitney, *State and Revolution in Cuba*, op. cit, pp. 138-139.

21. Van Cott, "A Political Analysis of Legal Pluralism in Bolivia and Columbia," *Journal of Latin American Studies*, Vol. 32, No. 1, Andean Issue, February 2000, pp. 207-234.

22. Díaz-Polanco, *El canon Snorri. Diversidad cultural y tolerancia*, p. 364.

23. Zellen, *The Other Side of the Arctic; A Western Arctic Odyssey, 1988-2000* (forthcoming).

24. Paul Collier and Anke Hoeffler, *Greed and Grievance in Civil War*; Donna Lee Van Cott, *500 Years of Confrontation: Indigenous Peoples and Security Policy in Latin America*.

25. Hendrix, "Memory in Native American Land Claims," *Political Theory*, Vol. 33, No. 6 (December, 2005), pp. 780-781; Steven Newcomb of the Indigenous Law Institute has pointed to a larger problem, noting that, "The categories and metaphors used in anti-Indian rhetoric are wrapped in language that reflects a number of values shared by millions of Americans. Terms and phrases such as "One Nation,' 'equal rights,' 'liberty,' 'justice,' 'equal justice under the law' and so forth seem quite normal to the average person in the United States. To a non-Indian audience, arguments that are put together through the use of such terms and phrases may seem to merely reflect common sense. Thus, one challenge we face as Indian people is how to formulate meaningful responses to anti-Indian messages without seeming to defy mainstream 'common sense' and deeply held American values. . . . When we as Indian people use the English language, we often find ourselves in the paradoxical predicament of attempting to express indigenous cultural and political understandings by means of concepts and categories that carry the baggage of a European cultural mentality, cultural context and values. A dominant-society audience will automatically interpret our messages within their own mental framework using their own cognitive and cultural background," in Newcomb, "Anti-Indian rhetoric in the 21st century," *Indian Country Today*, February 2, 2007.

26. Hvalkof, "Privatization of Land and Indigenous Communities," op. cit, pp. 2, 4, 14-15.

27. See, for example, Thomas K. Rudel, Diane Bates and Rafael Machinguiashi, "Ecologically Noble Amerindians? Cattle Ranching and Cash Cropping among Shuar and Colonists in Ecuador," *The Latin American Studies Association*, Vol. 37, No. 1, 2002..

28. The Goldman Environmental Prize announcement is online at: http://www.goldmanprize.org/2009/southcentralamerica.

29. Kinhide Mushakoji, "Development and racism in Asia and the Pacific," in Michael Banton ed., *Six Continents: Race and Unequal Development*, pp. 15-30; Milagros Salazar, "Peru: Indigenous people, ignored even by the statistics," *Inter Press Service*, Oct. 10, 2006; Andrew Buncombe, "Mahogany imports 'are wiping out Peru tribes,'" *Independent* (U.K.), June 27, 2006; Philip Howard, "The history of ecological marginalization in Chiapas," *Environmental History*, July 1998, p. 13.

30. Becker, "Ecuador: Indigenous Struggles and the Ambiguities of State Power," op. cit., p. 37.

31. Diego Cevallos, "Latin America: Second Chance for Indigenous People after "Lost Decade," *Inter Press Service* May 18, 2007.

32. "El rostro perverso del buen salvaje ecológico: La construcción occidental de los mitos sobre el indígena," *Pukara*, No. 27, December 7 to January 7, 2008, http://www.periodicopukara.com/articulo-del-mes.php.

33. "Ecuador's new constitution 'leaves the past behind,'" Habitat for Humanity, September 28, 2008, available online at: http://www.habitat.org/lac_eng/newsroom/2008/09_28_08_ Ecuador_eng.aspx.

34. James Cockcroft, "Historic Changes Across Latin America; Indigenous People Rising," *Counterpunch*, November 28-30, 2008; "Bolivia: Indigenous for Planetary Safety," *Prensa Latina* (Cuba), Oct. 13, 2007.

35. Rudel (et al.), "Ecologically Noble Amerindians?" op. cit., p. 144; The original panning of indigenous peoples as "ecologically noble" is contained in Kent Redford, "The Ecologically Nobel Savage," *Cultural Survival Quarterly*, Vol. 15, 1991, pp. 46-48; "Mapuche Put Earth First: An Interview with Floriano Cariqueo Colpihueque," Multinational Monitor, November 1995, Vol. 15, No. 11, available online at: http://multinationalmonitor.org/hyper/mm1195.09.html.

36. These were some of the recommendations contained in the "draft recommendations" of the 9th National Conference on Science, Policy and the Environment: *Biodiversity in a Rapidly Changing World*, December 8, 2008, online at: http://www.ncseonline.org/Conference/Biodiversity/Recommendations/Breakout%20Rec ommendations%201st%20edited%20draft.pdf.

37. Shorris, *The Death of the Great Spirit*, op. cit., pp. 58-59.

38. Deloria and Lytle, *American Indians, American Justice*, pp. 136-137.

39. See, for example, *Like a Loaded Weapon: The Rehnquist Court, Indian Rights and the Legal History of Racism in America*, by University of Arizona law professor Robert A. Williams (2005).

40. Martin Edwin Andersen, "Thankful for renewed rights; Native Nicaraguans needed protection," *The Washington Times*, November 22, 2001.

41. Tullberg, "Securing Human Rights of American Indians and Other Indigenous Peoples Under International Law," op. cit., p. 68.

42. Amb. Jorge Skinner-Klee, quoted in Josh Nelson, "U.N. Ambassadors experience Meskwaki culture," *WFCCourier.com*, October 16, 2007.

43. Bordewich, *Killing the White Man's Indian*, pp. 10-11.

44. See Deborah House, *Language Shift among the Navajos: Identity Politics and Cultural Continuity*, especially chapters 3 ("The Revitalization of Navajo Culture"), 4 ("Narratives of Navajo-ness"), and 5 ("Navajo-ization of Schools").

45. Carol Perry and Patricia Anne Davis, "Dineh Sovereignty Is Spiritual Empowerment and Self-Identity" (public hearing, Window Rock, Ariz, August 16, 2001, cited in Lloyd L. Lee, "The Future of Navajo Nationalism," *Wicazo Sa Review* 22.1, 2007, p. 60; The successful examples of indigenous Hawaiian societies (Maori and Kanaka Maoli) can also be of benefit for those tribes seeking to help sustain their cultural identity by means of language revitalization programs, whether through schools or in society as a whole, see Kauanoe Kamana and William H. Wilson, "Hawaiian Language Programs," National Clearinghouse for English Language Acquisition and Language Instruction

Educational Programs, http://www.ncela.gwu.edu/pubs/stabilize/ additional/ hawaiian.html, cited in Lee, "The Future of Navajo Nationalism," op. cit., p. 65. For an interesting historical perspective of the similarities and contrasts between Native American and native Hawaiian experiences, see Linda S. Parker, *Native American Estate: The Struggle over Indian and Hawaiian Lands*; Parker is a Western Cherokee.

46. Tullberg, op. cit., p. 65.

47. President Richard M. Nixon, *Special Message to Congress on Indian Affairs*, July 8, 1970.

48. López Bárcenas, "Indigenous Movements in the Americas: From Demand for Recognition to Building Autonomies," op. cit.

49. Tullberg, op. cit., p. 54.

50. Deloria and Lytle, *American Indians*, op. cit., pp. 136-137, listed as "weaknesses", among others, the courts' "susceptibility to political influence," "summary justice," a "need for qualified personnel," and "inadequate tribal laws."

51. *Nat'l Farmers Union Ins. Companies v. Crow Tribe of Indians*, 471 U.S. 845, 856-57, 105 S.Ct. 2447, 2454, 85 L.Ed.2d 818 (1985).

52. Janet Reno, "A federal commitment to tribal justice systems," 79 *Judicature* 113, 114, 1995.

53. Cohen, *Handbook of Federal Indian Law*, pp. 122-123.

54. *United States v. Antelope*, 430 U.S. 641 (1977).

55. Michael Riley, "Indian Justice; 1885 law at root of jurisdictional jumble," *The Denver Post*, November 11, 2007; A so-called "Montana rule" means that tribes and their courts do not have a presumption of civil jurisdiction over non-members unless the latter consent or unless it can be shown to all but threaten the continuing existence of the tribe. Indian police officers also cannot arrest a non-Indian person on tribal land.

56. The State of Louisiana, whose laws are based on the Napoleonic Code, the French civil code enacted in 1804, is an exception to this rule.

57. Deloria and Lytle, *American Indians*, op. cit., p. 118.

58. Robert Yazzie, "Life comes from it: Navajo justice concepts," *24 New Mexico Law Review*, 1994.

59. M. Wesley Clark, "Enforcing Criminal Law on Native American Lands," *FBI Law Enforcement Bulletin*, April 2005; Michael L. Barker, "American Indian Tribal Police: An Overview and Case-Study," Ph.D. dissertation, School of Criminal Justice, State University of New York at Albany, Summer 1994.

60. Michael Riley, "Promises, justice broken; A dysfunctional system lets serious reservation crimes go unpunished and puts Indians at risk," *The Denver Post*, November 11, 2007; Riley, "Justice: Inaction's fatal price: Delays and missteps in Indian Country criminal cases can give offenders a free pass. The consequences can be tragic," *The Denver Post*, November 12, 2007; Riley, "Principles, politics collide; Some U.S. attorneys who emphasize fighting crime on Indian lands have seen themselves fall out of favor in D.C.," *The Denver Post*, November 13, 2007; Riley, "Path to justice unclear; Empower the tribes, or beef up the federal role? Each side has its own history of failure," *The Denver Post*, November 14, 2007; "Indian Country Hit Twice With Budget Cuts," *U.S. Federal News Service*, Feb. 7, 2006.

61. Sam Vaknin, "Interview with Barry Scott Zellen: Arctic Lessons," *Global Politician*, June 5, 2008.

62. Zellen, *On Thin Ice* (forthcoming), pp. 47, 50; Sweetgrass, "Make Canada see the oppression," *The Globe and Mail,* June 28, 2007; Margaret Wente, "Trapped in the aboriginal narrative," *The Globe and Mail,* June 28, 2007; Frances Widdowson and Albert Howard. *Disrobing the Aboriginal Industry—The Deception Behind Indigenous Cultural Preservation.*

63. International Work Group on Indigenous Affairs, *Yearbook 1988,* p. 159; Zellen, *On Thin Ice,* op. cit., p. 45.

64. Vaknin, "Interview with Barry Scott Zellen," op. cit.; Zellen, *On Thin Ice,* op. cit., pp. 31, 35, 42.

65. Zellen, *On Thin Ice,* op. cit., p. 45; Vaknin, "Interview with Barry Scott Zellen," op. cit.

66. Burgete Cal y Mayor and Gómez Gómez, op. cit., pp. 348-356.

67. Burgete Cal y Mayor and Gómez Gómez, op. cit., pp. 356-362.

Chapter Fourteen

1. Barack Obama, "Message From Obama: Tribes Will Have Voice in White House," *Reznet,* October 25, 2008, http://www.reznetnews.org/article/message-obama-tribes-will-have-voice-white-house-23490.

2. Stuart J. Kaufman, "Spiraling to Ethnic War: Elites, Masses, and Moscow in Moldova's Civil War,' *International Security,* 21(2), 1996, p.151.

3. Shorris, *The Death of the Great Spirit,* op. cit., p. 90.

4. Goldstein and Pevehouse, *International Relations,* op. cit., pp. 163, 174.

5. Orin Starn, "To Revolt Against the Revolution," op. cit., p. 550.

6. Blight, *Race and Reunion: The Civil War in American Memory,* p. 219.

7. Simon Romero, *The New York Times,* February 3, 2009.

8. Jeffrey Gettleman, "Signs in Kenya of a Land Redrawn by Ethnicity," *The Washington Post,* February 15, 2008.

9. Posen, "The Security Dilemma," op. cit., p. 30.

10. Potter, *The Impending Crisis, 1848-1861,* p. 43, cited in the review of his work by Robert W. Johannsen, in *The Journal of Southern History,* Vol. 43, No. 1, February 1977, p. 104.

11. Alexis de Tocqueville, *Democracy in America,* Vol. 2, p. 261; Muller, "Us and Them, The Enduring Power of Ethnic Nationalism," *Foreign Affairs,* March/April 2008, p. 1.

12. Serafin Fanjul, "¿Indigenismo? No gracias," *Libertad Digital* (Spain), June 13, 2006.

Bibliography

Books and Reports

Albó, Xavier, and Raúl Barrios, eds. *Violencias encubiertas en Bolivia,* La Paz: CIPCA, 1993.

Anderson, Benedict. *Imagined Communities: Reflections on the Origin and Spread of Nationalism (Revised Edition).* London: Verso, 1991.

Anderson, Thomas. *Matanza: The 1932 'Slaughter' that Traumatized a Nation. Shaping U.S.-Salvadoran Policy to this Day.* Willimantic, Connecticut: Curbstone Press, 1992.

Assies, William, et al., ed. *The Challenge of Diversity: Indigenous Peoples and the Reform of the State in Latin America.* Amsterdam, Netherlands: Thela Thesis, 2000.

Austin, Raymond D. *Navajo Courts and Navajo Common Law; A Tradition of Tribal Self-Governance.* Minneapolis: University of Minnesota, 2009.

Becker, Marc. *Indians and Leftists in the Making of Ecuador's Modern Indigenous Movements.* Durham, N.C.: Duke University Press, 2008).

Bernstein, Alison R. *American Indians and World War II; Toward a New Era in Indian Affairs.* Norman, Oklahoma: University of Oklahoma Press, 1991.

Bantjes, Adrian A. *Cárdenas, Sonora, and the Mexican Revolution.* Wilmington, Del.: Scholarly Resources, Inc., 1998.

Bhabha, Homi K., ed. *Nation and Narration.* London: Routledge, 1990.

Bland, Douglas L., *Outbreak,* Toronto: Blue Butterfly Book Publishing Inc., 2009.

Blaser, Mario, et al., ed. *In the Way of Development; Indigenous Peoples, Life Projects and Globalization.* London: Zed Books, 2004.

Bonfil Batalla, Guillermo, ed. *Utopia y revolución: El pensamiento politico de los indios en América Latina.* Mexico City: Editorial Nuevo Imagen, 1981.

Booth, John A., and Mitchell A. Seligson. *The Legitimacy Puzzle in Latin America: Democracy and Political Support in Eight Nations.* Cambridge: Cambridge University Press, 2009.

Bordewich, Fergus M. *Killing the White Man's Indian.* New York: Anchor Books, Doubleday, 1996.

Briggs, Charles L., and John R. Van Ness, ed. *Land, Water, and Culture: New Perspectives on Hispanic Land Grants.* Albuquerque: University of New Mexico: 1987.

Bryce, James. *South America.* New York: The Macmillan Company, 1914.

Brysk, Alison. *From Tribal Village to Global Village, Indian Rights and International Relations in Latin America.* Stanford: Stanford University Press, 2000.

Carman, Robert, ed. *Harvest of Violence: Guatemala's Indians in the Counterinsurgency War.* Norman, Oklahoma: University of Oklahoma Press, 1988.

Case, David S. and David A. Voluck. *Alaska Natives and American Laws (Second Edition).* Fairbanks: University of Alaska Press, 2002.

Chapin, Mac, *Indigenous Peoples and Natural Ecosystems in Central America and Southern Mexico.* Washington, D.C.: National Geographic Society, 2003.

———. *"Recapturing the old ways: traditional knowledge and Western science among the Kuna Indians in Panama."* In *Cultural Expression and Grassroots Development: Cases from Latin America and the Caribbean,* ed. C.D. Kleymeyer. Boulder: Lynne Reinner, 1994.

———. *La Población Indígena de El Salvador.* San Salvador: Ministerio de Educación, Dirección de Publicaciones e Impresos, 1990.

Chua, Amy. *Worlds on Fire.* New York: Doubleday, 2003.

Clavero, Bartolome, *Freedom's Law and Indigenous Rights.* Berkeley: Robbins Collections Publication, 2005.

Clech Lam, Maivan. *At the End of the State: Indigenous Peoples and Self-Determination.* Ardsley, New York: Transnational Publishers, 2000.

Cohen, Felix. *Handbook of Federal Indian Law.* Washington, D.C.: Government Printing Office, 1942.

Collier, George A. *Basta! Land and the Zapatista Rebellion in Chiapas, Third Edition.* Oakland, California: Food First Books, 2005.

Paul Collier and Anke Hoeffler. *Greed and Grievance in Civil War.* Policy Research Working Paper, No. 2355. Washington, D.C.: The World Bank, 2001.

Commission for Historical Clarification *Guatemala, Memory of Silence: Conclusions and Recommendations.* Guatemala City: CEH, 1999.

CONAIE. *Las nacionalidades indígenas y sus derechos colectivos en la Constitución,* Quito: 1999.

Connor, Walker. *Ethnonationalism, The Quest for Understanding.* Princeton, N.J.: Princeton University Press, 1994.

Coordinadora Andina de Organizaciones Indígenas. *Preso por defender a la Madre Tierra, Criminalization del Ejercicio de Derechos de los Pueblos Indígenas,* 2008.

Cojtí Cuxil, Demetrio. *Ri Maya' Moloj pa Iximulew: El Movimiento Maya.* Guatemala City: Editorial Cholsamaj, 1997.

———. *Configuración del Pensamiento Político del Pueblo Maya.* Quetzaltenango, Guatemala: Asociación de Escritores Mayances de Guatemala 1991.

Cranston, Alan. *The Sovereignty Revolution.* Stanford: Stanford University Press, 2004.

Crooke, Alastair. *Resistance: The Essence of the Islamist Revolution.* London: Pluto Press, 2009.

Deere, Carmen Diana and Magdelena León, *Empowering Women: Land and Property Rights in Latin America.* Pittsburgh: University of Pittsburgh Press, 2001.

Degregori, Carlos Iván, et al., ed. *Las Rondas Campesinas. La Derrota de Sendero Luminoso* (Lima: IEP, 1996).

Degregori, Carlos Iván. *Ayacucho 1969-1979. El surgimiento de Sendero Luminoso.* Lima: IEP, 1990.

Deloria, Jr., Vine, and Clifford M. Lytle, *American Indians, American Justice* Austin: University of Texas Press, 1983.

Deloria, Jr., Vine. *Custer Died For Your Sins; An Indian Manifesto.* New York: Avon Books, 1969.

De Arístegui, Gustavo. *Contra Occidente; La emergente alianza antisistema.* Madrid: La Esfera de los Libros, 2008.

De la Cadena, Marisol. *Indigenous mestizos: The politics of race and culture in Cuzco, Perú, 1919-1991.* Durham, N.C.: Duke University Press, 2000.

DeShazo, Peter, et al., *Colombia's Plan de Consolidación Integral de la Macarena; An assessment.* Washington, D.C.: Center for Strategic and International Studies, 2009.

Deutscher, Irwin. *Accommodating Diversity; National Policies That Prevent Ethnic Conflict.* Lanham, Md.: Lexington Books, 2002.

Díaz-Polanco, Héctor. *Elogio de la diversidad. Globalización, multiculturalismo y etnofagia.* Sinaloa, México: Siglo XXI, 2006.

———. *El canon Snorri. Diversidad cultural y tolerancia.* México: Universidad Autónoma de la Ciudad de México, 2004.

Dobyns, Henry F., Paul Doughty, and Harold Lasswell, ed. *Peasants, Power, and Applied Social Change: Vicos as a model.* Beverly Hills, London: Sage Publications, 1971.

Edwards. Laura F. *Gendered Strife and Confusion; The Political Culture of Reconstruction.* Urbana: University of Illinois Press, 1997.

Elton, Charlotte. *Panamá: Evaluación de la sostenibilidad nacional.* Panama City: Centro de Estudios y Acción Social Panameño, 1997.

Enloe, Cynthia H. *Ethnic Soldiers.* Athens, Georgia: University of Georgia Press, 1980.

———. *Police, Military and Ethnicity.* New Brunswick, N.J.: Transaction Books, 1980.

Falk, Richard A. *Human Rights Horizons: The Pursuit of Justice in a Globalizing World.* New York: Routledge, 2000.

Falla, Ricardo. *Quiché Rebelde: Religious Conversion, Politics, and Ethnic Identity in Guatemala.* Austin: University of Texas, 2001.

Faron, L.C. *Mapuche Social Structure: Institutional Reintegration in a Patrilineal Society of Central Chile.* Urbana: University of Illinois Press, 1961.

Fischer, Edward F., and Peter Benson. *Broccoli and Desire: Global Connections and Maya Struggles in Postwar Guatemala.* Palo Alto, California: Stanford University Press, 2006.

Fischer, Edward F., and R. McKenna Brown. Maya Cultural Activism in Guatemala. Austin: University of Texas Press, 1997.

Friedrich, Paul. *Agrarian Revolt in a Mexican Village.* Englewood Cliffs: Prentice Hall, 1970.

Foner, Eric. *Reconstruction: America's Unfinished Revolution, 1863-1877.* New York: Harper & Row, 1988.

Garfield, Seth. *Indigenous struggle at the heart of Brazil: State policy, frontier expansion, and the Xavante Indians.* Durham, N.C.: Duke University Press, 2001.

Gellner, Ernest. *Nations and Nationalism.* Ithaca, New York: Cornell University Press, 1983.

Goldstein, Joshua and Jon Pevehouse. *International Relations.* New York: Pearson, Longman, 2009.

Gomez, Augusto, and Ana Cristina Lesmes and Claudia Rocha. *Caucherias y Conflicto Colombo-Peruano; Testimonios 1904-1934.* Bogotá: Disloque Editores, 1995.

Grant, Shelagh D. *Arctic Justice.* Montreal: McGill—Queen's University Press, 2005.

———. *Sovereignty or Security? Government Policy in the Canadian North, 1936-1950.* Vancouver: University of British Columbia Press, 1988.

Green, Linda. *Fear as a Way of Life: Mayan Widows in Guatemala.* New York: Columbia University Press, 1999.

Greet, Michele. *Beyond National Identity; Pictorial Indigenism as a Modernist Strategy in Andean Art, 1920–1960.* University Park, Penn: Penn State Press, 2009.

Gutiérrez, Natividad. *Nationalist Myths and Ethnic Identities: Indigenous Intellectuals and the Mexican State.* Lincoln, Nebraska: University of Nebraska Press, 1999.

Hansen, Roger D. *The Politics of Mexican Development.* Baltimore: The Johns Hopkins University Press, 1971.

Harvard Project on American Indian Economic Development. *The State of the Native Nations: Conditions Under U.S. Policies of Self-Determination.* Cary, N.C.: Oxford University Press, 2007.

Hernandez, Isabel. *Autonomia o ciudadania incomplete: El pueblo mapuche en Chile y Argentina.* Santiago: CEPAL, 2003.

Hobsbawm, E.J. *Nations and Nationalism since 1780: Programme, Myth, Reality.* Cambridge: Cambridge University Press, 1990.

Horowitz, Donald L. *Ethnic Groups in Conflict.* Berkeley: University of California Press, 1985.

House, Deborah. *Language Shift among the Navajos: Identity Politics and Cultural Continuity.* Tucson: University of Arizona Press, 2002.

Howe, James. *A People Who Would Not Kneel: Panama, The United States, and the San Blas Kuna.* Washington, D.C.: Smithsonian Institution Press, 1998.

Hoxie, Frederick E. *A Final Promise: The Campaign to Assimilate the Indians, 1880-1920.* Lincoln, Nebraska: University of Nebraska Press, 1984.

Human Rights Watch. "Undue Process: Terrorism Trials, Military Courts and the Mapuche in Southern Chile." October 27, 2004.

Huntington, Samuel. *Political Order in Changing Societies.* New Haven: Yale University Press, 2006.

Hutchinson, George, and Anthony D. Smith. *Nationalism: Critical Concepts in Political Science, Volume 4,* London/New York: Routledge, 2004.

Hylton, Forrest and Sinclair Thomson, *Revolutionary Horizons: Past and Present in Bolivian Politics.* London: Verso, 2007.

Ignatieff, Michael. *Blood and Belonging.* London: Chatto & Windus, 1993.

Johansen, Bruce E. *Forgotten Fathers, Benjamin Franklin, the Iroquois and the Rationale for the American Revolution.* Ipswich, Mass.: Gambit, Incorporated, 1982.

Joseph, Gilbert M., and Daniel Nugent, ed. *Everyday Forms of State Formation: Revolution and the Negotiation of Rule in Modern Mexico.* Durham and London: Duke University Press, 1995.

Jung, Courtney. *The Moral Force of Indigenous Politics: Critical Liberalism and the Zapatistas.* Cambridge: Cambridge University Press, 2008.

Kamenskii, Archimandrite Anatolii. *Tinglit Indians of Alaska.* Fairbanks: University of Alaska Press, 1985.

Kearney, Michael. *Reconceptualizing the Peasantry: Anthropology in Global Perspective*. Boulder: Westview Press, 1996.

Kedourie, Elie. *Nationalism, Fourth, Expanded Edition*. Malden, MA: Blackwell Publishers, Inc., 2000.

Knight, Alan. *The Mexican Revolution: Vol. 1, Porfirians, Liberals, and Peasants*. Cambridge: Cambridge University Press, 1986.

Kruger, Peter. *Ethnicity and Nationalism: Case Studies in Their Intrinsic Tension and Political Dynamics*. Marburg, Germany: Hitzeroth, 1993.

Krujit, Dirk and Kees Kooning. *Armed Actors*. London: MacMillan, 2005.

Laclau, Ernesto. *Politics and Ideology in Marxist Theory*. London: New Left Books, 1977.

Langer, Erick D., and Elena Muñoz. *Contemporary Indigenous Movements In Latin America*. Wilmington, Del.: Jaguar Books on Latin America/Scholarly Resources, Inc., 2003.

Larson, Brooke. *Cochabamba, 1550-1900: Colonialism and Agrarian Transformation in Bolivia, 2nd. Ed*, Durham, N.C.: Duke University Press, 1998.

Leibner, Gerardo. *El mito del socialismo indígena de Mariátegui*. Lima: Fondo Editorial de la Pontificia Universidad Católica del Perú, 1999.

Leoussi, Athena S. and Steven Grosby, ed. *Nationalism and Ethnosymbolism; History, Culture and Ethnicity in the Formation of Nations*. Edinburgh: Edinburgh University Press, 2007.

Luna-Firebaugh, Eileen. *Asserting Sovereignty, Seeking Justice*. Tucson: University of Arizona Press, 2007.

Mallon, Florencia. *Peasant and Nation: The Making of Postcolonial Mexico and Perú*. Berkeley: University of California Press, 1995.

Mander, Jerry and Victoria Tauli-Corpuz, ed. *Paradigm Wars; Indigenous Peoples' Resistance to Globalization*. San Francisco: Sierra Club Books, 2006.

Mann, Charles C. *1491: New Revelations of the Americas Before Columbus*. New York: Vintage, 2006. ·

Mann, Charles C. 1491: New Revelations of the Americas Before Columbus. New York: Vintage, 2006.

Markovits, Andrei S. *Uncouth Nation: Why Europe Dislikes America*. Princeton: Princeton University Press, 2007.

Marti I Puig, Salvador, ed. *Pueblos Indígenas y Política en America Latina, El Reconocimiento de sus Derechos y el Impacto de sus Demandas a Inicios del Siglo XXI*. Barcelona: Fundacio CIDOB, 2007.

Martin, David. *Tongues of Fire; The Explosion of Protestantism in Latin America*. Cambridge: Blackwell Publishers, 1990.

Martin, Terry. *The Affirmative Action Empire; Nations and Nationalism in the Soviet Union, 1923-1939*. Ithaca: Cornell University Press, 2001.

Massey, Douglas, et al., ed. *Return to Aztlan; The Social Process of International Migration from Western Mexico*. Berkeley: The University of California Press, 1987.

McIlwaine, Cathy, and Caroline Moser. *Violence in a Post-Conflict Context: Urban Poor Perceptions from Guatemala*. Washington, D.C.: The World Bank, 2001.

Meadows, William C. *The Comanche Code Talkers of World War II*. Austin: University of Texas Press, 2002.

Means, Russell, and Marvin J. Wolf. *Where White Men Fear to Tread; The Autobiography of Russell Means*. New York: St. Martin's Griffin, 1996.'

Merrell, James H. *The Indians' New World; Catawbas and their Neighbors from European Contact through the Era of Removal.* New York: W.W. Norton & Company, 1989.

Millett, Richard L., and Jennifer S. Holmes and Orlando J. Perez, ed. *Latin American Democracy; Emerging Reality or Endangered Species?* New York: Routledge, 2009.

Miranda, Roger and William Ratliff. *The Civil War in Nicaragua.* New Brunswick: Transaction Publishers, 1993.

Mires, Fernando. *Al Borde del Abismo; El Chavismo y la Contrarevolución Anti-Democrático de Nuestro Tiempo.* Caracas: Random House/Mondadori, 2007.

Mortimer, William Golden. *Perú: History of coca, "The divine plant" of the Incas.* New York: J.H. Vail & Company, 1901.

Naimark, Norman. *Fires of Hatred: Ethnic Cleansing in Twentieth Century Europe.* Cambridge: Harvard University Press, 2001.

Nietschmann, Bernard. *The Unknown War: The Miskito Nation, Nicaragua and the United States.* New York: Freedom House, 1989.

Osorno, Diego Enrique. *Oaxaca Sitiada; La Primera Insurreción del Siglo XXI.* Mexico City: Random House Mondadori, 2007.

Parker, Linda S. *Native American Estate: The Struggle over Indian and Hawaiian Lands.* Honolulu: University of Hawaii Press, 1989.

Plant, Roger, and Søren Hvalkof. *Land Titling and Indigenous Peoples in Latin America.* Washington, D.C.: Inter-American Development Bank, Technical Paper Series, 2001, online at http://www.iadb.org/sds/doc/IND-109E.pdf.

Portocarrero, Gonzalo. *Razones de Sangre. Aproximaciones a la violencia política.* Lima: Pontificia Universidad Católica del Perú, 1998.

Prashad, Vijay, and Teo Ballvé, ed. *Dispatches from Latinamerica; On the Frontlines Against Neoliberalism.* Cambridge, Massachusetts: South End Press, 2006.

Prieto, Mercedes. *Liberalismo y temor: imaginando los sujetos indígenas en el Ecuador postcolonial, 1895-1950.* Quito: FLACSO Sede Ecuador-Abya Yala, 2004.

Purnell, Jennie. *Popular Movements and State Formation in Revolutionary Mexico; The Agraristas and Cristeros of Michoacan.* Durham and London: Duke University Press, 1999.

Rabasa, Angel, et al. *Ungoverned Territories: Understanding and Reducing Terrorism Risks.* Santa Monica, Calif: RAND, 2007.

Rappaport, Joanne. *Intercultural Utopias: Public Intellectuals, Cultural Experimentation and Ethnic Pluralism in Colombia.* Durham, N.C.: Duke University Press: 2005.

Reuque Paillalef, Rosa Isolde, and Florencia E. Mallon. *When a Flower Is Reborn: The Life And Times Of A Mapuche Feminist.* Durham, N.C.: Duke University Press, 2002.

Roeder, Philip G. *Where Nation-States Come From.* Princeton: Princeton University Press, 2007.

Roncagliolo, Gonzalo. *La cuarta espada. La historia de Abimáel Guzmán y Sendero Luminoso.* Lima: Debate, 2007.

Rosenau, James. *Along the Domestic-Foreign Frontier. Exploring Governance in a Turbulent World.* Cambridge: Cambridge University Press, 1997.

Rossmiller, A. J. *Still Broken; A Recruit's Inside Account of Intelligence Failures, from Baghdad to the Pentagon.* New York: Ballantine Books, 2008.

Sábato, Ernesto. *El otro rostro del peronismo: Carta abierta a Mario Amadeo.* Buenos Aires: Private printing, 1956.

Sánchez, Enrique, ed. *Derechos de los pueblos indígenas en las constituciones de América Latina.* Bogotá: Disloque Editores, 1996.

Schirmer, Jennifer. *The Guatemalan Military Project: A Violence Called Democracy.* Philadelphia: University of Pennsylvania Press, 1998.

Selverston-Scher, Melina. *Ethnopolitics in Ecuador: Indigenous Rights and the Strengthening of Democracy.* Boulder: Lynne Rienner, 2001.

Seton-Watson, Hugh. *Nations and States; An Enquiry into the Origins of Nations and the Politics of Nationalism.* Boulder: Westview Press, 1977.

Shorris, Earl. *The Death of the Great Spirit.* New York: Simon and Schuster, 1971.

Sieder, Rachel, ed. *Multiculturalism in Latin America: Indigenous Rights, Diversity and Democracy.* Hampshire, England: Palgrave MacMillan, 2002.

Silko, Leslie Marmon. *Yellow Women and a Beauty of the Spirit.* New York: Simon and Schuster, 1996.

———. *Almanac of the Dead.* New York: Simon and Schuster, 1991.

Smith, Paul Chaat, and Robert Allen Warrior. *Like a Hurricane: The Indian Movement from Alcatraz to Wounded Knee.* New York: New Press, 1996.

Smith, Peter H. *Argentina and the Failure of Democracy, Conflict among Political Elites, 1904-1955.* Madison: University of Wisconsin Press, 1974.

Stern, Steve J., ed. *Resistance, Rebellion, and Consciousness in the Andean Peasant World, 18th to 20th Centuries.* Madison: University of Wisconsin Press, 1987.

Stoll, David. *Rigoberta Menchú and the Story of All Poor Guatemalans.* Boulder: Westview Press, 1999.

———. *Between Two Armies in the Ixil Towns of Guatemala.* New York: Columbia University Press, 1993.

———. *Is Latin America Turning Protestant? The Politics of Evangelical Growth.* Berkeley: University of California Press, 1990.

Ther, Philipp, and Ana Siljak, *Redrawing Nations: Ethnic Cleansing in East-Central Europe, 1944-1948.* New York: Rowman & Littlefield, 2001.

Thomson, Sinclair. *We Alone Will Rule; Native American Politics in the Age of Insurgency,* Madison: University of Wisconsin Press, 2002.

Tierney, Patrick. *Darkness in El Dorado: How Scientists and Journalists Devastated the Amazon.* New York: W. W. Norton & Company, 2002.

Tilley, Virginia. *Seeing Indians: A Study of Race, Nation and Power in El Salvador,* Albuquerque: University of New Mexico Press, 2005.

Tocqueville, Alexis de. *Democracy in America.* 2 Vols. New York: Vintage, 1960.

Townsend, Kenneth William. *World War II and the American Indian.* Albuquerque: University of New Mexico Press, 2000.

Van Cott, Donna Lee. *The Friendly Liquidation of the Past: The Politics of Diversity in Latin America.* Pittsburgh: University of Pittsburgh Press, 2000.

———. *From Movements to Parties in Latin America,* Cambridge: Cambridge University Press, 2006.

———. ed. *Indigenous Peoples and Democracy in Latin America.* New York: St. Martin's Press, 1994.

Van Dijk, Teun A., ed. *Racism and Discourse in Latin America.* Lanham, Md.: Lexington Books, 2009.

Vargas Llosa, Mario. *The Storyteller.* New York: Farrar, Straus and Giroux, 1989.

————, et al. *Informe de la Comisión Investigadora de los Sucesos de Uchuraccay.* Lima: Editora Perú, 1983.

Warren, Kay B. *Indigenous Movements and Their Critics: Pan-Mayan Activism in Guatemala.* Princeton: Princeton University Press, 1999.

Wauchope, Robert. *Lost Tribes and Sunken Continents; Myth and Method in the Study of American Indians.* Chicago: University of Chicago Press, 1962.

Weatherford, Jack. *Indian Givers; How the Indians of the Americas Transformed the World.* New York: Fawcett, 1988.

Whitney, Robert. *State and Revolution in Cuba; Mass Mobilization and Political Change, 1920-1940.* Chapel Hill, N.C.: University of North Carolina Press, 2001.

Wiarda, Howard J. *The Soul of Latin America.* New Haven, Conn.: Yale University Press, 2001.

Widdowson, Frances, and Albert Howard. *Disrobing the Aboriginal Industry——The Deception Behind Indigenous Cultural Preservation.* Montreal: McGill-Queen's University Press, 2008.

Wiewiorka, Michel. *El Espacio del Racismo.* Madrid: Paídos, 1992.

Williams, Jr., Robert A. *Like a Loaded Weapon: The Rehnquist Court, Indian Rights and the Legal History of Racism in America.* Minneapolis: University of Minnesota Press, 2005.

Yans-McLaughlin, Virginia, ed. *Immigration Reconsidered.* New York: Oxford University Press, 1990.

Yashar, Deborah J. *Contesting Citizenship in Latin America, The Rise of Indigenous Movements and the Postliberal Challenge.* Cambridge: Cambridge University Press, 2005.

Young, Crawford, ed. *The Rising Tide of Cultural Pluralism; The Nation-State at Bay?* Madison: University of Wisconsin Press, 1993.

———— *The Politics of Cultural Pluralism.* Madison: University of Wisconsin Press, 1976.

Zellen, Barry Scott. *On Thin Ice; The Inuit, the State and the Challenge of Arctic Sovereignty.* Lanham, Md.: Lexington Books, 2009.

————. *Breaking the Ice; From Land Claims to Tribal Sovereignty in the Artic.* Lanham, Md.: Lexington Books, 2008.

Articles

Abdo, Geneive. "Islamic Democracy; Two law professors offer very different assessments of sharia." *The Washington Post,* July 27, 2008.

Aguirre, Doris. "¿Quién dió la orden de desalojar a indígenas sin prevenir represalias?" *LaRepublica.pe,* June 12, 2009, online at: http://www.larepublica.pe/bagua-masacre/12/06/2009/quien-dio-la-orden-de-desalojar-indigenas-sin-prevenir-represalias.

Aiello, Kristina. "Peru's Cold War against Indigenous Peoples." *Worldpress.org,* July 19, 2009, online at: http://www.worldpress.org/Americas/3383.cfm.

Albó, Xavier. "La circunscripciones especiales indígenas." *La Razón,* April 6, 2009.

————. "And from Kataristas to MNRistas? The Surprising and Bold Alliance Between Aymaras and Neoliberals in Bolivia." In Van Cott, ed. *Indigenous Peoples and Democracy in Latin America,* New York: St. Martin's Press, 1994.

———. "From MNRistas to Kataristas to Katari." In *Resistance, Rebellion, and Consciousness in the Andean Peasant World, 18th to 20th Centuries,* ed. Stern. Madison: University of Wisconsin Press, 1987.

Albro, Roberto. "The Indigenous in the Plural in Bolivian Oppositional Politics." *The Bulletin of Latin American Research,* Vol. 24, No. 4.

al-Shisani, Murad. "Is al-Qaeda Seeking Allies in Latin America?" *Terrorism Focus,* Vol. 5, Issue 37, October 30, 2008, online at: http://jamestown.nvmserver.com/124/?no_cache=1&tx_ttnews%5Btt_news%5D=52 43&tx_ttnews%5BbackPid%5D=13&cHash=de76f08752.

Alvarez, Edwin. "Inaudito: Por primera vez en su historia el ejército boliviano recibe indígenas en sus filas." *El Tiempo,* August 8, 2005.

Alvarez, Ronald. "¿Rigoberta Menchú para presidenta?" *Tiempos del Mundo,* July 2006.

Andean Information Network. "Response to the Human Rights Foundation" Don't mistake lynching and other forms of vigilante violence for community justice." January 28, 2008, online at: http://ainbolivia.org/index.php?option=com_content&task=view&id=113&Itemid=31.

Andersen, Martin Edwin. "Flags of Their *Step*fathers? Race and Culture in the Context of Military Service and the Fight for Citizenship." In *Eastwood's Iwo Jima: A Critical Engagement With Flags of Our Fathers & Letters From Iwo Jima,* ed. Rikke Schubart. London: Wallflower Press (forthcoming).

———. "Latin American Indian Nationalism, Democracy and the Future of the Nation-State." In *Latin American Democracy: Emerging Reality or Endangered Species?* ed. Richard Millett, el. al. New York: Routledge, 2008.

———. "Failing States, Ungoverned Spaces and the Indigenous Challenge in Latin America." *Security and Defense Studies Review,* Volume 6, No. 2, August 2006.

———. "Thankful for renewed rights; Native Nicaraguans needed protection." *The Washington Times,* November 22, 2001.

———. "The Robespierre of the Andes." *The Washington Times,* September 2, 1999.

———. "Derecho Consuetudinario Consolidado y Revindicación Indígena en los Estados Unidos." presented at the Inter-American Development Bank's *Foro Nacional de Justicia* in Guatemala City, November 1996.

———. "Turning our backs on those who were here first?" *The Washington Times,* November 24, 1994.

———. "Chiapas, Indigenous Rights and the Coming Fourth World Revolution." *The SAIS Review,* Summer-Fall 1994, Vol. 14, No. 2.

———. "The coming of the plurinational state." *The Washington Times,* April 6, 1994.

———. "Early warning from Chiapas." *Los Angeles Times,* Jan. 6, 1994.

———. "Little-known Perú group gains public attention." *The Associated Press,* April 3, 1982.

———. "Peruvian officials are shaken by terrorist attacks." *Miami Herald,* March 11, 1983.

Andolina, Roberto. "The Sovereign and its Shadow: Constituent Assembly and Indigenous Movement in Ecuador." *Journal of Latin American Studies,* Vol. 35, Cambridge University Press, 2003.

Aponte Miranda, Lillian. "Uploading the Local: Assessing the Contemporary Relationship between Indigenous Peoples' Land Tenure Systems and International Human Rights Law Regarding the Allocation of Traditional Lands and Resources in Latin America." *FIU Legal Studies Research Paper Series,* No. 08-14, June 2009.

Arana, Ana. "Murder in Colombia: American Indians seek to avenge the murder of one of their leaders by leftist rebels." *Salon,* December 14, 1999.

Astor, Michael. "Brazilian Supreme Court Warns of Civil War in Part of Amazon Region." *The Associated Press,* August 5, 2008, online at: http://www.huffingtonpost.com/2008/08/05/brazilian-supreme-court-w_n_116981.html.

Azcui, Mabel. "Bolivia excluye el pasado criollo en el bicentenario de la independencia." *El País.com,* July 17, 2009.

———. "Evo Morales promulga una nueva ley electoral para los comicios de diciembre." *El País,* April 14, 2009.

———. "La milicia indígena de Morales." *El País,* February 19, 2007 online at: http://*www.elpaís.com/articulo/internacional/milicia/indígena/Morales/elpepuint/20 070219elpepiint_16/Tes.*

Azocar, Gerardo, et al. "Conflicts for control of Mapuche-Pehuenche land and natural resources in the Biobio highlands, Chile." *Journal of Latin American Geography* Vol. 4, No. 2, 2005.

Bajak, Frank. "Fighting the odds to keep Indian tongues alive." *Associated Press,* November 7, 2009.

Balbi, Mariella. "Entrevista: Yehude Simon; Renunciar sería desleal al país." *El Comercio.com.pe,* June 14, 2009.

Ballvé, Marcelo. "'Mother Coca' Wins in Bolivia — Can Evo Morales Foster World Coca Market?" *New American Media,* December 21, 2005, online at: http://news.newamericamedia.org/news/view_article.html?article_id=99b24b3ff23a 2b115a2802b7bf85117f.

Balmford, Andrew, et al. "Conservation Conflicts Across Africa." *Science,* New Series, Vol. 291, No. 5513, March 20, 2001.

Balch, Oliver. "The 'win-win' solution failing the rainforests; Market-based answers to deforestation in Latin America are backfiring, say conservation groups." *The Guardian,* October 20, 2008.

Banton, Michael. "International norms and Latin American states' policies on indigenous peoples." *Nations and Nationalism,* Vol. 2, Part 1, March 1996.

Barbassa Madera, Juliana. "Immigrants from Mexico's indigenous groups work to preserve traditional health care." *The Associated Press,* December 29, 2005.

Barrionuevo, Alexei. "A Tribe in Brazil Struggles at the Intersection of Drugs and Cultures." *The New York Times,* December 6, 2008.

Battaleme, Juan, and Eduardo Martin Cuesta. "Los límites de la cooperación displicente: autonomia e integridad territorial en Bolivia." *Observatorio de Bolivia,* CAEI, No. 10, 2008.

Bebbington, Anthony. "Modernization from below: An Alternative Indigenous Development?" *Economic Geography,* Volume 9, No. 3, Environment and Development, Part 1, July 1993.

Beck, Scott H., and Kenneth J. Mijeski. "The Electoral Fortunes of Ecuador's Pachakutik Party: The Fracaso of the 2006 Presidential Election." *The Latin Americanist 52.* No. 2, June 2008.

Becker, Marc. "Ecuador: Indigenous Struggles and the Ambiguities of State Power." In *The Resurgence of Latin American Radicalism: Between Cracks in the Empire and an Izquierda Permitida,* ed. Jeff Webber and Barry Carr. Lanham, MD: Rowman and Littlefield Publishers, forthcoming.

————. "Mariátegui, the Comintern, and the Indigenous Question in Latin America." *Science & Society,* Vol. 70, No. 4, October 2006.

Benavente, Andres, and Jorge Jaraquemada. "Conexiones politicas de las agrupaciones mapuches." In *La cuestion mapuche: aportes para el debate,* Santiago: Fundación Libertad y Desarrollo, 2003.

Benito, Irene. "La cumber del optimismo y resolución indígenas." *El País* (Spain), May 29, 2009.

Benjamin, Thomas. "A Time of Reconquest: History, the Maya Revival, and the Zapatista Rebellion in Chiapas." *The American Historical Review,* Vol. 105, No. 2, April 2000.

Bensman, Todd. "Iran making push into Nicaragua." *San Antonio Express-News,* December 16, 2007.

Birnir, Jóhanna Kristín, and Donna Lee Van Cott. "Disunity in Diversity: Party System Fragmentation and the Dynamic Effect of Ethnic Heterogeneity on Latin American Legislatures." *Latin American Research Review,* Vol. 42, No. 1, February 2007.

Bola, Burton. "Bolivia's Indian Majority Goes to College." *The Chronicle of Higher Education,* Vol. 52, No. 45, June 14, 2006.

Borrás, Saturnino M. "The Underlying Assumptions, Theory, and Practice of Neoliberal Land Policies." online at: www.landaction.org/gallery/NeoliberalLandPolicies.doc.

Bostock, Matt. "Indigenous Rights Bloodily Suppressed for Oil and Gas Returns." *The Santiago Times,* June 18, 2009.

Boucher, Stephen R., Bradford L. Barham and Michael R. Carter. "The Impact of 'Market-Friendly' Reforms on Credit and Land Markets in Honduras and Nicaragua." *World Development,* Vol. 33, No. 1, 2005.

Bowley, Graham. "Declaring Something a Lot Like Dependence." *The New York Times,* March 2, 2008.

Brechner, José. "Bolivia, Israel, and the Muslims." March 2, 2009, online at: http://brechner.typepad.com/jose_brechner/2009/02/bolivia-israel-and-the-muslims.html.

————. "Latin America—waiting for Allah." September 19, 2006, online at: http://brechner.typepad.com/jose_brechner/2006/09/latin_america_w.html

Bremner, Faith. "Lakota group pushes for new nation." *Argus Leader,* December 20, 2007.

Breton Solo de Zaldivar, Victor. "From Agrarian Reform to Ethnodevelopment in the Highlands of Ecuador." *Journal of Agrarian Change 8,* No. 4, October 2008.

Brodzinsky, Sibylla. "Colombia's Indians bank on coca drink becoming the real thing." *The Guardian,* December 14, 2005.

Brubaker, Rogers, and David D. Laitin. "Ethnic and Nationalist Violence." *Annual Review of Sociology,* Vol. 24, 1998.

Bruneau, Thomas C.. "Ecuador: The Continuing Challenges of Democratic Consolidation and Civil-Military Relations." *Strategic Insights,* Volume V, Issue 2, February 2006.

Brysk, Alison. "Turning Weakness into Strength: The Internationalization of Indian Rights." *Latin American Perspectives,* Vol. 23, No. 2, Ethnicity and Class in Latin America, Spring, 1996.

Buchanan, Patrick J. "Globalism vs. Ethno-nationalism." *Human Events,* January 30, 2009.

Buncombe, Andrew. "Mahogany imports 'are wiping out Perú tribes,'" *Independent* (U.K.), June 27, 2006.

Burgete Cal y Mayor, Araceli, and Miguel Gómez Gómez. "Multiculturalismo y gobierno permitido en San Juan Cancuc, Chiapas: tensiones intracomunitarias por el reconocimiento de 'autoridades tradicionales.'" In *Governar (en) la diversidad: experiencias indígenas desde América Latina. Hacía la investigación de co-labor*, ed. Xochitl Leyva, et al. Mexico City: Facultad Latinoamericana de Ciencias Sociales, 2008.

Calderon, Edgar. "Investigaran infiltracion del crimen organizado en el Estado guatemalteco." *EFE Spanish News Agency*, August 3, 2007.

Calhoun, Craig. "Nationalism and Ethnicity." *Annual Review of Sociology*, Vol. 19, 1993.

Cánepa, Gisela. "The Fluidity of Ethnic Identities in Perú." Centre for Research on Inequality, Human Security and Ethnicity (CRISE) *Working Paper No. 26*, June 2008.

Canessa, Andrew. "Contesting Hybridity: *Evangelistas* and *Kataristas* in Highland Bolivia,: *Journal of Latin American Studies*, Vol. 32, pp. 115-114.

Canessa, Gen. (Ret.) Julio. "El dilema mapuche: Integrar o segregar." *Revista UNOFAR*, No. 8.

Cárdenas, Victor Hugo. "View: Bolivia divided." *Daily Times* (Pakistan), January 30, 2008,   online   at: http://www.dailytimes.com.pk/default.asp?page=2008%5C01%5C30%5Cstory_30-1-2008_pg3_6.

Caracas Gringo. "Bolivarian Revolution in Peru." June 16, 2009, online at: http://caracasgringo.wordpress.com/2009/06/16/bolivarian-revolution-in-peru/.

Carrion, Julio F.. "The Persistent Attraction of Populism." In *Latin American Democracy: Emerging Reality or Endangered Species*, ed. Richard Millett, et al. New York: Routledge, 2008.

Carter, Jimmy. "Obama's Human Rights Opportunity." *The Washington Post*, December 10, 2008.

Casafranca Tinoco, Edith. "Finalizó Primer Congreso Politico Indígena Peruano." May 5, 2007, www.nodo50.org/pachakuti/textos/campanas/indígenas/nace_masa.html.

Cayuqueo, Nilo. "Guest Column." *Indian Country Today*, August 10, 2005.

CEPAL Comunicado de Prensa, 2000. "Situacion de indígenas y afro americanos en America Latina y el Caribe." July 18, 2000, http://www.eclac.org/cgi-bin/getProd.asp?xml=/prensa/noticias/comunicados/7/77/P77.xml&xsl=/prensa/tpl/p6f.xsl&base=/prensa/tpl/top-bottom.xsl.

Cevallos, Diego. "No indigenous woman has every held a seat in the Mexican Congress; Congress Closed to Indigenous Women." *Inter Press Service*, May 1, 2009.

———. "Challenging the tradition in Oaxaca; Indigenous Women on the Offensive." *Inter Press Service*, April 1, 2009.

———. "Indigenous Candidate denounces discrimination; Indigenous Candidates Disqualified Because 'Not a Man,'" *Inter Press Service*, March 13, 2008.

———. "Latin America: Second Chance for Indigenous People after 'Lost Decade,'" May 18, 2007.

Chaves, Juanita. "Criminal Justice and Indigenous People in Colombia." *Indigenous Law Bulletin*, online at www.austlii.edu.au/au/journals/LIB/1999/73.html.

Chávez, Franz. "Bolivia: Indigenous leaders beaten and publicly humiliated." *Green Left Weekly*, Issue # 753, June 4, 2008, online at: http://www.greenleft.org.au/2008/753/38930.

Chávez, Guillermo. "Bolivia: Too Many Obligations, Too Few Rights for Aymara Women." *Inter Press Service News Agency*, August 26, 2009.

————. "Aparece vocero de 'Comando Trizano' y amenaza con 'hacer volar' a dirigentes y lonkos indígenas." *El Austral,* July 30, 2009, online at: http://www.australtemuco.cl/prontus4_noticias/site/artic/20090730/pags/200907300 03325.html.

Ching, Erik, and Virgina Tilley. "Indians, the Military and the Rebellion of 1932 in El Salvador." *Journal of Latin American Studies,* Vol. 30, No. 1, February 1998.

Chomsky, Avi, and Cindy Forster. "Who is Indigenous? Who is Afro-Colombian? Who Decides?" *Cultural Survival Quarterly,* Vol. 30, No. 4, 2006.

Clark, M. Wesley. "Enforcing Criminal Law on Native American Lands." *FBI Law Enforcement Bulletin,* April 2005.

Cockcroft, James. "Historic Changes Across Latin America; Indigenous People Rising." *Counterpunch,* November 28-30, 2008, online at: www.counterpunch.org/ cockcroft11282008.html.

Colchester, Marcus, et al. "A Survey of Indigenous Land Tenure: A Report for the Land Tenure Service of the Food and Agriculture Organization." online at: http://www.Forestpeoples.gn.apc.org.

Conversi, Daniele. "Mapping the Field: Theories of Nationalism and the Ethnosymbolic Approach." In *Nationalism and Ethnosymbolism; History, Culture and Ethnicity in the Formation of Nations,* ed. Athena S. Leoussi and Steven Grosby. Edinburgh: Edinburgh University Press, 2007.

Cook, Michelle. "Navajo peacemaker, walking in beauty in Iran." online at: http://bsnorrell.blogspot.com/2008/07/navajo-peacemaker-walking-in-beauty-in.html.

Coronel, Gustavo. "The Hezbollah Venezuelan Metastasis." *Venezuelatoday,* September 4, 2006.

Coronel, José. "Violencia política and respuestas campesinas en Huanta." In *Las Rondas Campesinas. La Derrota de Sendero Luminoso,* ed. Carlos Iván Degregori, et al. Lima: IEP, 1996.

Corral B., Fabián. "Lo 'étnico' contra lo 'ético'." *El Comercio* (Ecuador), May 4, 2009, online at: http://www.elcomercio.com/noticiaEC.asp?id_noticia=274570&id_seccion=1.

Cordova-Claure, Ted. "Cuidado con el latente fundamentalismo indígena." *BIP,* September 14, 2006.

Corr, Edwin G.. "Whither Bolivia: The ethnic, cultural and political divide." *World Literature Today,* March-April 2006.

Corry, John. "On 13, Sandinistas vs. Miskitos." *The New York Times,* July 29, 1986.

Crary, David. "Countdown begins for Canada's new territory." *Associated Press/Juneau Empire Online,* March 29, 1998, online at: http://www.juneauempire.com/stories/032998/canada.html.

Curtis, Jessicah. "Colombia Calls Cocaine Users 'Predators of the Rain Forest,'" *The Huffington Post,* December 8, 2008.

Dabovich, Melanie. "Border agroterrorism workshop heads to tribal land." *El Paso Times,* April 13, 2009.

da Gamma, Francisca. "La Internacional Comunista, Mariátegui y el 'descubrimiento' del indígena." *Anuario Mariateguiano,* Vol. 9. No. 9, 1997.

Dawson, Alexander S. "From Models for the Nation to Model Citizens: *Indigenismo* and the 'Revindication' of the Mexican Indian, 1920-40." *Journal of Latin American Studies,* Vol. 30, No. 2 , May 1998.

De Vos, George. "Ethnic Pluralism: Conflict and Accommodation." In *Ethnic Identity: Cultural Continuities and Change*, ed. George de Vos and Lola Romanucci-Ross. Palo Alto, Calif.: Mayfield, 1975.

Diez Canseco, Javier. "Complot." *La República* (Peru), July 13, 2009.

Dunbar-Ortiz, Roxanne. "Indigenous Resistance in the Americas and the Legacy of Mariátegui." *Monthly Review*, September, 2009.

———. "Indigenous Peoples and the Left in Latin America." *Monthly Review*, July-August, 2007.

Environment News Service. "'Crude,' the Film Explores Oil Giants' Crude Conduct in Ecuador." October 22, 2009.

Escobar, David. "The invisible Indians of California." *El Tecolote*, June 17, 2006, online at: http://www.marinij.com/ci_3481971?source=most_emailed.

Escobar, Ramiro. "Indigenous Women, Invisible Citizens: News from Regional Summit of Indigenous Women." July 3, 2009, online at: http://www.latinamericapress.org/articles.asp?art=5894.

Espindola, Roberto. "New Politics, New Parties?" in *Latin American Democracy: Emerging Reality or Endangered Species*, ed. Richard Millett, et al. New York: Routledge, 2008.

Espinosa, Daniel. "El 2007 mujeres indígenas podrán entrar al ejército." *Bolivia.com*, June 10, 2006.

Espósito Guevara, Carla. "El discurso del movimiento Autonomista." *BolPress.com*, September 4, 2008, online at: http://www.bolpress.com/art.php?Cod=2008090411.

Estrada, Daniela. "Mapuche Land Conflict Stained with Blood." *Inter Press Service*, January 3, 2008.

———. "Latin America: Indigenous Peoples Gaining Ground (On Paper)." *Inter Press Service*, December 5, 2006.

Fabbri, Ana Maria, and Eduardo García. "Interview-New Bolivian governor to press for autonomy." *Reuters*, July 11, 2008.

Fanjul, Serafin. "¿Indigenismo? No gracias." *Libertad Digital* (Spain), June 13, 2006; online at: www.libertaddigital.com/index.php?action=desaopi&cpn=25560.

Farah, Douglas. "Into the Abyss: Bolivia under Evo Morales and the MAS." International Assessment and Strategy Center, June 17, 2009, online at: http://www.strategycenter.net/docLib/20090618_IASCIntoTheAbyss061709.pdf.

Fearon, James D., and David D. Laitin. "Explaining Interethnic Cooperation." *American Political Science Review*, 1996.

Febbro, Eduardo. "Felipe Quispe habla de Evo Morales."*Pagina/12*, Nov. 16, 2003.

Ferguson, Yale H.. "Ethnicity, National and Polities Great and Small." *Mershon International Studies Review*, 1994, Vol. 38.

Fleming, Tabitha. *Associated Content*. "Lakota Indians Declare Sovereign Nation Status, online at: http://www.associatedcontent.com/pop_print.shtml?content_type=article&content_type_id=496203.

Flores, Paola, and Carlos Váldez. "Indians Challenging Morales in Bolivia Face Dangers." *The Associated Press*, March 18, 2009.

Fontaine, Phil. "Protect the Lives and Rights of Indigenous People." *Americas Quarterly*, Fall 2008.

Ford, Dana. "Peruvian prime minister asks the left for a truce." *Reuters*, October 17, 2008; "Peru's PM vows to stamp out terrorism." Reuters, online at: http://tvnz.co.nz/view/page/536641/2210427.

Forero, Juan. "In Deeply Split Honduras Society, a Potentially Combustible Situation." *Washington Post,* July 15, 2009.

———. "Peru Report Says 69,000 Died in 20 Years of Rebel War." *The New York Times,* August 29, 2003.

Francia, Fernando. "Indígenas exigen pronta aprobación de ley de autonomía." *Informa-Tico* (Costa Rica), January 28, 2009.

Friedlander, Judith. "The National Indigenist Institute of Mexico Reinvents the Indian: The Pame Example." *American Ethnologist,* Vol. 13, No. 2, May 1986.

Fraser, Barbara J.. "Work remains in struggle to repair human rights violations in Peru." *Catholic News Service,* August 22, 2008.

Fredes, Iván. "Nueva unión de grupos mapuches impulsa estrategia de tomas para presionar por tierras." *El Mercurio,* August 15, 2009.

———. "Empresarios piden al Gobierno aplicar 'mano dura' por los atentados mapuches en el sur." *El Mercurio,* October 22, 2008.

Fund for Peace, *2007 Failed States Index (FSI),* online at: http://www.fundforpeace.org/web/index.php?option=com_content&task=view&id=99&Itemid=140.

Gaynor, Tim. "Mexico drug gangs muscle border tribe out of homes." *Reuters,* December 2, 2007.

García Linera, Alvaro. "Indianismo and Marxism: The mismatch of two revolutionary rationales." *Atlantic Free Press,* January 30, 2008, online at: http://www. atlanticfreepress.com/index2.php?option=com_content&task=view&id=3341.

Garfinkle, Adam. "Autumn Note: The Future of Jewcentricity." *The American Interest,* September-October 2009.

Garrigues, Lisa. "Ecuadorian Native movements turn up the heat." *Indian Country Today,* February 19, 2007.

———. "La Paz hosts continental indigenous encounter." *Indian Country Today,* October 27, 2006.

———. "Morales' victory brings indigenous leaders to Bolivia." *Indian Country Today,* February 10, 2006.

Gettleman, Jeffrey. "Signs in Kenya of a Land Redrawn by Ethnicity." *The Washington Post,* February 15, 2008.

Godoy, Angelina Snodgrass. "When 'Justice" is Criminal: Lynchings in Contemporary Latin America." *Theory and Society,* Vol. 33, No. 6, December 2004.

Gomez, Magdalena. "Bolivia: tequio del pensamiento." *La Jornada,* March 28, 2006.

Gonschor, Lorenz. "Rapa Nui." *The Contemporary Pacific,* Volume 20, Number 1, Spring 2008.

González, Daniel. "A man of the (indigenous) people." *The Arizona Republic,* January 26, 2008.

González, Gustavo. "Latin America: 'War on Terror' Has Indigenous People in Its Sights." *Inter Press News Service Agency,* June 6, 2002.

Good Fox, Julia. "Palestine: Stop the re-creation of 'Indian country' in the Holy Land." *Indian Country Today,* January 13, 2009.

Govan, Fiona. "ETA leader arrested in France." *Telegraph,* November 17, 2008, online at: http://www.telegraph.co.uk/news/worldnews/europe/spain/3472076/Eta-leader-arrested-in-France.html.

Granger, Sarah. "Guatemala Drug Trade Leaves Trail of Local Addicts." *Reuters,* August 26, 2009.

Gray Molina, George. "Ethnic Politics in Bolivia: 'Harmony of Inequalities,' 1900-2000." paper prepared under auspices of the Center for Inequality, Human Security and Ethnicity (CRISE) and presented at the Third Forum for Human Development, Paris, January 17-19, 2005.

————. "The Offspring of the Bolivian National Revolution: Exclusion and the Promise of Popular Participation" In *Proclaiming Revolution: Bolivia in Comparative Perspective*, ed. Merilee Grindle and Pilar Domingo. Cambridge, Mass.: Harvard University, 2003.

Grillo, Ioan. "Zapatista leader touring Mexico." *The Associated Press,* January 3, 2006.

Gutíerrez Chong, Natividad. "Ethnic Origins and Indigenous Peoples: An Approach from Latin America." In *Nationalism and Ethnosymbolism; History, Culture and Ethnicity in the Formation of Nations,* ed. Athena S. Leoussi and Steven Grosby. Edinburgh: Edinburgh University Press, 2007.

Habyarimana, James, et al.. "Is Ethnic Conflict Inevitable? Parting Ways Over Nationalism and Separatism." *Foreign Affairs,* July/August 2008.

Hackenberg, Robert A., and Beverly H. Hackenberg. "Notes Toward a New Future: Applied Anthropology in Century XXII." *Human Organization,* Winter 2004.

Halevi, Jonathan D., and Ashley Perry. "Hizbullah's global reach; Shiite group's reach extends far beyond Lebanon, poses global threat." online at: http://www.ynet.co.il/english/articles/0,7340,L-3580047,00.html.

Hall, G. Emlen. "The Pueblo Land Grant Labyrinth." In *Land, Water, and Culture: New Perspectives on Hispanic Land Grants,* ed. Charles L. Briggs and John R. Van Ness. Albuquerque: University of New Mexico: 1987.

Hart, Natalie. "Born Guilty—Chile's Hidden War Against the Mapuche." *The Patagonian Times,* August 25, 2008.

Harwood, John. "A Lot Like Home; Campaign Strategists Give Foreign Elections That American Cachet; They Arrive From the U.S. With Slick TV Ads and Centrist Platforms." *The Wall Street Journal,* March 24, 1999.

Haynes, Brad. "Chile: United Nations Investigates Mapuche Police Violence." *The Santiago Times,* November 2, 2009

Hearn, Kelly. "Chavez seen behind unrest in Peru." *The Washington Times,* July 6, 2009.

————. "For Peru's Indians, Lawsuit Against Big Oil Reflects a New Era." *The Washington Post,* January 14, 2008.

Hendrix, Burke A.. "Memory in Native American Land Claims." *Political Theory,* Vol. 33, No. 6, December, 2005.

Hernández Castillo, R. Aída, (translated by Mariana Mora). "Commentary; Gendered Violence and Neocolonialism; Indigenous Women Confronting Counterinsurgency Violence." *Latin American Perspectives,* Issue 158, Vol. 35, No. 1, January 2008.

Hernandez Gonzalez, Cynthia. "El Islam de Chiapas." *WebIslam,* September 13, 2006, online at: http://www.webislam.com/noticiatema_imp.asp?idt=5719.

Herrera, Natalia, and Douglas Porch. "'Like going to a fiesta'—the role of female fighters in Colombia's FARC-EP." *Small Wars & Insurgencies,* Vol. 19, No. 4, December 2008.

Hobsbawm, Eric J. "Ethnicity and nationalism in Europe today." *Anthropology Today,* Vol. 8., No. 1, February 1992,

Hooghe, Liesbet, and Gary Marks. "Unraveling the Central State, but How? Types of Multi-Level Governance." *The American Political Science Review,* Vol. 97, No. 2, May 2003.

Horowitz, Donald L. "Patterns of Ethnic Separation." *Comparative Studies in Society and History*, Vol. 23, No. 2, April 1981.

Houghton, Juan, and Beverly Bell. "Latin American Indigenous Movements in the Context of Globalization." *Americas Program Policy Report*, October 11, 2004, online at: http://americas.irc-online.org/am/1369.

Howard, Philip. "The history of ecological marginalization in Chiapas." *Environmental History*, July 1998.

Human Rights Watch. "Bolivia: Unequivocally Condemn Mob Violence: Politically Motivated Attacks Threaten Rule of Law." March 12, 2009.

Hvalkof, Søren. "Privatization of Land and Indigenous Communities in Latin America: Tenure Security or Social Security." Danish Institute for International Studies (DIIS) *Working Paper No. 2008/21*, online at: www.diss.dk.

———. "Colonization and Conflict in the Amazon Frontier: Dimensions of interethnic relations in the Peruvian Montaña." In *Frontier Encounters: Indigenous Communities and Settlers in Asia and Latin America*, ed. Daniel Geiger. Copenhagen: International Work Group for Indigenous Affairs (IWGIA) and University of Zürich, 2008.

Hutchinson, John. "Warfare, Remembrance and National Identity." In *Nationalism and Ethnosymbolism; History, Culture and Ethnicity in the Formation of Nations*, ed. Athena S. Leoussi and Steven Grosby. Edinburgh: Edinburgh University Press, 2007.

International Work Group for Indigenous Affairs. "Definitions of Indigenous Peoples." online at: http://www.iwgia.org/sw251.asp.

Introvigne, Massimo. "Chávez and the Strange Story of the Shi'ite Indios in Venezuela." *il Domenicale. Settimanale di Cultura*, March 24, 2007, online at: http://www.cesnur.org/2007/mi_03_24_en.htm.

Isbell, Billie Jean. "Shining Path and Peasant Responses in Rural Ayacucho." In *The Shining Path of Peru*, ed. David Scott Palmer. New York: St Martins Press, 1992.

Jackson, Jean E.. "Culture Genuine and Spurious: The Politics of Indianness in the Vaupés, Colombia." *American Ethnologist*, Vol. 22, No. 1, February 1995.

Jenkins, Chris L.. "Islam Luring More Latinos; Prays Offer a More Intimate Link to God, Some Say, *The Washington Post*, January 7, 2001.

Jevec, Adam. "Semper Fidelis, Code Talkers." *Prologue Magazine*, The U.S. National Archives & Records Administration, Winter 2001, Vol. 33, No. 4.

Johansen, Bruce. "Commentary on the Iroquois and the U.S. Constitution." *Ethnohistory* 37 (1990).

Johnson, Stephen. "Bolivian Election Reveals Need for Broader Engagement." *Heritage Foundation Executive Memorandum # 988*, January 26, 2006.

Karmon, Ely. "Iran and its Proxy Hezbollah: Strategic Penetration in Latin America." Elcano Royal Institute, Madrid, Spain, April 8, 2009.

———. "Hezbollah America Latina: Strange Group or Real Threat?" online at: http://www.instituteforcounterterrorism.org/var/119/35195-Hezbollah%20iin%20LatinAmerica_Dr%20Karmon.pdf.

Kaufmann, Chaim. "Possible and Impossible Solutions to Ethnic Civil Wars." *International Security*, Vol. 20, No. 4, Spring 1996.

———. "When All Else Fails: Ethnic Population Transfers and Partitions in the Twentieth Century." *International Security*, Vol. 23 No. 2, Fall 1998.

Kaufman, Stuart J.. "Spiraling to Ethnic War: Elites, Masses, and Moscow in Moldova's Civil War,' *International Security*, 21(2), 1996.

Kearns, Rick. "Indigenous leaders call for President Zelaya's return." *Indian Country Today*, July 13, 2009.
———. "Seeking justice, Latin indigenous leaders come to testify." *Indian Country Today*, April 6, 2009.
———. "Indigenous and Latin American leaders optimistic about Obama." *Indian Country Today*, November 21, 2009.
———. "From slavery to government; The rise of Ache Guayaki Chief Margarita Mbywangi of Paraguay." *Indian Country Today*, October 3, 2008.
———. "Indigenous languages added to new Ecuadorian constitution." *Indian Country Today*, August 22 and September 10, 2008;
———. "Protection of indigenous media sought at the UN." *Indian Country Today*, May 19, 2008.
———. "News Analysis on indigenous Latin America." *Indian Country Today*, March 3, 2006.
Kempe, Frederick, and Clifford Krauss. "Flawed Approach; U.S. Policy on Indians in Nicaragua Damages Anti-Sandinista Effort." *The Wall Street Journal*, March 2, 1987.
Kenny, Kevin. "Diaspora and Comparison: The Global Irish as a Case Study." *The Journal of American History*, June 2003.
Kiernan, Sergio. "El IncaPaz." *Pagina/12*, February 20, 2005.
———. "'Mi Lucha, versión andina." *Pagina/12*, January 29, 2006.
Kingsbury, Benedict. "'Indigenous Peoples' in International Law: A Constructivist Approach to the Asian Controversy." *The American Journal of International Law*, Vol. 92, No. 3, July 1998.
Klein, Hilary. "A Second Look at the EZLN's Festival of Dignified Rage." *The Narco News Bulletin*, February 23, 2009.
Kovalik, Dan. "Honduran Coup Government Continues Attack on the Poor with Plan to Seize Indigenous Hospital." *Huffington Post*, August 7, 2009, online at: www.huffingtonpost.com/dan-kovalik/honduran-coup-government_b_254033.html
Kraul, Chris. "Peru's indigenous people win one round over developers." *The Los Angeles Times*, June 25, 2009.
Lacey, Marc. "Complex defeat for Nobel Winner in Guatemala." *The New York Times*, September 11, 2007.
Lavie, Mark. "Israeli document: Venezuela sends uranium to Iran." *The Associated Press*, May 25, 2009.
Lakshmanan, Indira A.R.. "Evangelism is luring Latin America's Catholics; Charismatic sects focus on earthly rewards." *The Boston Globe*, May 8, 2005, online at: wwww.rickross.com/reference/fundamentalists/fund161.html.
Langewiesche, William. "The Border (Part I)" *The Atlantic Monthly."* May 1992, online at: www.theatlantic.com/issues/92may/border.htm.
Lee, Lloyd L.. "The Future of Navajo Nationalism." *Wicazo Sa Review* Vol. 22, Number 1, 2007.
Lemoine, Maurice. "Ecuador's unknown president." *Le Monde Diplomatique*, January 20, 2007.
Logan, Sam. "Iran courts Latin America." *ISN Security Watch*, January 22, 2007.
López Bárcenas, Francisco. "Indigenous Movements in the Americas: From Demand for Recognition to Building Autonomies." translated from "Autonomias Indígenas en

America: de la demanda de reconocimiento a su construcción." Center for International Policy, February 26, 2008.

Lucas, Kintto. "Latin America: Native Groups Express Solidarity with Bolivian Leader. " *Inter Press Service,* September 23, 2008, online at: http://insidecostarica.com/special_reports/2008-09/latam_native_groups.htm.

Lucero, Jose Antonio. "Review: We Alone Will Rule: Native Andean Politics in the Age of Insurgency by Sinclair Thomson." *Latin American Politics and Society,* Vol. 46, No. 2, Summer, 2004, pp. 176-181.

Luna Amancio, Nelly. "Grupos politicos radicalizan un discurso etnico aimara en Puno." *El Comercio,* January 13, 2008.

Mailer, Norman. "Superman Comes to the Supermarket." *Esquire,* November 1960.

Mallon, Florencia E.. "Indian Communities, Political Cultures, and the State in Latin America, 1780-1990." *Journal of Latin American Studies,* Vol. 24, Quincentenary Supplement: The Colonial and Post Colonial Experience. Five Centuries of Spanish and Portuguese America, 1992.

Mamani, Pablo. "Las estrategias del poder indígena en Bolivia." *Rebellion,* April 24, 2006.

Marhikewun, R. "Indigenous Leaders Speak Out: R. Marhikewun of Chile." In *Contemporary Indigenous Movements in Latin America,* ed. Erick D. Langer and Elena Munoz. Wilmington, Del.: Scholarly Resources, Inc., 2003.

Markovits, Andrei S.. "The European and American Left since 1945." *Dissent,* Winter 2005, Vol. 52, Issue 1.

Marks, Thomas. "Making Revolution with Shining Path." In *Shining Path of Peru,* ed. David Scott Palmer. New York: St. Martin's Press, 1994.

Martin, Terry. "The Origins of Soviet Ethnic Cleansing." *The Journal of Modern History,* Vol. 70, No. 4, December 1998.

McClintock, Cynthia. "An Unlikely Comeback in Peru." In *Latin America's Struggle for Democracy,* ed. Larry Diamond et al. Baltimore, The Johns Hopkins University Press, 2008.

Méndez G., Cecilia. "Populismo militar y etnicidad en los Andes." *Iconos, Revista de Ciencias Sociales No. 26,* Facultad Latinoamericana de Ciencias Sociales (Flacso), Sede Quito, September 2006.

———. "'Incas Si, Indios No' Notes on Peruvian Creole Nationalism and Its Contemporary Crisis." *Journal of Latin American Studies,* Vol. 28, No. 1, February 1996.

Meschkat, Klaus. "Helpful Intervention? The Impact of the Comintern on Early Colombian Communism." *Latin America Perspectives,* Issue 159, Vol. 35, No. 2., March 2008.

Mayer, Enrique. "Peru in Deep Trouble: Mario Vargas Llosa's 'Inquest in the Andes' Reexamined." In *Rereading Cultural Anthropology,* ed. E. Marcus. Durham, N.C.: Duke University Press, 1992.

Migdal, Joel S. "The State in Society." In *State Power and Social Forces: Domination and Transformation in the Third Worlds,* ed. Migdal, Atul Kohli and Vivienne Shue. Cambridge: Cambridge University Press, 1994.

Mills, John A. "Legal constructions of cultural identify in Latin America: An argument against defining indigenous peoples." *Texas Hispanic Journal of Law & Policy* Vol. 8, No. 49 (2002).

Ministerio de Relaciones Exteriores (Venezuela). "Posición del Ministerio de Relaciones Exteriores sobre los derechos de los pueblos indígenas." *El Nacional,* November 9, 1999.

Montalvo, José, and Marta Reynal-Querol. "Ethnic Polarization, Potential Conflict, and Civil Wars." *The American Economic Review,* Vol. 95, No. 3, June, 2005.

Morales, Lorenzo. "Colombia- Los indígenas desafían al narcotráfico." *Semana.com,* August 9, 2009, online at http://www.semana.com/noticias-conflicto-armado/indígenas-desafian-narcotrafico/126360.aspx.

Morris, Stephen D. "Reforming the Nation: Mexican Nationalism in Context." *Journal of Latin American Studies,* Vol. 31, No. 2, May 1999.

Muller, Jerry Z. "Muller Replies." In "Is Ethnic Conflict Inevitable: Parting Ways Over Nationalism and Separatism." *Foreign Affairs,* July/August 2008.

———. "Us and Them, The Enduring Power of Ethnic Nationalism." *Foreign Affairs,* March/April 2008.

Muratorio, Blanca. "Indigenous Women's Identities and the Politics of Cultural Reproduction in the Ecuadorian Amazon." *American Anthropologist,* New Series, Vol. 100, No. 2, June 1998.

Murillo, Mario A. "No end in sight: Indigenous and popular minga continues, debate with Colombian president stalls." November 3, 2008, online at www.prensarural.org/spip/spip.php?article1626.

Mushakoji, Kinhide. "Development and racism in Asia and the Pacific." In *Six Continents: Race and Unequal Development,* ed. Michael Banton. Tokyo: IMADR Yearbook: Peoples for Human Rights 1992.

Nagel, Beverly. "Indigenous Movements and Their Critics: Pan-Maya Activism in Guatemala." *Latin American Politics and Society,* Spring 2002, online at: http://findarticles.com/p/articles/mi_qa4000/is_200204/ai_n9041826/.

Neils Conzen, Kathleen, and David A. Gerber. "The invention of ethnicity: A perspective from the U.S.A.." *Journal of American Ethnic History,* Fall 1992, Vol. 12, Issue 1.

Nelson, Josh. "U.N. Ambassadors experience Meskwaki culture." *WFCCourier.com,* October 16, 2007.

Nepstad, D., S. Schwartzman, et al. "Inhibition of Amazon Deforestation and Fire by Parks and Indigenous Lands." *Conservation Biology,* Volume 20, No. 1, 2006.

Nevaer, Louis E.V. "The Return of the Native Americans as Immigrants." *New American Media,* October 24, 2007.

Newcomb, Steven. "Anti-Indian rhetoric in the 21st century." *Indian Country Today,* February 2, 2007.

Nolasco, Margarita, and Miguel Ángel Rubio. "La Migración Indígena: Causas y Efectos en la Cultura, en la Economía y en la Población." online at: www.etnografia.inah.gob.mx/pdf/Linea5.pdf.

Norell, Brenda. "Indigenous Uranium Forum Denounces Mining, Militarization, and Hate Crimes in Indian Country." *Americas Program Report,* Center for International Policy, November 4, 2009.

———. "Censorship and the US brand of terrorism at the border." *Narconews,* February 25, 2009, online at: http://narcosphere.narconews.com/notebook/brenda-norrell/2009/02/censorship-and-us-brand-terrorism-border.

———."Navajo youth peacemaker to Iran." *The Narcosphere,* August 1, 2008, online at: http://narcosphere.narconews.com/notebook/brenda-norrell/2008/08/navajo-youth-peacemaker-iran.

Obama, Barack. "Message From Obama: Tribes Will Have Voice in White House." *Reznet*, October 25, 2008, online at: http://www.reznetnews.org/article/message-obama-tribes-will-have-voice-white-house-23490.

O'Leary, Brendan. "On the Nature of Nationalism; An Appraisal of Ernest Gellner's Writing on Nationalism." *British Journal of Political Science*, Vol. 27, No. 2, April 1997.

Olmos, Harold. "South American Indians Seek New Nation." *The Associated Press*, February 7, 2006.

Olzak, Susan. "Ethnic Collective Action and the Dynamics of Ethnic Enclaves,' unpublished paper, Department of Sociology, Cornell University, p. 3, cited in Charles Tilly. "Transplanted Networks." In *Immigration Reconsidered*, ed. Virginia Yans-McLaughlin. New York: Oxford University Press, 1990.

Orlove, Benjamin S., and Stephen B. Brush. "Anthropology and the Conservation of Biodiversity." *Annual Review of Anthropology*, Vol. 25, 1966.

Ortiz, Roman D. "Balkan-Bolivia." *HACER; Hispanic American Center for Economic Research*, September 29, 2008.

Otoya, Rocio. "Disturbios en la Amazonía revelan fractura social en Perú." *EFE Spanish News Agency*, June 6, 2009.

Padilla, Abdel. "Yo ordené la emboscada de Warisata." *Semanario Pulso*, May 28, 2006.

Pantin, Travis. "Hugo Chavez's Jewish Problem." *Commentary*, July/August 2008, Issue, 2, online at: http://www.commentarymagazine.com/viewarticle.cfm/hugo-ch-vez-s-jewish-problem-11455.

Patch, Richard. "Bolivia: The Restrained Revolution." *The Annual of the American Academy of Political and Social Sciences*, 1961.

Patzi, Félix. "¿División en el MAS?" *La Razón Edición Digital* (Bolivia), May 4, 2009, online at: http://www.la-razon.com/versiones/20090504_006717/nota_246_805493.htm.

Paz García, Javier. "Bolivia: Nacional Socialismo y Movimiento al Socialismo." *HACER; Hispanic American Center for Economic Research*, September 29, 2008.

Penaranda, Raul. "Is there a shift toward indigenous leaders in Bolivia." *Global Post*, February 24, 2009, online at: www.globalpost.com/print/271221.

Perez, Luis Enrique. "Error y arrogancia de Rigoberta Menchú." *Siglo XXI*, September 19, 2007.

Perry, Carol, and Patricia Anne Davis. "Dineh Sovereignty Is Spiritual Empowerment and Self-Identity, " presented at a public hearing in Window Rock, Arizona, August 16, 2001.

Petersmann, Ernst-Ulrich. "State Sovereignty, Popular, Sovereignty and Individual Sovereignty: from Constitutional Nationalism to Multilevel Constitutionalism in International Economic Law?" *EUI Working Papers, Law No. 2006/45*, European University Institute.

Phillips, Tom. "Healed by the Amazon angels." *Guardian Unlimited*, December 21, 2007.

Pineda Camacho, Roberto. "Pueblos Indígenas de Colombia: una aproximación a su historia, economía y sociedad." In *Un siglo de investigacion social: antropologia en Colombia*, ed. Jaime Arocha and Nina S. Friedemann. Santa Fe de Bogotá: Etno, 1995.

Pion-Berlin, David. "Defense Organization and Civil-Military Relations in Latin America." *Armed Forces and Society*, Vol. 35, No. 3, 2009.

Pipoli, Renzo. "García denies massacre and keeps laws; forces Native chief out." *Indian Country Today,* June 15, 2009, online at: http://www.indiancountrytoday.com/home/content/47921432.html.

Pomeraniec, Hinde. "Evo Morales, de pastor de llamas y sindicalista, a presidente de Bolivia, *Clarin,* January 23, 2006.

Tomás Ponce, Gonzalo. "Autonomía Departamental en Bolivia." *Observatorio de Bolivia,* CAEI, No. 10, 2008.

Portugal, Andrea. "Voices from the War: Exploring the Motivation of Sendero Luminoso Militants." *CRISE Working Paper* No. 57, October 2008.

Posen, Barry R. "The Security Dilemma and Ethnic Conflict." *Survival,* 35(1), 1993.

Powell, T.G. "Mexican Intellectuals and the Indian Question, 1876-1911." *Hispanic American Historical Review,* Vol. 48 (1968).

Powers, William. "Poor Little Rich Country." *The New York Times,* June 11, 2005.

Ramos, Wellington C. "Commentary: Honduras government takes over the only Garifuna hospital in the country." *Caribbean Net News,* August 19, 2009, online at: http://www.caribbeannetnews.com/news-18314--6-6--.html.

Ramirez, Elaine. "Chilean Mapuche Leader Acquitted." *The Patagonian Times,* June 16, 2008.

Redford, Kent H. "The Ecologically Nobel Savage." *Cultural Survival Quarterly,* Vol. 15, 1991.

Reel, Monte. "South America's Constitutional Battles." *Washington Post,* January 18, 2008.

———. "For Bolivian Majority, A New Promise." *Washington Post,* January 23, 2006.

Reno, Janet. "A federal commitment to tribal justice systems." 79 *Judicature* 1995.

Replogle, Jill. "Indigenous Taking Note of Morales' Rise to Power." *The Miami Herald,* October 8, 2006.

Rey, Gloria Helena. "Colombia: Indians neither museum exhibits nor tourist attractions." *Inter Press Service News Agency,* December 17, 2007.

Reynaga, Ramiro. "La Ropa de Evo Morales: Incongruencia entre vestimenta, palabra, acción." *Pukara,* No. 20, June 7/July 7, 2007.

Richards, Patricia. "The Politics of Gender, Human Rights, and Being Indigenous in Chile." *Gender and Society,* Vol. 19, No. 2, Gender-Sexuality-State-Nation: Transnational Feminist Analysis, April 2005.

Riding, Alan. "For Ecuador Indians, Pride and Profits in Weaving." *The New York Times,* May 15, 1984.

Riley, Michael. "Path to justice unclear; Empower the tribes, or beef up the federal role? Each side has its own history of failure." *The Denver Post,* November 14, 2007.

———. "Principles, politics collide; Some U.S. attorneys who emphasize fighting crime on Indian lands have seen themselves fall out of favor in D.C.." *The Denver Post,* November 13, 2007.

———. "Justice: Inaction's fatal price: Delays and missteps in Indian Country criminal cases can give offenders a free pass. The consequences can be tragic." *The Denver Post,* November 12, 2007.

———. "Promises, justice broken; A dysfunctional system lets serious reservation crimes go unpunished and puts Indians at risk." *The Denver Post,* November 11, 2007.

———. "Indian Justice; 1885 law at root of jurisdictional jumble." *The Denver Post,* November 11, 2007.

Rivera, Laura, and Jorge Barreno. "Acusan a los Mapuches de relacionarse con los terroristas de ETA y las FARC." *El Mundo*, September 5, 2009, online at http://www.elmundo.es/elmundo/2009/09/05/internacional/1252122031.html.

Rivera, Silvia. "La Raiz: colonizadores y colonizados." In *Violencias encubiertas en Bolivia*, ed. Xavier Albó and Raúl Barrios. La Paz: CIPCA, 1993.

Rivera Velez, Fredy. "Los indigenismos en Ecuador: de paternalismos y otras representaciones." *America Latina Hoy*, Julio, 1998, Vol. 19, Universidad de Salamanca.

Rizvi Tierramerica, Haider. "N. American tribal leaders energized by Morales meet." *Inter Press Service/GIN*, October 23, 2006.

Robinson, Eugene. "Economic Hardship. Sharpens the Racial Schism in Peru." *The Washington Post*, February 25, 1990.

Roe, Paul. "The Intrastate Security Dilemma: Ethnic Conflict as a 'Tragedy.'?" *Journal of Peace Research*, Vol. 36, No. 2, March 1999.

Rodgers, Tim. "Separatists Declare Nation of Moskitia." *Nica Times*, May 1, 2009.

———. "Mosquito Coast Bites Nicaragua's Ortega." *Time*, May 1, 2009.

———. "A tale of genocide in a year of politics." *Miami Herald*, June 19, 2006.

Rojas, Marce. "Indígenas pueden rehusarse a prestar servicio militar." *Generación Invisible* (Colombia), April 27, 2009.

Romero, Simon. "In Bolivia, Untapped Bounty Meets Nationalism." *The New York Times*, February 3, 2009.

———. "Fears of Turmoil Persist as Powerful President Reshapes Bitterly Divided Bolivia." *The New York Times*, September 28, 2008.

———. "A Radical Gives Bolivia Some Stability." *The New York Times*, September 18, 2007.

Ronen, Moshe. "Indian Summer; From the jungles of Peru to Ramla, Jewish immigrants of Indian descent prove nothing trumps need to connect with one's heritage." *Israel Jewish Scene*, March 30, 2008, online at: http://www.ynet.co.il/english/articles/0,7340,L-3522812,00.html.

Rosenberg, Mica. "Mob Justice on the Rise in Guatemala." *Reuters*, July 25, 2006.

Rosenberg, Tina. "Why Mexico's Small Corn Farmers Go Hungry." *The New York Times*, March 23, 2003.

Rosenthal, Elisabeth. "New Jungles Prompt a Debate on Rain Forests." *The New York Times*, January 30, 2009.

Ross, John. "Commodifying the Revolution: Zapatista Villages Become Hot Tourist Destinations." *Counterpunch*, February 12, 2009, online at: http://www.counterpunch.org/ross02172009.html.

Rothe, Thomas. "Mapuche Girl Seeks Political Asylum in Switzerland." *The Patagonia News*, October 21, 2008.

Ruano, Wendy. "Indígenas logran poder local." *PrensaLibre.com*, September 13, 2007.

Rudel, Thomas K., Diane Bates and Rafael Machinguiashi. "Ecologically Noble Amerindians? Cattle Ranching and Cash Cropping among Shuar and Colonists in Ecuador." *The Latin American Studies Association*, Vol. 37, No. 1, 2002.

Saez Paiva, Javier, *La crítica mapuche a la frontera chileno-argentina: antesala a una crisis binacional?* Tesis Magister en Seguridad y Defensa, Academia Nacional de Estudios Políticos y Estratégicos de Chile (ANEPE), Fall 2008.

Salazar, Milagros. "Peru: Indigenous People, Ignored Even by the Statistics." *Inter Press Service*, October 10, 2006.

Sanford, Victoria. "Between Rigoberta Menchú and La Violencia; Deconstructing David Stoll's History of Guatemala." *Latin American Perspectives,* Issue 109, Vol. 26, No. 6, November 1999.

Schmidt, Blake, and Marc Lacey. "Puerto Cabezas Journal: An Independence Claim in Nicaragua." *The New York Times,* June 10, 2009.

Schroeder, Kathleen. "Spatial Constraints on Women's Work in Tarija, Bolivia." *Geographic Review,* Vol. 90, No. 2, April 2000.

Seitz, Max. "Ponchos Rojos, Milicia Indígena?" *BBC Mundo.com,* January 24, 2009, online at :http://news.bbc.co.uk/hi/spanish/latin_america/newsid_7849000/7849147.stm.

Seligson, Mitchell A., and John A. Booth. "Predicting Coups? Democratic Vulnerabilities, the AmericasBarometer and the 2009 Honduran Crisis." *AmericasBarometer Insights 2009.*

Sharp, David. "Venezuela deal with Indians could be prelude to big announcement." *The Associated Press,* January 7, 2006.

Sheerin, Cathal. "Chile: U.S. Government Keeping Tabs on Mapuche 'Terrorists,'" *The Patagonia Times,* June 17, 2009.

Shorris, Earl. "Mad Mel and the Maya." *The Nation,* December 18, 2006.

Siddique, Haroon. "Ecuador referendum endorses new socialist constitution." *Guardian,* September 29, 2008.

Siegel, Robert. "Sayyid Qutb's America." *National Public Radio,* January 4, 2009, online at: www.npr.org/templates/story/story.php?storyId=1253796.

Silva, José Adán. "Segregationist treatment of indigenous and Afro-Caribbean women." *Inter Press Service,* March 20, 2009.

Simon, Walker. "Ecuador's Correa: New term will favor poor, Indians." *The Associated Press,* August 10, 2009.

Smith, Anthony. "The Power of Ethnic Traditions in the Modern World." In *Nationalism and Ethnosymbolism; History, Culture and Ethnicity in the Formation of Nations,* ed. Athena S. Leoussi and Steven Grosby. Edinburgh: Edinburgh University Press, 2007.

———. "National Identity and the Idea of European Unity, *International Affairs,* Vol. 68, No. 1, January 1992.

Smith, Fiona. "Bolivians Elect Assembly to Revise Constitution; Morales Wins Only Narrow Majority for Plan Touted as Step Toward Equality." *The Associated Press,* July 3, 2006.

Sohr, Raúl. "The Amazon in Conflict." *The Santiago Times,* June 18, 2009.

———. "Peru and the law of the jungle." *The Santiago Times,* June 18, 2009.

Stabb, Martin. "Indigenism and Racism in Mexican Thought." *Journal of Inter-American Studies* 1: 4 , October 1959.

Starn, Orin. "To Revolt against the Revolution: War and Resistance in Peru's Andes." *Cultural Anthropology,* Vol. 10, No. 4, November 1995.

Stefanoni, Pablo. "Arranca en Bolivia la Constituyente." *Página/12* (Argentina), August 6, 2006.

Steiml, Silke. "Fugitive Mapuche Activist Caught." *The Santiago Times,* August 7, 2009, online at: http://www.santiagotimes.cl/santiagotimes/index.php/2009080616836/news/latest/fugitive-mapuche-activist-caught.html

Stocks, Anthony. "Too Much for Too Few: Problems of Indigenous Land Rights in Latin America." *Annual Review of Anthropology*, Vol. 34, 2005.

Stoll, David. "Rigoberta Menchú and the Last-Resort Paradigm." *Latin American Perspectives*, Vol. 26, No. 6, If Truth Be Told: A Forum on David Stoll's "Rigoberta Menchú and the Story of All Poor Guatemalans." November 1999.

Stone, John, and Polly Rizova. "The Ethnic Enigma: Nationalism, Racism and Globalization." In *Nationalism and Ethnosymbolism; History, Culture and Ethnicity in the Formation of Nations*, ed. Athena S. Leoussi and Steven Grosby. Edinburgh: Edinburgh University Press, 2007.

Stratfor, *Annual Forecast 2008: Beyond the Jihadist War*.

———. *Geopolitical Diary: Geography and Conflict in South America*, March 6, 2008.

Strauss, Bob. "Adam Beach." *The Toronto Globe and Mail*, October 20, 2006, p. R35

Stroebele-Gregor, Juliana. "Culture and Political Practice of the Aymara and Quechua in Bolivia: Autonomous Forms of Modernity in the Andes." *Latin American Perspectives*, Vol. 23, No. 2, Ethnicity and Class in Latin America, Spring 1996.

Suggett, James. "Venezuelan Government Responds to Massacre of Indigenous Protestors in Peruvian Amazon." *Venezuelanalysis.com*, June 10, 2009, online at: http://www.venezuelanalysis.com/news/4510.

Sweetgrass, H. Freddy. "Make Canada see the oppression." *The Toronto Globe and Mail*, June 28, 2007.

Sznajder, Mario. "Ethnodevelopment and Democratic Consolidation in Chile: The Mapuche Question." In *Contemporary Indigenous Movements in Latin America*, Erick D. Langer and Elena Munoz. Wilmington, Del.: Scholarly Resources, Inc., 2003.

Taylor, Clinton W. "Hezbollah in Latin America." *The American Spectator*, November 30, 2006.

Tilley, Virginia Q. "New Help or New Hegemony? The Transnational Indigenous Peoples' Movement and 'Being Indian' in El Salvador." *Journal of Latin American Studies*, Vol. 34, No. 3, August 2000.

Tobar, Hector. "Guatemala's new president will assume great burden." *Los Angeles Times*, November 6, 2007.

Tockman, Jason. "Independent Candidate Challenges Chilean Political Establishment." *NACLA Report on the Americas*, July 24, 2009, online at: https://nacla.org/node/6010.

Thompson, Richard H. "Ethnic Minorities and the Case for Collective Rights." *American Anthropologist*, New Series, Vol. 99, No. 4, December 1997.

Torres Soriano, Manual R. "La Fascinación por el Exito: El Caso de Hezbollah en America Latina." *Jihad Monitor Occasional Paper No. 1*, Universidad Pablo de Olavide, Sevilla, Spain.

Troyan, Brett. "Gregorio Hernandez de Alba (1904-1973): The Legimitization of Indigenous Ethnic Politics in Colombia." *European Review of Latin American and Caribbean Studies*, Vol. 82, April 2007.

Tullberg, Steven M. "Securing Human Rights of American Indians and Other Indigenous Peoples Under International Law." In *Bringing Human Rights Home, Volume 3, Portraits of the Movement*, ed., Cynthia Soohoo, Catherine Albisa, and Martha F. Davis. Westport, Conn: Praeger, 2008.

Ugaz, Paola. "Indígenas peruanos, en guardia contra Alan García." *Terra Magazine,* May 12, 2009, online at: http://www.ar.terra.com/terramagazine/interna/0,,EI8867-OI3760404,00.html.

Vaca, Alexander. "Servicios ambientales: Un proyecto productivo y un proyecto de vida." *El Bosque, Publicación del Programa Familias Guardabosques y del Programa Proyectos Productivos,* November 2007-January 2008.

Vacacela, Alicia,"La migración indígena." *Boletín ICCI-ARY Rimay,* Año 4, No. 41, August 2002, online at: http://icci.nativeweb.org/boletin/41/vacacela.html.

Vacaflor González, Jorge Luis,"Reformas de Estado y esencia de las autonomías indígenas." *Pukara* (Bolivia), No. 36, October 7/November 7, 2008.

Vaknin, Sam. "Interview with Barry Scott Zellen: Arctic Lessons." *Global Politician,* June 5, 2008, www.globalpolitician.com/24862-environment-interview.

Van Cott, Donna Lee. "Andean Indigenous Movements and Constitutional Transformation: Venezuela in Comparative Perspective,' *Latin American Perspectives,* Vol. 30, No. 1, Indigenous Transformational Movements in Contemporary Latin America, January 2003.

———. "Indigenous Movements Lose Momentum." *Current History,* February 2009.

———. "A Political Analysis of Legal Pluralism in Bolivia and Columbia." *Journal of Latin American Studies,* Vol. 32, No. 1, Andean Issue, February 2000.

Varela, Alejandro. "Escrutinio electoral expone el fracaso de Menchú." *ElNuevoHerald.com,* September 11, 2007.

Varese, Stefano. "The Ethnopolitics of Indian Resistance in Latin America." *Latin American Perspectives,* Vol. 23, No. 2, Ethnicity and Class in Latin America, Spring 1996.

Vargas Llosa, Mario. "The story of a massacre." *Granta 9,* 1983.

Vergara, Eva. "Mapuches chilenos dialogarán sólo con la presidenta Bachelet." *The Associated Press,* August 25, 2009.

———. "Chile's Mapuches announce alliance to push fight." *The Associated Press,* August 15, 2009.

Walder, Paul. "Neoliberalismo y represión contra el pueblo mapuche." *ElClarín.cl,* August 8, 2009.

Wallace, Paul A. W. "People of the Long House." *American Heritage Magazine,* February 1955, Vol. 6, Issue 2, online at: http://www.americanheritage.com/articles/magazine/ah/ 1955/2/1955_2_26.shtml.

Watanabe, John. "Mayas and Anthropologists in the Highlands of Guatemala since the 1960s." In *Supplement to the Handbook of Middle American Indians,* Vol. 6. *Ethnology,* ed. John Monaghan. Austin: University of Texas Press, 1999.

Webber, Jeffery R.. "Left-Indigenous Struggles in Bolivia: Searching for Revolutionary Democracy." *Monthly Review,* Volume 57, Number 4, September 2005.

Wente, Margaret. "Trapped in the aboriginal narrative." *The Toronto Globe and Mail,* June 28, 2007.

Whalen, Andrew. "Amnesty: Peru's pregnant Indians get unequal care." *The Associated Press Online,* July 9, 2009.

Whitehead, Laurence. "State Organization In Latin America since 1930." In *The Cambridge History of Latin America,* Volume 6, Leslie Bethell, Cambridge: Cambridge University Press, 1994.

Whitten, Norman E. "Jungle Quechua ethnicity; an Ecuadorian case study." In *Ethnicity and Resource Competition n Plural Societies*, ed. Leo A. Despres. The Hague: Mouton, 1975.

Wickstrom, Stefanie. "The Politics of Indigenous Development in Panama." *Latin American Perspectives*, Vol. 30, No. 4, Struggle and Neoliberal Threats, July 2003.

Williams, Jr., Robert A. "The Algebra of Federal Indian Law: The Hard Trail of Decolonizing and Americanizing the White Man's Jurisprudence." *Wisconsin Law Review 219*, March 1986.

Yardley, Jonathan. "Exploring the roots of anti-Americanism among European elites." *The Washington Post*, March 4, 2007.

Yashar, Deborah J. "Contesting Citizenship: Indigenous Movements and Democracy in Latin America." *Comparative Politics*, Vol. 31, No. 1, October 1998.

Yazzie, Robert. "Life comes from it: Navajo justice concepts." *24 New Mexico Law Review*, 1994.

Yovera, Daniel. "Antauro Humala: 'Simon me pidió interceder,'" *Perú21.pe*, July 16, 2009, online at: http://peru21.pe/noticia/314820/antauro-humala-simon-me-pidio-interceder.

Zambelis, Chris. "Islamic Radicalism in Mexico: The Threat from South of the Border." *Jamestown Terrorism Monitor*, Volume 4, Issue 11, June 2, 2006.

Zamosc, León. "The Indian Movement and Political Democracy in Ecuador." *Latin American Politics & Society*, Volume 49, Number 3, Fall 2007.

Zapeta, Estuardo. "Guatemala Peace Talks: Are Maya Rights Negotiable?" *Abya Yala News*, Vol. 8; No. 4, Winter 1994, 26, 37, online at: http://abyayala.nativeweb.org/maya/ zapeta.html.

Zellen, Barry Scott. "500 Years after Columbus: The Liberation of Native Peoples." *The Sourdough*, December 31, 1992, online at: http://thesourdough.com/index.php?articleID=15787&sectionID=135.

Zhingri T., Patricio. "Interview with Marlon Santi, new president of Ecuador's indigenous confederation." January 15, 2008, *Upsidedownworld*, online at: http://upsidedownworld.org/main/index2.php?option=com_content&task=view&id=108.

Zibechi, Raul. "The Mapuche in Chile; What their resistance can teach us." *Znet*, August 1, 2007, www.zmag.org/content/print_article.cfm?itenID=13420&sectionID=20.

Academic Papers and Dissertations

Barker, Michael L. "American Indian Tribal Police: An Overview and Case-Study." Ph.D. dissertation, School of Criminal Justice, State University of New York at Albany, Summer 1994.

Burguete Cal y Mayor, Araceli. "Multiculturalismo constitucional en Chiapas: reformas huecas para nulificar derechos autonómicos." Paper presented at the American University conference. "Reconciling Liberal Pluralism and Group Rights: Oaxaca, Mexico's Multiculturalism Experiment in Comparative Perspective," February 19-20, 2009.

Danielson, Michael S. "Migration and Customary Practice in Oaxaca: Preliminary Findings from the '2008 Survey of Oaxaca, Mexico Customary Law Municipalities." Paper presented at the American University conference, "Reconciling Liberal Plural-

ism and Group Rights: Oaxaca, Mexico's Multiculturalism Experiment in Comparative Perspective," February 19-20, 2009.

"Draft Recommendations" of the 9th National Conference on Science, Policy and the
Environment: *Biodiversity in a Rapidly Changing World,* December 8, 2008,
http://www.ncseonline.org/Conference/Biodiversity/Recommendations/Breakout%2
0Recommendations%201st%20edited%20draft.pdf.

Kobrak, Paul Hans Robert. "Village Troubles: the civil patrols in Aguacatán, Guatemala." Ph.D. dissertation, University of Michigan, 1997.

Mattiace, Shannan. "Mexico's 'Tranquil' Indians: Indian Rights Legislation in Yucatán."
Paper presented at the American University conference, "Reconciling Liberal Pluralism and Group Rights: Oaxaca, Mexico's Multiculturalism Experiment in Comparative Perspective," February 19-20, 2009.

Gray Molina, George. "Ethnic Politics in Bolivia: 'Harmony of Inequalities,' 1900-
2000." Paper presented at the Third Forum for Human Development, Paris, France,
January 17-19, 2005.

Kelly, Phil. "South America as a 'Zone of Peace'; Facilitating a Geopolitical Model."
Paper presented at the Midwest Association of Latin American Studies (MALAS)
annual conference in St. Louis, November 3, 2006.

Nava, Elena. "Pataxós y Mixes apropriándose de las políticas de 'inclusión social,'" paper presented at the 2009 Latin American Studies Association Congress in Rio de
Janeiro, June 6, 2009.

Reichard, David A. "'Justice is God's Law,' The Struggle to Control Social Conflict and
U.S. Colonialization of New Mexico, 1846-1912." Ph.D. dissertation, Temple University, 1996.

Risør, Helene. "Twenty Hanging Dolls and a Lynching: Living Insecurity and Recognizing Dangerousness in the Margins of the Bolivian State." Paper presented at the
2009 Latin American Studies Association Congress in Rio de Janeiro, June 6, 2009.

Selmeski, Brian R. "Multicultural Citizens, Monocultural Men: Indigeneity, Masculinity,
and Conscription in Ecuador." Ph.D. dissertation, Graduate School of Syracuse University, 2007.

Spencer, David. *Reexamining the Relevance of Maoist Principles to Post-Modern Insurgency and Terrorism,* unpublished manuscript in author's possession, 2007.

Taber, Peter. "Resource-Making and Conservation Politics in Esmeraldas, Ecuador."
Paper presented at the 2009 Latin American Studies Association Congress in Rio de
Janeiro, June 6, 2009.

"The Declaration of Barbados: For the Liberation of Indians." *Current Anthropology,*
Vol. 14, No. 3, June 1973.

U.S. Congressional Testimony

Martin Edwin Andersen, Statement submitted on Chiapas and democratization in Mexico
to the Western Hemisphere Subcommittee of the House Committee on Foreign Affairs, February 2, 1994, *Federal Document Clearing House Congressional Testimony.*

————. Statement submitted on the plight of Brazil's indigenous peoples to the Western
Hemisphere Subcommittee of the House Committee on Foreign Affairs, July 14,
1993, *Federal Document Clearing House Congressional Testimony.*

Government Reports and Selected Publications

Anuario de Estudios Americanos XXXVI, Seville, Spain: Escuela de Estudios Hispano-Americanos, 1958.

Central Intelligence Agency, *Mapping the Global Future,* online at: http://www.cia.gov/nic/NIC_globaltrend2020_s3.html.

*Comisión para el Esclarecimiento Histórico/*Commission for Historical Clarification, 1999, Guatemala: Memory of Silence: Conclusions and Recommendations, 12 vols., Guatemala: Oficina para Proyectos de las Naciones Unidas.

Lamb, Robert D. "Ungoverned Areas and Threats from Safe Havens; Final Report of the Ungoverned Areas Project," prepared for the Office of the Under Secretary of Defense for Policy, U.S. Department of Defense, 2008.

Marcella, Gabriel. "War Without Borders: The Colombia-Ecuador Crisis of 2008," Strategic Studies Institute, December 2008, online at: www.strategicstudiesinstitute.army.mil/pdffiles/PUB891.pdf.

Nixon, President Richard M., *Special Message to Congress on Indian Affairs,* July 8, 1970

Presentación del libro: "SEMBRAMOS Y AHORA RECOGEMOS: Somos Familias Guardabosques," discurso del Sr. Sandro Calvani , representante UNODC Colombia online at:www.unodc.org/pdf/colombia/discursos/DISCURSO%20libro.pdf.

Presidencia de Gobierno de Colombia. "$500 millones recibiran primeras familias guardabosques indígenas de Nariño," February 22, 2004, online at: http://www.presidencia.gov.co/prensa_new/sne/2004/febrero/23/09232004.htm.

República del Ecuador. "Constitución de 2008," online at: http://pdba.georgetown.edu/Constitutions/Ecuador/ecuador08.html.

"UN Forum urges inclusion of indigenous peoples' concerns in global anti-poverty goals," *United Nations News Center* (www.un.org), May 26, 2006.

Van Cott, Donna Lee. *Defiant Again: Indigenous Peoples and Latin American Security.* Washington, D.C.: National Defense University, Institute for National Strategic Studies, 1996.

———. *500 Years of Confrontation: Indigenous Peoples and Security Policy in Latin America,* McNair Paper Number 53, Washington, D.C.: Institute for National Strategic Studies, October 1, 1996.

———. "Matrimonio de Conveniencia: El movimiento indigenista mexicano y la rebelion Zapatista," *Airpower Journal,* www.airpower.maxwell.af.mil/apjinternational/apj-s/1998/2trimes98/vancott.htm.

———. "Las poblaciones indígenas y la politica de seguridad en America Latina," *Airpower Journal,* http://www.airpower.maxwell.af.mil/apjinternational/apj-s/1997/4trimes97/vancott.htm.

Index

About the Author

Martin Edwin "Mick" Andersen has a long history working with, advocating the rights of, and reporting on Native Americans in the United States and in Central and South America and Mexico. Andersen has worked under the direction of cultural anthropologist Henry F. Dobyns on tribal development issues on the Kaibab Paiute Indian reservation in Arizona (1975) and was a founding board member of the Amazon Alliance for Indigenous and Traditional Peoples (1993). He has covered Indian issues as a reporter in Madison, Wisconsin, and from Washington, D.C., where his Op-Ed submissions have regularly appeared in newspapers such as the *Los Angeles Times* and the *Washington Times*. In 1981, he was one of the first non-Peruvian journalists to cover the Shining Path insurgency from their mountain stronghold in Ayacucho. Andersen consistently sought to bring indigenous rights issues to the fore at the New York-based human rights group, Freedom House, where he served as senior analyst on Latin America and the Caribbean from 1997 to 2006. He has also twice provided written testimony before the U.S. House of Representatives on indigenous rights issues. In 2009, he served as the lead consultant on native peoples in the Western Hemisphere to the Democracy Project for the Organization of American States (OAS).

As a professional staff member of the Senate Foreign Relations Committee, working directly for Senate Majority Whip Alan M. Cranston (D.-Calif.), Andersen was the staff author of a bill, signed into law by President George H.W. Bush in 1992, that required coverage of the rights of indigenous peoples in the annual State Department country reports on human rights. He has also worked with Indian groups in Guatemala as a consultant for the Washington Office on Latin America (WOLA). In 1995 Andersen produced an on-site study as a consultant in La Paz, Bolivia, for the Criminal Division of the U.S. Department of

Justice, which provided for the creation of a rural police force that incorporated that country's indigenous peoples on their own terms, offering them the means and authorities for their physical and juridical security while protecting their lands and natural resources.

Andersen is the author of several scholarly works on Indian issues, both in the United States and in Latin America, including "Chiapas, Indigenous Rights and the Coming Fourth World Revolution," *The SAIS Review*, (Summer-Fall 1994); "Derecho Consuetudinario Consolidado y Reivindicación Indígena en los Estados Unidos," presented at the Inter-American Development Bank's *Foro Nacional de Justicia* in Guatemala City, November 1996; "Failing States, Ungoverned Spaces and the Indigenous Challenge in Latin America," in the Center for Hemispheric Defense Studies' *Security and Defense Studies Review* (August 2006), and "Indian Nationalism, Democracy and the Future of the Nation-State in Center and South America," in *Latin American Democracy: Emerging Reality or Endangered Species*, ed. Richard Millett, et al. (Routledge, 2008). He is the author of two books on Argentine history—*La Policia: Pasado, Presente y Propuestas para el Futuro* (Sudamericana, 2002) and *Dossier Secreto: Argentina's Desaparecidos and the Myth of the "Dirty War"* (Westview, 1993), the latter praised by *The New York Times* as "a tour de force." During his time as director for Latin American and Caribbean programs at the National Democratic Institute for International Affairs (NDI), and the founder of their Civil-Military Project, he was the editor of *Hacía una Nueva Relación: El papel de las Fuerzas Armadas en un Gobierno Democrático* (1990).

A graduate of the Johns Hopkins University's School for Advanced International Studies (SAIS) and the University of Wisconsin-Parkside in Kenosha, Andersen also holds an M.A. in American history from the Catholic University of America, where he is enrolled in the history department's Ph.D. program. He is a board member of the Washington, D.C.-based Center for Ethnic Research (CER) and serves as the vice president of the Midwest Association for Latin American Studies (MALAS).

Breinigsville, PA USA
31 January 2010
231613BV00003B/16/P